Globalization, Institutions and Social Cohesion

Springer
Berlin
Heidelberg
New York
Barcelona
Hong Kong
London
Milan
Paris
Singapore
Tokyo

Maurizio Franzini · Felice R. Pizzuti
Editors

Globalization, Institutions and Social Cohesion

With 19 Figures
and 29 Tables

 Springer

Prof. Maurizio Franzini
University of Siena
Dip. Economia Pubblica
Piazza S. Francesco, 7
53100 Siena
Italy
franzini@unisi.it

Professor Felice R. Pizzuti
University of Rome "La Sapienza"
Dip. Economia Pubblica
Fac. Economia
Via del Castro Laurenziano, 9
00161 Rome
Italy
pizzuti@dep.eco.uniroma1.it

The foreword by D. Tosato, the introductions by. F. R. Pizzuti and M. Franzini, as well as
the articles by: M. de Cecco, F. Sanna-Randaccio, L. M. Milone, M. Franzini, R. Schiattarella,
F. R. Pizzuti, P. Onofri, C. A. Ciampi, F. Farina have been translated by Robert Barone.

The original Italian edition is: Felice Roberto Pizzuti (**editor**):
"Globalizzazione, istituzioni e coesione sociale", Donzelli editore, Roma, 1999.

ISBN 3-540-67741-0 Springer-Verlag Berlin Heidelberg New York

Library of Congress Cataloging-in-Publication Data
Die Deutsche Bibliothek – CIP-Einheitsaufnahme
Globalization, Institutions and Social Cohesion / Maurizio Franzini; Felice R. Pizzuti ed. – Berlin;
Heidelberg; New York; Barcelona; Hong Kong; London; Milan; Paris; Singapore; Tokyo: Springer,
2001
   Einheitssacht.: Globalizzazione, istituzioni e coesione sociale <engl.>
   ISBN 3-540-67741-0

MIC 2001

Springer-Verlag Berlin Heidelberg New York
a member of BertelsmannSpringer Science+Business Media GmbH

© Springer-Verlag Berlin · Heidelberg 2001
Printed in Germany

Hardcover-Design: Erich Kirchner, Heidelberg

SPIN 10724892   42/2202-5 4 3 2 1 0 – Printed on acid-free paper

Foreword

The Department of Public Economics of the Rome University "La Sapienza", in keeping with its primary task of promoting research, not only inside the Department, but also through an exchange of ideas with scholars from Italian and foreign research institutions, periodically organizes conferences and meetings on the important topics of economic theory and policy. Economic globalization clearly belongs to this category. Just consider the widespread effects and consequences of globalization, the range of tools that its analysis requires as well as its impact on the welfare of the populations involved, and the new difficulties it brings about in terms of methods and results of public and regulatory interventions.

Therefore, on this very subject, the Department of Public Economics invited a group of scholars, who have been deeply involved with the questions raised by economic globalization, to a direct confrontation. The aim of this conference was to deepen awareness of the phenomenon and its specific impact on the advanced economies of our continent, as well as to formulate proposals for action on both the national and super-national level. This volume, which collects the contributions presented at this meeting, gives an account of the deliberations that took place at the Conference "Globalization, Institutions and Social Cohesion" held at the Faculty of Economics of Rome University "La Sapienza" from the 15th to the 17th of December 1998.

The Conference was organized with both passion and intelligence by Felice Roberto Pizzuti and Maurizio Franzini – who deserve the hearty thanks of the Department for their profound commitment. Professor Pizzuti's introduction gives a very useful synthesis of the subjects treated, of the concerns that were expressed, and of the positions outlined. Anyone who, like me, had the opportunity to follow the works of the conference and who can now revisit it by reading the articles collected in this volume, would certainly be struck by the range of ideas and research that emerged. On the level of analysis, the articles invite us to question the special aspects that distinguish the current phase of the globalization process from the rapid development that occurred in previous episodes of international trade and of economic integration. The articles also propose an examination of the theoretical analysis that is best adapted to evaluate the dimensions and the distribution of costs and benefits that derive from globalization, and of the consequences for macroeconomic equilibrium of the single economies in reference to the nature of the productive structure and of the labour market. In terms of economic policy, the articles invite us to reflect on the measures and the means of support towards those who risk becoming emarginated; and, on the new equilibrium that is being sought between public intervention and private initiative, on the one hand, and between regulatory powers entrusted to national and super-national authorities, on the other. It is specifically on these last points that the thoughts expressed by the then President of the Interim Committee of the International Monetary Fund and Minister of the Italian Treasury, Carlo Azeglio Ciampi, who is now President of the

Italian Republic, take on a special importance. On behalf of the Department, I want to thank President Ciampi once again for his valuable contribution to the works of the Conference.

And with the certainty that the ideas that emerged from the conference on "Globalization, Institutions and Social Cohesion" will continue to be fruitful, the Department of Public Economics is proud to present this volume to the attention of the academic world.

Domenico Tosato
Director of the Department of Public Economics
Rome University "La Sapienza"

CONTENTS

Introduction

Markets and Institutions in Neo-Globalization

Felice Roberto Pizzuti

To Maria Luisa,
who helps me even when she doesn't know it

1. An Overview [1]

The topics covered in this book[2] address the new wave of worldwide economic integration processes that have been taking place over the last quarter of the twentieth century, usually referred to as "globalization" of the economy or, as proposed herein, as "Neo-Globalization". More specifically, they analyze the consequences of these processes for the labor market and the redistribution of income, for the economic policies of the individual nation states, for the macro-regions (particularly the European Union) and supranational bodies, for the functions of the welfare state and the changes in social cohesion in the advanced countries. Reference is made also to issues that affect significantly emerging and

---

[1] I would like to thank N. Acocella, M. Franzini and L.M. Milone for their comments to a previous version of this introduction; of course, responsibility for its contents rests with the author.

[2] This book, now in its English version co-edited with Maurizio Franzini (based on the Italian version "Globalizzazione, istituzioni e coesione sociale" edited by F.R. Pizzuti, Donzelli Editore, Rome, 1999) is the outcome of the conference on "Globalization, Institutions and Social Cohesion" that was organized by the Department of Public Economics of "La Sapienza" University of Rome, in cooperation with Bank of Italy, European Commission, National Research Council, E.N.I. S.p.A. and under the auspices of the Italian Society of Economists. The conference was held in the Faculty of Economics from December 15 to December 17, 1998. The Scientific Committee was made up of N. Acocella, M. Baldassarri, M. Di Matteo, M. Franzini, G. Gandolfo, F. Hahn, G. Hughes, L. M. Milone, M. Nuti, F.R. Pizzuti, R. Schiattarella, D. Tosato, F. Vianello. The Organizing Committee consisted of M. Franzini and F.R Pizzuti. The articles published reflect mostly the papers presented at the conference, although with some editing. I would like to express my heartfelt thanks to the above institutions and the authors in this volume for giving me the opportunity to experience a scientific and cultural journey that, hopefully, might represent a useful contribution to the debate on the issues covered. A special thanks to Giancarlo Gandolfo for his contribution to the publishing of the present English edition and to Robert Barone who translated from and into English the contributions for both the Italian and the English editions. Both the organization of the conference and the preparation of the Italian and the English version of the present volume were made possible by the professional and pleasant cooperation of Dr. Annarosa Arista. Finally, many thanks to my wife, to whom my time and effort to see this book completed is dedicated. Her contribution was paramount for the actual involvement in the organization of the conference, but I am even more grateful for her unwavering and patient support to my work and because she helps me even when she doesn't know it.

developing countries.

The overall question dealt with in this volume is what should the relationship be between markets and institutions (national, regional and supranational) within the economic and social context determined by Neo-Globalization.

The term globalization has gained prominence over the past years but its meaning is not well defined or, at least, is not univocal. This state of indeterminacy gives rise also to manipulations concerning the interpretation of phenomena, platitudes on the resulting economic policy recommendations and even terminological abuses that ride on a cultural fashion.[3]

Making a concise attempt, the globalization under way may be defined as the increasing pace of supranational economic activities that has been occurring since the 1970s, consisting in the growth – to a varying degree – of the movement of goods, services, capital, workers and direct investments among different countries[4].

It is not a completely new phenomenon in economic history, even though its present version does have some significantly original elements.

The use of the term to define this phenomenon is relatively recent[5]; in any case, it has been adopted after the resurgence of economic integration processes over the past few decades. However, considering the qualitative and quantitative similarity of the processes under way with those that took place a century ago, and taking into account that their historical recurrences go hand in hand with not-so-casual revivals of neo-liberalist economies, the current phase of economic integration might be defined as "Neo-Globalization", in keeping with the new *laissez-faire* mood.

Neo-Globalization has both technological and production as well as historical and institutional causes.

The former include the impressive progress of transportation and communications, the ensuing reduction of costs and the greater ease with which production input and output are shipped, the development of techniques for breaking down production processes and relocating them to other countries.

The latter include the significant role played after the second World War by international institutions and agreements designed to foster economic relationships among countries, the abatement of protectionism in emerging countries as well, the fall of communist regimes which has led to an enlargement of the scope for international economic relations, the development of multinational enterprises, which, by definition, tend to spread their production and commercial activities worldwide.

The consequences deriving from globalization processes, or attributable to

---

[3] Suffice it to say that many publishers actively encourage the use of the "magic word" in the titles of the books they publish, even though the content does not warrant it all together.

[4] Cf. Acocella, N.(1999): Politica economica e strategie aziendali. Carocci, Roma, and the references cited therein.

[5] Cf. Oppenheimer's essay in this volume.

them anyway, are many.

The potentially positive ones include the increase of international trade and competition; the greater ease and rapidity with which information and technological applications travel; the ability to derive greater benefits from existing comparative advantages in each geographic area; the overall improvement of manufacturing efficiency. The effects that, to a varying degree, are cause for concern include possible imbalances in national labor markets (especially those in the most advanced countries); the increase in income disparities, among both geographic areas and different worker classes (particularly workers with different skills); the risk that a "race to the bottom" both of work conditions and social security might determine an overall decline (also in emerging and developing countries) of social cohesion, manufacturing efficiency and economic growth.

What are and will be the main effects of Neo-Globalization? The answer to this question depends on the analytical approach adopted, on the economic policy and political recommendations that may result and on the courses of action that are and will be taken.

No attempt is made to foresee which of these actions will (or will not) be implemented and what their outcome will be.

The following pages of this introduction will provide an overview of a substantial set of positive and policy elements related to Neo-Globalization, drawing also on the different contributions included in this volume.

While the different essays stand out for their own individual characteristics, it is this writer's opinion that they make it possible to make a number of general considerations, some of which are summarized below.

The most original elements (albeit not the only ones) that set the current economic integration processes apart from those at the beginning of the century is certainly not the growth of international trade (in some respect still lower than the past one) but the development of foreign direct investments (FDI); the breakdown of production processes and the localization of the different phases in areas outside the enterprises or group of enterprises' national borders by sub-contracting or outsourcing work; the huge movement of capital flows in search, among other things, of lower tax rates or higher yields.

The little empirical data on the trade of finished products between emerging economies and advanced economies as a percentage of GDP do not support the widely-held notion of social dumping, whereby lower salary levels and smaller welfare systems would give an advantage in terms of competitive pricing to the former that puts the latter in the position to push downward their labor costs, particularly the benefits.

While the idea that "everybody can produce everything" has no firm ground to stand on – although it might be necessary to assume so in order to validate the competitive pricing advantage – it might be more appropriate to regard trade between countries at different stages of development in light of an international labor division based on the different technological and qualitative characteristics of the two countries' production systems. On the other hand, the social dumping thesis implies, as a second necessary condition, that welfare expenditures are a form of non-productive consumption; this is a marked contrast with the likely role of expenditures for social goods and services as the structural cause of a greater and more qualified productive capacity by advanced countries.

A more controversial issue is instead that of the effects on the labor market and on the welfare systems of advanced countries attributable to a higher level of FDI, to a production organization based on outsourcing, and to the asymmetry between capital mobility and worker mobility.

To this end, two types of consideration can be made on the basis of the contributions in this volume.

Based on those of the first type, the localization of phases of manufacturing processes can be seen as a confirmation of the international division of labor. The problem of advanced countries would not be so much reducing salaries and welfare expenditures as keeping a quality advantage for its manufacturing system, and being able to shift to "higher" stages of the international division of labor, trying not to lag behind with products subject to the competitive pricing of emerging countries. With their contribution to the improvement of human capital, to an ongoing skill-upgrading process and to the financing of the socio-economic safety net necessary to mitigate the serious problems due to the restructuring of production systems, welfare expenditures are an important tool to foster the qualitative and quantitative upgrading of production capacity. Thus, more than reduced, these expenditures should be reallocated as a result of changed production, economic and social requirements; besides, if welfare systems are not restructured they may lose their *raison d'être* for efficiency purposes.

The second type of considerations on the effects of Neo-Globalization highlights that while on one hand there is a growing economic and social instability, which gives rise to a greater need for social security nets, on the other there are new problems related to the financing of national welfare systems.

These problems are due mainly to three new elements: a much greater capital mobility and the tax-base footloose behaviors of those who manage it in choosing the countries where to invest; the lower technical and institutional constraints on enterprises that want to relocate also a limited number of their production processes abroad in order to benefit from lower labor costs; changes in the labor market and a more marked difference in workers' salaries according to their skills.

The first two elements make it difficult for national states to tax capitals in absence of a coordination effort for their fiscal policies. However, beyond a certain level, it is difficult also to tax salaries without triggering a labor-cost rise.

More generally, the greater power of money managers and financial markets means that not only their interests gain strength but also their vision of the economy and society, whereby state intervention is a source of inefficiency that distorts market forces and their ability to achieve growth and progress. The diffusion of these neo-liberalist economies views among economic operators, as well as among the public opinion and their representatives, increases the difficulties for the single states to adopt economic and social policies different from that theoretical approach and from the interests which are identified with it.

The increase of salary differentials among workers with different skills may generate some negative dispositions toward welfare expenditures and financing also among workers. Those in higher income brackets might come to regard the market as an efficient provider of social goods and services for their needs; if this were to happen, however, workers with lower incomes would be forced into low-protection social systems and without the financial resources to tap private alternatives.

The instability and inequalities growth, as well as the parallel decline of social security nets, might reduce social cohesion in advanced economies, thus encouraging reactions against the globalization processes that would extend also to their most positive aspects. There might be negative consequences also in developing countries if advanced countries, thanks to their influence in international bodies, were to introduce protectionist measures, perhaps disguised as "humanitarian" labor standards.

The basic problem is how to make the most of the potentially positive aspects of economic integration without running the risks related to the Neo-Globalization processes.

Even discounting possible differences in their views, theoretical and empirical contributions on market and non-market "failures" highlighted why a cooperation between public and private sector is beneficial for efficiency and equity purposes.

The supranational scope of markets and corporate decisions presents a problem of alteration of the conditions in which a balance between public and private choices has to be found. The asymmetry between the public and private economic areas poses the need to identify, at the supranational level as well, a balance between spontaneous economic tendencies and the policies necessary to achieve equity and efficiency goals that cannot be otherwise attained by adopting the individualistic approach.

Market limits – such as those that stem from imperfect information and the resulting behaviors, which prevent it from considering individual interests as a unified whole in order to allocate, produce and distribute in a way that maximizes society's welfare – are still an issue. Actually their significance has somewhat increased due to the transition of economic relations from a national to a supranational dimension.

The tax base footloose approach of money managers is an example of free riding on a territorial larger scale.

In the hope of promoting economic growth in single areas through competitive reductions of labor costs, some economic policies are characterized by non-cooperative behaviors, such as that prevailing in the European integration process, where everyone undercuts everyone else in a growing climate of social unrest and deflation.

Thus, a fair and efficient allocation of resources in an increasingly global economy calls for transnational markets to be met with both some forms of coordination of existing national institutions (e.g. in the area of macroeconomic policies, tax harmonization and social policies) as well as the creation of supranational bodies capable of providing the "public goods" necessary to the new level of social and economic relationships (peaceful and orderly international relations, economic, financial and social safety nets, effective and efficient monetary systems capable of meeting growth and development goals, dissemination of information, rules and regulation, etc.).

Of course, not everybody shares each and every one of these views. Supporters of neo-*laissez-faire*, for instance, tend to consider Neo-Globalization as the "revenge" of the market whereas this, by overcoming national barriers, breaks loose from institutional constraints and makes any sort of regulation impossible more than useless.

This volume gives the impression that, in effect, there is some kind of "revenge" taking place in Neo-Globalization processes, and/or in their analysis; however, this involves the negative components of an overall phenomenon that has some positive aspects, which should not be sacrificed to a predictable indiscriminate reaction to its inequitable and destabilizing effects.

To this end, the conclusion of President Carlo Azeglio Ciampi's essay is particularly clear: "Globalization has brought to all of us not only a growth in the liberty of choice, but also in new duties and tasks that would be irresponsible to neglect or to face individually. It is not possible to have a social order based on the exclusive consideration of individual preference, and it is not possible to build a global society without a culture of reciprocity, or a sustainable economy without a *polis*".

The next four sections will provide a description of the specific issues dealt with here, and the thread that links the contributions of the different authors, in a more detailed and systematic way. This will be done by following the same order as that in which the topics are presented in the book.

The strand of, and the connections among, the different essays in terms of contents and positions will be outlined even though, as is to be expected, the analyses present in each of them may, at least in part, differ from one another, which will be more evident after reading them.

2. Precedents and Prospects of the Globalization Processes under Way

The first question this volume is faced with concerns the description and the definition of the globalization processes that have been taking place over the quarter of the century (Neo-Globalization) to analyze its nature and its actual original elements, compared with similar phenomena in other and not-too-distant phases of capitalistic development.

Actually, Marcello de Cecco traces an important example of globalization back to the Graeco-Roman age, which led not only to a vast commercial integration, and to a subsequent division of labor, but also to the largest monetary union before modern experiences.

The integration under the Roman empire extended also to the inter-ethnic mixes fostered by the movement of people and the diffusion of a common language, the extent of which has been equaled only by that achieved nowadays by the English language.

Subsequent examples of globalization were the attempts by the Italian Republics to establish large trade areas up to the 15th century. The successive geographic discoveries and colonial expansions opened the new age of the globalization processes centered on the New Continent.

Focusing the attention on modern age, it is clear that the current globalization processes have quantitative and qualitative aspects in common with those spanning the beginning of the 1900s. However, de Cecco suggests a distinction in the manners in which modern globalizations have been historically organized: initially as the result of an action by nation states characterized by the roles of bureaucracies, then as a result of the increasing power of merchants and financiers, namely of supranational market forces. Perhaps the distinguishing qualitative feature of the present experience – a process that is still under way – compared with that at the beginning of the 1900s, is the very transformation.

With special emphasis on the financial aspects, the alternative and the fluctuations between an integration controlled by the individual economies under the supervision of national and supranational institutions and an integration process based on a more pronounced market autonomy is the conceptual framework outlined by de Cecco to understand the evolution of the debate and the actual experiences related to the globalization processes of this century.

Peter M. Oppenheimer stresses the fact that, regardless of the contents, the term "globalization" began to gain currency at the end of the 1950s to describe the desirable tendency for governments' trade policies to become more homogeneous. The meaning attributed today to the term is akin to "interdependence", an expression denoting in the 1960s the opening of the economies to trade and investment flows (as well as to the tendency for national policies to become homogeneous).

Like de Cecco, Oppenheimer too underscores the large number of qualitative and quantitative similarities between the integration processes at the beginning of the century and the current ones, extending them also to the regionalization processes taking place in Europe in both periods. There are differences, however, in the current greater geographic size of the industrialized world and in the number of countries involved in foreign direct investments (FDI), in the "shrinking" world brought about by recent technological advances in the communication field, in the current predominance of multinational corporations and financial institutions in international trade and investments.

According to Oppenheimer, the present globalization thrust should be seen also as a reaction to the preceding sustained enlargement of the role of states (whose number, by the way, is quadrupled over the past half century) in national economies. The reaction to this enlargement of the role of states is also one of the reasons for the new forms of regionalization. These are often characterized by a drive toward a devolution of powers to local authorities and a tax federalism within the individual countries ("downstream" regionalism) in the hope that a greater autonomy might be conducive to a more favorable climate to attract foreign investments within a context of a greater liberalization of trade and FDI.

The present regionalization trends, however, are also marked by some "upstream" movements, whereby national governments try to optimize their influences in a world of freer trade and transnational production processes. Thus, while the influence of globalization on national states is multifaceted, the process is not a one-way street[6].

Another difference between the current situation and that at the beginning of the century is that while then wages were leveled by a major migration process (increasing them in countries emigrants left behind and decreasing them where they settled), now mobility involves mainly capital and commodities, instead of workers. As a result, there is a widening gap among the salaries of workers with different skills and/or greater unemployment in the developed countries, as well as a greater effort by the latter to restructure their productive systems in order to move "upmarket".

As will be seen, these last aspects attributed to Neo-Globalization are paramount to assess their effects on the tasks of the welfare state.

The quantitative and qualitative development of FDI, already indicated by Oppenheimer as a distinctive feature of the present globalization, is analyzed in depth by Francesca Sanna-Randaccio.

Thanks to a radical change in national policies, from the restrictions of the 1970s to the liberalization of the 1980s in about a decade (1985-1997), the worldwide size of the FDI stocks is more than quintupled. The most interesting aspect, however, is the greater geographic diversification of the phenomenon and an increased balance in cross-investments whereby emerging countries have witnessed a considerable growth of their share of outward FDI stocks (from 1% in 1960 to 9.7% in 1997). A notable exception to this trend is Japan, as it continues to receive a low investment inflow due to the structural barriers to both imports and foreign investments.

In the nineties, also developing countries encouraged investments by multinational corporations, which have, in turn, become increasingly important in the creation and international transfer of technology.

Sanna-Randaccio suggests that the increased balance of investment flows should be considered as an important element in the homogenization of the diverse national interests with respect to worldwide economic integration. This should discourage potential protectionist stances, an outcome consistent with the historical pattern of international economic relations.

---

[6] The last section will cover in greater details the relationships between globalization and institutions as well as regionalization in particular.

The greater diffusion of FDI compared with other types of short- and long-term investments is regarded as an element of stabilization of the international system and of its globalization. The debate on FDI should include whether it is appropriate or not to set rules on the basis of international agreements. This, however, has already been attempted, even though in a less than impeccable manner and ending up in a failure, with the Multilateral Agreement on Investments (MAI) by the OECD.

3. Neo-Globalization and the Labor Market

One of the most significant aspects of Neo-Globalization this book is focusing on involves its consequences on the labor market, on income distribution and on the degree of social cohesion in advanced countries.

To this end, Luciano Marcello Milone analyzes the distribution implications and some consequences for the management of welfare state deriving specifically from the links between globalization and the localization of economic activities highlighted by recent literature on the "new economic geography" (NEG).

Whereas it started out by analyzing the causes of the clustering and geographic concentration of manufacturing processes, NEG has shown recently the presence of other forces that push in the opposite direction. The localization of manufacturing activities would be the outcome of the combined action of all these opposing thrusts: the economies of scale of individual firms and industries account for the centripetal forces while the geographic distribution of demand, transportation and marketing costs are some of the important reasons underlying the centrifugal movement.

The downward trend of transportation and communication costs brought about by technological advances fostered, at one point, the concentration of manufacture, albeit within the national borders and within single regional areas due to tariff and non-tariff barriers.

Eventually, this multi-centered balance was altered by the effects of trade and capital-movement liberalization policies and by the growth of FDI.

The localization of manufacturing activities that utilize unskilled labor in countries where this input is cheaper has allegedly determined in advanced countries a widening salary gap, to the detriment of unskilled workers, and a higher unemployment due to resistances to the related salary adjustments.

However, Milone points to a large number of empirical studies to underscore that the actual problems arisen in the labor markets of developed countries often have only a tenuous link with either trade liberalization or the growing movement of capital. According to many scholars, the main cause of those problems lies in the tendency of technological progress to dispense with unskilled labor.

The significant novelty emerging from the Neo-Globalization processes would be, instead, that, beyond a certain level, a further reduction of transportation costs, together with the ability to break down and relocate manufacturing processes, would fuel centrifugal movements instead of encouraging manufacturing concentration. This phenomenon would materialize in the tendency to localize those phases of the manufacturing process requiring unskilled labor to geographic areas where this is cheaper; hence, the increase of sub-contracting and outsourcing that, in developed countries, would exacerbate the redistribution tendencies detrimental to unskilled workers already triggered by the development of unskilled-labor-saving technologies.

It should also be noted that, in developed countries, the demand curve for unskilled workers would not only shift downward as a result of the above effects, attributable to manufacturing relocation and to the related competition of low-wage countries, but would become increasingly elastic owing to the greater interdependence among the national labor markets of the most advanced countries.

This latter circumstance would worsen the situation of unskilled workers in terms of job security and working conditions. These developments would make for greater problems of social cohesion and stability and the need for a welfare state. Meanwhile, however, by increasing the mobility of capital and the difficulty for single governments to levy taxes on it, Neo-Globalization poses a problem in terms of financing the welfare state. Hence, the need, as indicated by Milone, to coordinate policies at a supranational level and the appropriateness of restructuring welfare systems.

Maurizio Franzini reiterates the concern for the negative effects of Neo-Globalization on social cohesion. According to this author, this phenomenon is not investigated in depth as, by underestimating the significance of outsourcing, no account is taken of one of the main systems through which Neo-Globalization may affect income distribution, particularly unskilled workers.

Thus, utilizing a concept typical of neo-institutionalism and of transaction cost economics, Franzini stresses that, in the current globalization phase, firms not only have to decide whether to make or buy but also where and how to make and buy.

The choice between the possible combinations depends on the cost of each alternative and the related changes. Franzini maintains that recent developments reduced the so-called governance costs, making it relatively easier to relocate abroad some manufacturing phases (more than make or buy everything abroad and more than make everything in the home country). These developments would encourage a greater reliance on outsourcing, resulting in a change in the products manufactured in developed countries that would, in turn, reduce the domestic demand for unskilled workers and their salaries to the levels prevailing in the countries where localization occurs. According to this view, governance costs, namely the costs built in the manufacturing process, would be much more important than the natural barriers to the mobility of the factors which, instead, most scholars have been focusing on.

According to Franzini, if globalization is characterized by the outsourcing phenomenon, then its effects on salary differentials due to skill differences, as opposed to the general effects of unskilled-labor-saving technological advances, can no longer be separated.

In conclusion, manufacturing segmentation and relocation of its low-skill-labor-intensive stages to low-wage countries would level salaries at the international level in the same way the migration of unskilled workers did during the other globalization at the start of the century. It is not by accident that the movement of goods and factors is said to perform the same balancing functions as prices and salaries.

The conclusion of the analysis is that the impact of Neo-Globalization on unskilled workers in developed countries may turn out to be so dramatic as to generate reactions capable of undermining the potential benefits of the international economic integration.

Franzini reviews a number of possible actions and shows the difficulties related to each of them. Particularly, he dwells on the problem of financing possible measures and states that there are reasons to believe that a sharp conflict between skilled and unskilled workers may come to pass in advanced countries with respect to redistribution policies and attitudes toward globalization. There are no easy solutions to these problems, yet there is scope for effective policy action.

This leads us to the relations between Neo-Globalization and social policies. This link, however, will be frozen for the time being; this in order to explore further the effects of the new manufacturing organization based on geographic segmentation and sub-contracting as well as to analyze the consequence of this process, as indicated by several scholars, that these organizational developments by firms means that international specialization is no longer tied to products but to their production processes.

More generally, this reference to the international division of labor makes it possible to open a bird's eye view on the labor market of developed countries in order to assess the effects of Neo-Globalization on it. To that end, Roberto Schiattarella's article analyzes the nature and the effects of relocalization processes, with special emphasis on the empirical aspects of the Italian experience in the so-called "Made in Italy" sector.

Schiattarella too criticizes the view of part of the current literature whereby there is a link between the decline of unskilled workers' salaries in developed countries and the increase in international trade. The link with the labor market becomes more significant, instead, if reference is made to the relocalization processes and the outsourcing phenomenon; in fact, to understand these, more than international trade theories, a more fruitful approach might be to analyze international productive and technological developments as well as the awareness that in the processes under way there is an overlapping of market elements, cooperation and hierarchical relationships.

The analysis of the effects of relocalization on the labor market is even more meaningful if reference is made not to the choices made by individual firms but to the internationalization of whole systems or firm networks, as is the case with our "districts".

In the "Made in Italy" case, a label encompassing the textile, garment and shoe industries, relocalization processes abroad gathered momentum in the nineties, even though the effects on employment levels do not seem to be consistent with the findings of the current literature on the effects of Neo-Globalization. More than a crowding out of the manufacturing activities and workers, relocalization has triggered a process of international specialization by manufacturing stage. The Italian regions where the relocation abroad of manufacturing activities has been more pronounced did not experience any unemployment crisis; actually, there has been an increase, both in absolute and relative terms, of better-paid and high-skilled jobs.

Schiattarella's empirical results support the view, shared by other essays in this book, that globalization and relocalization phenomena should be regarded against the backdrop of the changes taking place in the international division of labor and the resulting re-definition of the tasks of each national production system. This dynamics does not entail a deterioration of occupational levels but a thrust toward their development in qualitative terms. Of course, the quantitative change of employment levels in each country is tied to the ability of its own production system to maintain its position within the hierarchy of production and commercial capabilities.

As already mentioned, the book focuses basically on the effects of Neo-Globalization in developed countries. A matter which concerns mainly developing countries is that of international labor standards (ILS) and the relevant actions that should be taken as a result of economic integration.

This issue has been dealt with by Kaushik Basu. He shows that if on one hand ILS are presented as a kind of humanitarian guarantees to prevent such questionable practices as the massive use of child labor, on the other they are criticized as a form of protectionism by developed countries to relate cinically to possible competition problems by developing countries.

Basu's criticism of the commonplace whereby low labor standards in developing countries cause unemployment in developed countries is very apt. Actually, many emerging countries export to developed countries less than they import from them; protectionist measures would inevitably reduce the overall trade level to the detriment of all. At any rate, child labor, or in any case labor characterized by low regulatory standards, is utilized in manufacturing activities widely spread in developing countries, but not present in developed countries, and as such do not constitute a competitive threat. According to Basu, some measures to be assessed carefully would be those designed to penalize some specific manufactures characterized by the use of child labor. There might be worse effects if, as happens often, some industries or countries were discriminated against, actually favoring others that use child labor anyway, perhaps to a much greater extent and in a more worrisome manner. The risk would be to set off some free riding behaviors among manufacturers of developing countries, which would be prompted to shift and utilize child labor in non-exporting industries or, at any rate, in activities not subject to the labeling requirement for their labor content. Basu recommends a flexible approach, which might factor in the use of child labor – considering that in many developing countries this is essential for the survival of families – subject to some sort of regulations for the number of working hours and, at the same time, promoting school attendance.

International controls and possible enforcement might be entrusted to the ILO (International Labor Office) more than to the WTO (World Trade Organization); this in order to highlight the approach to safeguard the needs of developing countries rather than furthering a trade-based agenda that might result in protectionist measures erroneously designed to favor developed countries.

4. Neo-Globalization, Welfare State and Social Cohesion

The central section of this volume is devoted to the interaction between Neo-Globalization and social cohesion and, within this framework, to the role of the social state. This interaction should be analyzed particularly with respect to the characteristics of the economic integration processes under way and their consequences on the labor market as examined in the preceding sections.

An argument with analytical and policy aspects on how the interaction between Neo-Globalization and social cohesion should be interpreted is that of the so-called social dumping. This argument, thanks to its apparent straightforwardness, typical of conventional wisdom, is widely spread also at the public opinion level.

Critically analyzed in this writer's essay, the main point of this thesis is that, by pitting against each other countries with labor costs variously saddled with social welfare payments, trade integration would undermine the competitiveness of countries, such as the European ones, with more developed welfare systems. It follows that, in order to preserve growth and employment levels, it is necessary to reduce welfare state expenditures.

In effect, the social dumping argument is founded on two conditions – each necessary but not sufficient – that are not adequately supported, either by analysis or by experience.

First, contrary to what would be necessary for this argument to be valid, price competitiveness is not a decisive factor in trade relations between developed and developing countries; besides being almost irrelevant for rich countries, from a quantitative point of view, these relations are basically subjected to the different manufacturing abilities of the individual countries and by the resulting international division of labor.

On the other hand, welfare economics has been able to deliver results in areas where public intervention can be more efficient than the market, and many of these areas involve social goods and services. The birth and development of the welfare state is thus a response to a demand for both efficiency and equity. The presence of well-developed welfare systems generally represents a cause of the high and highly qualified productive capacity, of the competitiveness and wealth of those countries, not a consequence that is slowly turning into an unbearable burden. The latter may still be a possibility, however, in presence of organizational and opportunistic malfunctions of welfare systems.

According to this writer, the relocalization phenomenon should not be regarded so much in terms of price competitiveness as a confirmation of the greater importance of the qualitative capacities of production systems and of the appropriateness for each national system to adapt to changes in the international division of labor. Given the new set of needs arising from Neo-Globalization, it is up to the welfare state to enable the market to perform its functions. It is exactly its role as an input for the system as a whole, considering also the lead time required to yield a profit, the welfare state should certainly be adjusted (not reduced) to the changes in economic and production relationships as well as from social and demographic transformations.

By enlarging the market's scope, Neo-Globalization stretches and amplifies some of the issues related to it, such as free riding, which at the international level occurs, among others, disguised as tax-base footloose behaviors by financial investors, in picking the countries where to invest on the basis of their tax legislation.

Just as public intervention has been generally credited with making up for the inefficiencies generated by free riding and, more generally, by the so-called "market failures", also at the supranational level there is a problem related to the coordination of institutions so as to enable them to interact with market forces in order to optimize their potential and to reduce their inefficiencies; the latter have the same nature as those that arise at the national level, but with effects amplified by globalization.

One of the "market failures" amplified by Neo-Globalization is a greater inequality. This gives rise not only to fairness problems but also to some consequences in terms of productive efficiency. In their essay Jean-Paul Fitoussi and Xavier Girre analyze the current globalization processes, with emphasis on their effects on inequality.

These two authors stress first and foremost how economic integration processes were analyzed in the seventies paying special attention to their consequences on the relationships between North and South of the world and, more specifically, to the risks of a growing gap between rich and poor countries. The debate on the globalization under way is much more concerned with its effects on the socio-economic systems of the most developed countries.

Second, despite the smaller attention being paid nowadays to developing countries, it is noteworthy that if on the one hand the current economic integration processes bolster their growth, on the other they subject them to a strong dependency on international markets, particularly the financial ones.

Third, the influence of Neo-Globalization on the equality conditions prevailing in labor markets varies, depending on whether an economy is advanced or emerging. Whereas in the former there is a favorable tendency for skilled workers, and hence towards the stressing of wages differentials connected to the degree of specialization; in the latter there is a higher demand for low-skilled workers, a trend leading to lower inequality.

Fourth, financial globalization determines the so-called structural inequalities, as they create a new distribution among the different income groups.

More generally, the massive and rapid increase of capital movement is considered responsible for contributing to the destabilization of economies and capitalist societies.

While they have the potential to increase competition and consumption possibilities, Neo-Globalization processes have been developing hand in hand with a progressive fall of growth rates in industrialized countries, which in turn results from lower productivity gains, employment levels and effective demand.

The basic reason for these negative trends might be attributed to the growing power of capital suppliers, a condition that has forced firms to reduce costs and salaries drastically, with the resulting higher unemployment and lower domestic demand, which is still the most powerful growth propeller. Governments, for their part, have had to cope with greater social welfare costs and lower tax revenues; the resulting increment of public deficits has affected their economic policies, highlighting their dependence on the pressures of financial markets and the latter's interest in encouraging tight monetary policies and high interest rates. This overall picture translates into a dynamic inefficiency of economic systems or in a decline of the accumulation path and wealth creation.

According to the two authors, the best way out would be to gain the ability to set policies to control the economic trends stemming from the financial aspects of Neo-Globalization; the objective should be to prevent greater inequalities and the resulting lower social cohesion from hampering the economic growth fostered by the positive aspects of globalization.

Guy Standing considers the mid-70s, the period in which Neo-Globalization processes started, as a sort of great divide between the so-called "statutory regulation", started after the second World War, and the age of "market regulation" (that is shaped by market needs) currently under way. The former was characterized by different socio-economic aspects, including the tendency to the "decommodification" of labor as an effort toward the "de-monetization" of "social income", namely the reduction of the monetary component in favor of a greater availability of social services and insurance. Proceeding with an analysis of the models prevailing in the different regions of the world in the two periods, Standing notes, in the transition between the two periods, the progressive detachment of the economy from its social dimension, greater inequalities and the resulting lower job and income security. Particularly, Standing highlights three aspects. First, a shift in focus of labor regulations in favor of a more individualistic approach, less concerned with the collective dimension. Second, a reduction of social safeguards, which become more selective and tend to be provided by private organizations. Third, a new distribution of society in different social and income strata, at the top of which there are groups that are increasingly uninterested in social protection and, thus, less inclined to defend its principles, while at the bottom there are groups that feel deprived of that kind of safety that was traditionally provided by the public welfare system.

The challenge is, according to Standing, how to include social and redistribution justice in the economy to deal with the dangerous loss of safety and social cohesion that goes hand in hand with the greater economic instability born of Neo-Globalization and market regulation.

Paolo Onofri deals with the relationship between globalization and social cohesion, with special emphasis on the European Union and its need to revive and re-position its production system also in presence of its ageing population. The risk is that welfare state might be regarded as a burden to finance in alternative to economic growth.

For all their differences, the socio-economic reorganizations undertaken individually by Great Britain and The Netherlands in the eighties are evidence of the shift of attention from social solidarity to markets. Is the EMU as a whole set for a similar experience?

Onofri analyzes several possibilities; however, in each instance he makes a case for the harmonization, albeit gradual, of the macroeconomic (coordinated demand stimulation) tax and social (contributions and minimum common standards) policies of the different countries, with the intent to set up an increasingly important supranational budget.

In order to reconcile growth and social cohesion, it will be necessary to adjust the existing welfare systems and to correct some of their distortions that, in turn, translate into disincentives to face new market challenges.

The quest for a greater efficiency will entail a more pronounced transparency of the safety-net mechanisms and may require also a bigger use of market resources, although without falling into the temptation to devolve the coverage of social risks from the scope of political decisions to that of individual decisions, as this activity will always imply the compliance with equity and subsidiarity criteria.

The restructuring of the social state will inevitably meet with political and union-related problems but Europe, according to Onofri, would not be able to manage the adjustment of its socio-economic structures demanded by Neo-Globalization and its ageing and economic maturity problems without the support of the political power and trade unions.

In his contribution Ferruccio Marzano deals with the question of the "crisis of the growth model" in Europe. In his view a proper way to face such a problem is by adopting an approach in terms of "targets" and "instruments" of economic policy.

Actually one needs to refer to two kinds of alternatives: on the one hand, that between the harmonization at the European Union level versus the coordination of national welfare policies; on the other hand, the alternative between the liberalization versus the re-regulation of the labour market in each European country. Since four different combinations of such policies exist "in principle", the problem is which one of those will prevail in each country.

Anyway, the future of the welfare state cannot be dealt with but in connection to the problems of the labour market.

As to the structural problems of different productive sectors in Europe, Marzano believes that a relevant distinction is to be made within the present large tertiary sector, viz that between its traditional areas and the new and advanced areas.

In the first areas it will be difficult to avoid a dicrease in empoyment and thus social security policies will continue to be needed. On the contrary, in the second areas the forecast can be made to the effect of an increase in employment; but, in Marzano's opinion, this needs not to be accomplished within the public sector. It may well be the case that most of the new and advanced services may be provided within the so called "third sector", so that in Europe we shall be increasingly confronted with the shrinkage of the Welfare State and the expansion of the so called "Welfare society" or "Welfare community".

Finally Marzano deals with the crucial relationships between the problems of productive and social changes in Europe and the really demanding question of the economic development of poor countries in the world arena. In his opinion, in rich countries we should not really be worried by the social dumping problems in poor countries; on the contrary, the real problem cannot but be that of the help that we can give them in order that they may strive for both economic growth and social promotion in the near future.

A significant instance to examine some specific effects of Neo-Globalization, particularly those of FDI on the labor market and on pension coverage in the countries of destination, is the Irish experience. Over the past forty years, Ireland has received a substantial inflow of productive resources by foreign firms, which today represent a significant share of the country's output and employment. By referring to the different behavioral models (stylized by Hirst and Thompson) of multinational and globalized corporations in terms of industrial relations and provision of retirement benefits, Gerard Hughes analyzes the behavior of foreign firms operating in Ireland and compares it with that of local companies.

The comparison between actual behaviors and stylized ones shows that, at least for the past, the prevailing attitude in foreign companies was that of the multinational corporation, rather than that of a globalized company, that is based on the adoption of behaviors in line with those of local firms and without any particular conflict with the country's interest. In the retirement area, large multinationals have been more inclined, compared with the Irish ones, to provide the same benefits to all their employees and, with the exception of US companies, do not have a particular preference for defined contributions schemes, which pass insurance risks onto the insured parties. Also for the future, multinationals seem to be inclined to continue along a line that spares them any conflict with government policies. A significant exception, however, is represented by the loss of national control over the investments of retirement savings; pension funds, in fact, follow the pattern prevailing in international financial markets and prefer to invest in other countries. To this end, Hughes suggests that the creation of the EMU might foster a number of agreements to place international financial flows under the control of supranational institutions.

5. Neo-Globalization, the Institutions and Experience of the European Integration

As already noted, if on the one hand Neo-Globalization fosters the conditions for growth – such as open markets and a faster dissemination of technological innovations – on the other it creates serious difficulties. For instance, the instability of economic systems increases, starting from that of financial markets. The first section already stressed the asymmetric development of the geographic sphere of influence of the market as opposed to that of the institutions and the problem arising from the latter's inadequacy within the context of a globalized economy. Starting from the analysis of the Asian crisis triggered by the devaluation of the Thai baht, Carlo Azeglio Ciampi's essay highlights how the ripple effect that affected the rest of the world was attributable not so much to the corrective macroeconomic policies (which are normally necessary, anyway) as to a failure by the mechanisms of a global market lacking adequate regulations . " The recent crisis has definitely shaken the belief that the financial markets, left to the spontaneous forces in which they operate, are capable by themselves of achieving stability or of allocating resources efficiently. The crisis reminds us of a reality often obscured by an unquestioning faith in the redeeming capacity of the market ; the market requires a solid foundation in the form of rules, institutions, codes of conduct of the operators, widely shared standards, and consolidated procedures".

To make up for market failures, such as those deriving from imperfect information, it is necessary for Neo-Globalization to adopt more effective economic policies at the international level and that the relevant institutional instruments be created as a result of an agreement between industrialized and emerging countries.   To this end, Ciampi indicates four areas: better universally-accepted standards of transparency in bank supervision activities, the creation of international "safety nets" to ensure the proper working of financial systems balanced by the need to make individual operators accountable, efforts by national economic institutions to strengthen internal financial markets to countervail the effects of their openness to foreign financial inflows, the adoption of a sustainable exchange-rate regime, characterized by flexibility and the possibility to align currencies in case of problems due to external shocks that would require corrective actions to the detriment of internal fiscal and income policies, whose possible traumatic effects – more likely in emerging and highly-indebted countries – could threaten the stability of the international monetary system.

The lack of a set of consistent rules for the proper working of the international economic system is Pier Carlo Padoan's starting point. Over the past thirty years, the absence of a hegemonic power, capable of unilaterally providing the international community with the "public goods" necessary to regulate it, and the higher demand for supranational rules, required by the growing pace of globalization, have given rise to an actual "institutional imbalance". According to Padoan, Neo-Globalization is proceeding hand in hand with the development of regionalism. This represents a level of coordination and/or integration that stands between the worldwide one and the nation-state one. Regionalizations are an attempt to respond to the lack of international public goods, namely the attempt to meet a demand for institutional instruments by identifying a level more pliable to cooperation efforts, without a hegemonic power.

Regional coordination and integration require policies that are both suitable and inclined to restrict the national autonomies in the economic, political and social areas. This price, however, should be made more acceptable by the realization that the implementation of regional standards are a source of comparative advantage for member countries, as these are better sheltered from the instability phenomena made worse by Neo-Globalization.

Regionalism, namely agreements entered into by a limited number of parties, is not necessarily consistent with a greater degree of world cooperation and with the corresponding creation of institutional instruments that reduce the current "imbalance". This result, however, could be achieved thanks to a climate more conducive to agreements. Padoan makes it clear that this positive outcome is only one of many possibilities, and that it is not merely an optimistic goal as, given some alternatives, being aware of the potential to reach more desirable goals might actually result in the adoption of policies more in line with the final objective.

Regional coordination and integration policies are the grounds upon which the EMU and the European Central Bank (ECB) were established in Europe. Annamaria Simonazzi and Fernando Vianello on one side and Francesco Farina on the other analyze this important experience, the results achieved so far and the prospects attributable to it.

So far, the European integration process has met with a growth slowdown and higher unemployment. The conventional explanation for these evolutionary characteristics, which are rather different in the US experience, is that the labor market is rigid and that the European welfare systems too generous. Consistent with the other essays in this book and the view prevailing in it, Simonazzi and

Vianello think that the explanation lies in the diverse economic policies adopted in the two continents. More specifically, these authors state that, in the USA, it is actually the greater awareness of a lack of a social safety nets that led economic policies to focus more on employment levels. In Europe, instead, a much wider social safety net did not cause higher unemployment, but made it more bearable, thus making it possible to adopt highly restrictive policies. These policies reflected the conceptual framework of the German neo-mercantilist development model which, however, when applied to the entire continent, generated an overall deflation that affected Germany as well. For the future, fixed exchange rates, a single monetary policy and the little scope for the implementation of corrective fiscal policies at the local level – together with the constraints on the number of choices that can be made at the national level as a result of capital mobility – represent the elements of a "straitjacket" that, by ignoring differences, might determine a homogenization of economic policies along a deflationary path, without any regard for the high costs that this approach entails. Labor mobility, salary flexibility based on geographic locations and, more generally, the deregulation of the labor market are the most common recommendations to get out of the tunnel. However, without considering the social aspects related to a further reduction of salaries, this policy may not be successful because it could set off a downward spiral in an uncooperative game that could leave everyone worse off, given that everyone's relative position at the end would be unchanged

However, the outlook might not be that pessimistic, if the European Union can shake off the foreign constraint that acts on development policies, a constraint that penalized mostly individual countries, owing to their small-to-medium size and their greater openness compared with the USA and Japan.

Farina's essay analyzes in depth the positions expressed during the debate that took place when there were choices to be made during the European integration process that led to the EMU.

In Europe, the main obstacle to the goal of monetary stabilization, pursued with the integration process started with the creation of the EMS, was the inflation differential between the countries in the "periphery" and those in the center, particularly Germany. To make fixed exchange rates credible and to neutralize the opposing forces originating from the countries in the "periphery", it was deemed necessary to rely on the anti-inflationary reputation of the Bundesbank, thus pegging the values of all the other currencies to the Deutsche mark. According to the "new classic macroeconomics", the credibility problems of the fixed rates established with the EMS, highlighted by the differentials between the interest rates prevailing in Germany and those in the periphery countries, were due to the lower "inflation-avert" inclination of the latter and to market expectations whereby these countries would attempt a "surprise increase" of the money supply. According to this view, to dissolve these expectations on the policies of periphery countries, it became necessary not only to peg their currencies to the Deutsche mark but also to delegate to the Bundesbank the task of managing the money supply for the entire area.

Actually, this situation determined a German hegemony in the EMS which translated into an asymmetric allocation of the burdens for the adjustments necessary to keep exchange rates stable, as such adjustments did not take into account the currency that deviated from the framework set by the fixed exchange rates agreement. The resulting penalization of the periphery economies worsened their competitiveness, thereby creating devaluation expectations in markets more realistic and credible than those related to the alleged lower "inflation aversion" of the authorities of those countries.

The lower growth and employment levels in periphery countries should then be attributed not so much to the distortions of the relevant markets, as to the deflationary influence stemming from a more burdensome foreign constraint determined by the loss of competitiveness and by the interest rates differentials due to the "asymmetric" working of the EMS.

According to Farina, this deflationary experience which led to the 1992 crisis of the EMS could happen once again in the new situation that has arisen as a result of the Euro and the European Central Bank, should the same "asymmetries" take shape again.

Introduction to the English Edition

Maurizio Franzini

In the short time that has passed since the conference was held, and on which this volume is based, the adversaries of globalization seem to have become more numerous and outspoken.

We need only remember the clashes that took place at the end of November 1999 in the streets of Seattle during the World Trade Conference; this institution was considered, rightly or wrongly, the very incarnation of the globalization process. But there are also other signs, less vociferous and more institutional. In some countries, including those that started enthusiastically on the path of globalization, there has been a growing orientation towards caution and even opposition. The case of New Zealand is, perhaps, the most interesting in this respect.

As is well known, this country, with its historic social-democratic traditions, began a radical reform in 1984 (originally during the term of the Labour government) against state intervention and in favor of the "free market". This reform, primarily justified by the changes in the international context introduced by globalization, initially produced good results. With the passage of time, however, significant difficulties emerged that culminated in a political crisis that necessitated new political elections last November.

The Labour party put forward a program that assigned to the state the role of reducing inequalities. This program was in clear contrast with the party at the head of the government, the National Party, which upheld the position that international competitiveness warranted whatever sacrifices were necessary (Economist 1999). The Labour Party received the relative majority of votes. These elections seem, therefore, to signal an about face in comparison to the trend of the last fifteen years – or, at least, they represent a standstill. This outcome reflects a changed attitude in popular opinion concerning globalization – or, at least, concerning some negative developments attributed to globalization.

The New Zealand case, however, is not an isolated one. Other countries, medium or small sized, that firmly believed in the path of liberalization and that gave priority to international competitiveness in their economies are displaying by means of their own democratic institutions, signs of having second thoughts. This is the case, for example, in Chile, Peru, Mexico and Venezuela; but even in many advanced countries, the popularity of globalization does not appear to be in the best of health.

According to a survey conducted in the United States in mid-1999 by the Pew Research Center, 43% of Americans think that the global economy will give them a higher standard of living, but more Americans have the opposite belief (52%). Beyond this fact, it is interesting to note that the optimists are concentrated among those who have the highest incomes; they are, in fact, made up of 63% that have an annual family income above $75,000 dollars and only 37% that earn less than $50,000 dollars. Other surveys reached the conclusion that about two-thirds of Americans feared that globalization implied the transfer abroad of the best jobs – which helps to clarify the meaning of these findings.

Scholars of globalization – as demonstrated in some of the essays contained in this volume – have for some time pointed out the danger of a reaction or backlash against globalization. While it is certainly excessive to interpret the aforementioned signals as proof of a reaction already well underway, it would, however, be a serious mistake to underrate the significance of this backlash; keeping in mind – as several commentators have noted – that the Seattle demonstrators did not enjoy any democratically recognized position. Globalization – whatever the term means – in spite of its undoubted merits does not automatically guarantee advantages for everyone; on the contrary, it generates dissatisfaction, disillusion and even defeat. This is important to recognize, and it is equally important to avoid viewing the dissatisfied, disillusioned and defeated simply as stubborn and egoistic enemies of progress.

There are many motivating forces behind this opposition to globalization and not all are related to the fear of a worsening in their own economic situation. There are, in fact, ideological adversaries who fear the total domination of the economy in the social and political organization of diverse countries, and who are concerned about the progressive reduction in the variety of institutional solutions and of cultural models. There are, moreover, those who are against globalization because they consider it to be a serious threat to the conservation of natural resources, to the protection of the quality of the environment and to the care of human health. You could, strictly speaking, say that these concerns relate to phenomena that have a rather weak link to globalization. And this is probably true; however – keeping in mind the variety of positions among scholars in this respect – it should not be surprising that globalization has many and, sometimes, vague definitions[1].

What we mean by "globalization" is also important in identifying, strictly in economic terms, those who can be damaged by the process. It is, in fact, very different to examine the problem based on the idea that globalization consists essentially in the removal of barriers that "directly" obstruct the free circulation of goods, and to consider factors in which a more ample definition is adopted that includes those sets of changes that some indicate – often on the basis of unproven

---

[1] In their recent and accurate book, Held et al., propose to define globalization "as a process (or a set of processes) which embodies a transformation in the spatial organization of social relations and transactions – assessed in terms of their extensity, intensity, velocity and impact – generating transcontinental or interregional flows and networks of activity, interaction and the exercise of power" (Held et al. 1999, p. 16). The attempts to define globalization run two contrasting risks: the first is that of being overly generic, and, consequently, globalization appears as a phenomenon without any specific or particular characteristics; the second is to be too specific, and this leads to a definition that is overly conditioned by those who want to interpret globalization as they see it. In the example of Held and his associates, they seem to have run the second type of risk.

assumptions – as necessary in order to reinforce the predicted positive effect of the reduction of "direct" barriers.

This distinction tends to highlight the fact that globalization may not be simply understood as the phenomena of progressively reducing the obstacles to free trade, to the free circulation of capital and of people; in reality, globalization has recently been increasingly identified with the project of creating a free market economy. Naturally, there are a great many differences between free trade and free market – as recently clarified by Gray (1999) – but the link was made possible by those who believe that the free market economy is indispensable in producing the maximum expected benefits in the opening of national economies to the world market and, specifically, in the emphasis placed on the necessity of significantly reducing the tax burden on companies and public spending, above all, spending that goes to the Welfare State.

These positions, as seen in some of the essays contained in this book, are anything but impervious to criticism. In particular, the evidence of the existence of a negative correlation between the growth rate of the economy and the size of the public budget is not very convincing.

At the end of his recent and exhaustive analysis of the different empirical approaches to the problem, Atkinson stated: "The results of econometric studies of the relationship between social transfer spending and growth rates are mixed: some find that high spending on social transfer leads to lower growth, other find the reverse. The largest of the estimated effects – in either direction – do not, however, seem believable" (Atkinson 1999, p. 184).

Therefore, caution is necessary in order to avoid the error of "an excess of certainty" for purely ideological reasons. This caution is especially necessary since the risk is that of increasing – and not reducing – the groups who feel threatened by globalization and its supposed "laws". If, to go back to our example, the changes to the welfare state in the last few years had not led to a dramatic worsening of the position of the Maori in New Zealand – who make up a quarter of the population – the outcome of the election may have been different.

The adversaries of globalization, therefore, would be different and more numerous if the movement towards what we have defined here as "free trade" – a necessary and opportune movement – was also accompanied by a strong attempt to bring about, with more or less success, a free market economy.

Rodrik, after having carefully examined the economic performances of many countries in the period following the Second World War, writes: "Openness by itself is not a reliable mechanism to generate sustained economic growth" (Rodrik 1999, p. 13). More precisely, he affirms: "Countries that have done well in the postwar period are those that have been able to formulate a domestic investment strategy to kick-start growth and those that have had the appropriate institutions to handle external shocks, not those that have relied on reduced barriers to trade and capital flows" (Rodrik 1999, p. 13). Therefore, international openness is not by itself sufficient to insure economic growth; there must be other conditions as well. Rodrik believes that these conditions are made up of measures and institutions that necessitate a well-calibrated public intervention and not by the realization of the free market economy.

The growth of the GNP is certainly an objective of fundamental importance; it would be a mistake, however, to think that this objective incorporates every other desirable objective, or that an elevated rate of development is a necessary condition for other desirable goals – the reduction, for example, of inequality or greater protection of the environment. There exist good reasons for maintaining that the growth patterns can in the long run increase social inequality and that this inequality in the long term can itself become an obstacle to further growth. The political reaction of the victims of this inequality is precisely one of the means by which this last consequence can be expressed.

Therefore, neither the goals of growth or of equality (which, moreover, are intertwined with that of growth) seem to make necessary, even in an era of globalization, the reconstruction of a free market economy. This statement would have even greater weight if growth is seen as a condition for the development of other goals as well, for example, an increase in the real freedom of individuals, as Sen has recently sustained (1999)[2] .

One of the chief messages that leaps out of this volume is that to enjoy the benefits of globalization in the long run and in a context of equity, it is necessary to develop institutions that are capable of supporting growth and of providing an acceptable level of equality. This is, naturally, not an easy task, since new forms of coordination are needed at the international level. The recent incident in Seattle gives a clue to just how difficult it is to achieve this coordination.

On the subject of child labour and of work standards – which is treated in depth in the essay by Basu – there was a harsh conflict between the developing countries and the richer, developed ones. The richer countries – especially the United States – wanted a ban on child labour; they also wanted the developing countries to adopt a generally more advanced legislation concerning work standards. On their part, the developing countries were not without some suspicions about this concern about their workers, and they expressly stated that the only scope of these requests was to block the process of growth, and of eliminating the competitive advantage that they have in comparison to the richer countries.

This is, therefore, a real dilemma: one form of justice (the concern for workers, both children and adults) seems to be in contrast with another form of justice (the improving of the standards of living in often very poor countries). One of the most interesting aspects of globalization is the opportunity for economic and social growth that it appears to offer to countries that are further behind in the path

---

[2] In particular, Sen affirms: "The levels of real income that people enjoy are important in giving them corresponding opportunities to purchase goods and services and to enjoy living standards that go with those purchases. But as some of the empirical investigations presented earlier in this book showed, income levels may often be inadequate guides to such important matters as the freedom to live long, or the ability to escape avoidable morbidity, or the opportunity to have worthwhile employment, or to leave in peaceful and crime-free communities. These non-income variables point to opportunities that a person has excellent reasons to value and that are not strictly linked with economic prosperity". (Sen 1999, p. 291).

towards development. It would be a grave mistake if we do not succeed in finding a solution to this apparent conflict between economic growth and social emancipation. In order to achieve this goal it is indispensable that the rich countries underwrite at least a part of the "cost" of social progress in the more backward countries; in other words, the rich countries must take up the burden of part of the damage that more strict work standards would generate in the poorer countries. All of this would require a strong coordination among the policies of diverse countries, which at the moment would seem difficult to achieve. Many times, however, the search for a solution becomes easier when the goals to achieve are clearly defined.

Competition in a globalized world where decent conditions of life and of work were guaranteed to more people would certainly create fewer obstacles and would promote greater consensus and agreement. But, as recent events demonstrate, the problem emerges from the fact that the mechanism of international competition pushes, all too often, in the direction of lowering the standard of living (even if only in relative terms, but dramatically evident) of many people. In the free market economy there is no space for many subtle distinctions between "good forces" and "bad forces" in competition. However these distinctions appear to be of fundamental importance, especially for the prolonged survival of globalization itself.

As we see in this volume as well, much discussion is given over to the relationship between the current phase of globalization – which Pizzuti in his introduction correctly proposes to call "Neo-Globalization" – and the numerous past episodes of strong integration among the various national economies. A distinctive element of the globalization of today is, most likely, the importance that the ideology of the free market plays in this version of globalization. As Amartya Sen recently wrote in his usually impeccable way: "There was a time – not very long ago – when every young economist 'knew' in what respect the market systems had serious limitations: all the textbooks repeated the same list of 'defects'. The intellectual rejection of the market mechanism often led to radical proposals for altogether different methods of organizing the world…without serious examination of the possibility that the proposed alternatives might involve even bigger failures than the markets were expected to produce…The intellectual climate has changed dramatically over the last few decades, and the tables are now turned. The virtues of the market mechanism are now standardly assumed to be so pervasive that qualifications seem unimportant…. One set of prejudices has given way to another – opposite – set of preconceptions. Yesterday's unexamined faith has become today's heresy, and yesterday's heresy is now the new superstition. The need for critical scrutiny of standard preconceptions and political-economic attitudes has never been stronger".

The essays that are presented in this volume, which refer to the problems posed by globalization and the prospects that it opens before us, are meant to be a contribution to the "critical scrutiny" of which Sen speaks.

References

Atkinson, A. B. (1999): The Economic Consequences of Rolling Back the Welfare State. The MIT Press, Cambridge, MA.

The Economist (1999): Labour Wins in New Zealand. December 4th, 1999, p. 69.

Gray, J. (1999): False Dawn. The Delusions of Global Capitalism. Granta Books, London.

Held, D., McGrew, A., Goldblatt, D., Perraton, J. (1999): Global Transformations. Polity Press, Cambridge.

Rodrik, D. (1999): The New Global Economy and Developing Countries: Making Openness Work. Overseas Development Council, Washington D.C.

Sen, A. (1999): Development as Freedom. Oxford University Press, Oxford.

PART I.

Precedents and Prospects of the Current Processes of Globalization

1. Comparing 2000 with 1900: How Does Today's Globalization Differ from Yesterday's Free Trade?

Peter M. Oppenheimer

Half a century ago the late Gilbert Ryle, Waynflete Professor of Metaphysical Philosophy at Oxford, published a celebrated book, "The Concept of Mind". Although Ryle himself denied being a behaviourist, most readers would say that his book was concerned to put forward a behaviourist theory of mind. That is, in Ryle's own words, to refute the notion of "a ghost in the machine", a mind-body duality as a fundamental structural feature of human beings. Capacities, dispositions and habits do not, he argued, require us to infer that there is a unifying intangible object called "the mind" in which they all reside. Indeed, to talk about the mind as an entity is to display a form of conclusion, like the confusion of the parent who asks his child's schoolteacher to tell him when the child, alongside its lessons in mathematics, history, english language and so on, is going to have its "thinking" lessons. I wouldn't claim to do for globalization what Gilbert Ryle did for the mind. In any case, while everybody agreed that Ryle was very clever, few people actually believed him. But I do want to try to put globalization into its proper, limited perspective.

According to the Oxford English Dictionary, the word "globalize" first appeared at the end of the 1950s. At that time, however, it referred not to market phenomena, but to government commercial policies. Import quotas were to be "globalized", rather than formulated on a country-by-country basis which risked perpetuating discrimination.

The ancestor in the 1960s of today's globalization was "interdependence".[1] Both comprise, or hint at, two elements. One is economic openness to trade and investment flows. The other is limitations on national diversity, of both policy and experience. Globalization is claimed to take the process very much further - under both heads - than interdependence.

The claim is plausible enough as regards openness. Global networks are of growing weight in the decisions of individual economic agents (producers and consumers). As regards the scope for national economic policy, and for variety as against uniformity in economic conditions across the world, the position is far less clear.

Before enlarging on this assertion, I emphasise that the paper is concerned with empirical (positive) issues, not with evaluative (normative) ones. The aim is neither to welcome nor to condemn globalization, but to elucidate its place in

---

[1] Cf. the title of Richard N. Cooper's influential volume of 1968 "The Economics of Interdependence: Economic Policy in the Atlantic Community".

contemporary discussion of economic policy. It happens to be an area where inconsistencies of view are commonplace. For example, a free-market US economist opposed to government intervention in the United States economy may nonetheless object to external constraints on the US government's freedom of action in economic matters.

I refrain also from discussing areas other than the economic. For example, decisions by the British authorities (House of Lords plus Home Secretary) in mid-December 1998 to allow the Spanish government to bring extradition proceedings against the former Chilean head of state, General Pinochet, were hailed by some commentators as presaging "a fundamental revolution in international law. At long last universalism and extra-territoriality are being recognised as necessary conditions for the efficiency of justice. Sovereignty is slowly giving way, or at least fighting a rearguard battle..." (Dominic Moisi, Financial Times, 14 Dec. 1998).

Sticking to economics, relevant historical comparisons need to go back to before 1914. This is because of the extraordinary turmoil to which international economic relations were subjected in the half-century after 1914. It was a story of stress, collapse and hard-won recovery and re-emergence. The personal memory of today's analysts and policymakers does not go back beyond the period of re-emergence in the 1950s and 1960s. They are therefore inclined to exaggerate the degree to which the world economic regime of the 1990s is unprecedented.

* * *

Available evidence suggests that the openness of major national economies in the gold standard era was very comparable to the situation in the most recent quarter century. Likewise the scope and degree of regionalisation in Europe. The last point is particularly interesting, given the strong contrast drawn in recent literature between the "new regionalism" of the 1980s and 1990s and the older post-1945 regionalism founded on Article XXIV of the GATT and Vinerian customs union theory. The possibility of Vinerian trade diversion is by no means absent from current discussion, particularly in relation to regional arrangements in Latin America.[2] But there is now greater emphasis on the role of regionalism and regional incentives in influencing the location of multi-national enterprise in a world of substantially but not totally free trade.[3] I return to this point below.

The ratio of external trade in goods and services to GDP in the principal

---

[2]MERCOSUR has come under repeated criticism in this respect. See, for instance, Yeats, A. (1998): Does MERCOSUR's Trade Performance Raise Concerns About the Effects of Regional Trade Arrangements? World Bank Economic. Review. For criticisms of Yeats' view see. Nagarajan, N. (1998): MERCOSUR and Trade Diversion: What Do the Import Figures Tell Us? European Commission, Economic Papers No. 129, July.

[3]See *inter alia* the work of Bagwell, K., Staiger, R.W., Ethier, W.(1998): The New Regionalism. Economic Journal. And (1998): The International Commercial System. Princeton Essays. International Finance No. 210, September, Princeton, NJ. Both give a valuable overview and bibliographies. See also Pier Carlo Padoan in this volume; and the references cited by him.

trading countries is thought to have been not hugely different in 1880-1914 from the level of the past two decades. Table 1 showing merchandise trade ratios is taken from a recent article by Robert Feenstra.[4] Inclusion of trade in services (if figures were available for pre-1914) would of course raise all the ratios; and probably the post-1970 ones by more than the pre-1914 ones, although this is by no means certain.

Table 1: Ratios of merchandise trade to GDP (percent).*

Country	1890	1913	1960	1970	1980	1990
Australia	15.7	21.0	13.0	11.5	13.6	13.4
Canada	12.8	17.0	14.5	18.0	24.1	22.0
Denmark	24.0	30.7	26.9	23.3	26.8	24.3
France	14.2	15.5	9.9	11.9	16.7	17.1
Germany	15.9	19.9	14.5	16.5	21.6	24.0
Italy	9.7	14.4	10.0	12.8	19.3	15.9
Japan[a]	5.1	12.5	8.8	8.3	11.8	8.4
Norway	21.8	25.5	24.9	27.6	30.8	28.8
Sweden	23.6	21.2	18.8	19.7	25.0	23.5
U K	27.3	29.8	15.3	16.5	20.3	20.6
United States[b]	5.6	6.1	3.4	4.1	8.8	8.0

* Merchandise trade is measured as the average of imports and exports, except as noted below.

[a] Data for 1890-1950 uses three-year averages.

[b] Data recorded under 1980 is for 1889, and along with that in 1913, measures the ratio of merchandise exports to GNP.

Source: R.C. Feenstra, op.cit.

At the same time, there was before 1914 a world-wide capital and credit market centred on London. Long-term capital exports from Britain – mainly to the Americas, but also including Europe and some parts of the British Empire – accounted for a proportion of British saving (25-40 percent) far larger than that of any capital-exporting country in the post-1945 period, when corresponding percentages were 5 percent or less. Most long-term capital flows before 1914 took place via the bond market. Foreign direct investment (FDI) was relatively low, and nearly all in primary production.[5] On the eve of World War I Britain's net external assets amounted to an estimated £4bn. Converting into dollars and indexing up by the US nominal GNP, this total is the equivalent of about $400 bn. in 1980 - which, as it happens, was approximately the value of the low-absorbing OPEC countries' external asset holdings at that date. By comparison with pre-1914 Britain, the OPEC countries acquired their assets over a much briefer time-span than Britain - and subsequently spent them over a much briefer time-span as well.

[4] Feenstra, R.C. (1998): Integration of Trade and Disintegration of Production in the Global Economy. Journal of Economic Perspectives, Vol. 12, No. 4.

[5] Anderson, P.S., Hainaut, P. (1998): Foreign Direct Investment and Employment in the Industrial Countries. BIS Working Papers No. 61, November, p. 4. Also, . Bordo, M. Eichengreen, B., Kim, J. (1998): Was There Really an Earlier Period of International Financial Integration Comparable to Today? NBER Working Paper No. 6738, September .

The pre-1914 period also witnessed numerous minor – and not so minor – wars and political turmoil; debt defaults; and a "Great Depression" from the mid-1880s to the mid-1890s. Latin American debt defaults even triggered a Baring Crisis in 1890, though on that occasion the bank was rescued for its existing owners.[6]

As for regionalism in Europe, there was a substantial measure of economic integration: complete freedom of movement for labour; passport-free travel (up to the borders of the Russian Empire); no restrictions on cross-border establishment of businesses; and of course monetary union in practice via the gold standard. Absent, interestingly, was free trade in goods. There were significant tariffs among European countries on both industrial and agricultural products.[7]

However, given the far smaller weight of taxation in the economies of that period, it can be argued that such tariffs were of no greater significance from the viewpoint of economic integration than are differences in VAT or income tax rates in the 1990s – especially as the tariffs in question were anyhow imposed partly for revenue rather than protectionist reasons. To be sure, disparities in national tax rates across the EU have recently (1998) come under criticism. But this reflects, more a power-play on the part of certain European politicians and Brussels Commission officials than a deep-seated imperative of European integration. Federal states such as the USA or Switzerland have not found measurable differences in tax regimes among their constituent parts to be incompatible with close economic and political unity.

* * *

How then does the international trading and financial system of today differ from that of 100 years ago? There are at least three differences. First, the industrialised world covers a much wider area of the globe. The reference here is not simply or even mainly to the NICs, although they must certainly be mentioned. In the words of Anderson & Hainaut (op. cit., p.5): "FDIs involve more countries. Although stocks and flows are still dominated by the industrial countries, the role of emerging market countries has recently grown. By the end of 1996 these countries accounted for about 30 percent of inward stocks [of FDI] (and) they are also becoming increasingly active as source countries". Quite apart from the NICs, however, most of today's industrial countries other than Britain were only semi-industrialised a century ago and did not complete their industrialization until after

---

[6]The classic studies are Ford, A.G. (1962): The Gold Standard 1880-1914: Britain and Argentina. Oxford and Ferns, H.S. (1960): Britain and Argentina in the Nineteenth Century. Oxford.

[7]See Boltho, A. (1996): The Return of Free Trade. International Affairs, Vol. 72, No. 2; and Williamson, J.G. (1998): Globalization, Labour Markets and Policy Backlash in the Past. Journal of Economic Perspectives, Vol 12, No. 4, p. 66f. Citing also the work of K.H. O'Rourke and M. Tracy, Williamson points out that European import tariffs on grain after 1870 were (i) a response to the "grain invasion" from overseas and (ii) a precursor of the EU's Common Agricultural Policy.

World War II.[8] That, and the growing differentiation and sophistication of industrial products, must encourage a much denser and, above all, more multilateral and balanced pattern of international investment. Continental European countries have in fact been relatively slow to develop their own outward investments, whether in each other or wider afield. Switzerland is the exception.

Secondly, late twentieth-century technological progress in transport and in ICT (information and communications technology) has produced the "shrinking world" phenomenon often referred to in contemporary discussion. Of course trends in this direction were already operative a century ago, but the quantitative change since that time is nonetheless enormous.[9]

Thirdly, today's international trading and investment relations are dominated by multi-national enterprises on the one hand and financial institutions on the other. My main focus in this paper is on the 'real' sector, so I shall not dwell on financial aspects. Nevertheless a brief word is necessary if only because the two overlap. In the pre-1914 era the main channel of capital exports from Britain was through purchases of bonds in the London market by individuals. Institutions concerned with the marketing of securities hardly existed. Those that did were unregulated, and their honesty could not be relied upon. Merchant banks were – as their name implies – concerned with trade finance more than with long-term capital provision. Nowadays not only do banks play a much broader role, transmitting funds between countries through the world-wide interbank network, but cross-border placements in shares and bonds are undertaken predominantly by insurance companies, pension funds and other intermediaries such as investment funds (in US parlance; "trusts" in Britain). This has its roots in the greater wealth of the lending population, and the associated expansion of savings and pension schemes. One of its consequences is to make foreign capital available to a wider range of recipients than in the late nineteenth century, although governments, utilities and real-estate continue to occupy a large place.

As regards (non-financial) multinational enterprises, defining these as firms engaged in FDI, they have been estimated to number about 40,000 in the late 1990s and to account for about 1/3 of non-agricultural world output and for a considerably higher fraction of world trade in non-agricultural goods.[10] They are of importance too in non-financial services - business consultancy, law, accountancy. Associated with

---

[8] This proposition was central to the analysis in Nicholas Kaldor's celebrated Inaugural Lecture, "Causes of the Slow Rate of Economic Growth of the United Kingdom" (Cambridge, 1966). The relevant economic indicator is the proportion of a country's labour force employed in agriculture.

[9] Obstfeld, M. (1998): The Global Capital Market: Benefactor or Menace. Journal of Economic Perspectives, Vol. 12, No. 4, p. 11 notes that the laying of the first trans-Atlantic cable in 1866 reduced settlement time for intercontinental transactions from 10 days to a few hours. Jeffrey Williamson, op. cit., p. 51, cites the finding by O'Rourke and himself that real maritime freight rates fell by 1.5 percent per annum between 1840 and 1910. For earlier similar discussion see Imlah, A.H. (1958): Economic Elements in the Pax Brittanica.Cambridge, Mass.

[10] Dunning, J.H. (1997): Governments and the Macro-organization of Economic Activity. In: Dunning, J.H. (ed.): Governments, Globalization and International Business. Oxford.

them is a growing tendency for production to be organised transnationally, at least in certain sectors (automobiles, electronics). In other words, rather than just producing vehicles in several countries (perhaps even different models in each), or basically producing in one country but assembling them in several others, car manufacturers nowadays source components from a number of countries and also undertake different stages of assembly in more than one (transnational) location, so that the final product is in the literal sense of the word a multinational product.

The process is bound up with the changing nature of industrial output compared with a century ago: much lower raw material content, much greater contribution to value added from processing and knowledge.[11] In other words, technological development not only, as already noted, in ICT and transport, but in numerous other sectors of production: vehicle building, machine tools, medical and other specialised equipment, pharmaceuticals, printing etc . It is well-established that many forms of applied knowledge or productive skill are bound up with particular corporate cultures and organisations, and are not satisfactorily exploited merely thorough licensing agreements or shared training facilities. Problems of incomplete contracting and asymmetric information (moral hazard) abound. Hence, enterprises feel the need to extend their physical presence into all or most markets where they either sell their output or can usefully purchase labour inputs.

At the same time, lower transport costs facilitate geographical fragmentation of the production process ("slicing up the value-added chain", as Krugman has called it)[12] between different locations, allowing comparative advantage to be more efficiently exploited stage-by-stage. So there is much more re-exporting and re-importing, and the ratio of merchandise trade to merchandise value added has risen much more steeply in the past thirty years than has the ratio of trade to GDP. This is shown by the data in Table 2, again taken from Feenstra, op. cit. Although the broad tendency is not in doubt, the figures probably exaggerate its extent because of the tendency of modern firms to outsource services such as planning, maintenance, security or transport to separate enterprises, when in earlier decades such services would have been more often provided in-house and therefore recorded as contributing to merchandise value added. Likewise, comparisons with the pre-1914 period exaggerate the change for those countries which were only semi-industrialised a century ago, and where the rising ratio of trade to merchandise value added is therefore influenced by the relative decline of agriculture.

---

[11] This trend and its analysis have a long history. It featured prominently in Ragnar Nurkse's Wicksell Lectures of 1954, Patterns of Trade and Development. A recent summary is Stephen J. Kobrin, "The Architecture of Globalization: State Sovereignty in a Networked Global Economy". In: Dunning, J.H. (ed.) op. cit.

[12] Krugman, P. (1995): Growing World Trade: Causes and Consequences. Brookings Papers on Economic Activity.

Table 2: Ratios of merchandise trade to merchandise value-added (percent).*

Country	1890	1913	1960[a]	1970	1980	1990[b]
Australia	27.2	35.6	24.4	25.6	32.4	38.7
Canada	29.7	39.4	37.6	50.5	65.6	69.8
Denmark	47.4	66.2	60.2	65.9	90.0	85.9
France	18.5	23.3	16.8	25.7	44.0	53.5
Germany	22.7	29.2	24.6	31.3	48.5	57.8
Italy	14.4	21.9	19.2	26.0	43.1	43.9
Japan	10.2	23.9	15.3	15.7	25.8	18.9
Norway[a]	46.2	55.2	60.0	73.2	70.9	74.8
Sweden	42.5	37.5	39.7	48.8	72.9	73.1
U K	61.5	76.3	33.8	40.7	52.6	62.8
United States[c]	14.3	13.2	9.6	13.7	30.9	35.8

* Merchandise trade is measured as the everage of imports and exports, except as noted below. Merchandise value-added combines agriculture, mining and manufacturing for the U.S., and these sectors plus construction and public utilities for most other countries.

[a] Value for Australia refers to 1962, and for Canada refers to 1961.

[b] Value for Canada refers to 1988, for germany to 1989, and for the U.K. to 1987.

[c] Data recorded under 1890 is for 1889, and along with that in 1913, measures the ratio of merchandise exports to industry value-added.

Source: R.C. Feenstra, op. cit.

In addition, a growing share of capital commitments involves large-scale R & D. To undertake this is risky enough even for near-monopolists, let alone for competing firms which have to confront greatly enhanced market risks as well technological ones. One result is that formerly or even currently competing firms form strategic alliances for the development of, say, new aircraft (the European Airbus) or bigger memory chips. In other cases R & D costs create pressure for a global marketing organisation, even though production of the new output itself may not involve important scale economies. Pharmaceuticals are an obvious example. Conversely, the scale factor alone may bring about alliances, or indeed mergers, when little or no R & D is involved. This is the case in the upstream (exploration and production) segment of the oil industry; and – to return to the finance sector – in the history of banking over the past century and a half, where merger pressure arose primarily not from operational technology but from the exigencies of risk spreading in the face of ever larger debtor clients. The spread of international banking networks has likewise been stimulated by the spread of multinational enterprises, and is to that extent a second-stage outcome of changing patterns of manufacture.

* * *

The changes in productive structures and work habits associated with globalization are chiefly confined to the private sector. Not all of them have attracted attention, because their link with globalization has been insufficiently recognised. In particular, the working hours of many business professionals are now longer, sometimes much longer, than they were a generation ago. This is basically a result of modern communications linking financial markets and enterprises in different time zones and thus creating expectations of quicker decision-taking.

What globalizing tendencies have evoked, however, is a vague sense of anxiety about the position of the nation state. If this seems not to have been parallelled before 1914, the explanation is simple. Globalization would hardly be viewed as a kind of termite gnawing away at the economic foundations of the nation state, had not that state itself, or rather its government sector, acquired such enormously increased economic functions over the past century. In other words, by the standards of 1900 the main trespasser or source of disturbance in the late twentieth century has been not the external economy but internal state power. The increase in government economic functions is conveniently classified under (once again) three heads.

One is the growth of general government expenditure (and taxation) – from 10 or 12 per cent of GDP to 40-50 percent of GDP in Western Europe; and even in the USA and Japan to around 30 percent. These proportionate increases alone are far larger than any parallel increase in the openness of the economies in question. The second head is the growth of economic policy responsibilities beyond the traditional Adam-Smithian ones of law enforcement, defence, minimum poor relief and a stable currency (seen as part of the legal infrastructure). This category covers fluctuating governmental involvement with employment, economic growth, urban or environmental planning and income distribution. It also includes public ownership of enterprises in the utilities and other sectors. The third head concerns public regulation of market activities, designed to safeguard or promote probity in finance, health and safety at work, consumer protection, clean air and other environmental values, non-discrimination in employment and numerous other social and economic desiderata.

National governments play a bigger role in today's world not only because they claim wider economic and regulatory responsibilities, but because there are many more of them[13]. Without going back all the way to the Austro-Hungarian Empire, in the past half century alone membership of the United Nations has increased almost fourfold to 185 states. This is a result of decolonization and break-ups of existing states (such as the USSR – even though it had three members of the UN from the start; Yugoslavia; Pakistan).

Aside from globalizing tendencies in the organisation of production, several trends in the politics and economics of the late twentieth century are, in one way or another, reactions to the enlarged ambitions and activities of government in the economic sphere. Among these reactions are:

---

[13] For some incisive reflections on this phenomenon, see Moynihan, D.P. (1993): Pandaemonium: Ethnicity and International Politics. Oxford.

– thatcherism;

– devolution, or federalisation downwards, sometimes labelled "Europe of the Regions" in the EU context;

– the 'new regionalism', referred to earlier, or federalisation upwards, as seen in the development of bodies such as the EU, NAFTA, MERCOSUR, ASEAN, APEC and so forth.

Thatcherism is a shorthand term for political and social backlash against the mixed economy and state welfare systems. The following summary is parochially British, but many features have their parallels in other industrial countries, sometimes in conscious imitation of the British example. Mrs. Thatcher herself as Prime Minister of the United Kingdom spoke of the need "to roll back the economic frontiers of the state."[14] What this turned out to mean in practice was mainly the privatisation first of public housing and then of previously nationalised industry, primarily utilities (telephones, gas, electricity, water) but also transport enterprises (British Airways, British Rail) and some manufacturers, notably of motor vehicles and of defence supplies.

Such privatisation of production units, however, while widening share ownership and (somewhat to the UK government's own surprise) considerably enhancing economic efficiency in the areas concerned, had only short-lived or peripheral effects on government expenditure and taxation levels. There was a once-only boost to revenues from the actual sale of public-sector assets; thereafter, minor savings in public expenditure on housing maintenance, and probably little net change in Treasury revenues, as earlier profits or losses of nationalised industries were replaced by tax receipts from the newly privatised firms.

A separate and distinct aspect of Thatcherism, therefore, is the cultivation of political resistance to taxation, combined with attempts to limit government-sector spending. In terms of the aggregate numbers (ratios of government revenue and government spending to GDP) these policies had little tangible result. But there were structural and institutional changes, at any rate in Britain. The weight of personal taxation shifted markedly from direct to indirect (VAT and excise duties) imposts.[15] The management of public expenditure was altered in various ways, indicative of a new emphasis on parsimony and supposed efficiency. Performance or "value-for-money" audits of publicly financed institutions such as hospitals and universities became fashionable.[16] In the civil service ancillary functions such as cleaning and maintenance were tendered out to private firms, matching the trend in private

---

[14] Among the extensive literature on Thatcherism, an item which focuses concisely and informatively on this theme is a special number of the Journal of Law and Society, Vol,. 16, No. 1, reprinted as Andrew Gamble and Celia Wells eds, Thatcher's Law (GPC Books, 1989).

[15] In the process the tax burden was shifted significantly from the better off to the less well-off. Mrs. Thatcher's most radical effort in this direction, however – namely, the replacement of local real-estate taxes by a poll tax – not only proved unsustainable but was the cause of her expulsion from office by her own party in 1991.

[16] For a full discussion see Power, M. (1997): The Audit Society: Rituals of Verification. Oxford.

industry; and non-policy-making parts of the service were re-organised as free-standing "executive agencies", such as the Contributions Agency of the Department of Social Security or the Highways Agency of the Department of Transport.

Attempts were also made, with little success, to trim social security payments by curbing entitlement to unemployment benefits and by intensifying measures against fraudulent claims. The most important aspect of British arrangements in this domain, however, did not have to be invented by Mrs. Thatcher, although she reinforced it. This is the subordinate role of the state in relation to retirement pensions. By comparison with many other industrial counties, a large part of British pension provision is private and is financed through participation in profits rather than by adding to costs.

Interestingly, this type of pensions mechanism provides a partial answer to fears that pressure for reduced taxes on capital arising from international capital mobility and globalization of production will prove incompatible with democratically determined financing norms for social welfare.[17] Pensions form a sizeable fraction of society's welfare outlays. Yet British pension funds not only benefit from low taxes on corporate income but are free to invest abroad as well as in the United Kingdom.[18] It should also be said that Mrs. Thatcher's abolition of UK foreign exchange control in 1979 is the only example of relaxation of a regulatory regime by her Government. In other areas – the labour market, education, health care, financial services, the privatised utilities – government regulation was extended or tightened.

The foregoing "partial answer" is in addition to other, quite different answers to the same worry. One is that – as Thatcherism itself illustrates – the operative constraints on welfare spending and taxation may well reside in domestic politics rather than in external factors. Another answer is that the effective incidence of corporate profits tax (i.e. who ultimately pays it) is uncertain; and that shifting it on to consumers may be desirable on efficiency grounds (promoting saving and investment). A third answer is that pressure for inter-country convergence of corporate tax regimes – and of social security provision – is only partial, given that international mobility of enterprise activities is also partial.[19]

---

[17] Such fears are expressed in Rodrik, D. (1997): Has Globalization Gone Too Far? Institute for International Economics, Washington D.C.

[18] Until the corporate tax changes announced in 1998 by Tony Blair's Chancellor of the Exchequer, Gordon Brown, UK pension funds had since the 1960s been wholly exempt from tax on UK company profits. For a full study on pension funds, see Philip Davis, E. (1995): Pension Funds. Oxford. Their prominence in the Swiss and Dutch cases is comparable to the United Kingdom.

[19] Supporting this, recall the earlier comment that there are significant variations of tax even within individual federations such as the United States or Switzerland. Maurice Obstfeld, op. cit. p. 20, mentions the US case. He also notes the efficiency argument for low taxes on capital earnings, citing Lucas, R.E. (1990): Supply-Side Economics: an Analytical Review. Oxford Economic Papers, April.

* * *

Thatcherism purports to aim at a reduction in the economic functions of government. By contrast, the federalising tendencies also cited in the previous section reflect arguments not about reducing those functions, but about the most advantageous way of exercising them. Consider first devolution or "downward" federalism. This is exemplified with varying degrees of seriousness by Scotland (and to a much lesser degree Wales) in the United Kingdom, by Catalonia in Spain and by Padania in Italy. At the extreme it spills over into demands for full autonomy, as instanced by the Scottish National Party and by support for independence in Quebec. It is thus a part of the decolonization and self-determination trend in world affairs, which has so sharply multiplied the number of nation states.

It seems obvious, although not strictly provable, that pressures for devolution would be much less if the economic functions of the state were confined to those of a century ago. There would be so much less substance to argue about, particularly where the regions concerned already possess their own languages or cultural institutions (like the Scottish legal and educational systems).

Devolution pressures reflect consciousness of local common interests in opposition to a dominant centre. Compare this with "upward" federalism. Establishment of regional organizations in world trade, such as the European Union, NAFTA, MERCOSUR and the rest, reflect attempts by the dominant centres themselves, i.e. national governments, to optimize their leverage in a world of extensively liberalised trade and transnational production. A liberal world trading regime means that geographical proximity, i.e. transport-cost advantage, is an import factor influencing the composition of regional economic organisations. (Contrast the situation in the protectionist world of the 1930s and 1940s, when the sterling area, and later the dollar area, were established. Geographical proximity was far less important). Cultural affinity also plays a part. More specifically, Wilfred Ethier, one of the leading analysts of the new regionalism, summarises it in the following terms:

– "The new regionalism is, in good part, a direct result of the success of multilateral liberalisation.
– Regionalism is the means by which new countries trying to enter the multilateral system (and small countries already in it) compete among themselves for the direct investment necessary for their successful participation in that system.
– Regionalism - by internalising an important externality - plays a key role in expanding and preserving the liberal trade order".[20]

The externality in question centres on the credibility of each country's commitment to an FDI-friendly policy regime, comprising free-ish trade not merely within the club but also *vis-à-vis* third countries, reasonable corporate taxation and so forth. Commitments are solidified by incorporation in a treaty, which simultaneously promises adherence to an identical regime by the entire group of signatory countries.

---

[20] Ethier, W. (1998): The New Regionalism. Economic Journal, op. cit.

This in turn encourages mutually interdependent foreign enterprises to develop branches or subsidiaries in the countries concerned.

International states, and groups of states, are likely to have somewhat differing objectives. So regional regimes vary from case to case. And each organisation may involve complicated coalitions. This is especially evident in the European Union. Motives of financial self-interest, anti-Americanism, policy leverage over otherwise dominant neighbours and political herd instinct vary greatly from one EU member country (or aspirant member) to another. Thoughtful Germans are spurred by their special anxiety about *Vergangenheitsbewältigung*, or perhaps more appropriately, *Zukunftsbewältigung*.[21] What is conspicuous, however, is the universal reluctance to transfer most nation-state economic functions to the central authorities. Brussels is allowed to spend between one and two percent of Europe's GDP – and even that looks excessive to most people, especially after the revelations in 1998-99 of high level corruption and fraud – while the constituent national governments spend 40 or 50 percent of GDP. Ethier (op. cit.) is therefore unjustifiably cavalier in referring to the EU as a single (large) country in the context of his model of regionalism. European currency union under the Euro is unlikely to prove compatible with the preservation of existing economic functions of national governments. Tensions between the two will be a major theme of European economic history in the period ahead.

* * *

Viewing globalization as synonymous with incipient subversion of the nation state or national governments is thus mistaken. A more legitimate association is between globalization and convergence, defined as a tendency towards equalization of income levels across countries. The question is which countries and by what process.[22]

The natural inclination nowadays is to view convergence in terms of a growth process. Starting from a relatively low income level, countries experience a burst of rapid growth in *per capita* incomes as they catch up – fully or partly – with the leaders. This was the experience of continental western Europe in the 1950s and 1960s, and of Japan a little later, and is currently running its course in much of eastern Asia including China and, less spectacularly, India. The catch-up episode involves extensive capital accumulation, as well as assimilation of leading-edge technology. It is adequately captured by a neo-classical growth model with exogenous technical progress.[23] The most advanced countries may themselves be continuing to grow at a slower but still significant pace because of endogenous technical progress.[24] An

---

[21] Respectively, "overcoming the past" and "overcoming the future".

[22] Convergence may also occur without participation in the international system - through rivalry in isolation, as it were. Soviet Russia's economic development between 1917 and, say, 1960 may be interpreted in this light.

[23] Barro, R.J., Sala-i-Martin, X. (1995): Economic Growth. McGraw-Hill New York, Chs. 10-12.

[24] Ibid., Chs. 4-6.

implication of this approach is that converging countries are those whose domestic conditions – social, cultural, technological – are such as to have carried them across the Rostow threshold of take-off into self-sustained growth, and whose governments also pursue policies conducive to such growth. The specific content of policy - how outward-oriented, how much deliberate government promotion of enterprise, and so forth - is itself a complex topic beyond the scope of this paper.

Convergence in the second half of the nineteenth century took a different form. Of course there was a certain amount of catch-up growth. But the main mechanism was international labour (as well as capital) migration, leading to cross-country convergence of real wages and the ratio of wages to land rents, raising them in the countries of emigration and lowering them in the countries of immigration. The relevant analytical framework here is not a growth model, but a static adjustment process in newly unified or quasi-unified markets. Capital accumulation plays a less prominent role, governed mainly by the need to adapt to the changing availability of labour in the respective territories.[25]

Jeffrey G. Williamson and his colleagues have done a great service in shedding fresh light on this issue, especially in emphasising (a) the centrality of factor-price adjustment rather than *per capita* GDP growth to migration-based convergence, and (b) the magnitude of the process in the pre-1914 period. In Williamson's own words:[26] "Mass migration after 1870 had augmented the 1910 New World labour force [in Argentina, Australia, Canada and the USA] by 49 percent, reduced the 1910 labour force in the emigrant countries around the European periphery [Scandinavia, plus Italy, Portugal, Spain and Ireland] by 22 percent, and reduced the 1910 labour force in the European industrial core [Belgium, France, Germany, Great Britain, Netherlands] by 2 percent. Mass migration by itself may explain about 70 percent of the real wage convergence in the late 19th-century Atlantic economy....."

These labour force figures put in perspective the international migration of the post-1945 period. This has been important for a few small countries, such as Switzerland, Israel, Persian Gulf oil exporters and Puerto Rico. In global terms, however, it has not remotely approached the nineteenth-century magnitudes, despite some conspicuous south-north movements within western Europe and within the Americas. To find a recent analogy with the nineteenth-century process, one must look rather at the reunification of East and West Germany after 1989 - and contrast it with the West German miracle after 1949.

The key role of factor price changes in the nineteenth century is further highlighted by the Williamson team's findings on income distribution:[27]

"Between 1870 and 1913, inequality rose dramatically in rich, land-abundant, labour-scarce New World countries like Australia, Canada and the United States; inequality fell dramatically in poor, land-scarce, labour-abundant, newly

---

[25] Williamson, J.G. op. cit., and the references there cited, especially Taylor and Williamson (1997): European Review of Economic History.

[26] Ibid., p. 60.

[27] Ibid., p. 62.

industrialising countries like Norway, Sweden, Denmark and Italy; inequality was more stable in the European industrial economies like Belgium, France, the Netherlands and the United Kingdom; and inequality was also more stable in the poor European economies which failed to play the globalization game, like Portugal and Spain."

In the absence of international migration, national factor prices and income distribution are liable to be affected by the global pattern of trade and production. This has been a central theme of Heckscher-Ohlin trade theory since the 1920s.[28] A development which has in varying degrees been attributed to it is the deterioration in the market position of unskilled workers in the older industrial countries in the final decades of the twentieth century. The argument is that the new industrial countries have taken over manufacturing processes intensive in unskilled labour, while the older countries specialize in skill-intensive ones. In other words, workers in Asia now undertake manufacturing tasks whose performance in a nineteenth-century world would have involved them in migrating to North America or Western Europe. Correspondingly, unskilled workers in the older countries suffer a period of declining real wages (as in the United States) and/or rising unemployment (as in Western Europe).[29]

The argument needs to be viewed against the background of world economic growth highlighted above. Technological advance provides older industrial countries with opportunities to restructure in "up-market" directions. International trade imparts momentum to the process by involving new countries who are entering the "catch-up" phase of their development. The catch-up is then quicker and more diffused (not so much of a "dual economy"), but less hi-tech and probably less capital-intensive, than it would otherwise have been. The precise implications for unskilled wages in the older countries depend on the opportunities there for factor substitution and on the pattern of wage-earners' consumer preferences, as well as on the overall pace of technological progress. Greater inequality, in the sense of a wider spread between high and low incomes, may go together with higher absolute real wages even at the bottom of the scale. Analysis of such possibilities depends particularly on going beyond basic Heckscher-Ohlin models, which allow for only two factors of production.[30]

---

[28] The Stolper-Samuelson theorem and the Factor Price Equalization theorem of Samuelson are the best known textbook propositions. See also Mundell, R.A. (1957): International Trade and Factor Mobility. American Economic Review. These theorems all depend on similar very restrictive assumptions.

[29] The fullest study is Wood, A. (1994): North-South Trade, Employment and Inequality. Oxford. See also Journal of Economic Perspectives, Summer 1995.

[30] Merely introducing a third factor employed in only one sector makes a big difference. See Bliss, C. (1998): A Non-Square Trade Model with Development Application. Nuffield College, Oxford, processed; and the same author's (1998): Stolper-Samuelson and the Corn Laws. In: Cook, G. (ed.): Freedom and Trade: The Economics and Politics of International Trade. Vol. 1 London.

* * *

Nineteenth-century globalization was brought to an abrupt end by World War I. We rightly speak, even in economic terms, of the "pre-1914" era. Up to that point interference with the liberal international economic order had amounted to no more than secondary blemishes. This applies both to import tariffs in Europe and to restrictions on immigration in the Americas and Australia.[31] The tendency towards de-globalization – "fragmentation" is perhaps a better term – was, however, drastically reinforced in the inter-war period and at that time went together with a widening of the economic role of governments. After 1945 the latter trend continued but the former was consciously rejected – albeit cautiously at first and mainly at US insistence. The importance of inter-government co-operation was recognised, along with governmental responsibility for domestic economic affairs. Government reaction was decisive on two conspicuous occasions in helping to prevent economic shocks from triggering a global slump. The crucial shock absorber in the aftermath of the first jump in oil prices in 1973-74 was the endogenous ("automatic stabilizer") widening of public-sector budget deficits in the oil-importing world. When the LDC debt crisis broke in August 1982, it was the leadership of Mr. Volcker at the US Federal Reserve, supported by other central banks, in forestalling moves by commercial banks to recall loans from LDC debtors.[32]

Less episodically, the GATT/WTO remains the accepted institutional framework for safeguarding free trade and settling commercial policy disputes. The IMF, despite appearing in recent decades to be somewhat at the mercy of events, remains the focal point for discussion of balance-of-payments issues and mobilisation of currency support operations.

In short, globalization depends on the community of nation states continuing to value it and pursuing policies consistent with it. World government is not in prospect. To be sure, we are dealing here with a collective good, a repeated prisoner's dilemma game which requires countries to adapt their co-operative behaviour to changing circumstances. Errors and setbacks may occur from time to time. But to claim that globalization is essentially undermining the nation state is tantamount to asserting that the world economic order is on a path to self-destruction. Such a pessimistic conclusion is warranted by neither logic nor evidence.

---

[31] Williamson, J.G. op. cit., p. 62f. One reason why grain import tariffs were globally unimportant is that Great Britain, overwhelmingly the biggest importer, did not impose them.

[32] Although a central bank rather than a government in the strict sense, the Fed was only established on the eve of World War I.

2. Financial Globalization : Specificity and Historical Differences

Marcello de Cecco

Whoever visits the beautiful Roman National Museum at Palazzo Massimo, stops in front of the sepulchre, found at Grottarossa, of a young girl of the II century AD. From information provided by the curator of the Museum, we learn that she was buried wrapped in a silk cloth from Egypt. Her necklace was made of precious stones from Ceylon, and the other jewelry that adorned her was made of amber that came from places scattered throughout southern Europe. Next to the sepulchre of Grottarossa, the curators of the Museum have placed a beautiful map of all the principal trade routes within the Roman Empire and those in territories beyond the frontiers, as well as a detailed list of the commercial products and the directions of trade traffic.

One gets the impression of a vast commercial network, which included a great number of products and a highly developed division of labor as well. This impression is reinforced by the research that Spanish archeologists have been carrying on for years on the remains of the olive oil amphorae of Mount Testaccio. They speak of a very strong dependence of the imperial capital on the importation of oil from the provinces, especially Spain. But other colonies like Volubilis, in Morocco, also develop in order to supply Rome with oil. And the supply of wheat from Egypt is widely known. A visit to the ruins of Ostia Antica gives a clear picture of the extent, quantity and regularity of shipping between Rome and her Empire.

The Roman Empire was also the largest area of a unified currency in the world, before the modern experience. On the two million Roman coins found in and beyond the borders of the Empire, as far as India and China, specialists perform fascinating research - comparing the place of discovery with the age of the coins and the mint that produced them. And legal historians have enlightened us on the profundity and completeness of the commercial institutions and of the Roman banks, and of the judicial institutions created to govern them.

It is not difficult, therefore, to speak of an experience of globalization that is comparable only with the current one; for the inclusion of a large part of the lands of the Old World, for the links to the East with lands not included within the Roman frontiers, for the unification and standardization of the judicial and economic institutions in all of the territory of the Empire, for the currency integration in the sole area of the Empire itself, and even for the standardization of architectural and urban styles of the cities of the Empire.

The statues displayed in the Roman National Museum furnish, moreover, clear proof of the profound ethnic melting pot that the Empire favored. We know from the literature and inscriptions that the Emperor who celebrated the millenium of Rome was named Philip the Arab. Just a visit to the museum reveals the clear

African traits of the head of Alexander Severus and of the other Emperors of his house. As for the mixture of religions of the four boroughs of the Empire, any map of the Roman city reveals temples of widely differing creeds that penetrated the Empire and spread throughout it. Christianity became the state religion, but the cult of Mithra and Isis and Osiris continue to exist; Aryanism and other cults, that replaced the ancient gods of Rome to the new monotheistic religion from the near east.

And finally we should recall linguistic hegemony, which finds an equal only in the current global domination of the English language.

But it is worth stating, before closing this brief evocation of an impressive episode of globalization, that it would be more correct to refer to this period as the Greco-Roman era, given the importance of the Greek element in nearly all the principal aspects of the period.

Where and when did today's globalization begin? It is clear that we may date its origins to the great geographical discoveries, and the colonial expansion that followed, from the fifteenth century onward. These put an end to the attempt to reconstruct the commercial framework of the ancient world, initiated by the Italian Republics and carried forward successfully until the beginning of the fifteenth century. The geographical discoveries and the colonial conquests definitively ended this era of a return to the ancient form of globalization, and of a revival of Greco-Roman trade routes and institutions, giving the Atlantic European nations the opportunity to begin a new and completely original globalization, from which today's globalization is a direct descendant. From the eighteenth century on, the heart of globalization moved to the American continent where it has remained up to the present, because a centre of civilisation had been created in a previously semi-populated place, and because America was, and still is, able to act as a fulcrum between Europe and Asia, in a much more fundamental way than had been possible for Europe itself.

One thing which is worth stating, leaving aside three of the five centuries which this era encompasses, is the similarities between each other that may be noted in the periods of accentuated globalization, which fall between the nineteenth century and twentieth century. The characteristics common to the two decades that straddle the First World War and the three decades that close the millennium may be easily identified in both the institutional and commercial field. I will deal here with financial globalization, limiting myself to comparing the two periods with respect to that sector. Before doing so however we should remember that the nineteenth century and the first half of the twentieth are also witness to the apotheosis of the nation state, particularly in its economic aspects. And the nation state may be seen in full bloom and in its two main varieties, the Euro-continental and the Anglo-American; each tied to a precise way of viewing political philosophy and the resulting consequences on economic and social organisation. We may say that the two world wars represented an attempt, in two phases, to resolve the conflict between these two models of the state which we could call the bureaucratic state and the merchant state. At the end of the millennium we can assign victory, with some doubt about the longevity of the victory, to the merchant state. Many fortresses, however, still remain to be completely conquered, such as Russia, China, Japan and other examples of Asian capitalism, before being able to be absolutely certain. And complete turnabouts are not to be excluded even within the core of the system, as occurred after the First World War.

It would be very misleading to attempt to confine the bureaucratic organisation of economic life within the boundaries of the national economic experience. The great bureaucratic states of the recent and distant past represent in fact an alternative way of organising globalization in which the international division of labour responds to the needs of the bureaucratic structures by which the national economic systems are organised. If we consider the entire history of our species on earth, and in particular the history of organised societies, we may conclude without a shadow of a doubt that the bureaucratic model has largely prevailed over the mercantile model. The globalization of the last five centuries may be viewed as a reversal of this tendency, but the experiences of capitalist development in the countries which pursued the leaders, starting with England, have been so strongly distinguished by state bureaucracy as to render it impossible to believe in the irreversibility of this same tendency. It may be said, however, that the predominance in a particular era of external over internal trade has led to the assertion of the mercantile class in each country, due to the difficulty for the bureaucrats of adequately controlling the activities entrusted to the merchants going or coming from abroad. The alternative model of globalization, therefore, seeks to reduce to a minimum commercial activities which require a large-scale intervention of fiduciary guarantees. There is an attempt in particular to limit and restrain the development of international financial markets which turn out to be very difficult to control. The globalization led by the mercantile classes instead is founded precisely on the development of a global financial market and the shrewder or more powerful mercantile states do all they can to have the heart and nerve centre of those markets situated within their boundaries and use all possible means to promote this trend. Where bureaucratic states coexist with mercantile globalization, they must confront these problems and they react either by seeking themselves to foster the establishment within their boundaries of the organisational headquarters of the financial globalization or by attempting to minimise its importance without renouncing the benefits deriving from commercial globalization. The first and second solution depend for their success on particular historical contexts but they are both always eminently unstable. One sees, for example, the attempt by France, renewed periodically, to make Paris an international financial centre. One notes the efforts of the Japanese to achieve the same aim from the mid-eighties. Or the similar cyclical in pursuing the same policy over the last century. These relate to the first solution. As to the second, we have a striking example in the period which runs from the years immediately following the First World War, which inaugurate the most important phase of state capitalism and bureaucratic control over economic life, up to 1960. It is an example which swayed not only the weaker countries in Europe and elsewhere, but also for some time the centre of the mercantile economy itself, England and the United States. Also in these two countries, where the mercantile class has always been in the forefront of political and economic life, those who control the great industries and the unions waver between the two alternative versions of globalization, that based on bureaucratic international cooperation and that founded on the financial markets and on the markets in general, for determining the international division of labour and resources. The advocates of mercantile globalization are thus obliged to engage in a protracted battle, lasting decades, to win the industrial and political classes, or at least important segments of them, over their vision.

To understand the affinity between the two main phases in the episode of globalization still going on, which we have placed in the two decades straddling the turn of the century and the last three decades of our millennium, we can cite contemporary authors of the early period as their words highlight the similarity to the current phase. First of all, it is worthwhile referring to, without necessarily quoting them since they are so well known, the statements with which Keynes described the two decades prior to the First World War. It is, however, necessary to quote some extracts from a work by Norman Angell that appeared in 1912 and was immediately translated into all languages. The reference is to "The Great Illusion", a prophetic book in which the author shows how military strength and even territorial conquest are of little use in an era of economic integration and international financial institutions. Unfortunately, he was not correct in demonstrating that international financial integration would succeed in impeding war. But he demonstrates clearly the uselessness of the German efforts to defeat the power of international finance by force of arms. The war was not avoided but Germany was defeated along with Austria. Angell demonstrated above all how international commercial integration had made each country dependent on the economic events in every other country. This was due to the prodigious development of the means of communication and transport in the latter half of the nineteenth century. This vital interdependence - he asserts- "which goes beyond all borders" could stand in large part for the work of the last forty years. The extent of the developments in this period was such as to create such a complex financial interdependence between the capitals of the world that a change in business transactions in New York would immediately provoke turmoil in the financial institutions in London; and in serious situations the London financial houses would be forced to cooperate with their New York counterparts in order to put an end to the crisis: and this was prompted not by altruism but by the necessity of self-protection. The complexity of modern finance makes New York dependent on London, London on Paris, Paris on Berlin and in much greater measure than had ever happened previously in history. This concrete situation is a consequence of the general use of the new and very recent technologies that civilisation offers us: express post, instantaneous spreading of financial and commercial news by telegraph, the incredible world-wide progress in speed of communications which has placed a half dozen European capitals in the closest of financial contact and rendered each of them more interdependent than the major English cities were less than a hundred years ago. To give greater strength to his arguments Angell quoted a passage from a French newspaper which reads: "The rapid development of industry has provoked the active interest of finance, which has become the "*nervus rerum*" and has come to play a dominant role. Under the influence of finance, industry has begun to lose its exclusively national character and to assume an increasingly international nature."

A very recent study by Michel Bordo and Barry Eichengreen, using the most advanced methods of quantitative analysis, confirms what emerges clearly from the brief citation that I have quoted from Angell's text. The two periods of greatest commercial and financial interpenetration are really the same in terms of the quantitative values of phenomena, and also in the surprise at the speed and depth of globalization pre-1914 expressed by those who directly observed it, withstanding even the most exacting quantitative tests, so as to lead the two authors to conclude that perhaps it remains the more important of the two periods.

It was clear to Norman Angell, as it was to his contemporary and compatriot Hartley Withers, author of the keenly perceptive and highly successful paper "The meaning of money", that the heart of the phenomenon of accelerated globalization which took place under their very eyes in the two decades straddling the turn of the century was identifiable in the expansion of the credit institutions and in the formation of a global financial market, having as its centre the English financial system. Moreover Withers understood better than Angell that the model was changing, it was transforming into one characterised by greater polycentrism, and that from this transformation a greater instability in the international financial market would result, due to the loss of power by the traditional centre unaccompanied by the assumption of equivalent power by some other centre.

Other contemporary observers pointed out that the traditional centre, the English financial system, was also undergoing change with a major expansion of the few clearing banks which had survived the enormous process of concentration which had taken place in the twenty years prior to the First World War, accompanied by the relative loss of importance of the Bank of England and the merchant banks which lived in symbiosis with it. Universal banks, moreover, were becoming more diffused in all the advanced nations and this further contributed to the growth in anarchy in the world financial system. Any political disturbance- as Angell shrewdly noted, seeing, however, only the positive consequences for world peace- was enough to cause nervous oscillating movements in the entire world financial markets. The ever greater mix of major deposit banks and manufacturing industry which characterised countries like Germany, the United States, France Italy and Austria-Hungary was viewed moreover by English observers as a harbinger of huge disasters. If it permitted impressive advances of credit, so as to allow for industrial investments capable of imposing an accelerated rate of industrial development in those countries, the fragility of its structure threatened to render ruinous financial crises which previously had been speedily resolved also because the central banks of countries with universal banks were obliged, for the reasons given earlier, to hold enormous reserves of gold which would allow a gradual unfreezing of long held positions adopted by the banks against deposits in current accounts or short-term interbanks. The internationalisation of investments and of the financing of world trade put the peripheral countries at the mercy of the business cycles of the centre-countries. When there was a higher rate of demand for credit in the centre-countries, capital moved back, leaving investment programs in peripheral countries half completed. Keynes in his first post war work began to complain about this feature of portfolio investment, that is the possibility for the investor to withdraw at any moment thereby causing a fall in value and thus threatening the carrying out and completion of related industrial projects, and he continued to highlight it until 1936 (in The General Theory). But it was already clear to contemporary observers during the pre-war period of large-scale globalization.

It is well known that, as Angell had foreseen, the international financial system collapsed even before the Austrian declaration of war against Serbia and certainly before England entered into the war. The closing of the New York Market, large debtor of the London Market, was sufficient to provoke in turn a suspension of trading in London and, consequently, in all the continental markets. The then already huge American economy indeed functioned without a central bank, because the Federal Reserve had come being only the year before, and was still incapable of carrying out its role. The demand and supply of funds was therefore balanced by attracting funds from London, where the Bank of England with its meagre reserves found itself also acting as central bank to the United States. And summer was the period in which funds moved from New York to the west to pay for the harvests. The explosion of the European political crisis provoked therefore a withdrawal of funds by London and London requested funds from New York, precisely when the latter was paying the west for agricultural products. The *moratorium* of New York, where the greatest part of English portfolio investments was concentrated, made the collapse of the Gold Standard inevitable.

The globalization of the markets was therefore substituted, for the entire duration of the war, by a globalization arranged by the bureaucracies. It is fascinating to note how the rationing of raw materials necessary to the war effort and the sustenance of the population was organised by the same people, influential members of the English merchant aristocracy, who had been at the centre of the previous system. This was revealed with great acumen by Silvio Crespi, the Milanese cotton industrialist placed at the head of the ministry for the war effort. But the collapse in the summer of 1914 served also to register the definitive changing of the guard at the centre of the world financial system. The war provisions were channelled through London but it was not the territories of the British Empire alone which supplied the goods. A large part came directly from the United States, which by staying out of the war almost until the end, and trading with both sides over that long stretch of time, succeeded in accumulating an enormous quantity of gold and credit in comparison to the Allies and the central powers.

At the end of the war the banner of freedom of commercial and financial transactions was taken up by the United States. It is important to note how, under pressure from the precariousness of the English financial situation, even the legendary governor Montagu Norman rapidly converted to a model of management of monetary affairs and international finance based on the recycling of scarce European gold reserves organised by the central banks and on a time scale of return to fixed exchange-rate parities on the part of the European countries which obliged these countries to respect the rotation so as to avoid instigating recourse to the reserves and scarce capital. The standard of gold exchange, that up until then had operated only for the colonial territories was extended to the whole of Europe (and today it has arisen again under the name of target zones) in the recommendations of the Genoa conference. The system devised by Norman was a sort of European monetary unification led by London, a cartel of countries without gold (and debtors of the United States) in order to return, notwithstanding the lack of gold, to a fixed rate exchange.

But it had a defect. By effectively closing the gold reserves market, it rendered the enormous gold supplies accumulated by the United States useless. And it showed that it had as its objective a common European exchange fluctuation against the dollar.

The American reaction to this sophisticated plan was predictable and very tough. Above all, defeated Germany was obliged to stabilise its currency with reference exclusively to gold. The government of the Republic of South Africa was then persuaded to do the same with the rand. The first decision gave competitive strength to the huge German manufacturing power that had remained intact after the defeat. The second prevented London from exchanging South African gold for sterling, as they had done before the war, in this way procuring reserves.

At that point, due also to little desire on the part of countries like Italy and France to adhere to a monetary union guided by England and to wait for the stabilisation of sterling before stabilising the franc and the lira, the English plan was rendered unusable. A European monetary union against the dollar proved to be impossible. The United States was the only country that was a net creditor, and its financial market was the only one in which one could obtain both short-term and long-term capital. Thus the twenties witnessed the triumph of a new American supremacy, totally imposed by the American merchant class on its own and on European governments. The freedom of movement of goods and capital was reaffirmed, given that it was expedient for the European countries who wished to obtain loans for the reconstruction and development of their industries and the American financial class who were convinced they were the natural heirs to the English in the operation of the free international financial market. The English model that emerged from the Genoa conference was based on a generalised European deflation, as the only way to return to fixed exchange rates without reserves or foreign loans. It would not be excessive to maintain that this was considered too costly by the ruling political classes, who instead saw a less austere way out in the American offer of colossal loans arranged by the great financial houses of New York and taken up on the enormous American financial market. The financing of the war had accustomed European banks to deal in and hold government stocks of short and very short maturity. The end of the war led them to transform that part of their business into equally short-term loans on the international financial market. In the meantime, it had become much easier to transfer money by telegraph or telephone, as many shrewd observers had noted before the war on the occasion of the 1907 crisis, the Agadir "incident" and the Balkan wars. Thus in the twenties we have the first signs of what modern international finance would be like. We find a handful of American bankers, reckless as much as inexperienced, competing with each other to lend to governments impoverished by the war, who use the loans for balance of payments reasons or to guarantee precarious " without tears" stabilisations. The centre-periphery financial mechanism, which prior to the war had been based on the relationship between the English and international cycles, accordingly shifted definitively to the United States. It was now the American financial class leading the dance, moving the loans from the internal to the international market following the cyclical phases of the American economy. Even in the first fifteen years of our century American interest rates had acquired the capacity to condition those of the rest of the world. But after the war with the arrival on the scene of the United States as a creditor country and of the American financial intermediaries as the principal dispensers of loans, this phenomenon became the bedrock of the international financial system.

It is not difficult to believe those who point the finger of blame at the Federal Reserve for the 1929 crisis and the depression that followed. When we look at our post war experience it is quite difficult to explain the crisis in the international financial and monetary system without looking at the behaviour of the Fed.

At the same time it would be impossible to explain those crises without considering the effects of the Fed's change of course on the American financial system. And most certainly without considering the structural transformations of that system over time. If we use the same method as that applied for the period between the wars we will realise that we have in our possession a powerful means of explanation. And the use of the post war methodology to explain the events of the twenties and thirties becomes even more appropriate if we note, as we already have, that most of the financial techniques which have been refined in recent decades were used and at times introduced in the decades between the wars.

Certainly the enormous development in the forward exchange market dates from those years, in particular from the twenties. The celebrated defence of the rate of exchange of the lira by Count Volpi, Italian minister for finance, who upon becoming aware of the American attempt to bring down the rate of exchange in coincidence with the bilateral negotiations on war debts, initiated a barrage of forward exchange contracts, using the expertise of the Banca Commerciale Italiana, which enabled him to maintain the rate of exchange until the end of the negotiations, which were concluded on terms very favourable to the Italians. The exchange rate then collapsed and its defence was very expensive for the state budget. But the strategic result had been obtained. It is not without significance that at the same time Montagu Norman attempted to convince the Italian authorities to follow his recipe for deflation and stabilisation. But the latter preferred to give Italian exporters another year of plenty, before subjecting them to cut backs with the *"Quota Novanta"*, which had as its main objective the obtaining of American resources to finance the construction of the Italian electrical industry and generally to equip basic industries, by their nature non exporting.

Anyone following the recent debates on the Asian crisis will find more than one possibility to draw a parallel with the events which we have recalled just now and with others which can easily be brought to mind from the period between the two wars.

What characterises the last decade as regards the international system is the very real explosion of the so-called derivative and securtization products. We can find some examples of these also in the period between the two wars or in the fifteen years prior to 1914, but in such a minor way as not to allow us draw parallels as we have just done in the case of forward exchanges. One of the reasons why it is not possible to draw comparisons resides in the fact that those instruments literally exploded as a response by the banks to their obligations to respect the capital requirements imposed as a result of earlier crises in the eighties. The cost of the expansion of the capital base required by the convention of Basle led the banks to invent or merely rediscover instruments that could be placed outside the balance sheet. As a result there was a huge growth in off balance sheet operations, becoming a matter of great concern for those very same regulators who by their operations had stimulated their growth. The fact that in these contracts the banks were exclusively involved as intermediaries between the contracting parties and thus excluded from all risk, began to be called into question.

A study of the crisis that concluded the period of euphoria and financial innovation of the twenties may however be instructive. Even the mere use of the options on forward exchanges was capable of leading to the collapses of 1929, 1931 and 1933, especially when linked to the consequences of the unrestrained competition among the American banks, to the surge of the Wall Street quotations and to the ill-advised monetary policy of the Fed. They provoked such a strong reaction as to oblige the governing classes to return to the instruments of control invented during the First World War and optimistically abandoned in the twenties.

The novelty may be found in the radical change in attitude by the American government in the Roosevelt years. The credibility of the Fed and of the banking classes in general (and those of New York in particular) having been destroyed by the financial debacle, the new alliance between capital intensive industry and the unions upon which the New Deal was based favoured the launch of measures of control and segmentation of the internal financial system, excluding investment banks from the collection of savings through deposits and deposit banks from dealing in securities. But also placing a ceiling on deposit returns with the aim of aiding the gathering of funds by the intermediaries who financed building loans and who were in the main themselves building societies.

Re-armament, the outbreak of war and its financing through government bonds solidified a new equilibrium in the American financial system, which saw the small and provincial banks utilising their funds to buy government bonds, now that businesses with a return to prosperity due to the war, did not have need of credit. The great New York banks, with the internal interbank market drying up in this way, only managed to survive by acting as intermediaries for the enormous amount of money which flowed to New York from Europe, in the form of a flight of capital to the only financial centre truly safe from foreign invasion.

Thus at the end of the war, Keynes and White, proponents of an idea inherited from Norman, of the necessity to reform the international monetary system basing it on fixed rates of exchange, at the same time protecting it from the turbulence of short-term capital movements, and thus organising a bureaucratic system of recycling reserves ridding the market of intermediaries, found themselves leading the dance for a brief two-year lapse, as is clear from the scheme adopted at Bretton Woods. But this scheme, closely examined by the New York bankers before being approved, in its final version was severely impaired by omitting from it the very regulations which penalised the short-term capital international market, sanctioning the compulsory recycling of reserves by countries who received short-term capital. Thus the new international monetary system operated within a frankly bureaucratic and government controlled framework, with the creation of two apposite international institutions, the IMF and IBRD but at the same time the international market in short-term funding was left free to recover when favourable circumstances recurred. The first evidence of this was provided by the cold war that precipitated a renewed flight of short-term capital from Europe, barely compensated for by the Marshall Plan funds as the contemporary Bloomfield acutely noted. But the true cause for the resurgence in the international short-term financial market should be found in the accumulation of funds by importers and exporters world-wide, who wanted to avoid controls of a fiscal nature on the part of their respective governments, in the American balance of payments deficit which very quickly became structural, compelling the monetary authorities of surplus countries to combat the threat of inflation (if they did want to revalue the currency) by favouring capital export and, from the sixties onward, in the circumvention by some of the great American banks of the compulsory ceiling on deposit returns and of the reserve requirements with the exploitation of the London Eurodollar market, invented by the English to try to maintain an international role at London despite the recurrent serious crises of sterling.

The comparison with the twenty years of the gold standard triumph became more frequent on the part of economists and other commentators. But in reality the comparison works better with the twenties and thirties, because the transformation of the international financial system in both periods depended in a crucial way on the strategies of the main bureaucratic organisms, at international and national level, whether they were guided by a spirit of central control or liberalisation. The authorities found themselves facing an international financial market which, already in the early seventies, had developed again to the point of placing in daily danger the Bretton Woods system, the parities which the countries in surplus absolutely did not wish to revalue given the circumstances taken into consideration by the monetary constitution of Bretton Woods.

The ruling American class, which had learnt from the events of the twenties, did not in fact wish to repeat the error of fighting for a low parity for the dollar and imposed on the defeated countries exchange rates that forced them to export to the United States. They therefore opened their market to tie the European producer class to them. But the explosion in European export capacity, together with foreign spending on defence, which had become structural for the American government following the establishment of a giant network of military bases, and spending on economic aid, very quickly made the European governments face the need to revalue. But it was those very groups who had been wisely given incentives by the United States who now refused to change the exchange rates out of fear of seeing their exports suffer. Nor did the United States government feel like insisting, because of a fear that a depreciation of the dollar would encourage accumulation of gold reserves by countries in surplus.

The gradual but continued overvaluation of the dollar from 1950 -1971 had to induce a capital export of capital from the United States. It established a powerful incentive towards multinationalization by American industrial concerns and to uprooting entire sectors of production. American banks thus found themselves obliged to follow their more important industrial clientele in their partial transfer abroad either by setting up foreign branch offices or perfecting offshore financial transactions which meant being nominally registered in some tax haven but managed by headquarters in America.

Both the industrial and financial leadership which the United States exercised over the rest of the world throughout this period resulted in every action by American entrepreneurs being copied by their competitors world-wide, even if only in the case of England was the imitation prompt and slavish. The other developed countries, in fact, resisted this drive toward multinationalization for almost too long, preferring to resolve their competitive and organisational difficulties through massive recourse to "macro-Fordist" solutions, with the participation of business, unions and government.

It may be said that up until the collapse of the Soviet Union it was difficult to draw comparisons with other historical periods, even with regard to international finance and currency, as in modern times it had never happened that one superpower organised a powerblock for such a protracted length of time as against another superpower (at least definable as such because of the possession of equal nuclear arms). How much did the form of the process of globalization in the last fifty years owe to developments in the relationship between the two opposing blocks? Without the Soviet Union would the United States have so quickly reconstructed the economic and military power of Germany and the economic power of Japan? Would they have allowed for so long that a group of rapidly industrialising countries, specifically Germany, Italy, Japan and then Korea, Taiwan and other Asiatic countries avail of financial repression to direct massive quantities of funds towards industrial investments which competed with American companies? In fact, notably, they began actively to call for the liberalisation of financial markets in these countries only after the end of the cold war.

The same question can be repeated in relation to European unification. This was vigorously encouraged, almost imposed on reluctant Europeans by the United States to create a barrier against the expansion of communism in Europe, on the assumption that the creation of a single market would have permitted the exploitation of economies of scale and the consequent strengthening of industries and welfare in Europe. For a long time the need to create and maintain a political and military unity induced the United States, at least partially, to give up playing a zero-sum game with the European economies, thus favouring their unification. While, in the same years, American foreign policy without any checks forced the dismantling of the sterling area, which included countries producing essential raw materials, traded in London. The United States did not allow itself to be deflected for a moment by cold war policy considerations when the destruction of English power was at stake, which they considered as a limit on their own power in the crucial areas of the production and trade in raw materials and international finance. But the destruction was accomplished specifically by the take-over of English businesses and banks, the location in Great Britain of European headquarters of American banks and businesses, and the complete subjugation of the English nuclear armaments industry to the provision of American parts and components.

Acknowledgements

I wish to thank the Director of the Roman National Museum for her kindness in providing me with the trade map of the Roman Empire, by Alessandro Bertini and Ida Anna Rapinesi, quoted in this article.

3. Globalization and Foreign Direct Investments: Towards a New Protectionism?

F21 F23
F13

Francesca Sanna-Randaccio

1. Introduction

(Related Countries)

The last two decades have witnessed an increasing globalization[1] of the world economy. The spectacular growth of foreign direct investment (FDI) by multinational companies (MNEs) represents the most distinctive feature of this period.

The international system has gone through other phases of rapid internationalisation. The high level of integration of product and financial markets at the end of the XIX century is well known (Maddison, 1991; Williamson, 1996). The intensity reached by this process in the years before 1914 can be illustrated by considering the ratio between the world FDI stock and world GDP, as an indicator of the extent of globalization. Only in the 1990s this ratio has reached a value comparable to that recorded at the beginning of the century (table 1). The dramatic experience of the First World War and the subsequent fragmentation of the international system during the 1930s, with the introduction of protectionist national policies on goods and capital, clearly shows that we are dealing with a process which is subject to swift changes. Williamson (1996) wonders whether the deglobalization of the world economy between the First and Second World Wars was itself a product of the forces set in motion by the previous phase of rapid integration and whether an alternating cycle of integration and disintegration in the world economy could nowadays reappear.

Thus, where is the current phase of globalization leading to? Until the beginning of the 1990s the prevalent view was rather optimistic. Most analysts underlined the presence of positive feedbacks between the liberalisation of international transactions and economic expansion, and expected such virtuous cycle to continue over time (Ohmae, 1990). Only a few dissenting voices were raised against this prevailing view. However, a sudden reversal to a pessimistic line of thinking has taken place after the Mexican crisis in 1994, and even more after the Asian crisis in 1997. Many analysts now predict that protectionist forces will come to the fore. Thus Gray (1998) holds that the world economy risks falling into a situation similar to that of the 1930s and speaks of an incipient crisis in world capitalism. de Cecco (1999) too is pessimistic about the future.

In this short paper I offer a few hints for evaluating whether we are moving

---

[1] This term *à la mode* from the mid-1980s is often used with different meanings. Some use it to indicate exclusively a strong increase in the international flow of goods and factors and the removal of obstacles to these flows. Others maintain that globalization exists when the above mentioned criteria are accompanied by the emergence of a close net of relationships (with or without equity participation) among enterprises which operate in different countries, and by the fact that multinational enterprises adopt a well integrated international division of labour among their subsidiaries. (Brewer & Young, 1998). See Dunning (1993) for a definition of global enterprise.

towards a new phase of disintegration of the international system, with a tendency for national governments to adopt restrictive policies on international transactions. My observation point is represented by foreign direct investment, given that this component of international integration has come to assume an ever-increasing importance.

My contention is that a new phase of restrictive national policies on FDI is unlikely, due to the characteristics of MNEs' activities in recent years. Furthermore, given the composite nature of FDI - which represents a package of resources such as technology, financial capital, and managerial skills - and the close ties between FDI and international trade, it is foreseeable that the favourable attitude of governments towards FDI will discourage the introduction of restrictive measures also on other types of international transactions. In section 2, I will illustrate why the characteristics assumed by multinational expansion in recent years reduce the likelihood of a recourse to protectionist policies. I will then briefly outline the changes which national policies have undergone and the most important recent developments in the area of international FDI rules (section 3). In section 4, I will conclude by suggesting which, among the issues currently unresolved, are the ones to be confronted with the greatest urgency.

2. The Characteristics of FDI in the 1990s

In this section, after a brief description of the size of the phenomenon, I will analyse why the characteristics nowadays assumed by multinational expansion make the reappearance of restrictive national policies less likely.

2.1. The Size of the Phenomenon

The rate of growth of FDI accelerated rapidly from the mid-1980s. World FDI stock, equal to $689 billion in 1985, more than quintupled in about ten years ($3,541 billion in 1997). While positively influenced by the expansionary phase of the world economy, the phenomenon was principally a reflection of a new tendency in business strategies, increasingly geared towards establishing production plants abroad. In fact, world FDI increased at a much higher rate than GDP or exports[2]. As a consequence, at the global level, the ratio between the stock of FDI and GDP rose sharply and equally the ratio between production abroad and exports (table 1). The growing tendency of enterprises to invest abroad emerges also from table 4, which shows the rise in the ratio between the outward FDI stock and GDP for a sample group of countries.

A variety of factors, some long-term and others specific to the late 1980s, have contributed to the fast acceleration in production activities abroad by MNEs. On the one hand, international rivalry in the high-tech industries escalated due to the emergence of new competitors: the Japanese firms to start with, followed by producers from the emerging Asian countries. This led to an acceleration in technological change in all

---

[2] In the period 1986-1990, the annual rate of growth - at current prices - of world direct investments was equal to 27% as against 11.1% for GDP and 14.1% for exports. The data relating to the period 1991-96 are as follows:17.1% for FDI, 6.4% for GDP and 7.4% for exports (UNCTAD-DTCI, 1997).

Table 1: The role of foreign direct investment in international economic activity (percentage).

	1913	1960	1975	1980	1985	1991	1997
World FDI stock as a share of world GDP	9.0	4.4	4.5	4.8	6.4	8.5	11.3
World sales of foreign affiliates as a share of world exports	n.a	84	97	99	99	122	148

Source: 1913-1991: UNCTAD-DTCI, 1994, p. 130; 1997: UNCTAD-DTCI, 1998, p. 2.

industrialised countries. As Petit and Sanna-Randaccio (1998,1999a,1999b) have demonstrated, multinationalization and innovation are interrelated phenomena which are mutually reinforcing. Thus higher spending on R&D has incentivated firms to increase their production abroad and vice versa. In addition, the characteristics of the new technologies, in particular the recent developments in information and communication technologies, have had a key role in promoting multinationalization, due to the introduction of flexible manufacturing and by facilitating long distance control of geographically dispersed activities.

These trends are closely tied to the liberalisation of national policies on FDI which had its beginnings in the early 1980s in many industrialised countries and later on in the developing world, as described in section 3. Furthermore, the completion of the Single Market in Europe, undertaken in 1986 (Sanna-Randaccio, 1996), and the imposition of non-tariff barriers in Europe and in the US against the flood of goods coming from Japan contributed to accelerate the growth of FDI.

2.2. The Growth in Geographic Diversification

The growing geographic diversification of FDI, as regards both home and host countries, represents a major characteristics of the new phase of globalization. Consequently, the phenomenon of cross-FDI acquires increasing importance. The aggregate figure on multinational activity (the ratio between the world FDI stock and GDP) would seem to suggest that we are witnessing a phenomenon similar to that which took place at the beginning of the century. However, a more in depth analysis -taking into account the geographic concentration of investment- indicates that we are dealing with quite different developments.

In 1914 the four major investing countries accounted for 87% of the world stock of FDI (table 2).

Table 2: Outward FDI stock by home country and region (percentage).

Investors	1914	1960	1980	1985	1990	1997
Developed countries	*100.0*	*99.0*	*97.1*	*95.7*	*95.6*	*90.1*
United States	18.5	49.2	42.0	36.4	25.5	25.6
United Kingdom	45.5	16.2	15.3	14.6	13.5	11.7
Netherlands	n.d.	10.5	8.0	6.5	6.4	6.0
Germany	10.5	1.2	8.2	8.5	8.9	9.2
France	12.2	6.1	4.5	4.6	6.5	6.4
Japan	0.1	0.7	3.7	6.4	11.8	8.0
Developing Countries	-	*1.0*	*2.9*	*4.3*	*4.4*	*9.7*
Asia (South East)	-	-	2.0	2.0	2.6	7.9
World	*100.0*	*100.0*	*100.0*	*100.0*	*100.0*	*100.0*
Four major investors	*86.7*	*82.0*	*74.3*	*66.5*	*60.6*	*55.5*
World ($bn)	14.3	66.7	524.6	688.9	1,704.5	3,541.4

Source: Elaboration from data in Dunning and Cantwell, 1987 and UNCTAD-DTCI,1998.

In 1960 the situation was not much different, even if the major economic power was now the US rather than the UK. By 1997 the picture had changed totally, with the share of the four leading countries falling to 56%. This change is mainly the result of the increased multinational activity by European enterprises, which began in the early 1970s[3], and by Japanese producers, particularly in the late 1980s. There was also a fast acceleration in the foreign expansion of companies based in countries such as Canada or Australia, that is countries which for a long period had been almost exclusively the recipients of foreign direct investment from abroad. Equally important is the fact that in the 1990s some developing countries (in particular the Asian NICs) began to invest abroad on a large scale. The share of developing countries in the world stock of outward FDI thus rose from 1% in 1960 to 9.7% in 1997.

With regard to recipient countries too, the geographical pattern of investment has become considerably more diversified during the last decades.

FDI is no longer a one-way flow, coming from a limited group of industrialised countries, and directed mainly towards developing countries, especially those rich in natural resources[4], but has become predominantly a two-way flow, with the same countries playing the role of origin and destination of FDI. Cross direct investment is not only a North-North phenomenon, but takes place also in a North-South and South-South context.

The ratio between inward and outward stock of FDI is therefore rather more balanced than it was in 1914 or even in 1960 (table 3).

---

[3] Germany in particular has regained its position as an important international investor which it had lost as a consequence of the two World Wars, when the foreign subsidiaries of German firms were seized as enemy-owned properties.

[4] FDI in the developing countries represented 63% of the world stock in 1914 and 30% in 1997.

Table 3: Inward FDI stock as a proportion of outward FDI stock.

Countries	1914	1960	1970	1980	1985	1990	1997
United States	0.55	0.22	0.18	0.38	0.74	0.91	0.79
United Kingdom	0.03	0.44	0.56	0.79	0.64	0.89	0.66
Germany	n.a.	2.20	2.02	0.85	0.69	0.73	0.42
France	n.a.	n.a.	0.50	0.94	1.07	0.79	0.77
Netherlands	n.a.	0.44	0.56	0.45	0.56	0.68	0.60
Japan	1.75	0.17	0.17	0.16	0.12	0.04	0.12
Canada	5.33	5.15	4.27	2.27	1.50	1.33	1.00
Australia	n.a.	8.84	9.88	5.80	3.80	2.45	2.41

Source: Elaboration from data in Dunning and Cantwell, 1987 and UNCTAD-DTCI,1998.

This ratio, equal to 0.03 for the United Kingdom in 1914 and 0.18 for the United States in 1960 - that is for the two leading countries during the period of the *pax britannica* first and the *pax americana* later on - rose in 1997 to 0.79 for the United States and 0.66 for the United Kingdom. At the same time this ratio fell from 5.33 in 1914 (and 5.15 in 1960) to 1.00 in 1997 for Canada, and for Australia from 8.88 in 1960 to 2.41 in 1997. Table 4 shows that for Australia and Canada the change was due not to a fall in inward investments but to a strong acceleration in the multinationalization of local enterprises. The case of the United States, on the other hand, indicates that for long-time investors the readjustment occurred not on account of a fall in outward FDI, but due to an acceleration in the rate òf incoming FDI. Also China, which represented an important recipient in 1914 (7.8% of the world inward stock), and is again a very important country of destination for FDI (6% of the inward stock in 1997), has begun to invest abroad. At any rate for this country, which has only recently made its reappearance on the international scene, the ratio between inward and outward FDI stock is still notably unbalanced (9.6 in 1996).

Japan is the real exception to this trend. Table 3 indicates that the ratio of inward to outward FDI stock for Japan continues to be rather low as compared to that recorded for other countries. Japan is atypical not on account of the rapid rise in its investments abroad, but for the exceptionally low level of inward investment, as shown in table 4. It is the same problem as in the field of international trade. Notwithstanding the abrogation of the laws which in the past limited foreign enterprises' entry into the Japanese market, a series of norms which regulate production activities in Japan and other structural barriers, which strongly discourage import and inward FDI, continue to operate. These structural barriers are linked to the characteristics and institutions of the Japanese economy (the relationship between enterprises, between enterprises and financial institutions, the regulations governing acquisitions etc.) and are therefore quite difficult to remove (Ostry, 1990).

The fact that a growing number of nations have become simultaneously source and recipient of direct investment has made their interests, and the problems which they must face, more similar in nature. This has contributed to lower the likelihood of a unilateral introduction of new restrictive measures.

2.3. The Sectoral Changes

Table 4: Inward FDI stock as a proportion of GDP (I/GDP) and outward FDI stock as a proportion GDP (O/GDP) (percentages).

Countries	1980	1985	1990	1996
United States				
I/GDP	3.1	4.6	6.9	8.3
O/GDP	8.1	6.2	7.6	10.4
United Kingdom				
I/GDP	11.7	14.0	20.8	20.5
O/GDP	14.9	21.9	23.4	30.7
Germany				
I/GDP	4.5	6.0	7.4	5.9
O/GDP	5.3	9.5	10.1	12.4
Japan				
I/GDP	0.3	0.4	0.3	0.7
O/GDP	1.9	3.3	6.8	5.6
Canada				
I/GDP	20.4	18.5	19.7	22.0
O/GDP	9.0	12.3	14.8	21.3
Australia				
I/GDP	8.7	15.6	25.2	29.7
O/GDP	1.5	4.1	10.3	11.7

Source: UNCTAD-DTCI, 1998.

Another important difference between the first phase of globalization and the most recent one concerns the sectoral composition of FDI. In 1914 the bulk of world FDI was concentrated in the primary sector. The turn of the century represented the heyday of plantations, many of which were located in the colonies. Investments were therefore primarily of the resource-seeking type, that is oriented to the production of primary agricultural or mineral resources for re-exportation. The activities of the multinationals were only in small part directed towards the manufacturing and services sectors[5].

Currently the world stock of FDI is concentrated in high technology manufacturing and in the services sector[6]. While from the 1950s to the mid-1960s the manufacturing sector represented the most dynamic area, since then investments in the services sector have registered the highest rate of growth. Simultaneously the composition of manufacturing FDI has changed, with a shift from traditional to high-

---

[5] Dunning, 1983 p. 89, estimates that in 1914 the composition of the world FDI stock was as follows: primary sector 55%; transport sector 20%; manufacturing 15%; distribution, finance and other services 10%.
[6] UNCTAD-DTCI, 1993 Table III. 1 indicates that in 1990 the composition of the world FDI stock was as follows: primary sector 11.2%; secondary sector 38.7%; tertiary sector 50.1%.

tech sectors, just as it has happened in world trade. The sustained FDI growth in the services sector may be traced not only to the revolution in communications and information technologies, but also to the deregulation which occurred at national level and to the liberalization of national policies on inward FDI, which initially was directed at manufacturing activities and only later extended to the services sector. Further stimulus to the liberalization of services, and therefore to the strengthening of competition and direct investments, has come from the general agreement on services (GATS) which was reached in the Uruguay Round.

The type of activities carried on by a foreign subsidiary - and thus the sectoral composition of FDI - affects the impact on the host country welfare and, as a result, influences national policies. According to Vernon (1966), the welfare impact of manufacturing FDI is generally more positive than that of investment in the primary sector. Foreign-owned subsidiaries operating in manufacturing generally create links with local enterprises, through relationships with suppliers and in the case of intermediate production with buyers, much stronger than those created by investment in the primary sector. These links amplify technological spillovers in the host country. In addition, manufacturing subsidiaries generally modify their production processes and introduce new products more frequently, leading to further technological spillovers. Also the foreign-owned subsidiaries operating in the services sector tend to become deeply-rooted in the host economy.

2.4. The Growing Importance of Multinational Enterprises in the Creation and International Transfer of Technology

Technological change has accelerated since the mid-1970s, and this has led to a rapid transformation in the composition of world production. The share of high-tech industries in the value added of the manufacturing sector has grown in nearly all the OECD countries[7]. In the fast moving global economy, a country must gain access to the new technologies not only to improve the living standard of its citizens but also to prevent its fall.

Multinational enterprises have a key role in the creation and international diffusion of technology, a role which has grown overtime. It is estimated that MNEs' spending on R&D currently represents around 75-80% of the total, if one excludes the defence sector (UNCTAD-DTCI, 1995). In addition, the international transfer of technology occurs principally within the multinational circuit, that is, it is linked to direct investment. If we consider the payments for the international sale of technology in the 1990s, we can see that intra-firm payments - those between mother companies and subsidiaries - represent more than 90% for Germany and around 80% for the United Kingdom and the United States. However even in the case of these last two countries, if we consider the transfer to developing countries, the payments due to intra-firm transactions constitute more than 90% of the total. Moreover, the relative importance of intra-firm transfers has grown since the mid-1980s, particularly for English enterprises (UNCTAD-DTCI, 1994).

---

[7] Italy represents the exception. See World Bank, 1999.

The increasing complexity of technology is a major determinant of the growing importance of internalized technology transfers, which emerges from the previous data. In fact, technological complexity enhances the difficulties of obtaining and absorbing advanced technological know-how through arm's length transactions, such as licences. This is one of the main reasons why governments in developing countries have modified their policies on inward direct investment, opening up their markets and begging to compete in order to attract the operations of foreign multinational enterprises.

The rise in technological alliances is another phenomenon resulting from the acceleration in technological progress and the increase in international competition. Due to these developments, enterprises based in industrialised countries, above all those which operate in the high-tech sectors, have begun to create tight networks of technological agreements, which contribute to the deepening of economic integration between countries.

2.5. The New Strategies of the Multinational Enterprises

The strategies of the MNEs have changed over time. Until the 1970s, manufacturing FDIs were prevalently market-seeking, that is designed to serve the local market. These foreign subsidiaries, which enjoyed a great independence in decision making, had the task of replicating in the host country the activities carried out by the mother company in its country of origin. Furthermore, a large part of the subsidiaries' output was sold in the local markets. In more recent years MNEs have begun to redefine their strategies. According to UNCTAD-DTCI (1994), MNEs are tending more and more to adopt complex strategies, integrating the activities controlled in various countries. These enterprises are transforming what began as a fragmentary system of production, which was formed by subsidiaries in different countries with few links between them, into a production and distribution network, integrated at regional or global level. Strategies of complex integration are also beginning to be applied in the financial services sector.

This efficiency-seeking strategy requires a close interaction between the subsidiaries located in different countries. The links created amongst geographically dispersed subsidiaries controlled by the same MNE may be vertical and/or horizontal ones, depending on whether these subsidiaries are specialized in a particular phase of production or in a given product to be sold on a regional or global market.

The increasingly important role assumed by the efficiency-seeking strategy is an additional element leading to the deepening of international economic integration. When an enterprise adopts a complex international division of labour amongst its subsidiaries, it encounters greater difficulties when divesting from a country, as the subsidiary to be sold is tightly interlinked with other production activities of the mother company. This leads to a lower volatility of FDI.

3. The Evolution of National FDI Policies: from Restrictions to Promotion

National FDI policies have undergone major changes from the late 1970s to the present. In this section I will briefly outline the key features of this evolution.

3.1. The Restrictions of the 1970s

While, in the immediate post-war period, reconstruction and recovery demands created a particularly favourable climate for incoming FDI, in the 1970s various industrialised and developing countries began to introduce restrictions on the entry and operations of foreign multinational companies. At the same time, new controls were also placed on outward direct investments. The rapid rise in nationalizations, recorded in the early 1970s, represents an indicator of the deteriorating relations between governments and multinationals.

This change in policies was the product of a multiplicity of interacting economic and political developments. To start with, the American Challenge, i.e. the massive and rapid foreign expansion of US firms in the 1950s and 1960s, had arose deep concerns in many countries. Several host developing countries had begun to fear that foreign direct investment might represent a threat not only to national control but also to national sovereignty. This attitude was a result of the widely shared view that US multinational companies had closed ties with their home governments[8] and of the evident interference by MNEs in the internal politics of individual countries, as exemplified by the clamorous case of Chile in 1973.

Moreover, several experts and policy makers began to question the role of multinational enterprises as a source of resources difficult to obtain in the open market. In order to explain that, it is necessary to recall that, at the end of the 1960s - i.e. in the final phase of the so called "golden age of capitalism"- the prevailing expectation was that rapid economic growth would continue in the next decade. Furthermore, this period was characterised by a strong reduction in the technological gap between the USA and its followers, a phenomenon known in the literature as convergence. This partly derived from a slow down in the rate of innovation in the United States, shown by the fall in the ratio of R&D spending to GDP recorded between 1967 and 1975 (see Pavitt 1987, table 2). Thus in the late 1960s, the expectation of rapid economic growth and the greater technological capabilities of local firms led potential host countries to consider as less crucial the bundle of resources that a MNE could offer (capital, technology and management). This was associated to the idea that the investment package could be successfully disassembled[9], as the Japanese experience seemed to suggest.

The change towards restrictive policies reflected also a broader political tendency prevailing in the late 1960s, critical of market forces and favourable to

---

[8] According to Bergsten, Horst and Moran (1978, p.31) it was generally recognised that in the case of the United States government there was a high coincidence between the interests of the multinationals and the country as a whole.

[9] United Nations, (1978): Transnational Corporations in World Development: a Re-examination. United Nations, New York, p.155.

assigning a greater role to governments in the process of resource allocation. Greater scepticism arose on the benefits of FDI, and that found intellectual foundations in several studies published at the time, which highlighted the undesirable consequences of foreign penetration. At the time most efforts of researchers and observers were directed to the restrictive practices enacted by MNEs, while little attention was devoted to the role of MNEs as an engine of technological change.

3.2. FDI Policy Liberalisation in the 1980s

The 1980s witnessed a major reversal in FDI policies in the industrialised world, and the beginning of such process in the developing countries. OECD countries removed all controls on outward direct investments and began to compete to attract inward investments through dismantling and/or reducing restrictions which had previously been imposed. Thus, we have a clear process of FDI policy convergence in the case of developed countries. The liberalisation of inward investments was not merely the result of measures specifically directed towards the attainment of this goal but was also the product of a broader trend which was directed at reducing government intervention in the economy, leading to privatisation and deregulation in many fields of activity. This had important repercussions on FDI, for example, allowing foreign firms entry into sectors from which they had been previously excluded. The move toward the elimination of sectoral restrictions was particularly pronounced in the case of financial services.

During the 1980s, governments increasingly focused their attention on technological innovation as a crucial determinant of economic growth. On the one hand, this tendency was the consequence of the rapid and pronounced successes achieved in high-tech industries by Japanese firms initially, and later on by producers based in Asian emerging countries. The Japanese success had a remarkable impact on the policies implemented in other major OECD countries. The new policy orientation was influenced by the view that the Japanese success was largely due to "created" comparative advantages, in other words that the Japanese government had piloted the transformation of the Japanese industrial structure from labour intensive light industry to capital intensive heavy industry first and then to high-technology sectors such as electronics. European and American firms had reacted to the increase in international competition by devoting greater efforts to innovation, and in fact technological progress went trough a renewed acceleration from the mid-1970s[10].

Moreover, by the early 1980s, governments had to accept that the "golden age of capitalism" had come to an end and that world economic growth would continue at a slow pace. In addition the so-called *Ronald Thatcher revolution* created a climate favourable to liberalization. In Europe too it began to be accepted that the changes brought by the appearance of new competitors and by technological progress could not be opposed. In many European countries "defensive" industrial policies, directed to support declining industries, were substituted by positive industrial policies aimed at accelerating structural change and stimulating new technologically intensive industrial activities.

---

[10] See Archibugi and Pianta, 1992, table 3,4.

These developments help to explain why the attitude of governments towards multinationals changed so suddenly and profoundly. Since MNEs have a central role in the process of both creation and international diffusion of technology, governments began to consider these companies as a factor which could facilitate and accelerate the process of industrial restructuring, by now regarded as inevitable. Multinationals thus began to be perceived no longer as the source of problems - and therefore subject to obligations and restrictions - but as part of the solution to the complex adjustment process that all countries had to confront.

In the case of the developing countries, it is also necessary to recall the difficulties they encountered when trying to raise funds on the international capital market, after the Mexican debt crisis in 1992. The importance of the lower volatility of FDI emerged clearly during this crisis as in later ones. Consequently, on the one hand the growing complexity of technology - which made rather problematic the acquisition of frontier technologies through arm's-length transactions - and on the other the consequences of the debt crisis induced developing countries to change their FDI policies, in a direction more favourable to foreign producers. Radical changes took place in Latin America, a region which in the past had adopted a very restrictive stand with regard to investments from abroad, and which was hit by the debt crisis more than other areas. Even more remarkable the opening up to inward FDI of China, a market previously closed to foreign firms' entry.

3.3. FDI Incentives in the 1990s

In the 1990s, both industrialised and developing countries actively compete to attract inward FDIs. The favourable attitude towards multinationals, begun in the previous decade, continues. Almost all governments now consider inward FDI as a factor which increases the competitiveness of the host country, contributing to foster economic growth (UNCTAD-DTCI, 1996). In the 1980s the principal tool for attracting investments from abroad was that of removing or loosening the restrictions in force, a process which continues also in the 1990s. However, given that the barriers to MNEs' entry and operations had been notably reduced, in this decade with growing frequency governments have used incentives in order to attract foreign firms to their territory, thus competing the one with the other. The welfare effects of these policies have been analysed by Sanna-Randaccio (1998). The other trend which characterises this period is the liberalisation of outward FDI by developing countries, a process largely completed in the industrial world.

Many of the determinants of the evolution of national FDI policies in the 1980s have continued to operate over the following decade. The ideological climate has become even more favourable to strengthening free market mechanisms, primarily after 1989. International competition has become even more fierce and at the end of the decade - after a slowing-down in the early 1990s - there has been a substantial rise in R&D expenditure by firms based in OECD countries, above all the United States[11].

---

[11] The Financial Times, 25 June 1998, points out that in 1997 spending on R&D by the world top 300 firms went up by as much as 13% with respect to 1996.

Furthermore, economic growth proceeds at a moderate rate, particularly in the most advanced areas. The increase in international competition is also the consequence of trade and FDI liberalisation during the 1980s. Policies of liberalisation-direct investments-technological progress interact and reinforce each other, thus accelerating the processes of economic change and internationalization.

In the 1990s the elimination of restrictions on inward FDIs results not only from unilateral policies adopted by individual countries but also from the multilateral agreements reached with the Uruguay Round. For instance, the agreement on trade related investment measures (TRIMs) will lead to the elimination of local content requirements, a practice quite widespread in developing countries primarily in the automobile sector. Moreover the GATS agreement has accelerated the services sector liberalization[12].

In this period therefore the emphasis is mainly on the role of MNEs in the process of creation and international diffusion of technology, with the underlining idea that the net effect on the host country is positive. There is also a tendency to downplay the potential restrictive effects of FDI on competition, in fact issues concerned with restrictive business practises are largely set aside.

4. Conclusions

The characteristics assumed by foreign direct investments in the 1990s - in particular the greater geographical diversification and the growing importance of MNEs in the creation and international diffusion of technology - lower the probability of a return to restrictive national policies on international transactions. Thus analysts like Gray (1998), according to whom we are falling into a situation similar to that of the 1930s, are unlikely to be proved correct. Moreover, the lower volatility of FDI relatively to other forms of capital flows, either short-term or long-term, helps to promote the stability of the international system.

The normative framework which is applied to FDI in different countries is however rather less coherent than in the case of trade. Whereas in the field of international trade, the liberalisation of transactions has been due to the creation of a well articulated set of multilateral rules, resulting from repeated rounds of GATT negotiations, the liberalisation of both inward and outward FDI policies was until a few years ago exclusively the result of unilateral decisions. Only in relatively recent years issues concerning foreign direct investments - and only as far as effects on international trade were involved - began to enter the GATT agenda (and now that of the WTO). The TRIMs and GATS agreements are the first important results in this field.

Experts are now debating on the necessity (and feasibility) to formulate international FDI rules, through an agreement at the international level. The path towards a multilateral agreement on direct investments (MAI) is rather arduous, as indicated by the recent failure of the MAI negotiations within OECD. This attempt was weakened by the fact that many of the interested parties (first of all the developing

---

[12] The Fourth Protocol to the GATS agreement on telecommunication services and the Fifth on financial services entered into force respectively in February 1998 and March 1999.

countries) were not involved in the negotiations. This certainly did not represent the only obstacle. In fact the thorniest questions have still to be resolved. Many of the FDI restrictions removed during the Uruguay Round - for example some TRIMs or the restrictions in the services sector - concerned policies principally of interest to developing countries. It is now necessary instead to face issues which are much more vital for the industrialised countries and their enterprises, such as financial incentives granted for attracting investment from abroad and restrictive business practices enacted by multinational companies. It is on these issues that the debate will centre over the next few years.

References

Archibugi, D., Pianta, M. (1992): The Technological Specialization of Advanced Countries. Kluwer Academic Publisher, London.

Bergsten, C. F., Horst, T., Moran, T.H. (1978): American Multinationals and American Interests. Brookings Institution, Washington D. C.

Brewer, T. L., Young, S. (1998): The Multilateral Investment System and Multinational Enterprises. Oxford University Press, Oxford.

de Cecco, M. (1999): Financial Globalization: Specificity and Historical Differences. In this volume.

Dunning, J.H. (1983): Changes in the Level and Structure of International Production: The Last One Hundred Years. In: . Casson, M. (ed.): The Growth of International Business. George Allen & Unwin, London.

Dunning, J.H., (1993): Multinational Enterprises and the Global Economy. Addison-Wesley, Wokingham.

Dunning, J.H., Cantwell, J.A. (1987): IRM Directory of Statistics of International Investment and Production. Macmillan, London.

Gray, J. (1998): Alba bugiarda. Ponte alle Grazie, Milano.

Maddison, A. (1991): Dynamic Forces in Capitalist Development: A Long-Run Comparative View. Oxford University Press, Oxford.

Patel, P., Pavitt, K. (1987): Is Western Europe Loosing the Technological Race? In:. Freeman, C. (ed.): Output Measurement in Science and Technology. North-Holland, Amsterdam.

Petit, M. L., Sanna-Randaccio, F. (1998): Technological Innovation and Multinational Expansion: A Two Way Link? Journal of Economics - Zeitschrift für Nationalokönomie 68, 1-26.

Petit, M. L., Sanna-Randaccio, F. (1999a): Endogenous R&D and Foreign Direct Investment in International Oligopolies. International Journal of Industrial Organization, forthcoming.

Petit, M. L., Sanna-Randaccio, F. (1999b): Innovation and Foreign Investment in a Dynamic Oligopoly. CIDEI Working Paper n. 56 .

Ohmae, K. (1990): The Borderless World. Collins, London.

Ostry, S. (1990): Governments and Corporations in a Shrinking World: Trade and Innovation Policies in the United States, Europe and Japan. Council on Foreign Relations, New York.

Sanna-Randaccio, F. (1996): New Protectionism and Multinational Companies. Journal of International Economics 41, 29-51.

Sanna-Randaccio, F. (1998): The Impact of Foreign Direct Investment on Home and Host Countries with Endogenous R&D. Technical Report 11-98, Department of Computer and Systems Sciences, University "La Sapienza", Rome.

UNCTAD-DTCI (1993): World Investment Report 1993. United Nations, New York.
UNCTAD-DTCI (1994): World Investment Report 1994. United Nations, New York.
UNCTAD-DTCI (1995): World Investment Report 1995. United Nations, New York.
UNCTAD-DTCI (1996): World Investment Report 1996. United Nations, New York.
UNCTAD-DTCI (1997): World Investment Report 1997. United Nations, New York.
UNCTAD-DTCI (1998): World Investment Report 1998. United Nations, New York.
Vernon, R. (1966): Restrictive Business Practices. United Nations, New York.
Williamson, J.G. (1996): Globalization, Convergence and History. The Journal of Economic
    History 56, 277-306.
World Bank (1999): World Development Report. Oxford University Press, Oxford.

Acknowledgements

Financial support from Consiglio Nazionale delle Ricerche is gratefully acknowledged.

PART II.

Neo-Globalization and the Labor Market

4. Globalization, Localization of Production Activities and Income Distribution in the Advanced Countries: an Overview

Luciano Marcello Milone

FII
RI2

1. Introduction

This paper intends to analyze the implications of globalization, in terms of income distribution, for the advanced countries on the basis of recent literature on the so-called "new economic geography" (NEG).[1] This theoretical approach has underlined, among other things, how the drive toward the unification of markets due to the progressive reduction of both "natural" and trade barriers to international transactions has been increasingly fostering, through the different forms of outsourcing, the fragmentation and dispersion of production activities that stand in contrast with the well-known concentration and agglomeration processes.

Special attention should be paid to these aspects, within the discussion on the possible impact of worldwide economic integration on the labor markets of the advanced countries. In fact, the relocation abroad of production is another mechanism - in addition to those usually depicted by the traditional theory of international trade - through which the opening of economies might exercise undesirable repercussions, particularly in the future, in terms of income inequality and job instability and insecurity. Moreover, all this may imply serious constraints in the management of the welfare state in the pursuing of equity and efficiency targets.

2. Agglomeration and Concentration Processes in the Analysis of the "New Economic Geography"

Originally, NEG provided a frame of reference to understand the geographic agglomeration and concentration processes of production activities at the regional level.[2] In recent years, in the presence of a growing integration of national markets, this approach has been utilized more and more to analyze the links between the trade of goods and services and the localization of production activities at the global level.

Very briefly, in terms of regional analysis, NEG stresses the simultaneous presence of forces that push toward the geographic concentration of production processes, generating clustering phenomena (centripetal forces), and forces that pull in the opposite direction, namely in favor of fragmentation and geographic dispersion of such processes (centrifugal or space diffusion forces). Thus, the localization of

---

[1] It is a well-known strand of thought that has been developing mainly since the early nineties. Pioneering work includes Krugman (1991a; 1991b). For an accurate and up-to-date review of this literature, see Ottaviano and Puga (1998).

[2] Center-periphery models were developed within this framework. See, for instance, Krugman (1991b).

production activities would be the resultant of these thrusts.

As to the factors underlying the drives toward concentration and clustering, they are basically the following:

- The presence of increasing returns to scale for individual firms. The context of reference then is not perfect competition.[3]

- The existence of economies of scale within the industry. Basically, these are Marshall's well-known external economies, with all the successive refinements. They represent the theoretical reference of local production systems and, most of all, the phenomenon of industrial districts. In this case, the analysis is consistent with the assumption of essentially competitive markets.[4]

An important reason for the centrifugal or diffusion thrusts, instead, are the high transportation, communication and information costs as these may lead firms to localize production activities near their final market. These costs contribute to a pattern whereby the geographic diffusion of demand is associated with the geographic diffusion of production activities. In addition to the space dispersion of demand, other centrifugal forces include external diseconomies (for instance, congestion phenomena) and lack of labor or other factor mobility.[5]

Still in terms of regional analysis, NEG underscores how the historical role played by technical progress in reducing transportation and communication costs has often determined the onset of centripetal forces which, in turn, have fostered significant concentration and agglomeration phenomena of the production activities.[6]

Nevertheless, until a relatively recent time, concentration and clustering phenomena showed a tendency to remain within national or regional borders, owing to the high segmentation of national markets due to, in addition to transportation and communication costs, the presence of significant (tariff and non-tariff) trade, cultural, psychological and language barriers. Given this context, reference was made to a polycentric equilibrium.[7]

However, in recent years, this scenario has radically changed. In fact, the increasing liberalization of international trade and capital movements, along with

---

[3] In this respect, NEG models are different from the neoclassical models of international trade, which assume constant returns to scale and perfect competition.

[4] It might be appropriate to remember that, according to Marshall's analysis (1920, pp. 222-231 in particular) economies of scale at industry level, and not for single firms, reflect factors such as: technological spillovers; cost benefits and other advantages related to the proximity of firms to their suppliers of intermediate goods and equipment; the local presence of specialized labor force (the so-called Marshallian triad).

[5] For a short discussion of this point, see Krugman (1998, pp. 8-9), among others.

[6] The impact of technical progress in transport and communications on the geographic distribution of industries was already analyzed by Marshall (1920), who noted: "Every cheapening of the means of communication, every new facility for the free interchange of ideas between distant places alters the action of the forces which tend to localize industries. Speaking generally we must say that a lowering of tariffs, or of freights for the transport of goods, tends to make each locality buy more largely from a distance what it requires; and thus tends to concentrate particular industries in special localities" (p. 227).

[7] On agglomeration as an interregional, rather than international, specialization factor, see Krugman and Venables (1996, in particular p. 960).

technological progress, brought about an overall cost reduction of international transactions, along with technological advancements. All this added momentum to the spreading and strengthening of the thrusts toward the concentration and agglomeration of production activities not just at the national and/or regional level, but at the global level as well. Basically, the drastic reduction of transaction costs made it increasingly beneficial for firms to meet foreign demand, wherever it arose, through exports rather than through the geographic dispersion of production activities.

Given these conditions, increasing returns to scale take on a growing importance as a variable explaining international specialization, along with the theory of comparative advantage based on the differences among countries in their relative endowment of production factors, in technological skills and in their endowment of natural resources, as the case may be.

The changes described so far have important distribution implications for the industrialized countries. In fact, we know that the increasing returns underpinning the processes of production concentration and the ensuing emergence of markets based on imperfect competition, together with other factors such as the technology gap between industrialized countries and developing countries and the remaining presence of "natural" in addition to trade barriers, make for a much more complex and articulate link between international trade and income distribution than suggested by the standard theory (Heckscher-Ohlin model; factor-price equalization theory, Stolper-Samuelson theorem).

In particular, the diffusion of market regimes markedly different from perfect competition, the technology gap among countries and the presence of "natural" barriers all contribute to hinder or, in any case, to weaken greatly the convergence processes among the different countries and the different economic areas toward the same level of absolute and relative factor prices, thus toward the same wage structure.[8]

Usually, these types of consideration are made in the discussion under way on the possible role of globalization - especially with respect to the growing trade integration with developing countries - as one of the main causes of some worrying trends that have emerged over the past two decades in the labor market of the industrialized countries, such as: the stagnation of average real wages; the progressive reduction of the relative wages of low-skilled workers, compared with high-skilled ones, in countries like the United States and Great Britain; higher unemployment rates,

---

[8] Following the Heckscher-Ohlin model, as well known, international trade affects factor prices, thus a country's wage structure, through changes in the relative prices of goods. In particular, according to the model's assumptions, some of which are highly restrictive, by leveling the relative prices of goods, international trade triggers a movement toward the equalization of production factors among the different countries. In this respect, international trade acts as a substitute for the international mobility of labor and capital. As for the "new" theories of international trade, the substitution relationship between the mobility of goods and services and that of factors is much more imperfect than assumed by the Heckscher-Ohlin theory. They also point out situations where the relationship is based on complementarity; in other words, instead of discouraging international trade, migratory flows and foreign direct investments contribute to increase it. For a brief discussion of this aspect see for instance Markusen, Melvin, Kaempfer and Maskus (1995, pp. 385-392).

particularly for unskilled workers in different countries of continental Europe.

The many empirical studies that in recent years have examined the cause-effect relationship between the above patterns in the labor markets of advanced countries and international trade mostly agree that the constant decrease in the demand for unskilled labor, as compared to that for skilled labor, underpinning both the increase in wage inequalities and the particularly high unemployment rates for less skilled workers, can be attributed only for a small part to the growing increase of imports of goods with a high component of unskilled low-wage labor from developing countries. [9]

Besides international trade, two channels through which the growing integration of developing countries in the world economy can generate some consequences on the wage structures and employment levels in the industrial countries are capital mobility, especially in the shape of direct investments, and workers' migration. Empirical tests, however, tend to infer that in general, even when their influence has not been marginal, both capital flows and the migration phenomenon are not the main explanation of the developments unfolding in the labor markets of those countries.

The prevailing opinion is that the structural changes in the demand for labor in the advanced countries, which have caused the position of unskilled workers to deteriorate, are due mainly to the development of labor-saving technologies (skill-biased technological progress) rather than international factors. [10]

3. The Drive to the Fragmentation of Production Processes

The development of NEG highlighted another aspect of the interrelations among globalization, international trade and localization of manufacture, which seems interesting for its possible income distribution implications, especially in the next future. In particular, it has been shown how the functional relationship linking the degree of geographical concentration of production activities with the cost of international transactions (transportation and communication costs, trade barriers) is not necessarily monotonic. It has been underlined how up to a certain point - by reducing the advantages of the territorial distribution of production activities as a result of the scattering of demand - the lowering of these costs effectively fosters the concentration processes of production and clustering. Beyond a given level, however, the further

---

[9] For a review and a comment on the best-known empirical contributions on this aspect see, among others, Cline (1997, pp. 35-150), Slaughter and Swagel (1997, pp.78-93) and Franzini and Milone (1999, pp.23-36).

[10] For a criticism to this position see Wood (1994; 1995) in particular. This author points out that technological progress is not an exogenous phenomenon and, most of all, cannot by itself provide an explanation without relating to international trade. In fact, according to Wood, firms in industrialized countries are led to search for innovations that might allow them to reduce their use of unskilled labor in order to compete effectively with imports from developing countries which make an extensive use of that resource. Considering this behavior, Wood talks about "defensive innovation".

reduction of these costs can trigger mechanisms, which pull in the opposite direction.[11] It has been observed, for example, how part of the benefits accruing to firms from their proximity to their suppliers of intermediate and capital goods (pecuniary externalities), so important in industrial district theory, can become negligible in the presence of a drastic decrease in transportation and communication costs. Likewise, the lower acquisition and technology-transfer costs can also reduce the benefits of the technological spillovers due to proximity (technological externalities). In essence, it can be said that there is a limit beyond which the lower transportation, communication and information costs can significantly weaken the drive to the geographical concentration of production processes.

In a context such as the one just outlined above, the localization of production activities depends mostly on other variables: considerations on the market for factors, and especially the labor market, take on a special importance. Thus, by making firms more mobile and more reactive to wage differentials, globalization, as Venables (1996, p.58) underscores, "reduces the sustainable wage gap between north and south".[12] Strong incentives are created for firms located in advanced countries to localize those segments of the production processes characterized by the intensive use of unskilled labor in low-wage countries by subcontracting work abroad. This is very broadly what is referred to as outsourcing.

In particular, based on the definition by Feenstra and Hanson (1996) and by Feenstra (1998), relocation abroad of production through outsourcing includes the import of intermediate goods manufactured both by foreign subsidiaries of multinational corporations and by foreign firms completely independent from domestic firms. In other words, outsourcing does not involve necessarily direct investments and, more generally, international capital mobility. Thus, international specialization tends to focus increasingly on phases or segments of manufacturing processes rather than on products.[13] In other words, it is a type of vertical integration at international level.[14]

Thus, the trend of markets to unify caused by the progressive reduction of 'natural' and trade barriers to international transactions sets off a fragmentation and scattering of production processes as opposed to the concentration and agglomeration

---

[11] On this point, Venables (1996, p. 57) notes: "[At] high trade costs industry will be dispersed in response to product-market considerations and the need to serve final consumers. At lower costs these needs are more easily met by exports, and agglomeration occurs. At still lower costs agglomeration forces may be weakened .... creating the break-up of agglomerations and dispersion of industry in response to factor-market considerations". See also Krugman and Venables (1995), Fujita and Thisse (1996, in particular p. 370) and Venables (1998, p.3).

[12] Noteworthy among the models that illustrate the case whereby wage differentials between one country and the rest of the world are such as to overcome the benefits of clustering, thereby setting off a transfer abroad of production activities involving first and foremost the most labor-intensive industries, are those by Krugman and Venables (1995) and by Puga and Venables (1996).

[13] Together with product differentiation, outsourcing is an important cause of intra-industry trade.

[14] As remarked by Feenstra (1998, p. 31), "[the] rising integration of world markets has brought with it a disintegration of the production process, in which manufacturing or services activities done abroad are combined with those performed at home".

processes described above.[15] This drive to scatter production on an international basis associated with the globalization phenomenon can occur also in absence of capital flows. In the presence of foreign direct investments the potential impact of de-localization of production is certainly enhanced.[16]

4. Some Distribution Implications

Implications of the fragmentation of production processes are here examined within the context of the debate on the effects of globalization on aspects such as the income distribution, the safeguard of labor standards and the new tasks of the welfare state in advanced countries. [17]

First and foremost, it should be noted that the processes involving localization abroad of production add a potentially strong convergence factor among countries and economic areas, in terms of income growth and distribution, as compared to what the standard theory of international trade points out.[18] According to the latter, the progressive decline of the demand for unskilled labor relatively to skilled labor, thus the trend toward the relative wage reduction for unskilled labor, in advanced countries, should be due to the expansion of highly skilled-labor-intensive industries to the detriment of those with a low-technology content and highly unskilled-labor intensive. In other words, the effects of trade integration with developing countries in advanced countries would be closely related to the size of the transfer of resources among the different industrial sectors.

In the presence of delocalization, the tendency by firms in advanced countries to transfer those production phases which require mostly unskilled labor to low-wage countries can further penalize wages and the employment level of unskilled workers, compared with the mechanism described above, as it causes a fall in the demand for

---

[15] The scenario described here induces to a reconsideration of the contents of the center-periphery models.

[16] On the relocation abroad of production through localization mechanisms not closely related to the presence of direct investments, see for instance Feenstra and Hanson (1996), Feenstra (1998) and Schiattarella (in this volume).

[17] As regards the effects of international trade on the labor markets of advanced countries, the need to give greater consideration to the share of trade in intermediate goods, and thus the diffusion of various types of "vertical specialization" among countries, is stressed by Feenstra (1988, p. 32) who notes: "The idea that globalization has a minor impact on wages relies on a conceptual model that allows only trade in final goods, thereby downplaying or ignoring the outsourcing of production activities".

[18] In the Heckscher-Ohlin model - as already noted - international trade affects the relative prices of production factors through changes in the relative prices of goods. In fact, there is a close relationship between the relative price of factors and the relative price of goods (except those cases in which a country achieves a complete specialization). Recent literature identified additional channels through which international trade can affect income distribution in a country, which do not necessarily entail changes in the relative prices of goods; outsourcing is one of these channels. In particular, as Feenstra and Hanson (1996, p.240) remark, ignoring outsourcing "misses an important channel through which trade affects the demand for labor of different skill types". On this point, see also Sachs and Shatz (1996).

such resource within the individual industries; i.e. both what usual clustering of sub-sectors classifies as highly unskilled-labor intensive as well as skilled-labor-intensive industries. As was noted, in this respect outsourcing has the same effects as those resulting from skill-biased technological progress.[19] On the other hand, international relocation of production has further effects in addition to the lowering of the relative demand for unskilled workers. As shown by Rodrik (1997), following the reduction of obstacles to trade and capital movements, the greater opportunity by firms to replace domestic workers with foreign workers through foreign direct investments and the imports of intermediate goods makes for a higher demand elasticity (particularly) for unskilled workers.[20]

It should be emphasized that such increase in the demand elasticity for unskilled labor is not specifically related to the growing competition by low-wage emerging countries but it is an outcome of a more general nature, due to the high interdependence among national labor markets. Such phenomenon, as Rodrik (p.26) specifies, "is a direct consequence of international economic integration, regardless of economic structure and the identity of the trade partners".[21]

The growing demand elasticity for unskilled labor in the advanced countries can be held responsible for consequences such as: the presence of higher welfare costs, in terms of wages and/or employment, for the preservation of high labor standards (for instance, work hygiene and safety rules, union rights and maximum number of work hours per day); a greater variability of compensation and employment, thus a lower job security; a lower bargaining power of national trade unions[22].

To the extent that globalization has negative effects on wages, employment

---

[19] See Feenstra(1998). According to the standard theory, as previously observed, trade with developing countries should cause highly unskilled-labor-intensive industries to shrink and highly skilled-labor-intensive ones to expand in advanced countries. Meanwhile, as a result of the fall of the relative wage of unskilled workers, one might expect firms to replace skilled workers with unskilled ones both in highly skilled-labor-intensive as well as in unskilled-labor-intensive industries. Actually, several empirical studies in the United States in the eighties, for instance, highlighted how, alongside the increase in skill premium, there was no systematic increase of the percentage of unskilled workers employed in the different sectors. Rather, the opposite was true. Many interpreted this phenomenon as evidence that, in the advanced countries, the deteriorated position of unskilled workers should not be attributed mainly to international trade but to the presence of skill biased technological change. In fact, this would make the use of a larger number of skilled workers more beneficial, despite the rise in their relative wages. In this respect, however, Feenstra indicates how the lower the breakdown by sector in an empirical research, the more it may happen that a rise in the number of skilled workers as a percentage of total workers observed in a given sector is due to some forms of outsourcing, instead of technical progress unskilled labor-saving. On this issue, see also Lawrence and Slaughter (1993, pp.193-195) and Feenstra and Hanson (1996, pp.241-243).

[20] On this problem, Rodrik emphasizes the growing asymmetry between highly mobile capital and skilled labor on one hand, and less mobile unskilled labor on the other.

[21] Still on this aspect, Rodrik (1997, p. 26) stresses how "the focus on trade with (and immigration from) low-wage countries ignores the fact that less-skilled workers in Germany or in France are also in competition with similar workers in the United Kingdom or the United States markets with which the former countries are considerably more tightly integrated than they are with India or China".

[22] See Rodrik (1997, pp.16-27).

levels and labor standards (especially) of unskilled workers, that it generates disparities in the distribution of income and, at the same time, that it makes jobs more unstable, the welfare state takes on greater redistribution and social security tasks. In reference to this point, it should be stressed that even some of those who think that the world integration process plays a limited, if not negligible, role in determining the recent trends of the labor markets in the advanced countries are certain that this factor will inevitably exercise a stronger influence in the future.

However, if on the one hand globalization creates needs the welfare state should deal with, on the other it triggers some mechanisms that make it increasingly difficult to finance the social expenditure necessary to meet these needs.[23] In particular, as fiscal pressure becomes stronger, the high mobility of capital and skilled workers tends to erode the tax base. In a context such as this, it becomes increasingly expensive in terms of economic growth for national governments to pursue policies, independently of other countries, aiming at coping with distribution inequalities and at making up for the greater risks that international openness entails in terms of instability and uncertainty, for some strata of society at least.

Considering these difficulties, and in order to reduce conflicts of interest among countries, the most appropriate solution is to resort to an effective coordination of social policies at the international level. Where this solution is not feasible, there is still room for independent action in pursuing traditional welfare goals by the individual governments, even though to a much more limited extent than in the past. In particular, if there are some obstacles to an expansion of the welfare state, especially where its size already tends to overcome that of other countries with which integration is higher, the solution of a significant restructuring appears both desirable and feasible.[24]

Within this framework, proposals calling for higher investments in human capital through education, so as to decrease the share of unskilled workers, and incentives to employ low-wage workers are particularly appropriate.[25]

References

Cline, W.R. (1997): Trade and Income Distribution. Institute for International Economics, Washington.

Feenstra, R.C. (1998): Integration of Trade and Disintegration of Production in the Global Economy. Journal of Economic Perspectives, no.4, 12, pp. 31-50.

Feenstra, R.C. and Hanson, G.H. (1996): Globalization, Outsourcing, and Wage Inequality. American Economic Review, Papers and Proceedings, May, 86, pp. 240-245.

Franzini, M., Milone, L.M. (1999): I dilemmi del *Welfare State* nell'epoca della globalizzazione: In : Acocella, N. (ed.): Globalizzazione e stato sociale. Il Mulino, Bologna.

---

[23] Rodrik (1997) shed a light on this twofold and contradictory pressure that globalization exercises on the welfare state.

[24] For an analysis of this aspect, see Franzini and Milone (1999).

[25] For a proposal to that effect, see in particular Phelps (1997).

Fujita, M. and Thisse, J-F (1996): Economics of Agglomeration. Journal of the Japanese and International Economies, December,10, pp. 339-378.

Krugman, P. (1991a): Geography and Trade. MIT Press, Cambridge, (Mass.).

Krugman, P. (1991b) : Increasing Returns and Economic Geography. Journal of Political Economy, June, 99, pp.483-499.

Krugman, P. (1998): What's New about the New Economic Geography? Oxford Review of Economic Policy, no. 2, 14, pp. 7-17.

Krugman, P. and Venables, A.J. (1995): Globalization and the Inequality of Nations. Quarterly Journal of Economics, November, 110, pp. 857-880.

Krugman, P. and Venables, A.J (1996): Integration, Specialization, and Adjustment. European Economic Review, April, 40, pp.959-967.

Lawrence, R.Z. , Slaughter, M.J. (1993): International Trade and American Wages in the 1980s: Giant Sucking Sound or Small Hiccup? Brookings Papers on Economic Activity (Microeconomics), no.2, pp. 161-210.

Markusen, J.R., Melvin, J.R., Kaempfer, W.H., Maskus, K.E. (1995): International Trade-Theory and Evidence. McGraw-Hill, New York.

Marshall, A. (1920): Principles of Economics, Macmillan, London.

Ottaviano, G.I.P., Puga, D. (1998): Agglomeration in the Global Economy: A Survey of the 'New Economic Geography'. The World Economy, August, 21, pp. 707-731.

Phelps, E.S. (1997): Rewarding Work. Harvard University Press, Cambridge (Mass.).

Puga, D. and Venables, A.J. (1996): The Spread of Industry: Spatial Agglomeration in Economic Development. Journal of the Japanese and International Economies, December, 10, pp.440-464.

Rodrik, D. (1997): Has Globalization Gone Too Far? Institute for International Economics, Washington.

Sachs, J. D. and Shatz, H.J. (1996): U.S. Trade with Developing Countries and Wage Inequality. American Economic Review, Papers and Proceedings, May, 86, pp. 234-239.

Schiattarella, R. (in this volume): International Relocalization and Employment: An Analysis for the Traditional Italian industries.

Slaughter, M.J. and Swagel, P. (1997): The Effect of Globalization on Wages in the Advanced Economies. In: Staff Studies for the World Economic Outlook, World Economic and Financial Surveys, International Monetary Fund, Washington, December, pp. 78-93.

Venables, A.J. (1996): Localization of Industry and Trade Performance. Oxford Review of Economic Policy, no.3, 12, pp.52-60.

Venables, A.J. (1998): The Assessment: Trade and Location. Oxford Review of Economic Policy, no.2, 14, pp. 1-6.

Wood, A. (1994): North-South Trade, Employment and Inequality: Changing Fortunes in a Skill-Driven World. Clarendon Press, Oxford.

Wood, A. (1995): How Trade Hurt Unskilled Workers. Journal of Economic Perspectives, no.3, 9, pp. 57-80.

Acknowledgments

I am grateful to Nicola Acocella for his helpful comments. I alone am responsible for any errors.

5. Globalization, Profits and Salaries

Maurizio Franzini

1. Introduction

One of the main causes of concern in the advanced countries over the past few years has been the slide of unskilled workers on the income ladder. This slide was due according to some authors, to globalization, while others maintain that it was technological progress which made it possible to dispense with unskilled workers.

The assessment of the impact of globalization has obviously been affected by the way it is deemed to act. In particular, emphasis has been placed on imports from developing countries while other possible significant influences have been neglected.

Therefore, in order to illustrate the connections between globalization and income distribution it seems necessary to identify first of all the peculiar features of this end-of-the-century phenomenon. Consistent with some recent contributions, this paper will underscore the role of the localization abroad of some production stages and it will be shown how this is founded on important changes in the benefits related to the way production is organized. This means that globalization cannot simply be regarded as the consequence of a liberalization process that has materialized thanks to the progressive lowering of the natural and legal barriers to the movement of goods and factors.

Following this line of reasoning, the pressure on unskilled workers' salaries can be explained by the disequilibrium resulting from the greater profit opportunities associated with the relocation abroad of production and the related attempt by firms to gain access to such profit opportunities.

A comparison with the globalization which took place approximately one century ago will show how now, as then, there are forces at work which tend to narrow the differential between the salaries of unskilled workers in advanced countries and those of the same types of worker in countries that are lagging behind. This difference concerns the manner in which such forces take shape; migration then, localization today.

The possible reactions of those who suffer from globalization and the more general quest for corrective measures to improve the position of unskilled workers will be discussed in the final part of the article. It will be seen that there are no easy solutions, nor can the old solutions be guaranteed to work. This is not surprising, however. In an age of innovations it would be rather strange if old solutions were to apply. Thus, it is necessary to find new alternatives. Especially if good old *laissez-faire* is not included among the new policy prescriptions.

2. Globalization, Barriers and Frictions

It is well known that globalization has many – perhaps too many – meanings. The identification of an element common to the different conceptions by scholars in the different fields is a tall order but, if an attempt were to be made, perhaps there would not be much progress with respect to the vague, though useful, "end of geography" referred to recently by Bauman (1998).

Economists have embraced the notion that globalization means the "end of geography" (or, at least, its rapid decline). This can be proved by providing a brief review of their positions on the causes of globalization, how the latter takes shape and its consequences.

The starting point is a drastic decrease of the legal and natural barriers to the international movement of goods and factors. Due mainly to technological developments, as far as natural barriers are concerned, and to important political changes, as far as legal barriers are concerned, this decrease is considered the cause of globalization, namely of the acceleration of trade and the transfer of production factors (in addition to technologies). Several consequences are associated with these globalization phenomena, which concern mainly economic growth, the power of national states[1] , the degree of equality in income distribution. This last is the question which concerns us the most.

In this review, the "end-of-geography" idea appears in the causes (the fall of barriers that separate the worlds), in the signs (the speed of travel, the mobility of goods and factors) and perhaps even in the consequences (the uniformity of the "political landscape", the impracticability of diversity).

Let us leave behind the idea of the "end of geography" and let us concentrate on the problem we are interested in: the relationship between globalization and income distribution in the advanced countries. Conventional theories lead to expect a significant worsening for unskilled workers. This is not surprising if we consider that lower barriers brought about such an economic integration with less developed countries, with their abundance of unskilled workers, as to have an effect similar to a sudden increase in the supply of this resource. However, the channels through which this effect can materialize are many and not all equally beneficial to the decision-makers involved. Thus, in performing empirical tests, the role of the selected channel will be paramount.

In the wide debate held recently on the relationship between globalization and income distribution the prevailing opinion was that, so far at least, the effects of globalization have been rather weak; in fact, many consider the responsibilities of technological progress as much more significant in determining the unquestionable worsening of the position of unskilled workers in a large number of advanced countries. Without delving into the content of a far-reaching debate[2], what has already been stated should be reiterated, namely that the results are definitely

---

[1] The alleged loss of sovereignty is so significant that some observers include it in the definition of globalization. See, for instance, Beck (1999, p. 24).

[2] For a review of this debate, see Franzini-Milone (1999).

influenced by the way globalization takes shape. If, as it happened, this is identified solely with the imports of finished goods from less developed countries there is the risk to underestimate the strength of the changes propelled by the "end of geography".

Some recent studies, particularly those by Feenstra and Hanson (1996), Feenstra (1998), have called the attention on the remarkable development of the international trade in intermediate products. This increase is likely to represent extensive outsourcing and relocation abroad of some "backward" stages of the production process. If attention were paid to these developments, and if they were considered as the expression of the globalization process, then there would be serious reasons to consider the latter much more detrimental to the income of unskilled workers than what emerges from the consideration on finished goods.

However, before dealing with this problem it is worthwhile to take some preliminary steps. First, the benefits accruing from an interpretation of globalization which takes into account the importance of localization phenomena should be recognized.

The importance attributed by economists to lower barriers was already mentioned. Obviously, no one can dispute the occurrence of such reduction and that it was a substantial one; however, it is difficult to agree with those who talk about "frictionless economy" as a feature of the global economy[3], basically to present this as an unprecedented age in history. Actually, as Rodrik remarked recently: " for reasons that are not fully understood, national borders continue to act as barriers to economic exchange even in the absence of formal restrictions" (Rodrik 1998, p. 5).

If localization were attributed the importance it deserves, our age would acquire a peculiarity of its own, without the need to state that frictionless and costless markets are becoming a reality at exactly the moment when – perhaps due to one of history's ruses – the most enthusiast boosters of such markets, economics textbooks, are turning away from them.

Pinpointing any novelty in our age without any reference to localization is actually rather hard. This is shown for instance by the founded criticism leveled at those who regard as unprecedented the present international factor movement and trade of finished goods. Data on the other historical period characterized by a strong international economic integration, namely that included between 1870 and the first world war, reveal in fact that international trade in finished goods, foreign direct investments and, most of all, migration were much more substantial in those years. If what is occurring today were an exact replica of the above phenomena then there would be good reasons to be wary of the claim that "nothing of the kind has ever been seen".[4]

One of the objections usually raised to this seems inadequate. In fact, for purposes of comparison between the two historical periods, it is argued that the

---

[3] It can be of interest to notice how frequently Bill Gates uses the term "frictionless economy" in his book "The Road Ahead".

[4] As aptly noted by Perraton et al. (1997), there seems to be a divide between enthusiasts and skeptics, between those who take for granted a gigantic hyper-globalization and those who see nothing new in the present historical phase. Neither of these positions seems to be on the mark for the reasons outlined in the article.

enormous expansion of the service sector (services by nature are not exportable) makes an indicator such as the ratio between international trade and Gross Domestic Product meaningless. A direct comparison would require to adjust the Gross Domestic Product to account for services; if this were done the situation would drastically change in favor of the present globalization.

This objection might lead one to wonder why the growing dependence of individuals, and their welfare, on immobile services cannot be considered a new and powerful obstacle to globalization. It seems rather awkward that the service expansion argument is used exclusively to support the globalization thesis and not also to weaken it.

It is this writer's opinion that if no attention is paid to localization it is hard to characterize this end-of-the-century globalization as really peculiar.

But there is a question that needs to be answered. In what way is localization a manifestation of globalization? Can it be identified with the acknowledged cause of globalization, namely the reduction of legal and natural barriers to the international movement of goods and factors? Is it not perhaps necessary to look for localization causes, part of them at least, in the production sphere and in the most advantageous ways to organize it?

The following section will try to show that localization can occur also regardless of the changes in the height of international barriers. This does not mean that their reduction did not play a role; rather it intends to show how localization – and all it means for globalization – might be the consequence of developments that fall entirely within the production sphere. Thus, the objective is to correct the overwhelming tendency to establish very close links between globalization and liberalization. Actually, adding the classical liberalization perspective to the one outlined above – which refers, in part at least, to the crisis of fordism and to vertically integrated factories – provides a greater insight into today's globalization, thus making it possible to give a fuller account of highly significant phenomena such as the worsening position of unskilled workers.

3. Localization and Governance Costs

In order to examine the problem of relocation abroad of some manufacturing phases I will follow the approach adopted by the neo-institutionalist economic analysis, with special reference to Transaction Cost Economics. Oliver Williamson, the main initiator of this type of analysis in the wake of Coase's very well-known work, summarizes one of the key issues with the following penetrating questions: "why can a large firm not do what a large number of small firms do, and more?" (Williamson 1985, p. 161). He provides an answer based essentially on the progressive weakening of the incentives that size entails.

For our purposes the crucial question is actually different: "Why do firms not "disintegrate" production into different production units located in such a way as to take full advantage of the cost opportunities, after allowing for any productivity difference, made available by the different areas in terms of production factors?"

As can be seen, this question is different from Williamson's, particularly because it starts from the differences that characterize national territories. In reality, it could be rephrased as follows: "If territorial differences count why do firms do not implement systematically what Krugman (1995, p. 333) called the slicing up of the value chain?"

In an international economy perspective, this question could be answered immediately: because there are barriers, namely because internationalization does have a cost. There are reasons, however, to doubt whether the costs of the disintegration approach are only those related to the crossing of national borders. This would be reasonable, for instance, in light of the consideration that for a long time the breakdown of production was not even carried out within national territories. Actually, in line with Transaction Cost Economics, it can be assumed that the decentralized approach does have some costs regardless of the international dimension of localization. High costs, *vis-à-vis* the centralized and integrated solution, may be the key to answering the question at hand. These, which I shall term governance costs, should be considered as paramount for analyzing localization.

Actually, a suitable analytical approach for such a complex problem should take into account at the same time the governance costs, the internationalization costs and the production costs related to the different alternatives available to our representative firm. The following is an extremely simplified way to do so.

First of all, let us suppose that the production process consists of two technologically distinct phases, the first unskilled-labor intensive and the second skilled-labor intensive. The firm has a higher number of organizational alternatives available than the traditional *make or buy* considered by neo-institutionalists, namely either vertical integration or purchase of first-phase output in the open market.

First, the clear consideration on the territory introduces the "where" question. That means that it is important to ask where to produce (all or part) and where, if this is the case, to buy the intermediate product.

Moreover, it is necessary to consider the possibility that production (*make*) might be organized in manufacturing units in geographically distant areas. In fact, it is possible that even though there are no purchasing arrangements (*buy*) the firm might disintegrate production. The international dimension of localization attributes a special importance to this alternative which concerns the so-called how of production (*make*).

Taking into account all the possible combinations among the *where, how, make and buy* there would be at least nine organizational alternatives. As far as we are concerned, the five most important are the following:
1. Integration of the two phases within the national territory (integrated national production: INP);
2. Integration of the two phases within a foreign territory (IFP);
3. Localize part of production within the national territory (localized production within national territory: LNP);
4. Localize part of production in a foreign territory (LFP);
5. Buy abroad intermediate products related to first phase (Foreign buying – FB).

In order to further simplify the analysis, we can neglect the LNP[5] alternative on the one hand and consider the last two (LFP and FB) as completely equivalent and a depiction of outsourcing, though only initially, on the other. This will make it much easier for me to explain what I consider the most important point.

In order to establish which of the three remaining solutions (INP, IFP and Outsourcing) is more beneficial to our firm, we should determine the costs of each. As already noted, these costs involve production, governance and internationalization. Let us review them briefly.

Since skilled workers available within the national territory are less expensive, not including productivity, while the opposite is true for unskilled workers, the best solution in terms of costs seems to be outsourcing. In other words, the breaking down production in different phases would seem to represent the most beneficial solution; however, it is necessary to consider the influence of the other two types of cost.

Naturally, internationalization costs put a nationally integrated solution in a favorable light. These costs include both legal and natural barriers; the latter in turn include not only transportation costs but also all the risks related to international relations (starting from those arising from the reliability, institutional and otherwise, of the foreign country).

Finally, governance costs are those that arise from the way production is organized and should considered as depending on several factors: from the technological ones to those that determine the size of the incentives. For instance, as already noted, Oliver Williamson argued that in a large vertically-integrated firm the costs related to lower incentives play a significant role. In the interpretation that will be outlined shortly the way these costs change is key.

If there is not much of as difference between the two "foreign" solution, and if production costs of the two integrated solutions are more or less the same, the problem is as follows: production costs push toward localization, internationalization costs toward a nationally integrated solution. Governance costs are then key. While not denying the importance of lower barriers, I will argue that to explain localization it is enough to assume that governance costs be significantly lower for the decentralized solution than for the integrated one.

Chart 1 shows the prevailing situation in the presence of high decentralized-governance costs; in our model, this is the starting position. In the profit-cost internationalization plane there are three straight lines. The horizontal one, which shows a profit independent of international barriers, refers to the profit that can be achieved through the INP solution. The downward sloping solid line concerns instead IFP: the profit associated with this alternative decreases as internationalization costs increase. Finally, the downward sloping broken curve represents profits that can be made by outsourcing production. If the differential in governance costs is sufficiently high in favor of the integrated solution, this curve will lie below that which depicts the profits obtainable through the IFP solution, as indicated by the chart.

---

[5] Actually, this alternative would make it possible to study the role played by a less developed area within an advanced country in presence of a strong localization thrust.

Fig. 1: National integrated profitability in the initial situation.

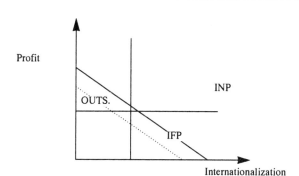

In the initial situation barriers are sufficiently high (for instance at level C*) so that the highest profit can be earned through the INP strategy. It should be noted that, based on the assumptions on governance costs, lowering barriers would tilt the scale in favor of the IFP solution and not outsourcing: this should prove that lower barriers are not a sufficient condition for localization. They are not even a necessary condition, as will be seen shortly.

Let us suppose now that governance costs change significantly and that, given the same internationalization and production costs, this causes profits associated with INP and IFP to fall on the one hand and profits related to outsourcing to rise on the other. The situation that would be determined under these assumptions is that depicted in chart 2: outsourcing is more profitable and firms will prefer that approach.

Fig. 2 : Outsourcing profitability after modification in governance costs.

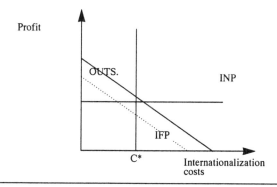

It should be noted that the profits the firm can achieve are much more substantial than the decrease in governance costs: the disappearance of the barrier represented by those costs makes it possible to gain access to much higher profits. Thus arise the conditions that lead firms to break the manufacturing process down into different phases and localize each of them according to the principle of comparative advantage. In particular, firms will try to localize abroad unskilled-labor-intensive production phases.

All this does not require lower international barriers, as was shown. If such reduction takes place, the localization phenomenon can gather strength, as indicated by our charts. However, according to what was already stated, this short analysis intends to give due recognition to the changes occurring within the sphere of production organization, which were overshadowed by the excessive emphasis on the liberalization processes.

Before ending this section, it seems appropriate to draw a short comparison between the two possible alternatives of localization abroad: make or buy. Up to now it has been assumed that the two alternatives are interchangeable, but this is very doubtful. If we are dealing with backwardness and thin markets, the risks associated with purchasing can be rather significant as the firm would depend on a single supplier that cannot be easily replaced. Of course, as market and development consolidate the situation changes. Following the Transaction Cost Economics approach, and adapting it to our case, it might be said that expanding markets reduce the risks related to specificity; this makes it increasingly beneficial to resort to the marketplace.

4. Profit Pressures on Unskilled Workers

In the previous section we analyzed what could be defined as the impact effect of globalization, the latter to be intended as a drive toward localization. The change in governance costs, possibly strengthened by the reduction of internationalization costs, alters the priorities of firms in terms of production organization and opens up an imbalance phase.

Firms undertake to achieve those profits that seem to be within their reach now; however, it would be wrong to assume, on the one hand, that localization is the only way for them to achieve this objective and, on the other, that firms almost automatically converge toward those solutions that guarantee a greater profit. Both questions are affected by the workings of the labor market of the country of origin.

Let us consider some possibilities.

If in the labor market there are rigidities, namely that it is difficult for firms to "terminate" their workers, the possibility to take advantage of profit opportunities through localization abroad will be significantly lower. Obviously, this does not apply to new investments. Thus, in this case the effects of globalization will show up much more slowly, though they will not fail to take shape in the long run.

If, instead, there is no such rigidity but there is a low downward flexibility of unskilled workers' wages, firms will take advantage of the new profit opportunities by localizing. In the short run unskilled workers will pay the price of globalization, while in the longer run it is highly likely that there will be effects on salaries as well.

The third possibility refers to the case whereby there is a full salary flexibility and firms can obtain the reduction required by simply threatening to localize abroad. In this case, higher profits are achieved without the need to localize, thus without triggering an additional stream of international trade. The exit threat is sufficient. This shows that at the foundation of the phenomenon there is a change in the relative positions of firms and unskilled workers: the most advantageous option available to firms improves their bargaining power and, in a market characterized by high salary flexibility, this translates rapidly into a different allocation of the surplus generated by cooperation.[6]

Besides the differences highlighted above, it is out of the question that the unbalance created by the higher profit opportunities made available by localization will end up exercising strong pressures on unskilled workers and that many firms will actually localize production. The road to a new equilibrium is in fact characterized by these phenomena, thus by the trend of the gap between the income of unskilled workers in advanced countries and those in developing countries to narrow.

Taking account of these considerations, one cannot help but agree with Feenstra (1998) when he criticized the approach most frequently utilized to determine empirically the effects of both globalization and technological progress on unskilled workers' income. Overlooking the outsourcing phenomenon may cause the role of globalization, or in other words the opportunities made available by world markets, to be underestimated and the impact of unskilled-labor-saving technologies to be overestimated. In fact:

• if the aspect of globalization examined is only that of the international trade in finished products and, in particular, imports coming from developing countries, while the trade of intermediate products is neglected, its effects on the unskilled workers' income will certainly be underestimated;[7]

• if, as it happened, every reduction of unskilled workers within specific industries is attributed to technological progress, forgetting that localization can be another cause of this phenomenon, then there may be an error in overestimating the impact of technological progress.[8]

Thus, evidence of the pressures globalization exerts on unskilled workers can be found also if account is taken of trade in intermediate products. Furthermore, if pressures arise regardless of actual localization, as might happen in some cases according to what was said above, then the overall impact might even be greater. There seems to be no doubt then that there are sufficiently strong forces to narrow

---

[6] These brief considerations then make it possible to outline some assumptions on the relationship between the use of outsourcing and characteristics of the labor market that call for a more detailed empirical analysis.

[7] For more on this, see also Slaughter e Swagel (1997, p. 78) .

[8] In commenting Feenstra's book, Rodrik wrote: "…The fact that skill upgrading has taken place *within* industries…. has been read as evidence in favor of the technology hypothesis and against the trade explanation If globalization results in the outsourcing of activities, with the least skill-intensive process *within* manufacturing shifting to developing countries, skill upgrading of the type we have observed would be the direct consequence of trade. In effect, trade and technological change could be observationally equivalent" (Rodrik 1998, p. 6).

the differential between the unskilled workers of advanced countries and those of developing countries, especially in absence of correctives or new obstacles.

Surely, this type of convergence is not a new development; Jeffrey Williamson showed that the same thing happened in the previous globalization phase (Williamson, 1998). Then, according to Williamson, the main mechanism that would have ensured this convergence was the mass migration from the old to the new world, namely from countries with an abundant pool of unskilled labor to countries that had a shortage of this resource. In particular, migration flows made it possible for the income of unskilled workers in Norway, Denmark, Sweden and Italy to rise, reducing income disparities in such countries. The opposite took place where these immigrants settled in countries such as the United States and Canada. In Spain and Portugal, which tried to steer clear of globalization, income inequality remained right where it was (Williamson, 1998, p. 62). There is a lot to learn from this historical experience, as we will see in the next section.

4. Reactions, Correctives and Conflicts

This section hinges on the following questions: can there be any reaction to the trends that will arise following the imbalance determined by the higher profits that can be achieved through localization? If governments wanted to intervene to prevent the conditions of unskilled workers from worsening excessively, what would the best measures to be adopted be?

Regarding the first question, reference should be made to the above-mentioned work by Jeffrey Williamson. During the other globalization, governments intervened as a result of the pressures by those who suffered from globalization in order to place a lid on the transmission channel whence the negative impulses were flowing. Thus, the United States introduced some restrictions on immigration while Continental Europe resorted to import tariffs.

Williamson blames measures of this kind for the de-globalization that characterized the years between 1914 and 1950; however, in concluding his essay, he maintains, though cautiously, that today the conditions for those events to occur once again are lacking. His views are based on three elements: the lower importance of the sector that produces tradable goods, the limited share of the agricultural sector (thereby limiting its importance, despite its being generously subsidized) and the incomparably lower importance of migration flows from developing to developed countries than that which took place in the period prior to the First World War (Williamson 1998, p. 69).

The considerations on localization outlined above, however, do not point to the same direction as Williamson's cautious optimism. The absence of significant migration flows does not guarantee a lack of significant pressures on the unskilled workers' income, so that if the reactions originate from a persistent and prolonged worsening there are good reasons not to share Williamson's conclusion. Actually, localization is different from immigration simply because companies go where cheaper unskilled workers are, instead of waiting for them in their countries of origin.

This does not make much of a difference, even though these workers are very much likely to prefer localization over migration by far.

Thus, strong pressures to introduce protectionist measures cannot be ruled out.[9] These measures can include outright brakes on international mobility or also the introduction of frictions in the labor market that might operate as the above obstacles to firm exits. Actually, some authors think that globalization will create a greater rigidity (Agell, 1999). As already mentioned, these types of measure alone are likely to do nothing more than delay the effects of globalization.

Obviously, in assessing the possibility that these interventions are carried out, it is necessary to consider also the interests of the beneficiaries and their lobbying ability. Beneficiaries do include firms, probably consumers (which is not an independent group and, in part, overlaps with unskilled workers) and probably skilled workers who might be interested in localization because, by increasing the price competitiveness of the firms they work for may make their jobs safer and better paid. In reality, as we will see presently, there is a risk that the interests of skilled and unskilled workers may clash also for other reasons.

From the standpoint of the unskilled workers in the advanced countries, one popular corrective action is to increase the cost of labor in developing countries. This result can be achieved by "exporting", as they would have it, a set of institutions, beginning from those related to social insurance and Welfare. The debate on labor standards for instance is headed in that direction. What was said before about the beneficiaries of localization can be applied also to this case. Contrary to what is normally stated, firms in developing countries are not the only ones whose interests run counter to these kinds of measure; anybody in the advanced countries that can benefit from localization are exactly in the same situation. Obviously, interests alone do not move people to action; it may be interesting, however, to know which way they drive them.

Another type of intervention is the attempt to change all workers into skilled workers. The emphasis placed on the formation of human capital in the debates on development strategies should be set within this context. Besides its unquestioned desirability, this intervention poses some problems: how long does it take to carry it out? Will there be actual job opportunities for all skilled workers commensurate with the investment made and the expectations raised? Who will finance this massive investment in human capital? This last problem is crucial and involves also the other interventions proposed.

Another corrective action is trying to raise in a selective and specific manner the productivity of unskilled workers, assuming that this could be done without investments in human capital, otherwise it would be the same as the intervention considered before.

In order to increase this productivity either private or public investments are necessary. As far as the former are concerned one wonders why firms should do it if they can reduce their costs simply by localizing. As to public investments, the question

---

[9] Rodrik argued that a greater openness of economies gave rise to an expansion of social protection mechanisms, in particular the welfare state, also as a result of greater insecurity (Rodrik 1997).

of financing them looms large. The pressure by unskilled workers to make these investments is likely to increase over time: these investments may be highly effective in protecting their incomes.

The last type of intervention is that designed to support workers' income through supplements *ex post*. In this case, the danger of adopting solutions that might turn into permanent obstacles to change – also and especially to the development of human capital in future generations – should not be underestimated. Actually, these types of experiment in the past did not yield appreciable results. I am referring, for instance, to the harm done recently to farmers by the economic integration in Europe. However, there are some interesting proposals that might significantly mitigate these risks. Noteworthy among these is that which calls for an income supplement to unskilled workers, which is strongly supported by Phelps (1997).

One of the main problems with this intervention – actually present in all the other interventions considered – is where to find the financial resources. Who should bear the cost of measures intended to protect unskilled workers?

In this respect, the situation is rather clear. Cutting into profits by way of taxation – and in particular doing it in a way that unskilled labor is not exempted – risks precipitating the localization processes. Thus, there is a catch-22 with this solution as it would generate the very problem it is trying to solve. This argument leads us to look into another direction to find those that will have to bear the costs to protect unskilled workers. These might be those who benefit from the services of the welfare state, or even skilled workers through the fiscal system.

Thus, the conflict between skilled and unskilled workers – which can be set against a larger backdrop involving the redistribution of income for salaried workers, beneficiaries of the welfare state, firms and investors – may become sharper. Its roots may reach down even further than those of the generational conflict, which is a matter of deep concern for many in several countries today.

Thus, it is not easy to devise corrective actions that do not have serious drawbacks, though the combination of some observations set forth in this section may indicate a practicable way out. A policy capable of preventing the most negative effects should, in any case, be coordinated at the international level, cast over the long term and structured along such a high number of issues as to limit the paralyzing burden of many, splintered, personal interests. Surely, it is not an easy task.

5. Conclusions

This paper has argued that in order to understand fully some of the most significant changes taking place now and, most of all, to identify the reasons why the situation of unskilled workers in industrialized countries is worsening, it is necessary to focus first and foremost on the extensive localization of manufacture under way. It was shown that the main cause of such change is the relative reduction of governance costs associated with the disintegration approach.

Taking localization into account makes for an easier identification of the effects of globalization on unskilled workers. These effects stem essentially from the much higher profits that firms can achieve by localizing production and replacing domestic unskilled workers with other, less expensive, workers; contrary to what happened in the preceding globalization, the use of this labor force does not require large migration flows but simply the relocation of whole production phases.

It was seen how the rigidities of labor markets can have a significant influence on the immediate and delayed effects of the localization thrust. In any case there will be substantial pressures, calling   for an adequate policy response to the likely reactions and to prevent the less socially desirable effects of globalization.

The analysis conducted in this respect indicated that there might be possible conflicts between skilled and unskilled workers within a wider context of income redistribution from salaries to profits. It was also underlined that a short-sighted redistribution policy and, especially, with little coordination at the international level can meet with some difficulties.

It is probable, to cite a well-known expression, that Rome's salaries are not set in Beijing. But surely a major political effort is necessary for them not to be affected too heavily by what happens in areas much closer to us, without causing harm of a different kind.

References

Agell, J. (1999): On the Benefits From Rigid Labour Markets: Norms, Market Failures, and Social Insurance. Economic Journal, 109, pp. 143-164.

Bauman, Z. (1998): Globalization. The Human Consequences. Polity Press, Blackwell Publishers, Cambridge-Oxford.

Beck, U. (1999): Che cos'è la globalizzazione. Rischi e prospettive della società planetaria. Carocci, Roma.

Feenstra, R. C., Hanson, G. H. (1996): Globalization, Outsourcing, and Wage Inequality. American Economic Review, Papers and Proceedings, 86, pp. 240-245.

Feenstra, R. C. (1998): Integration of Trade and Disintegration of Production in the Global Economy. Journal of Economic Perspectives, 12, n. 4, pp. 31-50.

Franzini, M., Milone, L. M. (1999): I dilemmi del welfare state nell'epoca della globalizzazione: In: Acocella, N. (ed.): Globalizzazione e stato sociale. Il Mulino, Bologna.

Krugman, P. (1995): Growing World Trade: Causes and Consequences. Brookings Papers on Economic Activity, n. 1, pp. 327-377.

Perraton, J., Goldblatt, D., Held, D., McGrew, D. (1997): The Globalisation of Economic Activity. New Political Economy, 2, n. 2, pp. 257-277.

Phelps, E. S. (1997): Rewarding Work. Harvard University Press, Cambridge (Mass.).

Rodrik, D. (1997): Has Globalisation Gone too Far? Institute for International Economics. Washington.

Rodrik, D. (1998): Symposium on Globalization in Perspective: An Introduction. Journal of Economic Perspectives, 12, n. 4, pp. 3-8.

Slaughter, M. J., Swagel, P. (1997): The Effect of Globalization on Wages in the Advanced Economies. IMF, Staff Studies for the World Economic Outlook (December).

Williamson, J. G. (1998): Globalization, Labor Markets and Policy Backlash in the Past. Journal of Economic Perspectives, 12, n. 4 , pp. 51-72.

Williamson, O. E. (1985): The Economic Institutions of Capitalism. Free Press, New York.

6. International Relocalization and Employment: an Analysis for the Traditional Italian Industries

Roberto Schiattarella

J31 | Italy |

F23 L23 F16

1. Introduction

The international integration of production processes has been accelerating since the second half of the eighties. As the extent of this phenomenon is the crucial aspect of what is termed globalization, scholars have been led, on the one hand, to develop analyses to assess the meaning of these processes and on the other to delve into the transformations thrust upon the economic structures of the advanced industrial countries and on their labor markets in particular.

The theory of international trade was the frame of reference of these analyses, as it was able to provide clues on both research strands. The literature dealing with the effects on the labor market, particularly the US one, highlighted the relative weak position of low-skilled workers in industrial countries determined by these processes. This weakness is due to the progressive specialisation in those industries and activities of the less developed countries that utilize low-skilled labor, which reflects in a contraction of the low-skilled component of the labor force and consequently in a decline of the related salaries.

Actually, research carried out in Europe did not yield equally clear-cut conclusions. However, there is no doubt that, since the Italian manufacturing sector specializes in the very industries that are considered traditional, and that are deemed to utilize low-skilled labor to a significant degree, the issue stands out as a sensitive one for Italy and as such it needs to be explored further.

The analysis that will unfold in the following pages will dwell on the transformation processes affecting the textile-clothing and shoe industries, that is the cornerstone of the so-called "made in Italy". The basic idea underlying the research is that the apparent stability of the Italian specialization model might have hidden, starting from the nineties, a transformation process of these industries that is hard to grasp, both because it is not taking place in the traditional shape of foreign direct investments and because of problems related to the gathering of information. These changes are altering the technological content of the manufacturing activities that continue to be performed in Italy. As a result, the question of the traditional Italian industries can be stated in less obvious terms and, most important, they make the effects of this processes on the internal labor market a rather compelling issue, which will be the focus of our analysis.

After a brief review of how the literature dealt with the question on the effects of international specialization, both through international trade and production (section 2), attention will be paid in particular to how to set the international relocalization processes against a theoretical background and to the related problems of measuring them (section 3). In the following section an attempt will be made to estimate the extent of these processes within the industries under review as a whole but also in the different Italian provinces. Finally, the fifth section will try to depict the various changes occurring in the regional and provincial markets of the areas mostly involved in international relocalization and of those where these phenomena have been either non-existent or irrelevant. In light of the growing importance of the phenomenon, the results obtained contribute to the understanding in particular of the impact of relocalization on the employment levels of low-skilled workers and their salaries.

2. International Trade, International Production and Labor Market

The literature on the effects of the globalization processes on the labor market of the advanced countries has witnessed a significant development since the second half of the eighties (among others, Grossman 1987; Revenga 1992; Bhagwati 1995; Bhagwati and Dehejia 1994). Right now, it is not necessary to review the milestones of a discussion that started in the United States and has involved European scholars. There are several particularly accurate reviews which can be referred to (among others, Franzini and Milone 1999; Faini, Falzoni, Galeotti, Helg, Turrini 1998).

This selfsame type of analysis has already highlighted both the significance and the limits of the assessments made within the framework of the standard international trade theory (Heckscher-Ohlin model, theory of equalization of production-factor prices, Stolper-Samuelson model). More recent research revealed that the evidence available is not sufficient to bear out the hypothesis that the progressive contraction of the share of low-skilled labor in the industrial countries should be linked to the growing trade integration put forth in early works. The displacement effects of low-skilled workers in the European countries have been relatively moderate. And whenever a displacement of low-skilled workers did occur, this could be attributed to international trade (Leamer 1996, among others) only to a limited extent, thus to the specialization of the advanced countries in more technology-intensive manufacturing activities.

Likewise, not only is the relative decline of the salaries paid to low-skilled workers not always evident (Lawrence and Slaughter 1993; Neven and Wyplosz 1996), but even when it is, according to most analyses, it cannot seem to be directly related to the changes in international trade. Both the growing demand for qualified labor as well as the widening of salary differentials due to skill premiums can apparently be explained first and foremost by the changes in technology and only indirectly in terms of trade composition between high- and low-income countries (since the evolution of technology can in turn be somewhat explained by international trade)[1].

As can be seen, most contributors have analyzed the question of the effects from the standpoint of international trade. This can be somewhat surprising since the most significant aspect of the so-called globalization phenomenon has been the very acceleration which has occurred in production integration and not in international trade. The direction of the debate is likely to have been affected to a large extent by a number of factors, viz.: a) the theory of international trade seemed

---

[1] On these points in particular see the literature review in Franzini and Milone (1999).

capable of providing plausible answers to the questions that kept cropping up; b) the short-run effects of the most common foreign investments in low-income countries – those intended to take advantage of low labor costs – are not too different from those indicated by the theory of international trade; c) researches conducted on multinational activities agreed in the conclusion that their link with the changes in the labor market of the advanced countries is rather weak, or almost non-existent (Krugman 1994; Lawrence 1994; Slaughter 1995). Or it is irrelevant, to say the least, if the international production activity is measured only in terms of foreign direct investments. The link between foreign manufacturing and changes in the labor market becomes important once again if, as Feenstra and Hanson (1996) do, the analysis focuses on that branch of international trade related with the development of outsourcing, that which hereinafter will be defined as international localization.

The analytical framework set up by these two authors poses two different problems. One related to the measurement of international production and the other to the definition of international production in broader terms than it is normally common in the literature. Let us consider the latter problem, which is also the more important. Thus the two authors: "we adopt a more general definition of outsourcing, which in addition to imports by U.S. multinationals, includes all imported intermediate or final goods that are used in the production of, or sold under the brand name of, an American firm (p. 92)"[2]. By international relocalization it is meant the displacement of manufacturing activities from domestic firms to firms located in foreign countries. These foreign firms can be owned by nationals of the localizing country or also by foreigners in case the output (both final and intermediate goods) is not sold on the market but is purchased by the domestic firm presumably to be resold under its own brand name. In other words, the key to defining outsourcing, thus international production, is that the firm that localizes production controls the activity of the firm abroad in the sense that it either utilizes the latter's products as intermediate goods or sells them under its own brand name.

Thus, something broader than the traditional manufacturing activity related to foreign direct investments (FDI), but also than international trade. In fact, the relationships among the parties in the international localization processes may be regulated by the marketplace – then we are faced with a "normal" specialization process among firms of different countries – or they may be of a hierarchical type – thus manufacturing relocation takes place through an FDI – or they may be governed by some sort of cooperation agreement[3]. Within the analytical frameworks normally utilized to study internationalisation processes, the relocation of production abroad is a complex phenomenon where market, cooperation and hierarchy elements overlap (see Ietto Gillies, 1991, among

---

[2] Feenstra and Hanson (1996 pp. 241-2).

[3] The authors that have been studying manufacturing relocation, at least as far as Italy is concerned, have focused mainly on the indicator - temporary exports (TE) - and failed to deal with the logical theoretical definition of the underlying phenomenon.

others).[4]

Since there is international production only in the presence of some hierarchical, asymmetrical relationship among firms (a firm has to have power over another located abroad and has to control its behaviors), the two authors' implicit assumption is that there can be a control situation regardless of the existence of legal ties (as in the case of foreign investments). A similar definition is also given by Cowling and Sugden (1986).

Besides, speaking of international relocalization of manufacture rather than dwelling separately on the traditional types of foreign involvement takes on a specific significance only when it is assumed – as in the Italian case - that the important dimension for analytical purposes is that of firm systems, local systems taken as a whole and not that of individual enterprises. That is to say when the rationale underpinning the system is not equivalent to the sum of the rationales of the single enterprises (Cantwell and Iammarino 1998). In fact, what is the meaning of a legally enforceable control when, by definition, what is important are the benefits and control that cannot be traced to individual enterprises as such? The idea of legal control calls for the identification of the firm that exercises this control; but it is no longer meaningful when control is exercised by a local system. When internationalization involves systems, enterprise networks, the forms of control on foreign manufacture become increasingly complex and do not necessarily entail legal control, which could not be attributed to the system as a whole anyway but to a firm which is part of the system.

Thus, there are reasons to believe that in some cases relocation abroad of manufacture might be likened to international production regardless of the legal form governing the relationships between firms that localizes manufacture and foreign firms. The question is of no small import when analyzing the effects of these processes on the labor markets of advanced countries. The ties that are established among firms, or rather within firm systems, that operate in different countries are more complex than those that arise from a simple international specialization. And if it is true that in the short-run the differences might be significant only because the rationale guiding the transfer abroad of manufacturing activities might vary, in the longer run the effects on employment levels might be much less predictable.

Our analysis will focus on a set of industries, the so-called "made in Italy", which consists of the textile, clothing and shoe industries, whose characteristics seem to provide enough material to ponder on what we have just said. The assumption that the development of the international involvement of the "made in Italy" sector which has taken place in the nineties has occurred within a context of international involvement of local enterprise systems is extremely plausible, owing to the fact that: a) these industries are characterized by a very high number of small

---

[4] Analyses do not always underline in full the FDI and TE elements that can possibly overlap. Most of all, the contrast between FDI, which is one of the possible form that internationalization processes can take, and the TE, which is a statistical aggregation of the different internationalization forms, is not convincing.

or very small firms, normally organized as local systems, the so-called districts;[5] b) these firms do not seem to enjoy any specific advantage other than their being located in Italy, which by the way is the aspect that identifies the industries.

The fast pace at which foreign development has been taking place – in light of what emerges from the statistics on temporary exports (TE) – makes the study of the internationalization of these industries' manufacturing activities particularly interesting to test the theories on the subject.[6]

Let us turn now to measuring problems. The traditional indicators utilized to measure international production, namely direct investments, seem completely inadequate because, by definition, they allow us to grasp only part of the so-called international localization of manufacture, because the control situations referred to previously in small-firm systems characterized by a strong integration and by system benefits is extremely problematic and, finally, because of problems related to survey techniques, at least in the Italian case.[7]

The measurement problem must then be solved by utilizing information without separating the different forms of internationalization, as in the case of TE, but that at the same time can overcome the incompleteness typical of this kind of information.[8] A choice was made to utilize the international trade series published by Istat, analyzed by province and by product (236), in the belief that an in-depth breakdown of these data can measure in a rather satisfactory manner the integration

---

[5] The district subject that has been unfolding since the end of the seventies has led many authors to deal with the question of international involvement of these systems. Notable among recent publications Belfanti and Maccabelli (1998).

[6] The question of the international restructuring of the "made in Italy" sector was dealt with also in not-so-recent researches. Cf., for instance, Zanfei (1985), Ginzburg and Simonazzi (1995).

[7] FDI measurement is based on newspaper sources which can grasp phenomena as long as international production involves large firms or in any case firms that are part of large groups. These sources are not completely reliable when the firms involved are small or very small. In cases such as these, in fact, it is much more difficult to collect information on cooperation agreements, on acquisitions or on greenfield investments abroad because newspapers are seldom notified by the companies or cannot easily access the relevant information. As in these industries the international localization of manufacture involves mainly small firms, it is reasonable to suppose that also statistical surveys based on newspaper sources are unreliable in the sense that the actual amount of FDI is underestimated.

[8] The quality of measurement improves considerably if use is made of the second source of information normally resorted to for these researches, the data on the so-called temporary exports. While presenting the advantage of taking localization as a whole into account, these data too tend to neglect an important part of international localization processes, first because firms do not often utilize this form of exports as it requires some sort of licenses whose issuance is subject to some bureaucratic constraints (Forti 1994); second, TE only measure vertical integration processes while neglecting the horizontal ones; third, because this indicator allows us to grasp the processes only when they unfold within individual firms. In other words, they measure the exports of semi-finished products and the subsequent re-imports of products that come back to the same company after they have been processed. This rationale makes sense if the firms involved are large . If, on the other hand, they are small or very small and operate within an integrated system, it is very probable or even possible that the exporting enterprise is not the same as that which re-imports the semi-finished product. Thus, TE only tell part of the story.

process under way between Italian and foreign firms.[9]

Considering that the reason for these industries to relocate abroad manufacturing activities is basically to take advantage of the low labor cost outside Italy, trade between Italian and foreign firms, as far as the different textile manufacturing stages are concerned, should consist in exports of raw material from Italy and imports of fabric, exports from Italy of yarns and imports of knitted wears and exports of fabrics from Italy and imports of sewn goods. In other words, it is possible that the relocation of manufacture in some cases concerns the initial stages of production – that involving the manufacturing of yarns or fabrics – but it is more likely that the manufacturing phases relocated abroad are those with the highest content of low-skilled labor, namely knitwear manufacturing and sewing. As to the stages of shoe manufacturing, one might expect exports from Italy of raw hides and skins and imports of leather, or exports from Italy of raw hides and skins and imports of vamps, or exports from Italy of raw hides and skins and imports of finished goods, namely shoes and gloves. The most reasonable of these alternatives is the relocation of vamp sewing, a phase which is known to require the highest content of labor which is not particularly skilled.

Table 1: Changes in the relocalization processes for the traditional sectors in the 1990s. In millions of lire.

	1990	1992	1994	1997
IMPDELV	388,383	889,626	2,087,135	3,749,704
IMPDELO	377,526	267,620	679,382	990,854
IMPDELT	766,388	1,157,244	2,766,517	4,740,558

IMPDELV = Imports related to vertical integration
IMPDELO = Imports related to horizontal integration
IMPDELT = IMPDELV + IMPDELO

Source: Our compilation on Istat data.

3. The Extent of Manufacturing Relocalization

The research spans the years from 1990 to 1997. Moreover, attention was focused on international trade between Italy and two groups of countries, those of the southern shore of the Mediterranean sea and the countries of Eastern Europe.[10]

---

[9] For a detailed analysis of the methodology followed, see the methodological note in the appendix in Schiattarella (1999).
[10] The first group of countries included the former Yugoslavia (in 1996, Croatia and Slovenia), Albania, Bulgaria, Poland, the former Czechoslovakia (in 1996, the Czech Republic and Slovakia), the former USSR (in 1996 Russia), Bulgaria, Poland and Hungary. The second group includes Morocco, Algeria, Tunisia, Jordan, Israel, Syria, Lebanon, Malta, Cyprus, Egypt and Turkey.

These countries were selected as, according to data on both foreign direct investments and TE, they are concerned the most with the relocalization phenomena involving these industries (based on the reasonable assumption that the TE is an acceptable relocalization indicator). A recent survey (Crescini and Mistri, 1996) showed that the "made in Italy" accounted for 95 percent of the TE for Italy and 85 percent of this was in the countries being considered.

Not only did the results of this survey bear out what emerged from the data on TE and on foreign direct investments, which signaled a strong growth, but they allow us to go a little further than this initial assessment. In 1997, the amount of imports for the industries analyzed which, according to our estimates, could be linked to the international integration of production – thus measuring the value of localized production – was greater than Lire 4,700 million (table 1). Of this, more than three-quarters should be related to specialization processes by stage, namely vertical integration processes, with the balance to specialization by product.

Over time, the fastest-growing localization component was that related to vertical integration phenomena. In 1990, this accounted for less than one-quarter of the entire phenomenon, increasing to almost 80 percent by 1997, as already mentioned.

The contribution of these processes to the competitiveness of such traditional industries can be appraised through the ratio of the total value of imports related to relocalization processes to (estimated) total sales of the industries. In 1997 such ratio was 2.6 percent of total sales. A rather minuscule percentage, which seems to point to a still marginal role of these processes within the organization of production in these industries, which makes it also difficult to explain their international success mainly – or to a significant extent – in terms of ability to organize international production.

Actually, it should not be forgotten that foreign sales per employee in the countries involved in the relocalization process is generally much lower than those in Italy, both because the cost of labor is lower and because only some phases of the production process are concentrated abroad. Based on data published by R&P[11], in 1996 the average sales per employee of Italian subsidiaries that operate in these industries (and in the countries we took into account) varied between Lire 25 million and Lire 35 million, namely between one-fifth and one-sixth of the Italian one in the same year. In other words, the percentage of internal sales replaced by imports related to localization processes was much higher than 2.6 percent of total sales for the industries and may be estimated at approximately 12-15 percent.

Such a percentage cannot be regarded as negligible, especially to understand what the meaning of what we have just seen is in terms of "exports" of jobs from our country, namely jobs created abroad as a result of the relocalization processes taking place within these industries. An estimate of these jobs can be reached by resorting once again to the estimated total sales per employee of the subsidiaries of Italian firms that operate in the same industries and in the same countries. The resulting data can only represent an indication also because there

---

[11] Cominotti and Mariotti, 1998.

are reasons to consider this estimate excessive[12], as there are reasons to consider it inadequate.[13] In order to quantify this uncertainty we computed employment for both sales amounts per employee, namely a minimum of Lire 25 million and a maximum of Lire 35 million. As can be seen from table 2, in 1997 total estimated foreign workers ranged from 130,000 to 180,000. Thus, considering that the number of workers employed in these industries in Italy was approximately one million, it can be inferred that in 1997, on the southern shore of the Mediterranean Sea, there was one worker for each six or seven workers employed in Italy.

Table 2: Estimated employment abroad related to relocalization processes. Total for traditional sectors.

	1990	1992	1994	1997
Estimated employment	33,000-45,000	50,000-70,000	100,000-140,000	130,000-180,000

Source: Our compilation on Istat data.

The most significant element of the data reported in the same table is that in less than a decade, a relatively short period of time, total foreign workers employed in localized manufacturing activities grew from approximately 33-45,000 to a number approximately four times as high.

A highly significant phenomenon in quantitative terms, which calls for a qualitative reflection. First of all, is there still a reason to define these as traditional industries, at least in the sense of industries with a large number of low-skilled workers? While the answer can only be positive if account is taken also of the foreign component, it becomes more difficult if only the part manufactured in Italy is considered. The phenomenon is still in full bloom but it is clear that when the push toward international relocalization peters out our country will be left mainly with activities that cannot be profitably carried out elsewhere and that can hardly be regarded as traditional.

The second problem is to understand the necessary consequences of such

---

[12] Account should be taken of the fact that almost 80 percent of re-imports is related to vertical integration processes. Thus, imported products are semi-finished goods with total sales per employee lower than the comparable figure for finished goods even though, as it emerges from this survey, the manufacturing phases performed abroad seem to be the downstream ones, thus with a sales amount per employee closer to that generated by finished goods.

[13] In fact, it should not be forgotten that the sales amount of re-imported products includes also the sales amount of exports from Italy (approximately 60 percent of the amount of imports related to vertical integration processes and slightly more than 40 percent of the overall amount of re-imports), thus a sales amount computed on the basis of Italian prices. The minimum estimate of Lire 25 million in sales per employee does not depart significantly from that by the Crei and reported in Scarso's article (1996). According to the Crei, which studies the situation in Veneto, the Lire 440 billion worth of contracts assigned by the fashion system to foreign firms (in 1995) represent "at least 20,000 jobs". Thus, the average sales per employee is Lire 22 million as against the Lire 25 million computed by the R&P survey.

a phenomenon on our country's labor market. We have seen above what indications emerged from the international literature. We also tried to shed a light on the limits of these theoretical tools when we are dealing with outsourcing, international relocalization and how in this case reference should be made to the theory of production instead of the theory of international trade.

As the extent of international relocalization processes in our country varied from one region to another, one way to gain an insight into the matter can be to compare the labor markets of the different areas. Table 3 takes a first step in that direction by showing the distribution of localization related only to vertical integration processes by region from 1990 to 1997. [14]

As was to be expected, the region where the relocalization phenomenon has been occurring more extensively is Veneto. This both in absolute terms as well as taking account of the role that the industries in question play in this region. More than one-third of the entire relocalization phenomenon is concentrated in this region, which accounted for less than 20 percent of total jobs. The second most important region was Lombardy with 21 percent. However, the fact that the number

Table 3: Make-up of international relocalization for the traditional sectors, by region of origin.

| | Vertical relocalization | | | | Employment |
	1990	1992	1994	1997	1996
Piedmont/V.A.	11.2	15.3	9.5	7.7	7.5
Lombardy	25.0	22.8	20.3	20.9	26.9
Liguria	-	-	0.1	0.5	0.5
Veneto	34.5	29.3	39.9	37.5	17.2
V. Giulia	4.6	0.3	0.5	0.3	1.3
Trentino	0.1	0.3	0.5	0.4	0.6
Emilia R.	3.8	8.7	6.3	5.9	7.2
Tuscany	17.9	16.8	10.9	13.9	12.3
Marche	0.2	1.2	3.2	4.8	7.4
Umbria	0.2	0.3	1.4	1.0	2.6
Latium	0.5	0.1	0.2	0.5	1.7
Abruzzo	-	1.1	1.9	2.9	2.6
Molise	-	0.1	0.1	0.3	0.3
Campania	0.1	0.8	0.6	0.5	4.0
Puglia	1.7	2.9	4.7	3.2	4.9
Basilicata	-	-	-	-	0.3
Calabria	-	-	-	-	0.8
Sicily	-	-	-	0.2	1.7
Sardinia	-	-	-	-	0.4
First 5 regions	93.2	92.9	86.9	85.9	71.3

Source: Our compilation on Istat data.

---

[14] No account is taken of horizontal relocalization as this was computed only for the provinces where the largest production centers of the industries are localized. For a clearer description of the method, see Schiattarella (1999).

of total jobs in the industries in this region is higher (27 percent) tells us that the propensity of this area to localize is markedly lower than the national average. The third region is Tuscany and the fourth is Piedmont, showing percentage rates not too different from those of total employment. In Emilia Romagna and the Marche, relocalization phenomena are pretty important but the propensity to localize is lower than the national average. Abruzzo is different as its propensity to localize is greater than the national average. A comparison with previous years reveals two patterns.

The first is a certain stability in the geographic distribution of the phenomenon. The second pattern that is taking shape over time is a geographic spreading of the phenomenon involving new regions, also in the South. Basically, international relocalization no longer seems to concern specific areas of the country or some industrial groups but it is always something that concerns the Italian industrial complex as a whole (in these industries). Noteworthy is that the presence of unemployed workers within the country, the greater opportunities to hire workers off the book or to pay relatively lower salaries do not seem to put a brake on the international relocation of manufacture.

4. International Relocalization and Effects on the Labor Market

Thus, in the room of seven years an exceptionally high number of jobs has been created outside our country, especially in light of the fact that the analysis is focusing on one area of the manufacturing sector alone. The size these processes have achieved over the years yields some very interesting information.

The analysis of these changes can be meaningful both in terms of aggregate data and, for some aspects in particular, if a comparison is made especially between the areas where the relocalization processes have been more pronounced and the other areas. In other words, it should not be difficult to spot features attributable to the relocation abroad of manufacture, or stages of manufacture, in the changes in the employment levels and composition within the industries at the beginning of the 1990s.

Let us focus the attention on the employment issue. Is the international development of enterprises a threat to domestic employment? Table 4 was built to try to find an answer to this question; it shows employment patterns by group of regions or provinces by utilizing two sources, Istat's regional accounting data and employment data provided by Inps. The regional accounting data are in labor units, Inps's in jobs. The former are available at the regional level until 1995 while the latter are so at the provincial level and until 1996 (with some problems related to the quality of information). Obviously, the area under consideration is that of the traditional industries.

In all the tables that follow, provinces (regions) are divided on the basis of the ratio of relocalization share of the country total and employment share of the total for the country. The provinces (regions) where this ratio is higher than 1 have been defined as areas with a high propensity to localize manufacturing abroad; the propensity to localize of those areas where the ratio is between 0.5 and 1 has been defined as medium, while those lower than 0.5 had a low propensity.

Table 4: International relocalization and employment changes in traditional sectors.

	Regional accounts		INPS (Social Security)	INPS Cograd index
	1980-90	1990-95	1990-96	
High propensity to relocalization	-13.1	-5.8	-17.3	
Medium propensity to relocalization	-9.5	-9.1	-13.5	
Low propensity to relocalization	-21.8	-7.4	-14.1	
				0.21

Source: Our compilation on Inps and Istat source.

The regional accounting data shown in table 4 reveal that there is no correlation between international relocalization and employment patterns, both if a comparison is made between the 1980s – with no international localization to speak of – and the 1990s as well as if a comparison is made among the areas that were variously concerned with this type of processes. Inps's employment data seem to tell another story. Actually, here the reduction of employment in the provinces that localize more is sharper, though to a limited extent. In reality the result of this group of provinces is strongly affected by a completely anomalous factor (also with respect to that which can be derived from regional accounting data) for the province of Milan.

To verify the apparent inconsistency between the results obtained utilizing the two different statistical sources, a rank correlation index between the imports (per employee) related to the international relocalization phenomena for each province and the employment changes in the industries under review in the nineties was computed by utilizing Inps's employment data. Spearman's rank correlation coefficient was 0.21. In other words, not only do Inps's data confirm that there is no positive correlation between relocalization and unemployment , as attested also by the regional accounting data, but it can also be observed that, if anything, this correlation would be negative. Thus, not only do the provinces that lose jobs are not those where international relocalization has been more marked but, to a limited extent, the opposite seems to be true.

Thus, as far as these industries are concerned, there is no evidence that the localization of manufacturing activities abroad entails a cost in terms of higher unemployment.

What is surprising, however, is that the areas where some production stages were localized until the eighties (Marche, Abruzzo, Molise, Puglia) – all located in the first two groups of regions – did not pay too high a price (in terms of higher unemployment) for the relocation abroad of these phases of the production processes.

These results can probably be explained with the lower costs related to localization; in fact, these seem to have caused such a higher competitiveness as to make up for any negative effect brought about by international localization. On the other hand, it is plausible to surmise that such results might have been affected by the different relationship between domestic and foreign jobs in an international production system.

As underlined above, theoretical analysis suggests that these processes displaced only low-skilled labor. If this is true then it can be inferred that what has taken place is a process whereby low-skilled workers have been replaced by high-skilled ones.

As the presence of such a phenomenon should determine a higher increase of average pay in the areas where international relocalization phenomena have been more significant, this assumption can be tested by utilizing once again both the regional accounting series as well as Inps's data (table 5). The data shown in the table are fairly consistent with one another and bear out the theory. In the provinces (or regions) where international relocalization processes have been more pronounced average pay has been growing faster in the nineties. Thus, relocalization processes seem to go hand in hand with a faster growth of average pay. A faster growth which is not related to any composition effect, as can be evinced from the last column of the same table, which lists the average change for each group of provinces (as opposed to the average change in the preceding column), but seems to be the expression of rather consistent patterns within the three areas.

What should be understood now is if this faster growth can be explained in terms of changes in the composition of the labor force in favor of higher-skilled labor (higher-skilled workers replacing the workers who performed the tasks which have been localized abroad), as the above results seem to suggest, or if, in addition to the composition effect, the related values have changed. In other words, if the greater demand for higher-skilled workers (and the lower demand for low-skilled ones) has had some effects on the pay differential between these two components of the labor force, as outlined by the theory.

Table 5. International relocalization and changes in the traditional industries.

	Regional accounts Regions 1990-1995	Inps Provinces 1990-1995	
		Weighted data	Non-weighted data
High propensity to relocalization	27.5	39.3	37.6
Medium propensity to relocalization	25.9	35.7	34.9
Low propensity to relocalization	20.9	34.4	33.8

Source: Our compilation on Inps data.

Inps's data allow us to perform a more in-depth analysis on the composition by skill, but only for blue-collar workers and clerks. No in-depth analysis can be conducted instead within the blue-collars' ranks. Table 6 shows the clerk share of total workers in 1990 and 1996 for the three groups of provinces already considered in the two preceding tables. The results seem to confirm the assumption that in the areas where the international relocalization of production has been more marked are those where the clerk share of total workers has been growing the fastest, both in absolute as well as in percentage terms. Thus, this is a further confirmation of the assumption that the main effect of these processes, at least as far as these industries are concerned, has been a specialization by phase which did cause the less skilled components of the labor force to be shed but which saw also a greater concentration in our country of the more skill-intensive stages of the production processes, thus an increase of high-skilled employment levels.

Table 6: International relocalization and changes in employment make-up in the traditional sectors. Share of clerical workers.

	1990	1996
High propensity to relocalization	15.0	18.0
Medium propensity to relocalization	14.9	17.0
Low propensity to relocalization	11.9	13.3

Source: Our compilation on Inps data.

It might be interesting to understand the tradeoff mechanisms between these two components of the labor force. Namely, whether new jobs are the result of internal upgrading (dictated by the market or related to the work of institutions) or are determined by a generation turnover. The information available cannot provide an answer to these questions. On the other hand, it can be seen that international relocalization did determine some effects on salary differentials.

As table 7 shows, the greater demand for clerical workers that materialized in the presence of international localization processes marched in lockstep with a rise in their pay, at least in relative terms; nothing similar occurred in the areas where the propensity to relocalize was relatively low. The differential widens by 11 points in the provinces with a high relocalization propensity, by 4 points in those with a medium propensity while in those with a low propensity it even narrows by 1 point. At this analysis level, it is difficult to tell to what extent these outcomes result from a change in the composition of skills (especially among clerks) and to what extent instead they can be explained in terms of a stronger market position of higher-skilled workers (as theory seems to suggest).

Table 7: International relocalization and changes in employment make-up in the traditional sectors. Salary differentials between blue-collar and clerical workers.

	1990	1996
High propensity to relocalization	1.45	1.56
Medium propensity to relocalization	1.41	1.45
Low propensity to relocalization	1.43	1.42

Source: Our compilation on Inps data.

5. Conclusions

- International relocalization is a multifaceted phenomenon where elements of market, hierarchy and cooperation all play a part. It makes sense to review international relocalization as such and not the single instances of foreign involvement, especially when the focus is on local production systems rather than single firms.
- The issue regarding the effects of international relocalization is far more complex than in the traditional literature on the so-called social dumping . The theory of international production may represent in these cases a better frame of reference, or an additional one in any case, as far as the long-term effects on the labor market are concerned.
- Not only did employment in Italy decrease to a much lesser degree that would have been reasonable to suppose in light of what the literature suggests, but its changes do not show any correlation with the international relocalization processes. If there is a correlation is very weak and even negative. Obviously these results have to be confirmed by more in-depth analyses. What seems to have happened in these specific industries is a strong specialization process by production phase at the international level. Italy is experiencing a growing concentration of skill-intensive production phases (which, by the way, command better pay) while those localized abroad require only low-skilled labor. Thus, in our country high-skilled labor is replacing low-skilled one. An apparently virtuous effect, at least in the short run, which not only has to be verified but whose meaning has to be evaluated also in light of what might be the long-run effects, of which much less is known.

References

Acocella, N., Schiattarella, R. (eds): 1989. Teorie dell'internazionalizzazione e realtà italiana. Liguori, Napoli.

Andersson, U., Fosgren, M., (1995): Subsidiary Embededdness and its Implication for Integration in MNC. In: Schiattarella, R. (ed.),: New Challenges for European and International Business. Urbino.

Belfanti, C. M., Maccabelli, T. (eds) (1998): Un paradigma per i distretti industriali. Grafo.

Bhagwati, J. (1995): Trade and Wages: Choosing among Alternative Explanations. Economic Policy Review 1:42-47.

Bhagwati, J., Dehejia, V. (1994): International Trade Theory and Wages of the Unskilled. In: Bhagwati, J., Kosters, M. H. (eds). Trade and Wages: Leveling Wages Down? Washington: American Enterprise Institute, pp 36 - 75.,

Balloni, V., Conti, G., Cucculelli, M., Menghinello, S. (1997): Modelli di impresa e di industria nei contesti di competizione globale. Paper presented at the X meeting by "L'industria". Bari.

Becattini, G., Rullani, E. (1993): Sistema locale e mercato globale. Economia e Politica Industriale n° 80.

Berman, E., Bound, J., Griliches, Z. (1994): Changes in the Demand for Skilled Labor within U. S. Manufacturing: Evidence from the Annual Survey of Manufactures. Quarterly Journal of Economics, 109:367-98.

Brainard, S. L., Riker, D. (1997): Are U. S. Multinational Exporting Jobs? NBER Working Paper n° 5958.

Cantwell, J., Iammarino, S. (1998): MNCs, Technological Innovation and Regional Systems in the EU. University of Reading. Discussion papers in: International Investment and Management, series b, vol.10, n.247.

Casson, M. (1992): Internalization Theory and Beyond. In: Buckley, P.J. (ed): New Directions in International Business. Elgar.

Cominotti, R., Mariotti, S. (various years) Italia multinazionale.

Conti, G., Menghinello, S. (1995): Territorio e competitività: l'importanza dei sistemi locali per le esportazioni italiane di manufatti. Un'analisi per province (1985-1994). Rapporto sul Commercio Estero, ICE, Roma.

Cowling, K., Sugden, R. (1987): Market Exchange and the Concept of Transnational Corporation: Analysing the Nature of the Firm. British Review of Economic Issues, 9 (20).

Coro', G.C., Rullani, E. (eds) (1998): Percorsi locali di internazionalizzazione. Franco Angeli, Milano.

Crescini, A., Mistri, M. (1996): Il Veneto e il traffico di perfezionamento passivo nel settore tessile, abbigliamento, calzature. Economia e Società Regionale, n° 3.

Dunning, J. H. (1981): International Production and the Multinational Enterprise. Allen & Unwin.

Dunning, J. H. (1993): Multinational Enterprises and the Global Economy. Addison-Wesley.

Faini, R., Falzoni, A. M., Galeotti, M., Helg, R., Turrini, A. (1998): Importing Jobs and Exporting Firms? A Close Look at the Labor Market Implications of Italy's Trade and Foreign Direct Investment Flows. Mimeo

Feenstra, R. C., Hansen, G. H. (1996): Foreign Investment, Outsourcing, and relative wages, in Feenstra R. C., Grossman G. M., Irwin D. A. (eds), The Political Economy of Trade Policy, M.I.T. Press.

Feenstra R. C., Hansen G. H., (1996): Globalization, Outsourcing and Wage Inequality. American Economic Review, papers and proceedings, May.

Forti, A. (1994): Il Traffico di perfezionamento passivo nelle nuove strategie delle imprese italiane del tessile-abbigliamento. In: Istituto Commercio Estero, Rapporto sul Commercio Estero.

Grandinetti, R., Rullani, E., (1996): Impresa transnazionale ed economia globale. NIS, Firenze.

Grossman, G. (1987): The Employment and Wage Effects of Import Competition in the United States. Journal of International Economic Integration, 2, 1-23, Spring.

Ginsburg, A., Simonazzi, A. M., (1995): Il settore tessile, abbigliamento, calzature in Europa. Conferenza CNA, Roma.

Krugman, P.(1991): Geography and Trade. MIT Press, Cambridge Ma.

Krugman, P. (1994): Does Third World Hurt First World Prosperity? Harvard Business Review, 72:13-121.

Krugman, P. (1995): Growing World Trade: Causes and Consequences. Brooking Papers on Economic Activity, 1.

Howells, J. (1998): Regional Systems of Innovation. In: Archibugi, D. et al. (eds): National Systems of Innovation or the Globalisation of Technology? CUP.

Ietto Gillies, G. (1991): International Production, Trends, Theories, Effects. Polity Press London.

Lawrence, R. Z., Slaughter, M. J. (1993): International Trade and American Wages in the 1980s: Giant Sucking Sound or Small Hiccup? Brooking Papers on Economic Activity, Microeconomics, 2:161-226.

Lawrence, R. Z. (1994): Trade, Multinationals and Labor. NBER, Working paper 4836.

Revenga, A. (1992): Exporting Jobs? The Impact of Import Competition on Employment and Wages in U. S. Manufacturing. Quarterly Journal of Economics, 107:255-84.

Scarso, E. (1996): La rilocalizzazione del processo produttivo nei sistemi locali del Veneto: evidenze dal settore moda. Economia e Società Regionale, n° 4.

Schiattarella, R. (1987): Nodi strutturali e problemi congiunturali di un sistema in ritardo. In: Politica Internazionale: L'internazionalizzazione dell'economia italiana, 6.

Slaughter, M. J. (1995): Multinational Corporations, Outsourcing and American Wage Divergence. NBER Working Paper, n° 5253.

Storper, M. (1995): The Resurgence of Regional Economies Ten Years Later: the Region as a Nexus of Untraded Interdependencies. European and Regional Studies, 2, pp.191-221.

Zanfei, A. (1985): Cambiamento tecnologico e strategie di internazionalizzazione delle imprese tessili italiane. Economia e Politica Industriale, n° 46.

7. International Labor Standards and Child Labor

Kaushik Basu

J13

J82

1. Introduction

'International labor standards' are meant to be policy measures aimed at helping poor nations achieve certain minimal living standards. What is remarkable about these measures is that the most consistent opposition to them has come from the alleged beneficiaries. The fear of the poor nations is that labor standards are a facade for hiding the true agenda of developed nations, to wit, that of protectionism. The fear is partly justified. The demand for labor standards, as it stands today, comes overwhelmingly from protectionist lobbies in industrialized nations.

While labor standards as they are conceived currently ought to be rejected, there is nevertheless, I will argue, scope for a minimal and differently conceived set of international labor standards. I call this the "third" formulation, not only to distinguish it from the two viewpoints most often heard—that labor standards as currently recommended are a must, or that labor standards ought to be shunned altogether—but because this approach argues that the labor standards should be devised so as to give voice to certain muted demands in the Third World. As such, the third formulation consists of a package, which helps poor countries collude, in order to maintain better standards for their workers. It is a construct meant to counter the problem of free-riding among developing nations. The role of the industrialized nations, that this approach envisages, is the rather ironic one of helping poor countries collude.

A notable feature of this third approach is that it does not consist of deontic rules, such as, child labor must never be used. Whether children are allowed to work or not will be dependent on the welfare consequences of such a decision. It is also compatible with the view—which I maintain—that, in general, the best way to help poor nations is to open the doors of industrialized nations so that there can be greater demand for goods and services (and therefore, indirectly, labor) from the Third World. Such openness would cause wages to rise in the developing countries, thereby increasing the bargaining power of the workers, which would then result in higher living standards.

The subject of international labor standards (ILS) has been debated extensively by policymakers, especially before the Uruguay round of GATT, and in the seminar rooms of the WTO and the ILO[1]. The US had campaigned for labor standards and a "social clause" in the Uruguay Round; and from some recent statements of President Clinton, for instance, his address to the Economic Club of

---

[1] The academic literature on this is very large. Here are some references to papers that discuss issues that I am concerned with here: Bhagwait (1995), Roderik (1996), Srinivasan (1996), Maskus (1997).

Detroit on January 8, 1999, it is evident that the US will continue to push for international labor standards. But ILS is not a unique set of prescriptions, and the portents are that the kind of ILS policy that is being mooted by the industrialized nations, if adopted, will be detrimental to the poorest nations.

The problem stems from the fact that the idea of minimal labor standards is a Trojan horse that not only has room for those who are genuinely concerned about the well-being of workers but is a convenient hide-out for those with a much more selfish, protectionist agenda. And, regrettably, the initiative for ILS has moved into the hands of the protectionist lobbies. This has driven a wedge between the interests of the industrialized nations and the developing countries. Yet it will be sad if this backlash against the current conception of ILS results in the rejection of the very idea of minimal labor standards.

2. North vs. South or South vs. South?

A myth, which has fueled support for protectionism among the uninitiated of the North, is that the low work standard in developing countries is robbing the jobs of adults in developed countries. First of all, what many people seem unaware of is that most of the so-called power houses among the developing nations import more from the industrialized nations than they export to them. In 1995 Korea's exports to the industrialized nations constituted 12.3 % of its GDP, while its imports from the industrialized nations were 13.9% of its GDP[2]. In brief, *vis-à-vis* industrialized nations, Korea ran a trade deficit of 1.6%. Indonesia in the same year also ran a deficit, of 2.2%; Malaysia ran a deficit of 11.8%; Thailand a deficit of 9.1%; Brazil a deficit of 1.4%. With a trade surplus of 1%, China is more the exception than the rule. Moreover, the Chinese surplus is relatively recent phenomenon. What all this means is that, if the exports of these countries are cut off, in all likelihood their imports from industrialized nations will go down as well, so the net effect on the industrialized nations will be negative, instead of positive, though of course some specific sectors may gain. So the fear that the developing countries with their cheap labor are swamping industrialized country markets is a myth. By and large they continue to buy more than they sell.

Secondly, the products which are manufactured in the worst conditions often using child labor, are not the sectors in which there is any serious competition between the industrialized nations and the developing countries. Consider the celebrated soccer ball industry. High-quality soccer balls entail leather panels to be hand-stitched into geometric patterns. This high labor intensity implies that the bulk of the soccer balls are produced in developing countries. In 1996 the US imported 34.2 million dollars worth of soccer balls. The top five suppliers of soccer balls were Pakistan, China, Indonesia, India and Thailand. These countries together supplied 96.9 percent of the soccer imports. It is also worth keeping in mind that the US do not produce any soccer balls. If any of these countries is banned from exporting to the US it is highly unlikely that the demand will shift to another

---

[2] The statistics cited in this paragraph are from Golub (1997).

industrialized nation. It will be some other developing country that will pick up the slack. It is therefore a completely erroneous view that there is competition between the child laborers of the Third World and the adult workers of the industrialized nations.

A nice natural experiment in this actually occurred in the carpet industry. Hand-knotted carpets are another classic example of labor-intensive production. Indeed it is widely believed that children have a relative advantage in this because of their "nimble fingers", though a recent ILO study of the carpet industry contests this belief as yet another myth (see Levison et al, 1998). For historical reasons, Iran was the largest exporter of hand-knotted carpets to the US. Then in the late eighties the US placed an embargo on imports from Iran. Did that boost production in industrialized nations? The answer is an unsurprising no. India, China, Nepal and other poor nations stepped in. India, which used to be a small exporter of carpets suddenly became a big player. In 1996, the US, which do not make any hand-knotted carpets, imported 316 million dollars worth of this product. The five biggest sellers were India (45%), China (25%), Pakistan (16%), Turkey (6.5%) and Nepal (2.9%). The competition is clearly much more acute among developing countries than between developing countries and the developed ones.

A natural consequence of this, often overlooked by the North, is that labor standards are a great concern within the developing countries. This concern is combined with a fear that any action on this front by any one country will cause a shift in production to some other developing country[3]. Indians point out how the lack of democracy enables China to use forms of forced labor, for instance, prison labor, which would not be feasible in India; China on the other hand worries how India's greater poverty pushes wages down and sends larger numbers of children into the labor force. And in today's world of mobile capital each of these countries is aware how capital can easily leave its territory and go to the other if its cost of labor goes up.

What ILS can do is to address this fear among the developing nations, which makes it difficult for each of them to act on its own in raising labor standards. This would however require us to think of international labor standards very differently from what we are used to. ILS according to this "third approach" has to be viewed as an instrument of collusion among the Southern countries for raising labor standards, which none of these nations can singly do, without driving out capital. Before spelling out this approach, let us take a quick look at some of the policy actions currently being espoused.

3. Child Labor, Legal Action and Product Labeling

The existing international efforts are of two kinds, which in Basu (1999) were called 'extra-national' and 'supra-national'. An extra-national effort is an action taken within the boundaries of an industrial nation, which creates incentives in the Third World to raise labor standards. A classic example of this is the Harkin's

---

[3]This point has been made by several commentators, for instance, Grimsrud and Stokke (1997) and Harvey, Colingsworth and Athereya (1998).

Bill in the US, which, by stopping the import of products made with child labor, tries to create incentives in the exporting nations to change their method of production. A supra-national effort, on the other hand, is a multi-country effort, executed through some international organization, such as the WTO or the ILO, to discourage whatever it is that we want to discourage.

Given the difficulty of mobilizing the opinions of several nations, it is not surprising that most of the action thus far has been in the area of extra-national effort. Despite rhetoric to the contrary, these have frequently and increasingly been used as weapons of protection. Nevertheless, being weapons of protection does not preclude them from having concomitant beneficial effects elsewhere. So irrespective of what they are used for, we need to evaluate their worth in terms of their impact on the Third World. But even by this measure they fail.

These instruments, especially in the context of child labor, suffer from two weaknesses. They fail to realize that parents who send their children to work do not do so out of sloth and meanness, but to escape extreme poverty and hunger for the household, including the child (Basu and Van, 1998)[4]. When child labor occurs as a mass phenomenon, it must be distinguished from child abuse. Secondly, these instruments are very sector-specific; they penalize a nation for using child labor in export industries. Put these two arguments together and it is evident why these policies are likely to fail. If implemented properly they are likely to drive children from the carpet industry or garment industry or soccer ball industry to other sectors, some of which are more dismal, such as prostitution or welding. Indeed there is some evidence from Bangladesh that in anticipation of such laws, children have been removed from some of these export sectors, resulting in a rise in child prostitution. Similarly, a UNICEF study found that between 5,000 to 7,000 young girls moved from the carpet industry to prostitution as a result of these policies.

Fortunately, there is increasing realization among academics and activists in the North that, if our real aim is to help the children, then extra-national action has to be much more nuanced than just banning the import of any product that has been tainted by child labor[5]. Some recent legislation, such as the Harkin-Sanders amendment to the Tariff Act of 1930, which prohibits the import of products which use forced or indentured child labor is a move in the right direction. As an aside it is worth noting that one of the first uses of this amended law, illustrates how the overwhelming tendency is to use such social legislation for self-interest. This law was recently cited to criticize Brazil's largest juice exporter, Sucocitrico Cutrale Ltd., for using forced child labor to pick oranges. However, what brought the charge was not new evidence of forced child labor but the fact that Cutrale bought up a Minute Maid processing plant in Florida and then went on to cut back its work force. The law was plainly being used as an instrument.

---

[4] In a recent paper (Basu, Genicot and Stiglitz, 1999) we analyse the more general proposition that in altruistic households the mere risk of unemployment of the primary wage earner may cause secondary earners (typically, women and children) to look for work.

[5] For a lucid statement of the need for a multi-pronged approach to policy see Fallon and Tzannatos (1998).

One policy that has found increasing favor among activists is that of product labeling, that is, pasting labels on products, with a message like: "Guarantee: manufactured without child labor". This is, in fact, the exact label used by Reebok on soccer balls manufactured in Pakistan and sold in the US. The reason why this has found favor is because the choice is laid at the door step of the consumer. He can decide, according to his own morals, whether or not to boycott imported goods which do not have such a label. This additional information and additional choice has a nice democratic flavor. For this reason, to argue against this is much more difficult.

There are several reasons why product labeling is not the right way to battle child labor. The authenticity of these labels is highly questionable. In many of the sectors in which child labor flourishes, production takes place in thousands of little sheds and homes. In order to avoid this problem, Reebok has actually decided to centralize its manufacture of soccer balls in Pakistan by setting up a large facility in Sialkot, despite the increased cost of so doing. The problem is however pervasive in a range of industries, including carpets and shoe uppers. The joke used to be that stitching product labels can be another industry for employing children.

Even if we can get around the authenticity problem with a reasonable degree of accuracy, there are several compelling reasons why product labeling is a bad idea. First, it shares with the Harkin's Bill the problem that it attacks child labor in a few export-goods sectors and is therefore likely to push children into indigenous productive activities, some of which are much more harmful to them.

Second, as suggested earlier, in some of the poorest economies, if we try to eradicate child labor suddenly (whether by law or by a consumer boycott of such products), we may push poor households into even greater poverty and possible starvation. In some countries such as Ethiopia, where 42.3% of all children in the age-group 10-to-14 years work, and per capita income is a precarious 110 dollars *per annum*, a sudden stoppage of child labor will have a devastating effect on many households. In countries like India and China (and certainly Thailand, Malaysia and other more prosperous Asian countries), where industrialization has proceeded further and the incidence of child labor has come down—it is 14.4% in India and 11.6% in China, a sudden ban will be difficult but one that the economies can take without getting derailed. So a refusal to import products which use any child labor will put the poorest economies of the world at a disadvantage, because they may not be in a position to overhaul their production structure in the short-run. More specifically, this policy is likely to shift advantage away from the African economies in favor of the Asian and Latin American ones. And herein lies another lesson for designing a good ILS policy. It must make allowances for variations across countries; and not create advantages in favor of the stronger.

Finally, even in nations like China and India, it is not such a good idea to try to eradicate child labor in one fell swoop. Field workers in India have reported that some areas are so poor that perhaps the best policy is to allow children to combine schooling with some work. Indeed doing some work and earning some money may be the only way that children can afford the opportunity cost of schooling. Recent work on Peru tends to confirm this view of some work making it possible for children to go to school. It is also sobering to recall that one of the first laws in the US to curb child labor, by the state of Massachusetts in 1837, prohibited firms from employing children below the age of 15 years, who had not attended school for at least three months in the previous year. Likewise in Britain, all the way up to 1861, both the incidence of child labor and of schooling continued to rise. In other words, what we need to do is to put a limit on the amount of a child may work, and be prepared to vary this according to the country's general economic condition. Such variations are difficult to capture on product labels (the labels would have to be too long and complicated) but an international organization can work out detailed outlines and at least try to enforce these. So ILS has to be a supra-national effort, if at all. It may be harder to do so, but it has to be mediated through international organizations as a collective effort.

4. The "Third" Approach

The third approach views ILS as an instrument for Third World countries to achieve what they want to achieve but cannot do so because of the lack of coordination among themselves and the consequent fear that they will drive capital out of their country. The three essential ingredients of the third approach to international labor standards are as follows.

First, it must be recognized that to look for a single set of standards for all countries is to have virtually no standards. ILS must be flexible enough to take account of the different stages of development of different nations. Second, we should abandon the idea of banning child labor (as implicit in the product labeling program or the Child Labor Deterrence Bill). Instead, there should be limits specified about the number of hours that a child is allowed to work and restrictions on the conditions of work. Finally, if a certain product is manufactured in a certain country in violation of whatever happen to be the agreed-upon international labor standards, punitive action should not take the form of boycotting that product alone, but be more generalized. This is to prevent driving children away from one sector into another.

To elaborate on these, what the first requirement says is that we will have to first decide whether there is a minimal set of labor standards which all countries should be required to adhere to, and be prepared to face the answer that this set may be empty. We may, for instance, decide that nations with *per capita* income below a certain level are exempt from all the ILS strictures. In the past, ILS discussions have run around in international fora, first, because they were motivated by the interests of the developed nations and, second, because of the insistence that there had to be a program common to all countries, irrespective of their level of economic development. What is being suggested here is that each item discussed in the many previous meetings of GATT and ILO will have to be considered explicitly from point of view of the interests of the developing nations. We may reach the conclusion that forced labor should not be allowed anywhere, but that legal minimum wages are not desirable for poor nations. In that case we must not have minimum wages as a part of international labor standards. Protectionists in industrialized nations will not be happy about this but, if we are to have an ILS, which does what it is ostensibly supposed to do, then we must resist the forces of protection.

A central element in most ILS discussion pertains to child labor. It is hard for people in developed nations to realize that child labor is a fact of life that cannot be wished away— there is enough evidence now to suggest that for very poor countries we cannot use the law to banish it, unless we are insensitive to the well-being of the children. The second ingredient of the Third Approach is a plea to recognize this and to work for steps which seek to curb child labor, leaving the idea of eliminating it to the long run. There should be steps taken to make it possible for children to work flexible hours so that they can, if they want, combine some child work with schooling. Of course 'collaborative' measures, such as school meals and subsidy for going to school can be used to make it attractive for parents to pull their children out of the labor force of their own accord. Industrialized nations can contribute to such an effort, and one possibility is to make such a commitment on the part of industrialized nations a part of ILS.

If we do decide to back up the standards with punitive action for their violation, these actions should ideally not be product specific. It is not clear that trade sanctions are a good way to deal with labor standards violation, but if we do decide to use them, the final condition suggests that these should take the form of sanctions being imposed no matter in which sector the violation occurs. A country must not go exempt from punishment because the violation occurs in a non-exportable sector. The present method of not buying a product, the manufacture of which violates an agreed-upon labor standard, drives some of the worst practices into sectors which have no connection with exports.

Let us now turn to the subject of enforcement. A question that has on occasions been discussed is who should be the enforcer of ILS (Bhagwati, 1995). In particular, should it be the WTO or the ILO? At an abstract level, this does not matter. As long as we agree on what the standards are and what the punishments are, how does it matter who does the enforcing? In reality, institutions come with a baggage of history, their own structures and modes of operation. So the same set of rules may be perceived differently whether the WTO or the ILO carries them out, and in this area perception matters. Moreover, even if we start from one set of rules, the evolution of these over time may be very different depending on who is entrusted with them.

There are two reasons that weigh against the WTO as an agency for carrying out this task. Given the history of GATT, in the WTO the battle lines have historically been drawn between the developed nations and the developing nations, with the ILS being viewed as what the North wants to impose on an unwilling South. Since the third approach to ILS is an attempt to reverse this, with the initiative being shifted to the countries supposed to be helped by the standards, it is doubtful whether our perceptions, rooted in history, can be changed adequately for old suspicions not to reappear. Secondly, it is not clear to me that trade sanctions (which is the domain of WTO) is the right way to deal with labor standards enforcement. The risk is that protectionism will again work its way back and thwart trade, once the door is opened to blocking trade for a limited class of actions.

On balance, ILS is better left to the ILO. Conventions, which nations are encouraged to sign and then are expected to adhere to, is the standard method that the ILO has used to orchestrate various kinds of labor rights. This is not a powerless instrument. In today's inter-connected world, with easy information flow, the violation of a convention that a nation has signed can have plenty of consequences without anyone having to orchestrate it. The mere 'news' of Nike having possibly violated some standards was like a negative advertisement and was enough to change manufacturing practices in a large number of multinationals. Moreover, one can back up the voluntary nature of conventions with some punitive ammunition. One can think of varying foreign aid flows according to whether a nation violated the ILS. One may also think of linking the ILO and WTO in enforcing labor standards, whereby the ILO drafts the standards and monitors them and the WTO is empowered to take action only after it gets the go-ahead from the ILO.

The policy of international labor standards is a dangerous one, where a desirable end can easily become a *conduit* for protectionism, which is likely to harm not only the developing nations but also the population at large in the developed countries. Hence, even if a particular action seems desirable today, one has to be conscious of the fact that one act can lead to another and somewhere along the line cross over into policies which hurt the very people they were supposed to help. In this essay I have tried to outline a minimal, pragmatic program and also the agency for implementing it, keeping in mind that this is an area where in designing policy one has to keep in mind not just economic desirablity but the risk of future misuse.

References

Basu, K. (1999): Child Labor: Cause Consequence and Cure with Remarks on International Labor Standards. Journal of Economic Literature, forthcoming.

Basu, K., Genicot, G., Stiglitz, J. (1999): Household Labor Supply, Unemployment and Minimum Wage Legislation. Policy Research Working Paper No. 2049, The World Bank, Washington.

Basu, K., Van, Pham H. (1998): The Economics of Child Labor. American Economic Review, vol. 88.

Bhagwati, J. (1995): Trade Liberalization and 'Fair Trade' Demands: Addressing Environmental and Labor Standards Issues. World Economy, vol.18.

Fallon, P., Tzannatos, Z. (1998): Child Labor: Issues and Directions for the World Bank. Human Development Network, The World Bank, Washington.

Golub, S. (1997): Are International Labor Standards Needed to Prevent Social Dumping? Finance & Development, December.

Grimsrud, B., Stokke, L.J. (1997): Child Labor in Africa: Poverty or Institutional Failures. FAFO Report 223, Oslo.

Harvey, P. J., Collingsworth, T., Athreya, B. (1998): Developing Effective Mechanisms for Implementing Labor Rights in the Global Economy. Mimeo. International Labor Rights Fund, Washington.

Levison, D. et al. (1998): Is Child Labor Really Necessary in India's Carpet Industry? In: Anker, R. et al. (eds): Economics of Child Labor in Selected Industries of India. Hindustan Publishers, New Delhi, forthcoming.

Maskus, K. (1997): Should Core Labor Standards be Imposed Through International Trade Policy? Policy Research Working Paper No. 1817. The World Bank, Washington.

Rodrik, D. (1996): Labor Standards in International Trade: Do They Matter and What Do We Do about Them? Policy Essay, No. 20. Overseas Development Council, Washington.

Srinivasan, T.N. (1996): International Trade and Labor Standards from an Economic Perspective. In: van Dyck, P., Faber, G. (eds): Challenges to the New World Trade Organization. Kluwer Publishers.

Acknowledgements

The author is grateful to Maurizio Franzini for comments.

PART III.

Neo-Globalization, the Welfare State and Social Cohesion

8. Globalization, Welfare State and Social Dumping

Felice Roberto Pizzuti

1. Introduction

The discussion on the growing role of the welfare state (WS) in advanced economies has been gathering steam again since the mid-70s, within a framework characterized by the renewed popularity of free market or pro-market economics (hence-forth: neo-liberalist economics) or neoliberalism and its strong criticism of state intervention in all sectors, including the social one. This period also witnessed the acceleration of the international economic integration referred to as globalization, or Neo-Globalization (NG)[1], a term utilized not only for markets but also for the non-economic aspects of society.

The association of these two trends raises two questions: are there any new theoretical elements and/or new empirical experiences that justify the stronger criticism leveled at the WS and make the traditional pro-market economics proposals to reducing it significantly more compelling? If so, is the presence of these new elements related to the NG phenomena?

The neo-liberalist criticism of the WS has a positive answer to both questions and uses social dumping (SD) as an analytical tool to support its positions.

This paper reaches conclusions which differ from those of neo-liberalism. The effects on the WS attributed to the NG phenomena are brought down to scale and the SD argument which considers those effects negative is criticized. meanwhile, new important developments in the social and economic systems over the last two decades are highlighted which have a stronger impact on the role of the WS and on the need for an adjustment of its functions in the more advanced economies.

The next section will describe shortly the SD argument and the political recommendations that result from the analysis. In the following section the argument will be reviewed, criticizing the underlying analytical assumptions and assessing the supporting empirical aspects as well as the policy recommendations. Within this context, on the one hand those criteria which mostly affect the trade relations between developed countries (DC) and emerging countries (EC) – or newly industrializing countries (NIC) – will be analyzed, on the other the economic role of the WS will be evaluated.

The WS has both economic as well as socio-political goals, but drawing a line between the two is not always easy. In fact, while economic growth fosters the solution of social problems, stability and social harmony provide a positive contribution to economic growth. On the other hand, a traditional position is that

---

[1] As I suggest in the introduction of the present volume it should be better to use the term "Neo-Globalization" in order to distinguish the new phenomena of globalization from those of the last century and to highlight the parallelism with the recurrent editions of free market economics (neo-liberalism referring to the present edition).

which sees a trade-off between growth and social equity. In section 4 the interaction between these two spheres will be explored with reference to the peculiarities of the economic and social context attributable to NG and to the related role of the WS.

Section 5 will consider other new elements, different from those commonly related to NG, but that exert even greater effects on the WS and on the need for its reform.

Some recommendations on the adjustments of the WS will be issued in the final part, taking into account both the needs arising from NG and the other new developments considered.

2. The Social Dumping Argument and its Policy Recommendations

According to the SD argument, as they have a lower level of public social expenditure and equally low social security contributions, NIC have lower labor costs, thus they are more competitive than countries with more advanced welfare systems.

On the other hand, NG, generating – among other things – lower transaction costs and greater ease of trade and foreign direct investments, enhances the competition between advanced and emerging economies. Ruling out protectionist policies designed to hamper economic integration, European countries in particular – traditionally characterized by the broader role of their social institutions – should need to reduce their labor costs and the constraints on its use. This objective should be pursued by trying to reduce exactly what is regarded as the main cause for the differential in competitiveness, namely by shrinking the edifice of the WS, in terms of both budgets and rules that limit the flexibility of the labor market[2].

According to some interpretations, the SD argument does not apply only to trade relations between advanced and emerging economies; it should be extended also to the relations between European countries on the one hand and US and Japan, on the other, as these are characterized by smaller WS systems, even though their level of private expenditure in the social area is higher[3].

As far as the European countries are concerned, the lesson that can be learned from an accurate interpretation of the SD argument is that not only does the average overall cost of labor have to be lowered, but also, and most importantly, the extent of the benefits and the related contribution costs have to be selectively reduced, distinguishing among the different worker categories on the basis of their type and degree of specialization. The need to reduce the cost of labor should be greater for low-skill workers (whose wages are, moreover, already below the average) and in any case for all those employed in the production of more mature products, which are more exposed to the competition of emerging countries. As the best way to reduce real salaries is the reduction of the contributions related to benefits, the recommendation to proceed more selectively by penalizing workers who are already at the bottom of the

---

[2] According to Alesina-Perotti (1997), the extent to which the higher labor tax linked to the greater social expenditure is passed on to firms – resulting in a loss of competitiveness – is related to the power of unions and to the degree of geographic concentration of union barganing.
[3] See for instance Saint Paul (1997).

remuneration ladder lends additional support to the notion that the welfare state has to be reined in. In fact, the goal of the WS is not only to distribute social goods and services but also to distribute them equitably so as to favor mostly low-income classes. The WS then represents a double roadblock for the recommendations of the SD argument: not only does it provide too many social services, which increase the average cost of labor, but it allocates the benefits and the relative costs on a criterion that runs contrary[4] to that deemed appropriate to counter the competitive pressures of emerging countries[5] A solution in line with the recommendations of the SD argument would be to allow the market to allocate social goods and services by adopting as selection criteria both the same price for all and the income and individual choices. Access to social goods and services would be freed from the reallocation rationale and from the direct approach to maximize social welfare typical of the WS and would depend on the individual salaries that the market pays for each worker's productive role.

As it is attested to by the historic, political and cultural context in which it began spreading, the SD argument is rooted in a neo-liberalist rationale.

Throughout this century, the state role in the social area, which eventually materialized into the WS systems, showed a continuous and substantial growth in most developed countries[6]; it found its *raison d'être* in both the theoretical and cultural debate as well as in the political events and social and economic changes that have marked the evolution of capitalist systems.

This trend witnessed a turning point in the 70s when, following a long and widespread economic, social and political instability at the international level, which ended in strongly inflationary pressures and in the ensuing thrust to normalization, the neo-liberalist position gained strength and popularity once again.

That time marked also the acceleration of economic integration among the different production systems known as globalization (Neo-Globalization).

The question that needs to be analyzed in depth is whether the NG processes have triggered significant changes in the composition and pattern of social and economic equilibria and if such changes are of some consequence (and how) for the discourse on state intervention in the economy, on the development of the sector of social goods and services and on the role of the WS[7].

More specifically, a review should be carried out of any theoretical and

---

[4] Obviously, what is important in terms of competitiveness is not the distribution of the services but the cost. If, for instance, the former were not strictly related to the latter it might be possible to be equitable by providing more services to low-income people without a corresponding cost increase. We will return on this subject; here it is only specified that in this way the re-distributive role of the WS would be more pronounced, a characteristic that is not consistent with the neo-liberlist approach of the SD argument which will be examined shortly.

[5] Holding the criteria for delivering the services and financing the WS equal, and given their inconsistency with the indications of the SD argument, demands for scaling down the welfare state go beyond the quantity that would be sufficient to reduce the average cost of labor to the extent required.

[6] Cf. Pizzuti (1994b).

[7] For an analysis of the evolution of the role of the state in the social area, regardless of the additional problems determined by NG, see Pizzuti (1994b).

empirical changes that justify the evolution of the debate and of the actual choices concerning the state role in the social area and if such explanations are those suggested by the SD argument.

The most appropriate method is to start by checking the consistency between the theoretical assumptions and the empirical findings that implicitly or explicitly support the SD argument; then, those changes will be examined which are unrelated to NG but that in any case concern the role of the WS.

3. Assessment of the Social Dumping Argument and of its Economic Policy Recommendations

3.1. The Insufficient Weight Assigned to Labor Productivity

Though it seems founded on a reasoning which is both straightforward and easily understood also by the layman – certainly a reason that contributed to its popularity – the SD argument rests on a number of theoretical assumptions that are neither a given in the economic literature nor borne out by adequate empirical findings. Moreover, the policy recommendations descending from this argument support reallocation processes that are far from equitable.

An initial consideration on the preoccupations related to the growing competition of low-wage countries is not to take sufficiently into account that the most appropriate parameter to evaluate the impact of the cost of labor on the competitiveness of manufactured goods is not the hourly rate but the cost per unit of output, which is of course also a function of labor productivity. If, for instance, the cost of labor in Italy is compared to that of other countries of the OECD area, it can be seen that, while it is lower than France's and Germany's (by more than 30%) as well as the USA's (by approximately 20%) and Japan's (by more than 50%), it is higher than Spain's and the United Kingdom's (by 10%) and Greece's (approximately 50%). However, while labor productivity in Italy is more or less similar to that of the USA and France and lower in the other countries considered – in Germany and Spain by approximately 15%, in Japan and United Kingdom by approximately 25% and in Greece by almost half – it appears that overall the cost of labor per unit of output (CLUO) is basically similar to the Greek one and to a varying extent lower than that of all the other countries mentioned, including Spain and Great Britain despite their lower hourly rates[8].

A labor productivity gap can then offset even significant differentials in hourly rates, such as that between Italy and Greece.

As we will see later, the expenditure for social goods and services shows a

---

[8] In particular, setting Italy's CLUO at 100, France's is equal to 137, Germany's 156, the USA's 144, Spain's 107, Great Britain's 115 and Greece's 96. These data – which refer to the private sector and determine productivity in terms of purchasing power parity of the GDP per unit of labor – were compiled utilizing statistical data published by the OECD for 1996 as reported by Delli Gatti et al. (1998).

positive correlation with labor productivity, due to the effects it exercises directly on workers' skills and indirectly on the social and working environment.

3.2. The First Analytical Assumption of the Social Dumping Argument: the Role of Competitive Pricing

Moving on to the analytical assumptions of the SD argument, a necessary, though not sufficient, condition for their soundness is that trade between structurally different countries – the developed countries (DC) with a higher labor cost due to high social security contributions on the one hand and the emerging economies (NIC) characterized by relatively low social expenditures and wages on the other – is essentially based on competitive pricing, or on the hypothesis that countries produce the same exportable goods and services. It is this hypothesis that makes significant and full of material consequences the combination of national differences in labor costs, the reduction of transaction costs and of the institutional obstacles to international trade brought about by NG.

The SD argument and the significant role played by the price-based competition would be empirically supported by the developments occurred in the DC's labor markets over the past two decades.

It is a well-known fact, as highlighted by the literature on the labor market in the past few years, that in DCs a pattern has arisen whereby workers command different wages depending on their level of specialization. The salary gap to the detriment of low-skill workers has been widening particularly in the USA; where that trend would be countered by a greater market regulation, as in continental Europe, the result being a higher unemployment rate that would have penalized mostly unskilled workers[9].

Based on the SD argument, the worsening of the unskilled workers' conditions[10] in the DCs would depend on NG which has fueled the competition of NIC workers with similar skills but lower salaries; this competition would take place both in the markets for goods as well as in attracting the direct investment in the NICs that would otherwise go to low-skill-labor-intensive activities in the DCs.

Starting from the empirical aspects, it should be noted that, despite the greater trade integration that has been taking place in the past few years, imports from NICs account for a very small share of the DC's GDP; Krugman (1995) shows that for the OECD countries that share is equal to 2%, quite an irrelevant figure; this, however, cannot explain the 30% skill-premium increase the USA have had since the 1970s.

According to Rodrik (1997b), among the effects of international integration on the increased wage differential related to labor specialization, consideration should be given to those determined by the migration of workers from NICs to DCs (of which,

---

[9] On the more or less significant effects exercised by globalization on the labor markets of the DCs see Gottschalk- Smeeding (1997), Milone-Franzini (1997), OECD (1997), Wood (1994, 1995, 1998).

[10] Other reasons for the worsening conditions of low-skill workers in the DCs were cited by Rodrik (1997b); we will return on this later.

admittedly, no empirical findings are available)[11] . A rather more important reason for the skill premium increase is definitely represented by technology changes and the resulting adoption in the DCs of more specialized labor intensive manufacturing techniques which caused the demand for low-skill labor, and the related wage level, to drop.

Obviously it should not be ruled out, as underlined by Wood (1994 and 1995), that the evolution in the choice of manufacturing techniques in the DCs has in turn been affected by the economic integration with the NICs ("defensive innovation"). This aspect is underscored by those, like Rodrik, who think that the effects of NG on the equilibria of the labor market in the DCs are not so small, as might be evinced from Krugman's analysis[12].

However, the very link between technological innovation and the need for the DCs to defend themselves from the competition of NICs in mature industries call the attention on the strong one-sidedness and the ensuing interpretation limits of a vision of trade between the two sets of countries founded on the assumption that both might produce all the types of goods they want and with the same techniques, thus giving rise to a price-based competition. A more meaningful depiction of the trade between structurally different countries would be that based on the international division of labor resulting from the differences existing in the technologies available, in the qualitative features of the production systems, of the goods manufactured and of the manufacturing techniques utilized. In a more realistic analytical context such as this, it seems clear that the greater breadth and qualification of production possibilities available puts the DCs in the condition to know and to be able to engage in production activities not subject, or with little exposure, to the competitive pricing policies based on low wages that might be implemented by NICs.

Among the technological developments that fostered the recent globalization processes are those that have made it possible to break down production processes in clearly different phases, some of which do not require skilled labor and may be easily contracted out. Outsourcing and the production of different parts of a product in several sites have become generally more important and with them the relocation to more cost-effective territories. There is no doubt that these technological and

---

[11] Citing papers by Bhagwati (1991) and Lawrence-Slaughter (1993), Rodrik (1997b) emphasizes that the difficulties of linking the fall of the relative prices of goods manufactured with low-skill labor to the rise of the skill premium makes it difficult to conclude that both international trade and immigration have had a significant role in the widening of the wage differential that has been occurring in the last few years. Also for Italy, Cipollone-Sestito (1997) report that the increment of international trade (which, by the way, is at the same level as at the beginning of the century) has not affected significantly labor market equilibria. The two authors show that greater effects might be attributed to other aspects of Neo-Globalization such as the tearing down of position rents for some worker categories and the relocation abroad resulting from the development of outsourcing and the finishing of products by firms. Schiattarella (1998) does not consider these two last NG aspects as equally significant. We will return on this at a later stage.
[12] Rodrik (1997b) agrees with Cline's analysis (1997) whereby 20% the growth of the wage differential which took place in the 80s should be attributed to international reasons.

organizational trends of the production processes from time to time cause some adjustment problems related to new production methods and to the quality of the labor force in the DCs; they constitute, however, neither a blurring of the lines along which international labor is divided nor a move toward a leveling of production possibilities. If anything, the breakdown of production processes shifts the stage of the international division of labor from the products to their production phases, leaving in any case the control of the overall process and of the phases that require adequate production contexts and more qualified labor force to countries with more advanced production structures.

Within the DCs, even in a productive system like the Italian one with relatively little in the terms of high-tech industries, there are some specific production capabilities that, so far at least, have crowded out low-wage competitors. Schiattarella (1998) shows in recent research that, over the last decade, the international integration of the Italian economy has grown significantly also through foreign direct investments[13] . Among the different aspects of this development, emphasis should be placed on two in particular: the first is that, though foreign direct investments in Eastern Europe rose substantially (also because before the fall of the communist regimes those countries were basically excluded from international trade) also those in Western Europe showed a marked increase, the latter being the area where most foreign direct investments are concentrated; this aspect bears out the limited importance of the competitiveness and the attractiveness of low-wage countries for production relocation purposes. Second, the production relocations in the "made in Italy" sector took place within the framework of a segmentation by phases of the overall production processes, which continue to be controlled from Italy; with reference to the sectors considered, the new jobs created abroad had little or no effects on the employment levels of the Italian regions from which the manufacturing stages had been relocated. Instead, in these regions there was an increase in productivity and salary level, which suggests that the labor force shifted to jobs requiring higher skills.

Going back to the general considerations on the SD argument, it might be said that in light of the little importance of the trade relationships between DCs and NICs, considering that they reflect mainly an international division of labor based on the different technological and qualitative abilities of the production systems, the role that can be attributed to the price-based competition as a result of low salaries seems rather small. Thus, one of the two necessary conditions for the SD argument is very weak.

While the trade relations between DCs and NICs are characterized by a division of tasks deriving mainly from their different degree of knowledge and skills, the presence of productive activities accessible to countries that are part of both classes should not be underestimated. This is more likely to occur in the phases of territorial rearrangement of the international division of labor, during which some emerging

---

[13] Though not very high, the Italian share of worldwide foreign direct investments more than doubled, from 1.42% to 3.33% [data from Mariotti-Cominotti (1998) as mentioned in Schiattarella (1998)].

countries (EC) gain access to new productive activities which had formerly been the exclusive preserve of DCs and some of the latter have difficulties or in any case experience delays in evolving toward production modes not open to ECs. At this stage competitive pricing is hard at work, but such circumstance does not mean that WS expenditures should be cut, as suggested by the SD thesis. The possibility of DCs avoiding competition with the ECs, by specializing in activities precluded to the latter, can in fact be facilitated by their very own WS institutions.

This leads to the evaluation of the economic function of the WS and to the second assumption of the SD thesis. Before moving on, however, it might be appropriate to touch briefly on one aspect of the globalization processes under way that is not given due consideration in the DS thesis: it is the regionalization phenomenon, namely the creation of supranational, though limited and constrained, territorial areas by institutional accords, especially in the economic and trade area.

Since these are countries in which geographic proximity has generally facilitated shared historic and cultural experiences, their institutions too differ relatively little; as a result, the SD argument applied to trade within regions is deprived of one of its analytical foundations. Besides, the economic competitiveness of these areas vis-à-vis the external world depends also on the degree of their internal social cohesion and their ability to maintain it, despite the presence of significant changes taking place in their social and productive organizations. Social cohesion is fostered by a certain level of equitable income distribution, by low unemployment and by the insurance against the risk of its increase, by the ability of social and training structures to manage productive changes and, more generally, by the satisfaction of a given level of social needs which is an integral part of the cultural traits that have historically emerged in an area.

These last considerations lead us to discuss the second necessary condition (which by itself is not sufficient) for the SD argument which, as a matter of fact, concerns the economic role of WS.

3.3. The Second Analytical Assumption: The Economic Role of the Welfare State

It has already been noted that, within the framework of the SD argument, the WS plays the role of a consumption good, or better of a luxury good[14] essentially accessible to the rich countries, but which inevitably generates a cost for their production systems. Since this is financed by firms and workers in proportion to the latters' salaries, the WS translates into a rise in the cost of labor – discouraging firms from hiring – and lower competitiveness on global markets. This interpretation of the WS's economic role is set within the more general neo-liberalist criticism of state intervention in the economy which, in its most radical expression, does not make any exception for the provision of social goods and services[15]. However, the economic

---

[14] Cf. Sala-i-Martin (1996).

[15] According to "social Darwinists", state intervention in the social area would not only be damaging from an economic point of view but would remove individual responsibility to the point that citizens would be unable to provide for their own needs which might result in their loss of freedom. Cf. Hayek (1960, 1982). For an analysis of these positions, see Artoni (1993).

discussion is marked by established positions, founded both on theoretical arguments and empirical findings which equate social expenditure not so much to unproductive consumption only as mainly to interventions that increase economic efficiency.[16]

The different functions carried out by the welfare state can be summarized. By guaranteeing healthcare services and education to all, it promotes the creation and dissemination of human capital, which constitutes a primary resource for production and productivity growth.

Most services rendered by the WS are transfers, such as pension payments, designed to stabilize individuals' incomes during their lifetime. This need which previously was met by social institutions such as the family, has always existed, however, following the diffusion of capitalist societies and economies, it became necessary – for reasons of effectiveness and efficiency – to resort to collective insurance schemes.

WS institutions protect incomes against risks such as unemployment, sickness, accidents, maternity etc., creating a social security net which tends to offset the uncertainty generated in market economies and enhanced by neo- globalization; in this way, labor mobility and flexibility increase and workers can cope more easily with the risk and the costs of their retraining and employment reallocations associated with the upgrading of production systems and productivity increases.

It is generally recognized that political stability, which finds fertile ground in a climate of greater social security, improves the productive capacities of an economic system and its performances[17].

Benefits and income protection financed by the WS, by making more payments during recessions and collecting higher tax revenues in phases of sustained growth, tend to stabilize the economic cycle whose fluctuations are a serious problem, typical of the workings of capitalist markets.

The positive economic effects that are credited to the WS are countered by the criticism on the distortions caused by its financing. In one recent contribution, Alesina-Perotti (1997) linked this thesis to labor unions and international trade, maintaining that   higher taxes levied on workers' salaries to finance higher WS expenditures lead labor unions to demand higher pay which in turn determine an increase in labor cost and a reduction in a country's international competitiveness.

This kind of criticism to the WS's role, a case made also against financing public expenditure in general, is rooted in the neoclassical model of an abstract economic system made up of perfectly competitive markets which attain first-best equilibria[18], altered only by labor unions. However, albeit within the neoclassical theoretical model and the Pareto efficiency criterion, welfare economics, with its first analyses of market failures started by Marshall and Pigou and with the more recent studies on the consequences of imperfect information, unearthed the existence of a

---

[16]Cf. Acocella (1998b), Atkinson (1995, 1995b), Barr (1992, 1993), Fitoussi (1995), Garrett-Mitchell (1996), Rodrik (1997, 1997b).

[17] Cf. e.g. Alesina et al. (1996), Atkinson (1995, 1995b), Barr (1992, 1993), Fitoussi (1995), Garrett-Mitchell (1996), Perotti (1996), Rodrik (1997, 1997b).

[18] Cf. Atkinson (1995b).

number of circumstances – particularly widespread in the sector of social goods and services – in which it is more economically advantageous to resort to state intervention; such advantage is demonstrated from the very proof that under those circumstances the market cannot achieve a first-best equilibrium. Other market failures have been shown to take place at the macroeconomic level by the Keynesian theoretical contribution, with reference to the existence of involuntary unemployment and the instability of capitalist economies. Also within the context of these issues the state's role in mitigating market inefficiencies is recognized particularly in the social area.

The analyses of both market failures, at the micro and macroeconomic levels, reveal that the operations of the WS are a tool to maximize economic efficiency.[19]

Atkinson also stresses that the theoretical models pointing to the negative economic role of the WS often do not take into account the institutional aspects that regulate it [20], thus missing some remarkable features of the workings of the different WS institutions. For instance, Atkinson (1995b) emphasizes that many labor market models, demonstrating that unemployment benefits constitute an actual disincentive to look for work, do not consider that benefits are paid provided, among other things, the recipient does not reject any job offer. Neglecting this institutional aspect which regulates the payment of unemployment benefits adversely affects the opinion on its role in terms of economic efficiency.

It is a well-known fact that the analysis of market failures has been matched by that of non-market failures which has stressed the limits of state intervention and the possibility that it cannot do better than the market, not even when this fails to achieve optimal equilibrium[21]. Some of the limits and difficulties concerning specifically the working of SW will be reviewed later.

Going back to the evaluation of the WS by the SD argument, it should be noted how this does not consider that widely available social goods and services, transfers and income redistribution determine not only specific efficiency increases but, more generally, are conducive to that economic and social stability which, according to several studies, has been on average underpinning capitalism development[22]; thus, even when the WS produces costs which do not yield immediate and adequate benefits, account should be taken of the advantages, economic and otherwise, which derive from a greater social cohesion and by the cooperative

---

[19] On the analysis of the causes of market failures of a micro and macroeconomic nature, see Acocella (1997), Atkinson (1995,1995b), Barr (1992, 1993), Pizzuti (1994b), Stiglitz (1986, 1989).

[20] It is well known that one of the criticisms leveled at classical economists by Keynes is their lack of attention to the institutional aspects that characterize the actual working of a capitalist economy; cf. Caffè (1978).

[21] For an analysis of non-market failures see, among others, Barr (1992, 1993), Le Grand (1991), Pizzuti (1994b), Stiglitz (1986, 1989), Woolf (1979,1988).

[22] Cf., for instance, Garrett-Mitchell (1996), Rodrik (1997b), Wilensky (1993) and the numerous studies cited by them.

behaviors that this determines.[23]

In scrutinizing the SD thesis, it is interesting to notice that, historically, the WS has actually developed hand in hand with capitalist markets and their international integration. Both in the past and in more recent times, many empirical studies have shown the positive space and time correlation between the degree of opening to international trade and the incidence of social expenditure[24]. Also in the past two decades – during which neo-liberalist policies have overwhelmed the Keynesian edifice and the general tendency toward a reduction of the overall public expenditure imposed itself – also in countries like the USA and Japan, where the state's role in the social sector is traditionally less pronounced, the social-expenditure component has only been growing at a lower rate, a confirmation of the inability in advanced market economies to curb the WS role.[25]

The different weight of the WS in the US and in the European countries has often been linked to the different performance of the economic systems of the two continents in the past few years to support the SD thesis. However, both the comparison between the two aspects and the results of such comparison raise a number of questions. First, the comparison between the USA and the countries of Europe highlights that, while the role of the WS in the former is more limited, the overall social expenditure (private and public) is similar to that incurred on average in the old continent[26]. Second, evidence does not seem to disprove the above-mentioned indications of welfare economics concerning the efficient role of the WS; in fact, the comparison between the two continents does not yield any proof or clue that the different compositions of public and private expenditures attribute a greater competitiveness to the USA, as maintained by the SD thesis and as suggested by studies such as those by Alesina-Perotti (1997) and Saint-Paul (1997). The comparison

---

[23] "The endogenous growth theory shows how the accumulation of human capital and the positive externalities created by some types of investment may lead an economy along a higher and more permanent growth path. Social cohesion is deemed to play in a society the same role as know-how in some of these models. A welfare state is likely to be the best way to encourage this team spirit and the positive externalities related to it.". Fitoussi (1995, p. 346). "Social disintegration is not a spectator sport – those on the sidelines also get splashed with mud from the field. Ultimately, the deepening of social fissures can harm all..... This is not a pleasing prospect, even for individuals on the winning side of the divide who have little empathy for the other side". Rodrik (1997b), p. 7.

[24] See Cameron (1978), Garrett-Mitchell (1996), Wilensky (1993), Rodrik (1997, 1997b); however, as will be seen later, this last author maintains that beyond certain levels of both social expenditure and international economic integration, an increase in the need for social security is matched by an increased difficulty in financing it.

[25] For an analysis by the author on the quantitative evolution of social expenditure broken down by single component cf. Pizzuti (1994); on these aspects see also Artoni (1997), Barr (1992), Rodrik (1997b).

[26] In 1993, based on computations by Artoni et al (1997), total social expenditure in the USA represented 27.9% of GDP, 43% of which was accounted for by private outlays. In the same year, in the European Union (then made up of 12 countries) total social expenditure amounted to 28.5% of GDP; in Italy that share was equal to 25.8%, of which (made it equal to 100), only 14% was incurred by private entities.

provides results that run contrary to these positions.

As to healthcare, Artoni et al. (1997) show that, despite the fact that the share of private outlays in the USA (approximately 45%) is larger than in Italy (approximately 38%), the cost borne by USA employers (equal to 3.5% of the GDP) is greater than that incurred by Italian employers (less than 2%). Two circumstances help to explain this difference. The first is that, even though 15% of the USA population is not covered by any type of insurance while the Italian population is fully covered, the total expenditure in the USA (equal to 14% of the GDP) is much higher than in Italy (8.2% of the GDP). The second is that in the USA most health-insurance premiums are paid by employers, thus representing part of a worker's compensation.

This example shows not only that entrusting healthcare to the public sector is more effective and less costly, but it shows also that, if it is not socially and economically desirable to dispense with some social goods and services, thinking to lower the cost of labor by reducing public-sector services and the related contribution costs is deceptive and self-defeating. If, as Alesina-Perotti (1997) surmise, the presence of unions and their pay demands pass the cost of benefits on to employers, there is no reason to think that those very unions do not press the same demands – asking employers for raises in take-home pay or indirectly the funds to pay for insurance premiums – so that workers can purchase in the marketplace the same healthcare services formerly provided by the state. Actually, given the same healthcare services, the replacement of public-sector intervention with more expensive private services will result in employers paying more for insurance premiums than they did for social security contributions, a change that will – without doubt – erode their competitiveness in international markets.

Analogous considerations could obviously be made for all the social goods and services that state intervention can provide more efficiently and at a lower cost.

From this point of view, there is the even more typical case of pension systems in which administrative costs and the uncertainty concerning pension payments increase markedly when compulsory state schemes are abandoned in favor of private pension funds selected by the individuals. The USA and Great Britain's experience where private and public pension systems live together, and the Chile case where the former replaced the latter, bear out the theory that the distribution of insurance risks is managed more effectively by the state[27].

---

[27] Stiglitz (1986) writes that in the USA, while the administrative costs of the public system account for less than 2% of the payments made, those of private companies represent more than 50%. The financial management of private defined-contribution pension funds in Chile amounts to approximately 30% of the contributions made. For more information on the Chilean experience cf. Diamond (1993), Diamond-Valdes Prieto (1993), Valdes Prieto (1994). In Great Britain, following a flurry of lawsuits related to lower-than-promised pension payments (and even lower than those paid by the public system whose abandonment had been sought) the Agency which supervises the financial markets, the Security Investment Board, mandated insurance companies to disclose their operating costs, whose share of premiums paid turned out to be very high (up to 24%), structurally greater than that of the public pension system. Noteworthy is that in Italy INPS's operating costs account for less than 2% of the pension payments made.For a more in-depth analysis of the evolution of pension systems and the comparison between public and private systems cf. Pizzuti (1999).

There was no evidence to confirm the negative effect on growth[28] of pension transfers by the WS; to this end, Barro's statement whereby "One puzzle in the empirical growth literature is that a measure of old-age transfers is not negatively related to subsequent growth and investment ".[29]

Returning to the general analysis of the WS, its economic efficiency and its influence on competitiveness, Wilensky wrote: "My analysis of the economic performance of nineteen rich democracies between 1950 and 1988 .... as well as papers by Cameron, Schmidt, Scharpf and others cast a doubt on the statements that the overall social expenditure is a threat to economic growth, the control of inflation or low unemployment or that the small welfare states of Japan and the United States give these countries some competitive advantages over those advanced welfare states which are saddled with huge social budgets."[30]

The comparative analysis of the performance of the US and European economies over the last few years should be investigated further, starting from a more accurate check, statistical and otherwise, of the real extent of the better results attributed to the American economy; in any case, the main explanation of the different results should be sought in the diversity of the economic policy guidelines followed in the two continents in the last few years rather than in the different flexibility of their labor markets[31].

In the comparison between WS and market, efficiency considerations should be accompanied by equity ones. Replacing the public provision with the private one, as suggested by the SD argument, would change the criteria for gaining access to social goods and services; in fact, there would be a shift from the collective interest in achieving the broadest and most equitable distribution of goods the enjoyment of which is socially meritorious and economically productive to the individual choices dictated not only by the individual income but also by the usually-limited individual information and awareness of social needs.

Concluding on the policy recommendation by the SD argument to replace the WS with the market, the resulting change in the manners for accessing social goods and services, in addition to leading to a socially inequitable redistribution, which is in

---

[28] For an analysis by the author on this subject and further bibliographical references cf. Pizzuti (1995).
[29] Barro (1996) p. 147.
[30] Wilensky (1993), p.49. As to the comparison between the performance of the USA economic systems and that of the countries of Europe, the conclusions of the report by Artoni et al. reflect views that can be concurred with:" If the term of comparison is the United States, we do not think that the deep causes for the different economic performance of Europe and United States in the 90s should be sought in the size, financing and organization of the social security net. The difference arisen over the past few years could be explained in a more satisfactory manner by some factors related to economic policy. Fitoussi holds that the true origin of the situation we are in is the abnormally high level, and for such a long time, of real interest rates (Fitoussi 1997, p.40). Somebody might reasonably think that the unsatisfactory economic performance in Europe during these years has been determined by its economic policy in general".
[31] Cf. Artoni et al. (1997) and Fitoussi (1995) as well as other studies cited therein.

itself a significant result, would abate the spreading of human capital and the social security that helps to cope with the individual and collective risks related to the diffusion of productive innovations, would lower social cohesion and would increase political instability to the detriment of the conditions that foster economic growth. The suggestion to change from WS to market does not take into account that the former developed exactly because the fulfilment of the growing individual demand of social goods and services satisfy the requirements of the community as a whole, since this activity goes well beyond the scope of the interests and awareness of individual economic agents. The satisfaction of some needs cannot be guaranteed by differentiating among individuals on the basis of income or labor productivity. A community is not the sum of isolated individuals; in some respects it is that too, but it is much more and something different, which affects significantly the overall quality of life in society and, as a result, the economic relationships and their efficiency.

4. New Developments in Today's Globalization and their Effects on the WS (Additional Considerations on the SD Argument)

4.1. Foreign Direct Investments

The analysis of the SD argument conducted so far, both of its theoretical assumptions and the empirical and historical aspects related to it, leads to believe that its validity is very limited. Its policy prescription to reduce the WS in the DCs might be justified under a limited set of circumstances; all it does is to list the cases of those WS expenses which, although they have a socially positive function, would hardly, if at all, affect the efficiency of the economic system and at the same time would bloat the operating costs of those DC activities, included in what is already a small component of their trade relations with the NICs, which compete on the basis of price.

However, further verifications are necessary to determine whether some developments attributed to the current globalization processes compared to past economic and commercial integration experiences add new elements to the role of the WS and on the validity of the SD thesis.[32] To this end, the discourse is marked by some new issues, including: the significant expansion of foreign direct investments (FDI); the greater mobility of capital compared to the labor force; new interrelation elements between growth and equity.

Contrary to the growth of international trade, which in quantitative terms does not constitute a development of historic proportions, there is a new phenomenon in the current globalization process, if only for its size: the growth of FDI. The greater number of opportunities and advantages for firms to relocate their factories abroad, in regions where labor is cheaper, might increase the competition by the labor force of these countries against the more expensive one in the DCs.

---

[32] Moreover, it should be verified whether, regardless of the NG processes, something has changed in the way WS institutions work and in the socio-economic environment in which they operate. The analysis of this second question – which since it has nothing to do with globalization cannot be related to the SD thesis – will be conducted in the following section.

We saw, however, in a preceding section that the development of FDI does not lend additional credibility one of the mainstays of the SD arguments, that whereby all goods can be produced in all countries so that the economic relationships between DCs and NICs would be regulated by a price-based competition. We have already seen instead that the FDI pattern is consistent with the international division of labor which, in this case, is forcing specialization up to the phases of the manufacturing processes. It is possible that the expansion of FDI accelerated the periodic territorial repositioning of the world production which accompanies its qualitative evolution thereby causing adjustment problems in the short run.

Such process makes it necessary also for DCs to adapt their productive organization and capacity, leading them to respond more dynamically by retraining their workforce, on pain of subjecting their areas of specialization to the price competition of NICs. Since some manufacturing activities are still carried out in DCs, while they are being taken up also in some NICs, in these readjustment phases of the international division of labor the scope of competition and price competition between the two types of countries increase, if only temporarily. In the international reallocation of productive activities, the difference in the time and manner of the readjustment which has occurred in each national productive system can also change their distance and hierarchy, creating new equilibria in international trade relations. Naturally, there are many causes that can determine advancements or deterioration of wealth in a territory; they are not only of an economic type and often can hardly be pinpointed. But as was indicated above, theoretical arguments and empirical tests indicate that social expenditure and WS institutions can facilitate the adjustment processes of the productive structure[33], thus disproving both the analysis and the recommendations of the SD argument which list the shrinking of the WS as one of the priorities dictated by Neo-Globalization.

Even in the presence of price-based competition (one of the necessary but not sufficient conditions for the SD argument), it does not follow that the WS causes the labor-cost per unit of output to rise (second necessary but not sufficient condition for the SD argument). On the other hand, the WS is not always a competitiveness factor. In particular, as will be seen better later, the WS institutions will also have to adjust in qualitative and quantitative terms to the new conditions determined both by the NG phenomena as well as by the other changes that affect social and economic systems.

4.2. The Asymmetric Mobility of Capital and Labor and the New Trade-off between Growth and Equity

According to Rodrik (1997b) an important but underestimated consequence of the NG process is that the competition among unskilled workers would increase not

---

[33] Rodrik (1997) analyzes the economic evolution of a large number of countries, particularly of the Far East, and in his conclusion underlines the primary role played by state intervention in the explanation of the apparently astonishing results achieved by some of them. More specifically, he shows empirical evidence of the beneficial role of public sector intervention in the social area which generates a situation of cooperation between state and market for development purposes.

only within the context of the relations between DCs and NICs but also and especially among the DCs[34]. Meanwhile the effect of NG on the labor market in the DCs would not be so much a downward shift to the left of the demand curve for low-skill workers, with the resulting reduction of their salaries and the increase in the skill premium[35]. The most important effect would be a gentler slope of the demand curve for low-skill workers, which would attest to a more pronounced sensitivity of their wages to foreign competition, the greater instability of their compensation and the overall worsening of working conditions. According to Rodrik, NG increases the risks related to the working of the market and consequently it determines an increase in the need for social security traditionally met by the WS. However, the greater need for the WS would clash with the problems related to its financing generated by another specific characteristic of modern globalization, namely the asymmetric international mobility of capital and labor.

The possibility of transferring capital in accordance with the relative tax advantages offered by different countries (tax-base footloose) would place their holders in the position to avoid the tax pressure necessary to finance the growing need of social services.

The alternative to levy additional taxes on salaried workers would be limited and in any case it would enhance the tensions already existing in the labor markets of the DCs, already subjected to the pressures of globalization and technological innovations.

Rodrik shows his concern in emphasizing the contradiction created by NG; this is given credit for the potential positive effects related to the enlargement of markets and their competitiveness. However, as we have just seen, international economic integration creates also new social tensions, stressing the conflicting interests of capital holders and highly-skilled workers on the one hand and low-skill workers on the other. The creation of a growing need for the WS and the simultaneous reduction of the possibilities of financing it generate a social and political unease which may turn against the entire globalization process, thus preventing also its positive effects from unfolding. Bringing up to date a position traditionally present in the economic literature[36], Rodrik's analysis puts forth a trade-off between growth and equity related to the activities of the WS which would be more evident and pronounced as a result of the additional and contradictory influences of NG.

The new terms of the trade-off would be the following: when the progress of

---

[34] As already noted, trade relations with the NICs continue to account for a very limited share of the total for the DCs.

[35] As noted above, given the low share of the NICs' trade relations with the EEs, there are other explanations (other than the effect of the competition by low-skilled workers in DCs) for the increase of the skill premium that has taken place in the latter countries based essentially on the development of new technologies and the diffusion of new production techniques that rely less on low-skill labor. However, Rodrik somehow includes also the application of new production techniques among the effects of NG. According to Rodrik, NG would affect labor markets in DCs also through immigration and following the reduction of the rent situations enjoyed by workers employed in low-competition sectors.

[36] Cf. Okun (1975).

NG is such as to cause the need for the WS to rise above a certain level, the growing difficulties related to its financing exceed its benefits thereby setting a limit to its expansion, despite the fact that it would be worthwhile to offset the higher social risks created by more integrated markets. The appropriate size of the WS varies from country to country, depending on the extent the different risk factors, including the degree of volatility of the terms of trade, related to the international openness are at work.[37]

Following a rationale in part similar to Rodrik's, the analysis of the trade-off between growth and equity related to the working of the WS in the presence of NG was depicted in a graph format by Franzini- Milone (1998). The optimal WS level is identified taking into account its specific qualitative characteristics – which are supposed to be more growth – or equality-oriented – and the degree of globalization of the country considered. A greater globalization has positive effects on growth, but it also increases inequality which, in turn, affects growth adversely; whether it is worthwhile to fight the trend toward a greater inequality caused by globalization, by enhancing the compensating role of the WS, depends on the initial qualitative and quantitative features of the latter. To this end, the "WS standard" is introduced, intended basically as the average WS present in the countries involved in the globalization process, to conclude that "The countries with below-standard welfare states will certainly benefit from economic integration.....while the opposite is true for countries with above-standard welfare states". [38]

4.3. The Effects of the New Aspects of Neo-Globalization on the Welfare State and the Role of International Coordination Policies

Rodrik's analysis of the relationships between NG and WS brings significant questions to the fore and the Franzini-Milone model constitutes an interesting way to study those and other issues related to the subject. Their restatement of the trade-off between growth and equity in a situation of globalization extended to many countries with small WS systems might give rise to new elements to assess the SD argument. This possibility and the underlying rationale should be further investigated.

First of all, it should be considered that the emphasis placed by Rodrik on the effects of NG on the demand of low-skill labor carries a qualification by the same author; if, on the one hand, the low incidence of trade with the NICs makes for a correspondingly small downward shift of the curve, on the other, there is no solid empirical support to its flattening caused by the competition among the low-skill workers of the DCs[39]. However, even though the latter aspect had some significance,

---

[37] Rodrik's empirical study reveals that for the countries characterized by a higher volatility of their terms of trade, a greater international openness is matched by an increase in social expenditure; the opposite is true for countries characterized by a lower volatility of their terms of trade.

[38] Franzini-Milone (1998).

[39] "How much has international economic integration raised the elasticities of demand for low-skilled labor in the relevant markets?... The answer therefore, is that we cannot be certain about the quantitative magnitudes. The basic research on these questions has yet to be undertaken". Rodrik (1997b), p. 27.

exactly because it is related to the greater economic integration of the DCs, namely countries with similar welfare systems, it would not warrant the WS cuts prescribed by the SD argument. On the other hand, as has already been noticed, NG is proceeding hand in hand with regionalization phenomena, namely an economic integration which is greater for countries close to one another not only geographically, but also in terms of history, socio-political development and social structures. Considering also the institutional aspects that regulate the formation of these macro-regions, the risks of social dumping related to economic integration are reduced not only by the social policies historically present in the countries whose economies are integrating but also by the economic policies implemented by them.

Thus, it is more likely that market competition within supranational economic areas, but institutionally and politically cohesive, takes place within a framework of economic and social structures and rules springing from a common tradition which, in the European case, certainly includes the strong role played by the WS.

The ease with which they coordinate their social and economic structures should help the countries involved in the regionalization processes to cope also with the other difficulty indicated by Rodrik, which derives from the asymmetric mobility of labor and capital. This asymmetry does represent a potential tax problem for each country and may create financing difficulties which, obviously, concern the entire public expenditure, regardless of its being economically or socially appropriate. But in those particularly widespread cases in the social area for which both theoretical arguments and empirical findings concur and attest to the benefits of state intervention, the effort of economic and institutional policies should be such as to remove all obstacles to its financing[40] . These efforts would be even more justified if their aim were to remove the free riding by some components of the community. In the case of the tax-base footloose practiced   by capital holders, since it is a form of free riding that can exist only at the international level and in presence of inconsistent tax laws, such practices and their very causes can be eliminated through agreements intended to harmonize tax treatments.

As has just been mentioned, in the case of the economic areas involved in the regionalization processes, the coordination of the national social and economic structures is in the order of things.

The WS financing problems originated by the asymmetric mobility of workers and capital indicated by Rodrik as a basic feature of the present globalization processes represent then an actual possibility; equally actual, however is the possibility to tackle those difficulties at an international institutional level, which is expected to grow stronger as a result of the regionalization processes that accompany NG. Besides, even among the countries belonging to diverse regional economic areas, there seems to be a growing awareness of the need to improve coordination in order to check the risks of the financial and economic instability that NG has made more serious and recurring.

---

[40] On the social and economic costs arising from choices between state and market other than those recommended by theoretical and empirical indications cf. Franzini-Pizzuti (1994).

The efficiency-equity trade-off traditionally related to the WS role is based on the distorting effect attributed to the taxation level necessary to finance state intervention, compared to the Pareto-optimality goal; but, as was already mentioned, the grounds for state intervention outlined by the analysis of market failures start from the very empirical and theoretical observation of the difficulties experienced by the market in some circumstances to ensure a Pareto-optimum equilibrium.

The trade-off set-up emerging from Rodrik's analysis is "more advanced", in the sense that it is compatible with the above-mentioned criticisms to the market; not only is the WS credited with an equitable redistribution function but also an efficiency role, even though it is mainly indirect, namely linked to the positive externalities generated by the climate of social and political stability fostered by social expenditure. According to Rodrik, for each given national reality (which includes both the quantitative and qualitative aspects of international economic integration as well as the characteristics of the services and the manner for financing the WS) there is an optimal WS size; it is as though there were a production function of the entire productive system in which the WS is an input with its own variable marginal productivity that can be used in optimal quantities.

The Franzini-Milone's description differs from Rodrik's analysis; their "welfare state standard" is not an optimal configuration of the WS as that depicted in the latter's analysis. As was seen, the two authors equate the concept of "welfare state standard" to the "average" configuration present in the countries whose economies are integrated by the NG process and point out that countries with lower-than-average WS will certainly benefit from economic integration. They add that: "If integration occurs among countries with similar Welfare States, the standard remains basically unchanged and no one can substantially deviate from it; as a result all the countries involved will benefit in terms of growth". "If, however, integration has a global character and involves widely differing economies, the welfare standard can easily experience a substantial drop and the consequences for countries with bigger Welfare States can be very serious."[41]

Fanzini-Milone's interpretation of the trade-off between growth and equity attributed to the WS seems to lie half way between Rodrik's and the traditional one. They agree both on the limited effects of NG on the labor market conditions of the DCs, as well as on the efficiency role of the WS, as borne out by different aspects of their depiction[42]. However, as was seen, they state that economic integration among countries with differing WS would benefit certainly those with a lower-than-average WS, adding that globalization "lowers significantly the welfare standard". Contrary to

---

[41] Franzini-Milone (1998).

[42] For instance, the curve they draw to establish a relationship between economic growth (measured on the ordinate) and the size of the WS (measured on the abscissa, along with its quality) is rising at the start, even though the longer portion is declining; a mention is made also of the possibility that, starting from a situation represented by a point on the declining portion of the curve, an attempt to increase the growth rate by reducing the WS (namely moving upward and to the left along the curve) can cause a negative "regime shift" which would reduce the growth rate instead of increasing it (the entire curve would shift downward, so that a lower size of the WS would be matched by a lower growth rate).

the former positions, these – not justifiably – weaken the conviction that the WS plays a productive role and partly follow in the tracks of the SD argument.

5. The Welfare State Problems (Independent of Neo-Globalization): Some Indications.

5.1. The Welfare State as a Production Input

The NG developments reviewed in the preceding section do not add significantly to the soundness of the SD argument, its analysis or its policy recommendations. In the critical examination of this thesis, based on the support of a vast and well-regarded economic literature, both theoretical and empirical, attention was paid to the efficiency role played by WS institutions within market economies. To express this function it was suggested that the WS be considered as a production input for the overall economic system. Besides, this concept entails that WS institutions should have well-defined quantitative and qualitative characteristics consistent with those of the economic systems in which they operate and with their role in the international context.

While the preceding consideration, whereby NG requires a qualified expansion of the WS, on the one hand counters the SD thesis, on the other it indicates that welfare institutions should be adapted to the changes of the socio-economic systems in which they operate. To this end, the additional question to be posed is whether, besides the NG phenomena already analyzed, there are other changes which require WS systems to adapt, possibly to a greater extent.

This problem has a much wider scope than the evaluation of the SD argument and cannot certainly be dealt with adequately in the final part of this paper. In the following notes it may be appropriate to draw attention to some of the developments that have been taking place over the past few decades which are more significantly connected to the functions that the WS is expected to take on, both immediately as well as in the short-to-medium run. Then some economic policy indications will be outlined.

5.2. The Problems of the Welfare State

It has already been mentioned that welfare expenditures have been constantly growing since they were established and not even the economic, political and cultural turning point of the 80s checked this trend.

There are many reasons for this. Some of them, already mentioned above, are structural in nature and involve the growing role of the WS, made necessary by the development of capitalist economies and societies.[43] As was seen, by expanding markets, NG causes a parallel increase in the need for the WS. There is then a growing financing problem even though its magnitude seems to be enhanced by circumstances

---

[43]"The postwar economic order was based on a bargain that John Ruggie has termed 'the compromise of embedded liberalism' " Rodrik (1997b), p. 65.

of an accounting and statistical nature. In fact, WS institutions have replaced other social institutions such as families and rural communities in the performance of the same type of functions which formerly were not reflected in any statistic or economic report[44].

Other reasons for the growing GDP share of social expenditure – as a whole and not only state outlays – are rooted in such technological aspects as those emphasized by Baumol[45]; reference is made to the lower productivity increases that have characterized on average the service sector, the increase in this sector's terms of trade and the rising share of the productive resources it absorbed regardless of the relative changes in the quantitative mix of the GDP.

Higher WS expenditures due to opportunistic behaviors by politicians, bureaucrats and beneficiaries are completely different in nature[46]. Higher expenditures were caused also by the improper use of social institutions, which have often been utilized to make up for the shortcomings of other state intervention tools such as industrial policy ones (e.g. early retirements)[47].

A structural cause that has strongly affected WS budgets, and will do so even more in the future, is the ageing of population in the developed countries, an unprecedented event in history in terms of intensity and rapidity, in periods untouched by catastrophes such as wars and epidemics. It originates from the simultaneous action of the strong and rapid reduction of the fertility rates and by an equally strong and rapid increase of the life expectancy at birth[48]. This is a phenomenon whose consequences go well beyond the problem of financing the welfare state; in short, it is a situation

---

[44] Cf. Pizzuti (1999).

[45] Cf. Baumol (1967).

[46]For a more detailed analysis by the author, see Pizzuti (1999).

[47] For an analysis of the Italian experience by the author, see Pizzuti (1990, 1994, 1995,1998, 1999).

[48] In Italy, the total fertility rate per generation dropped from 2.70 - the maximum value achieved after the Second World War in 1964 – to the current (1996) minimum of 1.18. For the future, the Italian Statistics Institute (ISTAT) assumes a spectrum of possibilities which includes both a further slight drop of the present value and its increase, significant as well; the life expectancy at birth rose from 63.71 years for men and 67.24 years for women in the second World War aftermath to 74.3 years and 80.7 years, respectively in 1994. Further and more or less consistent increases are predicted for the next two decades: between 76,9 and 80,1 for men and between 83,3 and 86,3 for women. The combined result of these two trends is that the ratio of sixty-five-year-olds to the total population grew from 9.5% in 1961 to approximately 16% in 1995. In the fifteen countries of the European Union, that ratio is expected to rise from 15.5% in 1995 to anywhere between 19.5% and 21.5% in 2025, depending on the scenarios utilized; in every scenario Italy and Germany rank consistently at the top of the list. (European Commission, 1996). In Italy, the old age dependency ratio (population older than 65 to the 15-to-64 years old population) should grow from the current 24.6% (1996) to 36.3% in 2020, to 39.17% in 2025 and to 57.6% in 2050 (ISTAT). In the European Union, the current 23% ratio should increase to anywhere between 31% and 40% in 2025 (European Commission, 1996). Obviously these are highly uncertain forecasts. For instance, the entire population of the fifteen countries of the European Union is expected to vary, depending on the scenario, from the 370.4 million of 1994 to 396 million in 2010 and then to 400 in 2025, or to 376 in 2010 and 371.6 in 2025. In any case, also the most dynamic assumptions foresee a stationary state in a not-too-distant future and then a demographic drop and at any rate the ageing of the population.

whereby a shrinking working population has to support an increasing share of pensioners. It is clear, however, that the unsettling rise of the old dependency ratio will exercise its effect starting from the problems of financing the WS and, in particular, the pension systems [49].

Over the past few years, in Europe at least, the rates of growth of the economy and employment levels have decreased[50]; as the prospects of an expansion of the total wealth have diminished, the shortsighted unwillingness to finance expenditures such as those for the WS – whose returns cannot be easily perceived by individuals, and in any case are postponed until some time in the future[51]– has increased.

5.3. Recommendations to Deal with the Welfare State Problems

As already noted, the actual workings of the WS fostered some opportunistic behaviors and some malfunctions which have yielded results that at times run counter the social and economic rationale of its institutions. The negative experiences of the WS have contributed to generate a lack of confidence in it which made it possible for the neo-liberalist criticisms to the state role to gain currency with the public opinion also in the social field. On the other hand, the theoretical arguments in favor of public intervention in this field are confirmed empirically by many other positive experiences. The overall assessment of these circumstances, which at times are also conflicting, constitute the grounds for two considerations. Certainly, the pragmatic suggestion should be accepted which is offered by the complex discussion on market and non-market failures to make some concrete choices which would lean toward the use of public structures, the private ones or a combination of the two depending on the case at hand[52]. However, if in practice there are specific obstacles to the adoption of the most advantageous theoretical solution, the short-term pragmatic choice designed to adopt the best solution should be coupled with the start of the action to remove the causes that prevent the optimal solution from being chosen.

The adoption of a non-optimal solution – such as would be, for instance, that of leaving to the market the task of meeting the need for some social goods and services – even if dictated by objective conditions, would entail a loss of efficiency by the economic system (to be attributed, for example, to possible malfunctions of the WS). However, failure to remove those malfunctions, indeed using them as an excuse for abandoning once and for all that which is theoretically the most efficient tool, would result in a wrong structural choice[53].

As already noted, NG makes state intervention in the social area a necessity; but it was also underlined that WS systems have to adjust qualitatively and quantitatively to the economic and social evolution of the societies in which they operate.

---

[49] For a more detailed analysis by the author, see Pizzuti (1999).

[50] Ibidem.

[51] Ibidem.

[52] Cf. Stiglitz (1989) and Rodrik (1997).

[53] For an in-depth review of this issue, see Franzini-Pizzuti (1994).

The financial problems related to the growing WS expenditures driven by the development of markets and their worldwide integration would indicate that the best approach would be for a country to expand the financing base to the entire spectrum of income-generating activities and not just wages and salaries. This solution would, on the one hand, be in keeping with the WS function which does not meet only the needs of a limited number of citizens but produces an atmosphere of security and collective social cohesion that represents a productive input for the entire economic system. On the other hand, taxing income in general would mitigate both the distorting problems that penalize the use of labor and the tax-base foot-loosing pattern by capital holders.[54] To this end, as state institutions from Adam Smith on have been conceived as the basic instrument to regulate domestic markets, in the age of NG agreements and institutions are necessary to regulate markets and international trade relations and to deal, also within such an enlarged scope, with the social and efficiency problems arising from market failures.

The changes under way in the organization of labor, legal and otherwise, are creating new worker figures, which actually continue to be employed by the companies they work for but are formally self-employed and less covered by the WS. The WS should then adjust to the new conditions in order to avoid inequalities and unfair competition among different worker figures which would not only result in an overall contraction of pension insurance but would also jeopardize social cohesion.

The faster pace of technological developments, of the reorganization of production processes and the periodical geographic regroupings of the international division of labor call for the WS to pay greater attention to education, training and skills upgrading needs. To this end, it is not only necessary to improve educational structures at the different levels, but also to ensure the prompt and effective response of the institutions that provide a guarantee against the loss of income during the phases of productive restructuring. The working of these institutions should be organized with a view to achieving two goals. The first is to strengthen the tasks of the social and economic security cushion necessary to offset the risks traditionally generated by the market, which lately have experienced a further increase as a result of a faster dynamics of the worldwide productive organization.

Second, the risk related to a possible conflict between the social and the economic functions that operate in a WS system should be kept to a minimum, as this might generate a dangerous tradeoff between equity and efficiency that would alter social cohesion. It is necessary for instance to minimize the need for unemployment benefits by utilizing those resources to promote new productive activities[55] which, however, should not be a disguise for handouts but should actually create new jobs to satisfy new unmet social and economic needs. Meanwhile other state expenditures, often financed by WS institutions, should be rationalized as, even though their stated

---

[54] The expansion of the tax base should not be confused with a "universal" and "minimum" WS that relies on the initiative and the possibilities of individuals to access supplementary insurance coverage. On the other hand, the introduction of a means test to determine eligibility for services should be weighted against the risk of creating a "Welfare State of the poor".

[55] Cf. Phelps (1995).

purpose is to create new jobs, they show up as revenues of firms which would have carried out their investment projects anyway. These activities have two flaws: on the one hand they adversely affect the state and the WS budgets; on the other they distort market workings, altering the competition between the firms that receive and those that do not receive the incentives.

As to the above-mentioned two reasons that contribute to determine the ageing of the population in the most developed countries, while a longer life span is obviously a desirable feature, it is hoped also that the low birthrate will reverse its trend. The Malthusian interrelation between demography and economy suggest the possibility that the worrisome effects of a strong and rapid ageing of the population might trigger some spontaneous reactions capable of mitigating or reversing the demographic trend[56] ; in any case, policies designed to assist families and children by helping women to cope with their family and professional lives can go a long way in reversing such trend.

An immigration planning and control policy, which is necessary anyway, can also contribute to lessening the ageing process in the most developed countries[57] However, countering the reduction of the working population would yield little results – actually it might even turn out to be detrimental – if the productive system were to continue providing insufficient employment opportunities. The present high unemployment rates in Europe, along with a low growth rate as is the case in Italy, show that there is a persistent difficulty on the part of the economic systems to utilize even the scant labor resources available. The resurgence of neo-liberalism in the 80s involved a widespread use of economic policies essentially devoted to the stabilization of the monetary equilibria and the expansion of the financial sector, thereby paying a lower attention to the real economy and, in particular, to growth and unemployment.

The continuing disappointment with neo-liberalist policies – whereby financial reorganization, lower salary increases and worker flexibility would have enabled the market to set the economies on new growth paths – makes it increasingly necessary to shift the focus of economic policies. During the two decades from the birth of the European Monetary System to the creation of the European Monetary Union, the European economy has been progressively affected by the "spirit of Maastricht" which has certainly helped the recovery of inflation and has led to the creation of the Euro but has also contributed substantially to doubling the unemployment rate and significantly reducing growth rates. Nevertheless, the very regionalization process Europe is undergoing, namely the passage from a set of very open small-to-medium economies to a single large economic system with foreign trade accounting for a smaller share of the GDP might reduce the traditional link between the balance of payments and the domestic growth rate and foster economic policies which, given the same monetary and financial objectives, pursue more aggressively goals related to the development of the real economy.

---

[56] For more details on this aspect see Pizzuti (1999).
[57] Cf. Aprile-Palombi (1998) and Pizzuti (1999).

Policies intended to create jobs, even though are likely to be unsuccessful if they do not operate within a context of macroeconomic growth also cope with specific problems. To this end, the strong ageing pattern and a corresponding growth of the old dependency ratio are not the right conditions to implement policies whose aim is to reduce unemployment by encouraging pre-retirements. From the standpoints of the workers nearing retirement age, the unemployed youth and firms these policies are somewhat attractive: the first exit the labor force early without any cut in pension benefits, the seconds find jobs, the last replace their older and more expensive workers with younger and less expensive (since they are at the initial stage of their careers) and perhaps more productive ones (depending on the activity in which replacement takes place).

From society's point of view, unemployment does not decrease, but a new cost is added to finance the pensions of early retirees, which is certainly higher than any saving generated by the lower disbursement of unemployment benefits. If the net financing requirements of the transaction are not met with new tax revenues, public debt will increase – and it might eventually become self-financed if the possible demand increase so obtained is capable of setting off a larger income growth without any inflationary effect. Of course, to raise demand – a highly desirable objective at this time – an alternative choice, more effective in terms of production and less risky on the inflation side would be to increase public (as well as private) investments. The two channels, to support consumption and investment, should be balanced and planned anyway within the framework of new economic policy orientations, no longer tied exclusively to the financial and monetary objectives that dominated the "Maastricht spirit". Actually, it is in this approach that hopes should be placed to improve the macroeconomic context necessary to reduce unemployment.

If all we did were to replace old workers with young workers, considering also the not-irrelevant financing problems indicated above, the positive results on the economic and social plane would be insufficient in view of the present and future problems which require instead a substantial increase in economic growth and employment levels.

Replacing old workers with young ones would generate more financial problems than would actually be solved in the real economy; furthermore, it would validate an intergenerational conflict which does not help in dealing with the problems posed by demographic ageing. The best way to tackle them without driving a wedge between young people and their elders is to accept the obvious consideration that if the latter have increased considerably, unless they are to be blamed for it, their income can only rise. But to prevent intergenerational conflicts it is necessary also to try to expand the overall income that has to be allocated to the whole population, young and old. The necessary intermediate steps to proceed along that road are the increase of employment levels and productivity.

To increase productivity it is necessary to manage the technological progress and its applications in the productive processes. To raise employment levels, beyond the adoption of more adequate economic policies that increase the labor demand, it is necessary to establish also what is the acceptable age divide between young and old to combat the reduction of the job supply for demographic reasons.

The longer life span and the improvement of health and labor conditions would make it easier and possible to move that divide up, were it not for the fact that it would result in a plain and unbearable extension of dreadful working activities, a road which is difficult to pursue.

On the other hand, retirement age cannot be regulated referring only to an issue such as youth unemployment which is certainly very important but that can be dealt with only through additional and more adequate economic policy alternatives.

If, besides lifestyle and demographic changes, account is taken of the new ways the production processes are organized, of the greater needs for education and training – both initial and continuing – it can be seen that all together these are important developments, which in turn make it necessary to rethink the organization and allocation of working hours as well as their combination with training time and leisure time, in reference both to daily and weekly hours as well as to the entire life span.

In light of such complex objectives, coordination of the different instruments of state intervention and its interaction with the market becomes important.

A more accurate combination of the social and economic functions of the WS, and a more effective focus on its part on growth and unemployment require a coordination of the work of its institutions with all the other activities implemented as a result of state intervention, and not only in the economic area; this coordination should take place in line with an overall plan that might optimize the role of the state as a supplement to the market.

6. Conclusions

Neo-Globalization (NG) has both the positive and negative aspects that are traditionally attributed to the market. In some respects NG moves into a larger geographical territory the debate on the capabilities and the limits of the market on the one hand and of state intervention on the other, which in this case not only involves the activities of national institutions but those of supranational institutions as well, both the existing ones and those that could or should be set up.

In this paper, the focus was mainly on some characteristics, new or allegedly such, attributed to the NG processes under way and on the consequences that would derive for the Welfare State (WS).

According to the social dumping (SD) argument, those consequences would be negative as the new context determined by NG would create competitiveness problems and obstacles to economic growth in those national productive systems that are characterized by advanced WS systems.

From an analytical point of view, the SD argument is based on two unlikely conditions, each of which is to be regarded as necessary but not sufficient: competitive pricing as the main factor on which trade relations between developing countries (DC) and newly industrializing countries (NIC) are based and the economic conception of the WS as a reason for a rise in labor costs.

It has been shown above that trade relations between DCs and NICs are mainly regulated by an international division of labor based on the different technological and qualitative knowledge in the two types of country. This means that only a limited number of productive activities could be carried out in countries belonging to both categories.

This and the fact that trade relations between DCs and NICs are of relatively little significance for the former keep to a minimum the international trade relations where the low salaries of the NICs constitute a competitive factor.

The development of foreign direct investment, one of the innovative aspects of the globalization under way, does not alter the substantial prevalence of trade relations based on the international division of labor over those based on competitive pricing. The relocation of productive activities, or of some of their phases, does not necessarily disprove the existence of an international allocation of productive tasks associated with different skills and a hierarchy among countries. Relocations constitute mostly dynamic demonstrations of the international division of labor which, more generally, may change its equilibria and cause alterations in the relative positions of the single countries. When new products and productive processes gain ground, and during the ensuing territorial rearrangement of responsibilities, it is possible that, at least in the short-run, there might be an increase of the productive activities accessible equally to some DCs and NICs, that are countries characterized also by significant differences in the cost of labor. However, also the more or less temporary presence of a larger number of trade relations based on competitive pricing is not sufficient to validate the SD argument. In fact, the validity of the second condition of the SD argument should be verified , namely whether the presence of a larger WS harms or helps the individual national economies in the upgrading and restructuring of their productive processes.

To this end, the results achieved by both the old and the new welfare economics theory, the theoretical and empirical analysis of the instability of market economies, the determination of the greater economic and social risks attendant to the international integration of the single economic systems are all elements that have led to the recognition of the important role played by WS institutions in terms of economic efficiency, which while on one side is independent of its equity and social stability function on the other is rooted in it.

The need for two highly unlikely conditions to occur at the same time reduces the explanatory and policy value of the SD argument. The efficiency and social stability role of the WS and the growing need for these characteristics prompted by the very NG could actually overturn the indications of that argument.

In the debate on qualitative and quantitative choices for the WS, account should be taken also of other aspects and developments – in some cases more significant than those attributed to NG – such as the acceleration of technological innovation in productive processes, demographic aging, the slower pace of economic growth and some significant faulty applications of state intervention.

These developments and those related to NG do not warrant the cuts, at times substantial, to the WS systems indicated as necessary for the most developed countries. The experiences and the changes occurred over the past two decades and the expectations for the near future indicate that the institutions of the WS can be better utilized, that they should, in any case, be adapted to the new economic and social needs but that it is not necessary to downsize them *a priori*.

This general result should however translate into specific recommendations on the qualitative and quantitative aspects of each national WS system. Each of these systems certainly constitutes the result of the past and present political and social preferences expressed in each country; however, they were and should be considered as actual general productive inputs that can be used in varying quantities – such as those related to the different production techniques – though not at random and should in any case be optimized with reference to both economic and social requirements.

The continuing growth of WS institutions raises the question of their financing. One solution might be the outright reduction of social goods and services, namely cuts in the expenditures of the WS without a corresponding increase of those made through the market. It was shown, however, how all the most developed countries are characterized by a large share of social expenditures and that these are in fact an irreplaceable development factor. The indication then is that such expenditures can rise also in the NICs, thereby fostering a socio-economic environment which is necessary to economic development.

Another solution for DCs would be to replace the activity of the WS with the market one; however, some comparative empirical tests between the USA and Europe bear out the theoretical indication that such approaches would be neither advantageous nor effective.

However, it was also seen that at the practical level WS activities in some cases did not live up to theoretical expectations; there have been excessive expenditures which must undoubtedly be eliminated. In the cases in which more time should be allowed for state structures to adopt socially and economically efficient behaviors, account should be taken on a case-by-case basis of the possibility to adopt the most effective and advantageous combinations between the public and private sectors.

It was underlined that, if on the one hand NG increases the need for the WS, on the other makes its financing more difficult by encouraging tax-base footloose behaviors by capital holders. This consideration however confirms the inevitable association between market mechanisms and free riding behaviors whose consequences in terms of inefficiency (in addition to social injustice) can be solved also through institutional interventions outside the market purview.

Neo-Globalization then extends the state-market problem to the international level, entailing an adjustment of the former to the supranational expansion of the latter.

The consideration on the collective utility of the WS and the need to reduce the distorting effects in the choice of production techniques suggest that, at the domestic level, its financing base be enlarged from salaries and wages to the entire GDP; at the international level that the tax systems be coordinated.

As to the functions performed, technological, productive, demographic, institutional and trade-relation developments demand that WS systems make some adjustments so as to give utmost priority to education and training as well as to the stability and social security tasks necessary to compensate for the growing risks generated by the expansion and integration of markets. An increased coverage of market risks – necessary also following the emergence of new legal arrangements in the labor market – should be pursued by minimizing potential conflicts between social equity goals and economic efficiency.

This can be achieved by keeping in check the need for unemployment benefits and reallocating those resources to support the creation of new productive activities capable of meeting the substantial number of unmet needs utilizing the large unutilized pool of labor resources.

The most important development the WS institutions will have to deal with are the needs generated by the rapid and significant demographic ageing in DCs. The higher old dependency ratio should be balanced through a series of actions. In addition to policies to increase economic growth and employment levels, helping women manage their family life and their careers simultaneously and allowing effective immigration plans, a new borderline should be drawn between active and retired workers. To this end, WS institutions should foster a reorganization in people's lives, in terms of time spent at work, time utilized for education and skill upgrading and leisure time.

Neo-Globalization and other important social and economic developments that characterize our time require an increasing coordination among markets and collective institutions, both at the national and supranational level. Within this framework, properly strengthened and adapted WS institutions will be able to continue their precious historical function of economic, social and civil progress.

References

Acocella, N. (1998): Foundations of Economic Policy. Cambridge University Press, Cambridge.

Acocella, N. (1998) (ed.): Globalizzazione e stato sociale. Il Mulino, Bologna.

Acocella, N. (1998b): Il dibattito sul welfare state. In: Acocella, N. (1998).

Alesina, A., Perotti, R. (1997): The Welfare State and Competitiveness. The American Economic Review, December, Vol. 87, No.5.

Alesina, A.,Ozler, S., Roubini, N.,Swagel, P. (1996): Political Instability and Economic Growth. Journal of Economic Growth, Vol.1 No. 2, June.

Aprile, R., Palombi, M. (1998): Flussi migratori e struttura demografica della popolazione italiana. Mimeo.

Aquino, A. (1997): Aspetti empirici essenziali del processo di globalizzazione. Report to the 38th annual scientific meeting of "Società Italiana degli Economisti". Rome, October 17-18.

Artoni, R. (1992): Componenti pubbliche e private nella produzione e nella fornitura di servizi sociali. In: Ente Einaudi: Il disavanzo pubblico in Italia: natura strutturale e politiche di rientro. Il Mulino, Bologna.

Artoni, R., Giuliano, Saraceno, P. (1997): Componenti allocative e distributive della spesa sociale: un confronto internazionale. In: Acocella, N. (1998).

Atkinson, A.B. (1995): Is the Welfare State Necessarily an Obstacle to Economic Growth? European Economic Review, No. 39.

Atkinson, A.B. (1995b): The Economic Consequences of Rolling-Back the Welfare State. Lectures to Centre for Economic Studies. University of Munich November.

Baldassarri, M., Paganetto, L., Phelps, E.S. (eds) (1995): Equità, efficienza e crescita. SIPI, Rome. Translated in English: Equity, Efficiency and Growth: the Future of the Welfare State. McMillan, London, Saint Martin Pres, New York, 1996.

Barr, N.(1992): Economic Theory and the Welfare State: A Survey and Interpretation. Journal of Economic Literature, Vol.XXX, June.

Barr, N. (1993): The Economics of Welfare State. Oxford University Press, Oxford.

Barro, R. J. (1996): Institutions and Growth, an Introductory Essay. Journal of Economic Growth, Vol.1 No. 2, June.

Baumol, W.J. (1967): Macroeconomics of Unbalanced Growth: the Anatomy of Urban Crises. The American Economic Review, vol. 57.

Bhagwati, J. (1991): Free Traders and Free Immigrationists: Strangers or Friends? Working Paper No.20. Roussel Sage Foundation, New York.

Caffè, F. (1978): Lezioni di politica economica. Boringhieri, Torino.

Cameron, D.(1978): The Expansion of the Public Economy. American Political Science Review, No.72.

Cipollone, P., Sestito, P. (1997): Globalizzazione e mercato del lavoro: il caso italiano. In: Acocella , N. (1998).

Cline, W. (1997): Trade and Wage Inequality. Institute for International Economics, Washington D.C.

Cominotti, R., Mariotti, S. (eds) (1998): Italia multinazionale 1996. F. Angeli, Rome.

Delli Gatti, D., De Novellis, F., Forti, A., Padoan, P. (1998): La competitività dell'Italia. In: CER-IRS, Competitività e regolazione. Il Mulino, Bologna.

Diamond, P., (1993): Privatization of Social Security: Lesson from Chile. NBER, Working Paper Series, n. 4510, Cambridge (MA).

Diamond, P., Valdes Prieto, S. (1993): Social Security Reforms. Paper presented to "Chilean Economy: Policy Lesson and Challenges", Conference at the Brookings Institution, April 22-23. 1993.

Dore, R. (1996): La globalizzazione dei mercati e la diversità dei capitalismi. Lecture by "Associazione il Mulino", Bologna.

European Commission (1996): Ageing and Pension Expenditure Prospects in the Western World. Brussels.

Ferrera, M., (1993): Dinamiche di globalizzazione e stato sociale: una introduzione. In:Ferrera, M (1993b).

Ferrera, M., (1993b): Stato sociale e mercato. Edizioni della Fondazione Giovanni Agnelli, Torino.

Fitoussi, J.P. (1995): Ridurre o eliminare lo stato assistenziale? Competitività e coesione sociale. In: Baldassarri, M., Paganetto, L., Phelps, E.S. (1995).

Fitoussi, JP. (1997): Il dibattito proibito. Il Mulino, Bologna.

Franzini, M., Milone, L. (1998): I dilemmi del welfare state nell'epoca della globalizzazione. In: Acocella, N. (1998).

Franzini, M., Pizzuti, F.R. (1994): La sfiducia nella politica e le scelte economiche. In: Pizzuti, F.R. (1994).

Garrett, G., Mithcell, D. (1996): Globalization and the Welfare State: Income Transfers in the Industrial Democracies, 1966-1990. Report presented at the Annual Meetings of the American Political Science Association. San Francisco, August 28-September 1.

Golini, A. (1989): Dinamiche demografiche e politiche previdenziali. INPS.

Gottschalk, P., Smeeding, T. (1997): Cross National Comparisons of Earnings and Income Inequality. Journal of Economic Literature, Vol.35, No. 2.

Hayek, A. von (1960): The Constitution of Liberty. University of Chicago Press, Chicago.

Hayek, A. von (1982): Law, Legislation and Liberty. Routledge & Kegan Paul, London.

INPS (1989): Novant'anni di previdenza in Italia: culture, politiche, strutture. Proceedings of the INPS conference held in Rome on October 19th 1989.

Lawrence, R.Z., Slaughter, M. (1993): Trade and U.S. Wages in the 1980s: Giant Sucking Sound or Small Hiccup? Brookings Papers on Economic Activity (Microeconomics).

Le Grand, J. (1991): The Theory of Government Failure. British Journal of Political Science, vol.21. Italian translation: La teoria del fallimento del settore pubblico. Problemi di amministrazione pubblica, n. 3, 1992.

Machin, S. (1997): The Decline of Labour Market Institutions and the Rise in Wage Inequality in Britain. European Economic Review, Vol.41, Nos. 3-5, April.

OECD (1997): Trade, Earnings and Employment: Assessing the Impact of Trade with Emerging Economies on OECD Labour Markets. Employment Outlook, OECD.

OECD (1988): Reforming Public Pensions. Paris.

Okun, A.M. (1975): Equality and Efficiency. The Big Trade-off. The Brookings Institution, Washington.

Perotti, R. (1996): Growth, Income Distribution and Democracy: What the Data Say. Journal of Economic Growth, Vol. 1, No. 2, June.

Phelps, E. S. (1995): Gli effetti collaterali negativi dello Stato sociale: come, perché e cosa fare. In: Baldassarri, M., Paganetto, L., Phelps, E.S. (1995).

Pizzuti, F.R. (1990): La sicurezza sociale tra previdenza, assistenza e politica economica. Liguori, Napoli.

Pizzuti, F.R. (ed.) (1994): L'economia italiana dagli anni '70 agli anni '90. Mc Graw- Hill, Milan.

Pizzuti, F.R. (1994b). Welfare state, economia e società. In: Pizzuti (ed.) (1994).

Pizzuti, F.R. (1995): Economia e politica della previdenza sociale. In: Castellino, O.: Le pensioni difficili. Il Mulino, Bologna. Translated in English: A Political Economy Approach to Pension Financing. In: Hughes, G., Steward, J. (eds) (2000): Pensions in the European Union: Adapting to Economic and Social Change.Kluwer Academic Publishers, Boston. In: Proceedings of the 1996 annual meeting of the European Network for Research on Supplementary Pensions, held in Münster 13-16 June. French translation: Les techniques de financemet des retraites: notes sur un approche fondée sur l'économie politique. In: Reynaud, E. (ed.) (1998): Les retraites dans l'Union Européenne. L'Harmattan, Paris.

Pizzuti, F.R. (1998): Pension Reform and Economic Policy Constraints in Italy. Labour, Vol.12, N.1, Spring.

Pizzuti, F.R. (1999): Trasferimenti intergenerazionali, previsioni pensionistiche e politica economica. In: Acocella, N., Rey, G.M., Tiberi, M.: Saggi di politica economica in onore di Federico Caffè. F. Angeli, Milan.

Rodrik, D. (1996): Why Do More Open Economies Have Bigger Governments? NBER Working Paper No. 5537. National Bureau of Economic Research. Cambridge, MA.

Rodrik, D. (1997): The 'Paradoxes' of the Successful State. European Economic Review, Vol. 41, Nos. 3-5, April.

Rodrik, D. (1997b): Has Gobalization Gone Too Far? Institute for International Economics. March, Washington DC.

Saint-Paul, G. (1997): Is Labour Rigidity Harming Europe's Competitiveness? The Effect of Job Protection on the Pattern of Trade and Welfare. European Economic Review, Vol.41, Nos. 3-5, April.

Sala-i-Martin, X. X. (1996): A Positive Theory of Social Security. Journal of Economic Growth, Vol.1 No. 2, June.

Sandmo, A. (1991): Economists and the Welfare State. European Economic Review, Vol.35, No2/3, April.

Schiattarella, R. (1998): La globalizzazione: miti, questioni aperte ed esperienza italiana. Mimeo.

Stiglitz, J.E. (1986): Economics of Public Sector. W.W. Norton & Company, New York.

Stiglitz, J.E. (1989): The Economic Role of the State. Basil Blakwell, Oxford.

Valdes Prieto, S. (1994): Evaluación de la reforma de la seguridad social en Chile. Paper presented at the meeting "Privatización, regulación y reforma de la seguridad social: experiencias colombiana y internacional". Bogotà, May 11th 1994.

Wilensky, H. (1993): Stato-nazione, politica sociale e andamenti economici. In: Ferrera, M. (1993b).

Wood, A. (1994): North-South Trade, Employment and Inequality: Changing Fortunes in a Skill-Driven World. Clarendon Press. Oxford.

Wood, A. (1995): How Trade Hurt Unskilled Workers. Journal of Economic Perspectives, Vol. 9, No. 3.

Wood, A. (1998): Globalization and the Rise in Labour Market Inequalities. The Economic Journal, Vol. 108, No. 450, September.

Woolf, C. Jr. (1979) : A Theory of non Market Failure. Journal of Law and Economics, n. 22.

Woolf, C. Jr. (1988) : Markets or Governments: Choosing between Imperfect Alternatives. Cambridge, Mass.

9. Globalization, Growth, Inequalities and Democracy : a New Perspective

Jean Paul Fitoussi, Xavier Girre (OECD)

Everyone feels that inequalities are steadily increasing. Simultaneously, many debates focus on these drastic trends' causes. We consider that globalization has a major impact on wealth's distribution because of its own characteristics and the context in which it happens.

Globalization is not only internationalisation of trade. It also implies free capital transfers. Globalization is not only free trade among developed countries. It also implies a free trade with developing countries. Globalization, as we have been experiencing it along the last decades, has been happening in a context of deep influence of the financial markets. Such a context contributes to create very brutal capital flows, which exacerbates inequalities. It has also been happening in a context of sudden and rapid technological changes.

There are not only theories and plausible assertions, but also facts, which show that globalization exerts a strong impact on inequalities by the conjunction of sudden capital flows and quick technological changes.

This situation leads to a paradox: globalization contributes to the development of capitalism all over the world, but, on the other hand, globalization causes new kinds of inequalities that hamper capitalism itself.

As Lester Thurow writes in "The Future of Capitalism", "The eternal verities of capitalism – growth, full employment, financial stability, rising real wages – seem to be vanishing just as the enemies of capitalism vanish".

It is therefore clear that globalization in a free capitalist economy creates drastic inequalities that jeopardise the social cohesion of capitalist societies. Markets put public policies under heavy pressure, which is a danger for democracy itself. That is why, the crucial point is to redefine the role of public policies, to alleviate the markets' pressure to enable a real autonomy of economic policies.

1. Globalization, Inequalities, Capitalism, Past and Present

1.1. Past Trends

We would like first to focus on the end of the nineteenth century. This period was one of deep trade integration thanks to the development of transport means (railways, steamships, etc.) and the European move toward free trade at the beginning of this period, in the wake of the 1860 Cobden-Chevalier treaty. Moreover, this period was one of massive migration trends, from the poorest Old World countries to the richest New World countries, and one of deep technological changes, due to the extension of the industrial revolution to many Northern countries. The protectionist tensions of the very end of the nineteenth century and of the beginning of the twentieth, which included France, Germany, Italy and Spain, did not change the global trend.

Finally, if we except the current crucial importance of capital flows, there are many similarities between this period and ours.

In such a context, the standard Hecksher - Ohlin trade model would argue that this international integration should lead to a convergence of factor prices. Moreover, the migrants being frequently unskilled workers, the massive migrations of that time should have led to increasing wages inequalities in the richest countries and to the contrary in the poorest countries. In a deep statistical study, J.G. Williamson showed that globalization and technological changes were two key factors for explaining the rising inequality in rich countries, and the declining inequality in poor ones[1]. He also highlighted the difficulty to decompose effects into trade and migration because of the very high correlation between migration's impact and initial labour scarcity.

If we now turn to the 1970s, we face a period in which globalization was once more deepened and got some new specific features, after the retreat from trade liberalism from 1913 to the end of World War II. During the 1950s and 1960s, the economic growth was rapid, and the European countries narrowed somehow their gap with the United States. Afterwards, in the 1970s, the increasing unemployment in many industrialised countries, and destabilising effects of the oil shock and of the currencies increasing volatility, renewed the debate about inequality. At that time, many authors considered that globalization would deepen inequalities between rich and poor countries. Advanced economies being able to produce and export manufactures at low prices would prevent developing countries from entering that market and confine them in the production and export of natural products or low value added productions. The claim that a global marketplace tends to widen inequality among nations was used to justify demands for aid and call for a new International Economic Order.

1.2. New Trends

If we now consider the current period, it appears that globalization is no longer the phenomenon of the 1950s, 1960s, or even the beginning of the 1970s. Three characteristics are commonly presented as knew. We would have swung :
- from an emerging trade among developed countries to a global trade among both developed and developing countries,
- from a growing trade of goods in a traditional industrial and agricultural world, to the integration of a world trade globalization and sudden and quick technological changes (new technologies of information and communication),
- from a growing trade of goods to a global trade of goods and capital, and a disequilibrium of these two kinds of trade : the daily capital transfers amount to the yearly German GNP (1,500 billion dollars).

In fact, these three characteristics that are so frequently stressed are not equally new. As highlighted earlier, trade at the end of the nineteenth century was also

---

[1] Williamson, J.G. (1997).

unbalanced, between some old traditional European countries and some industrialised countries, both in Europe and in the United States. On the other hand, technological changes have taken a new pace and form, being based on new technologies of information and communication. Moreover, the major increase in capital flows along the last decade is one of the newest and most important changes.

Therefore, in the current context, the globalization's impacts on inequalities may be defined along the three following lines :

- First of all, the 1970s debate about a North-South increasing gap fades. There are some evidence that globalization has two effects on the developing economies :

• it boosts their growth. For example, from 1965 to 1995, the real revenue *per capita* in the Asian new industrialised countries has been multiplied by seven. As a comparison, from 1973 to 1995, the nominal revenue *per capita* in the United States has been increased by one third.

• It submits these economies to the market's dependency, and especially to the financial markets' dependency. We could refer to the Mexican crisis of 1994/1995, and, of course, the current Asian crisis.

- Secondly, there is a fierce debate about the impact on the advanced economies of their trade with the developing countries.

Some academics stress that the impact of the trade with the developing countries should not be overestimated. Trade between developed and developing countries is very limited. During the 1990s, more than two thirds of the international investments took place in the OECD States. Only 3 % of French trade are done with developing countries.

But many economists refuse this theory. Pierre-Noël Giraud considers that these trends may explain 20 % to 40 % of the recent increase of wages inequalities in the United States[2]. Robert Reich stresses in his book "The Work of the Nations" that the net revenue of major CEOs in 1960 was 12 times as high as workers' revenue. In 1990 the same ratio amounted to 70. Adrian Wood showed in a deep empirical study[3], that the industrial jobs supply in Japan, the United States and Europe had been decreasing by 15 % because of the growing trade with the developing countries. Moreover, some developing countries, such as China, India or Brazil, may exert an increasing pressure on unskilled jobs in developed countries, because the skills of their workers and their technological abilities are rapidly improving.

- Thirdly, some traditional analyses infer some new consequences in the context of the current globalization. This is the case of the Hecksher-Ohlin trade model and the Stolper-Samuelson theorem. These theories founded geographical inequalities between countries, they may now infer dynamic inequalities among the different categories of workers in each country.

The international trade leads countries, or other consistent economic zones, to specialise on the basis of the distribution of the factors of production. The Hecksher-Ohlin trade model makes unambiguous predictions : every country exports those products that use abundant and cheap factors of production. People with high academic records being particularly numerous in the industrialised countries, these

---

[2] Giraud, P. N. (1998a, 1998b).
[3] Wood, A. (1994).

countries will specialise in high value added sectors, whereas the less developed countries will be obliged to specialise in low value added sectors that are intensive in less qualified labour force (textile, for example). Therefore, globalization in poor countries should favour unskilled labour, globalization in rich countries should favour skilled labour. In our developed countries, supply for less qualified jobs may decrease, and, as a consequence, the unemployment rate may rise for the less qualified people or their wages may decrease. As an example, in the United States, the average hour salary of people without any college degree was 11,83 dollars in 1973, and 8,64 dollars in 1993. Of course, we could focus on the other side of the coin, and, considering the situation in the developing countries, stress that the fate of the less qualified workers will be improved there. Globalization increases dynamic inequalities in our developed countries, but reduces them in the developing countries.

Finally, current globalization infers much more complex inequalities among workers than the basic Hecksher-Ohlin trade model would have led to, because it increases the impacts of technological changes and capital flows.

In 1993, Lawrence and Slaughter[4] explored the wage inequality induced by the standard Hecksher-Ohlin trade model. They concluded that there was little evidence to support the standard trade model explanation. They also concluded that technological change was an important source of rising wage inequality. However, it seems quite clear that globalization and technological changes cannot be separately analysed, as far as the inequalities are concerned. The global integration highlights and increases the impacts of the technological changes. We could of course refer to the theories of the endogenous growth which criticised the Solow's model of convergence by stressing that there were many sources of externalities and growing returns – among which technological changes – that prevented convergence.

Financial globalization creates what we could call structural inequalities, because it creates a new sharing of profits and wages in the industrialised countries. A major cause for this globalization is an improvement of the assets transfers' fluidity. For the first time, any product may be manufactured anywhere and also sold anywhere else. In this context, the assets will necessarily be transferred to the zones where they will produce the highest return. Such massive and quick capital flows destabilise economies.

Therefore, current globalization jeopardise social cohesion within each country. When boundaries are closed, the main inequalities do not appear in just one country, but in different ones. We could call them geographical inequalities. On the contrary, inequalities that are provoked by globalization tear the social tissue within each country. They are less geographical, more structural, dynamic and transversal.

2. Globalization, Growth, Capitalism and Democracy

2.1. Globalization, Growth and Convergence

If we refer to the classical theories, we could consider as a reasonable assertion

---

[4] Lawrence, R.Z. and Slaughter, M.J. (1993).

that globalization would stimulate growth thanks to an international specialisation.

There are some hints of such a tendency. From 1950 to 1996, the world exports' volume has been multiplied by 16, the volume of manufactures' exports has been multiplied by 31. From 1950 to 1996, the world production has been multiplied by 6, and the production of industrial goods by 9.

But on the other hand, the average growth of the OECD industrialised countries has been shrinking along the last decades. As an example, we could refer to France : French growth has been regularly slowing down since the 1960s. From 1965 to 1975, growth peaked to 4,4 %. Since 1975 it has reached only 2,3 %, and since 1990 only 1,1 %. 1998 has been a better year, growth coming back to 3,1 %. However, these last trends are too fragile to modify the global perspective. At a time when France has been continuously opening its frontiers, its growth has been continuously declining.

J.P. Fitoussi and O. Blanchard have shown in a recent report to the Conseil d'analyse Économique[5] that it results from a decreasing growth of the productivity trend (since 1975 it has been cut down by 50 %), a decreasing rate of employment, and a deficit of global demand since the beginning of the 1990s.

Table 1

	1	2	3	4	5	6
	Potential productivity[6]	Active population	Potential growth[7] (1) + (2)	Productivity Potential productivity	Employment Active population	Real growth (3) + (4) + (5)
1965-75	3.4%	0.9%	4.3%	0.3%	– 0.3%	4.3%
1975-85	1.8%	0.8%	2.6%	0.4%	– 0.7%	2.3%
1985-95	1.7%	0.5%	2.2%	0.2%	– 0.1%	2.3%

Source : J.P. Fitoussi and O. Blanchard (from OECD perspectives).

Moreover, globalization may induce a relative convergence.

Of course, we call refer to *naïve* analyses : natural resources are not equally distributed around the world. Therefore, people who are lucky enough to have been born in a rich country will profit from its products, people who are not among these happy few may starve.

Moreover, if there is no open trade, the low degree of competition among firms may create some national monopolies that would sell their products at a high price (and price would in no case be equal to the marginal cost). Therefore, people with low wages may be excluded from consumption. These hypotheses create huge inequalities, which are cancelled by globalization : if there is a commercial

---

[5] Fitoussi, J.P., Blanchard, O. (1998).
[6] Potential productivity is obtained starting from Solow's residual and dividing it by the wages in the production sector. Actually it is very difficult to measure the potential growth. Various studies proved that Solow's residual, calculated in this way, was independent from the global demand.
[7] The potential growth rate is equal to the sum of the potential growth rate plus the growth rate of the population in working age. Fitoussi J.P. et Blanchard O. (1998).

globalization, firms will export goods and enable anyone to get access to a great variety of products. Moreover, competition will force firms to reduce their prices at their marginal costs, which will facilitate an equal access to consumption.

We could even refer to Solow's analysis of growth. He stresses that there is in the long term a relative convergence as regards growth, and considers that international trade, and, why not, globalization, contributes to this convergence because it accelerates technological transfers from developed countries to developing ones. Moreover, Solow considers two different countries with the same savings rate but a different level of capital per agent. In that case, growth will be higher in the poorest country in capital because its capital productivity is higher. Therefore, there will be a progressive convergence towards the same level of revenue *per capita*. However, many authors, and especially those referring to the endogenous growth, criticised this analysis and stressed that such a convergence would not happen because of externalities and growing returns.

2.2. Globalization, Capitalism and Democracy

Industrialised countries, especially European ones, are suffering from a massive unemployment, and emerging countries are facing increasing inequalities. In the United States inequalities are also increasing despite an extraordinary period of rapid growth. All these situations have in common a collapse of the traditional national solidarity, and they cast a bleak light on the question of political choice in contemporary societies. Arguments based on globalization are used to justify the states' withdrawal from economic policies. Therefore policy falls far behind economy. There is only one strategy, one dominant opinion that gets rid of public debates and democracy. States are considered as firms, and they should have just one aim, based on the maximisation of their competitiveness.

But this analysis is based on drastic misunderstandings.

First, states are not firms. In his book "Pop Internationalism", P.R. Krugman has clearly shown that national policies to enhance competitiveness are doomed to fail because in each country national demand is still the major stimulus of growth and employment. He has stressed as an example that 90 % of goods manufactured in the United States are consumed in the United States, whereas a tiny proportion of a firm's production is consumed by its own staff. The stake is not the same, therefore policy and strategy must also be different.

Secondly, the current situation creates structural winners and systematic losers. This drastic bias is totally contradictory with democracy and, in the long term, with the market itself.

Globalization has extended market rules not only all over the world, but also to always more numerous activities and to capital flows. Nevertheless, it is clear that markets make failures as the agents themselves do. But their failures have drastic economic and social consequences. Some of these failures result from the complexity of the markets' role, but some others are created by the current mismatching between capital supply and capital demand, the former being much shorter than the latter. Therefore financial market is dominated by capital suppliers, who impose their will to all institutions and agents.

This unbalanced globalization has deep consequences on profit sharing and public policies.

Creditors and firms should not be in the same situation. Firms are usually net debtors, and therefore in conflict with creditors. But this game is biased because of globalization, which opens extremely wide opportunities to creditors. Capital demand is so high that creditors can easily select the highest returns and set aside many projects. Therefore, firms have reacted by accumulating increasing profits in order to be capital self-sufficient. This is a historical revolution the consequence of which is a cut in wages and costs, which increases massive unemployment. Many people are in a precarious position, which destabilise middle classes that are the main basis of our democratic societies.

Moreover, a widespread and unbalanced globalization infers what Jean-Paul Fitoussi calls *"la substitution des victimes"*. Firms make all the efforts to reduce their debt in order to alleviate the creditors' pressure on them. As a consequence, unemployment steadily increases and national demand is cut down. Therefore public authorities have to face decreasing fiscal revenues and increasing economic and social needs. As a consequence, public deficits and debts get a crucial importance. States fall under the financial markets' pressure. Their political room for *manoeuvre* is reduced : either they cut public expenditures or increase taxes to reduce their debt and their dependency from the creditors, or they adopt a restrictive monetary policy, which is imposed by creditors to guaranty the real net value of their asset.

Finally this situation may create a kind of dynamic inefficiency because it does not reach any Pareto equilibrium. In the long term, consumption may be higher (in the sense of the Golden rule) if today's level of accumulation and investment were higher.

This gloomy picture reflects exactly the current situation. It shows clearly that globalization in the context of unbalanced markets infers stiff inequalities that have drastic social and political consequences. What are really at stake are the cohesion and the stability of our societies and of capitalism itself.

As a conclusion, today's priority is to redefine a room for political decisions, to open public debate to find a new perspective. As such, cutting down deficits thanks to restrictive policies should not be the only answer to globalization's challenges.

Capitalism and democracy can very clearly overcome the tensions provoked by the new forms of inequalities. It is therefore necessary to find once again the way to structural factors of growth, such as education, training, an increasing capital stock, or new forms of solidarity. What is at stake is to take benefit of globalization to stimulate growth – globalization does not only create inequalities, it also boosts the economic growth and increases global wealth – and find room for a future better profit sharing.

References

Fitoussi, J.P. (1995): Le débat interdit , Arléa, pp. 49-81.

Fitoussi, J.P. (1996): Anatomie de la croissance molle. Revue de l'OFCE n. 59.

Fitoussi, J.P., Blanchard, O. (1998): Croissance et chômage . Rapport au Conseil d'Analyse Économique.

Giraud, P. N. (1998): Les causes des inégalités croissantes dans les pays riches. Études, janvier 1998.

Giraud, P. N. (1998): Les politiques économiques dans la globalization. Études, janvier 1998.

Hanson, G.H., Harrison, A. (1995): Trade, Technology and Wage Inequality. National Bureau of Economic Research, working paper n. 5110.

Krugman, P. R. (1996): Pop Internationalism . MIT Press, Boston, pp. 37-80.

Krugman, P.R., Venables, A.J. (1994): Globalization and the Inequality of Nations. Centre for Economic Policy Research, discussion paper n. 1015.

Lawrence, R.Z.,Slaughter, M.J. (1993): Trade and US Wages : Great Sucking or Small Hiccup? Brookings Papers on Economic Activity, Microeconomics, the Brookings Institution, Washington, vol. II pp. 161-226.

Leamer, E. (1994): Trade, Wages and Revolving Door Ideas. National Bureau of Economic Research, working paper n. 4716.

Reich, R. (1993): L'économie mondialisée. Dunod, Paris. (original edition: The Work of Nation, 1991).

Rodrik, D. (1997): Has Globalization Gone too far ? Institute for International Economics. Washington, pp. 11-48.

Thurow, L. (1996): The Future of Capitalism. Nicholas Brealey Publishing.

Williamson, J.G. (1997): Globalization and Inequality : Past and Present . World Bank Research Observer, vol. XII, n. 2.

Wood, A. (1994): North-South Trade, Employment and Inequality. Oxford.

10. Global Flexibility: Economic Integration, Social Disintegration ?

Guy Standing

"The certainties of one age are the problems of the next."
Richard Tawney

1. Introduction

The 20th century has been the century of the labouring man. It has been also the century when the working class scared rulers almost everywhere, has been twice decimated by world conflagrations, trudged out in support of two competing socio-economic systems ostensibly dedicated to its interests, and has ended the century by splintering in disarray.

There is another, classical way of looking at what has happened. Recalling Karl Polanyi's "The Great Transformation", and risking the appearance of functionalism in presenting the process in brief, industrial capitalism has evolved through eras of stability and eras of upheaval. The era of stability is when the economy is embedded in society, that is, when the state legitimises and facilitates mechanisms of redistribution. The redistributive system, and the state regulations associated with it, gradually over decades lead to "rigidities", which choke economic dynamism. Then there is an era of upheaval, when the economy is disembedded from society, when new forms of production and work organisation spread, and new forms of inequality and insecurity emerge.

After a while, those inequalities and insecurities become so great that they threaten the sustainability of the economic system. At that point, if economic progress is to resume, the state acts to re-embed the economy by introducing new forms of redistribution and new means of ensuring enough economic security for those near the bottom of society to ensure a sense of social legitimacy and sustainability.

With that imagery in mind, it is not too fanciful to see the 20th century as dominated by two labourist models by which states attempted to embed the economy state socialism and welfare state capitalism. Both, in different ways, made labour the fulcrum of their development strategy. In order to understand them in a way that facilitates analysis of recent developments and the challenge before us during what should be called "the second great transformation" (globalisation), this paper briefly describes the relevant characteristics of the two development models. It then considers the relevant characteristics of the recent period of upheaval, or what may be called the era of market regulation or second great transformation, and concludes with some speculations on what options lie ahead.

2. The Era of Statutory Regulation

"Labour is not a commodity."
ILO Philadelphia Declaration, 1944

The essence of the two models that competed during the middle decades of the century was that they promoted labour security at the cost of constraining liberty, albeit in different ways. Both were initially based on the needs and aspirations of labouring man. Under both communism and welfare state capitalism, full employment was seen as the major instrumental goal. Adherents of both models tried to export their model to developing countries. The most extreme version of labourism was the Soviet Constitution, which declared that "he who does not labour shall not eat." But we shall not dwell on the characteristics of the state socialism model here. The welfare state, of which there were several variants, had a rather similar orientation, linking entitlement to state-provided social protection to current or past performance of labour or willingness to perform it.[1]

The essence of social and development policy in welfare state capitalism was the promotion of seven forms of labour security, which are summarised as follows:
– *Labour market security* - Adequate employment opportunities, through state-guaranteed full employment;
– *Employment security* - Protection against arbitrary dismissal, regulations on hiring and firing, imposition of costs on employers, etc.;
– *Job security* - A niche designated as an occupation or "career", plus tolerance of demarcation practices, barriers to skill dilution, craft boundaries, job qualifications, restrictive practices, craft unions, etc.;
– *Work security* - Protection against accidents and illness at work, through safety and health regulations, limits on working time, unsociable hours, night work for women, etc.;
– *Skill reproduction security* - Widespread opportunities to gain and retain skills, through apprenticeships, employment training, etc.;
– *Income security* - Protection of income through minimum wage machinery, wage indexation, comprehensive social security, progressive taxation, etc.;
– *Representation security* - Protection of collective voice in the labour market, through independent trade unions and employer associations incorporated economically and politically into the state, with the right to strike, etc.

The economic, regulatory and social policies of the era were intended to achieve steady progress on all these forms of security, and generally did so. The model, underpinned by Keynesian economics, was based on a set of premises. Technical change was expected to be steady and moderate, and the production structure was

---

[1] The debate on forms of welfare state started with Richard Titmuss, and since Gosta Esping-Andersen's 1990 book has generated a huge debate on welfare regimes. See, for instance, Esping-Andersen, G. (ed.) (1996): Welfare States in Transition: National Adaptations in Global Economies. Sage, London.

expected to be stable or only change slowly, with enough time for employers and workers to adjust, without major fluctuations in employment and unemployment. The labour force was expected to be overwhelmingly in full-time, regular employment, with men comprising the primary or 'core' labour force. It was presumed that the economy of any country was essentially closed, in that trade was either a small part of the national economy or — where the traded goods were in competition — was conducted between countries in which there were similar labour rights and obligations, or involved trade along sectoral lines according to the preceding international division of labour in which developing countries mainly exported primary goods. The model depended on dividing the global economy into "three worlds" - industrialised, communist and the Third World - in which a static international division of labour was expected to prevail.[2]

The regulatory framework of the era was predominantly *pro-collective* and based on a mix of strong statutory regulations, epitomised by increasingly complex and comprehensive laws and procedures, coupled with strong voice regulation, exercised by formally legitimised trades unions and employer organisations, protected by measures to extend freedom of association, in many countries backed up by neo-corporatist "tripartite" mechanisms, at the pinnacle of which was statutory or negotiated incomes policy. Because the system relied primarily on laws and regulations, one might call the period from about 1945 to 1975 the era of statutory regulation.

There was a rough distributional *quid pro quo,* in which, in return for leaving the managerial right to manage virtually intact, there was expected to be 'redistribution from growth', gradually shifting income in favour of workers and lower-income groups. In that context, workers and unions struggled for what amounted to the "decommodification of labour", through raising the social income — not just raising money wages but shifting a growing share of remuneration onto enterprise and state benefits, as well as giving workers' implicit income in the form of labour protection. This was the focus of the distributional struggle. There was never a distributional consensus, because trade unions and workers were always pushing for a more rapid improvement in their social income while employers were always trying to arrest that process. It was the employers who made most of the concessions.

Labour decommodification is not an ideological slogan. It can best be appreciated by considering the concept of social income. Basically, any individual in any society may have up to five sources of income, which together constitute the person's social income. This may be defined as follows:

$$SI = W + CB + EB + SB + PB$$

where SI is the individual's total social income, W is the money wage or income received, CB is the value of benefits or support provided by the family, kin or the local community, EB is the amount of benefits provided by the enterprise in which the person might be working, SB is the value of state benefits provided, in terms of insurance benefits or other transfers, including subsidies paid to workers or through firms to them,

---

[2] Gunnar Myrdal was not only a pioneering spirit in the development of welfare state capitalism but saw the welfare state as ultimately protectionist and nationalistic.

and PB is private income benefits, gained through investment, including private social protection.

We can disaggregate the elements as follows:

$$SI = (W_b + W_f) + (FT + LT) + (NWB + IB) + (C + IS + D) + PB$$

where W_b is the base or fixed wage, W_f is the flexible part of the wage (bonuses, etc.), FT are family transfers, LT are local community transfers, including any income from charity, non-governmental organisations, etc., NWB are non-wage benefits provided by firms to their workers, IB are contingency, insurance-type benefits provided by firms to their workers, C are universal state benefits (citizenship rights), IS are insurance-based income transfers from the state in case of contingency needs, and D are discretionary, means-tested transfers from the state.[3]

We do not have good data on the distribution of social income, or of the relative weights of the several components. However, based on anecdotal and scattered data, we can probably guesstimate the prevailing patterns in the different regions of the world during the era of statutory regulation. In a stylised, rough way, relative to other regions and as a proportion of total personal income, in the era of statutory regulation the average values of the components of the social income, as expressed in the first identity above, were as follows:

Table 1: Relative structures of social income in era of statutory regulation, by region.

	W	EB	SB	PB	CB
Africa	Medium	Low	Low	Low	High
Western Europe	Medium	Medium	High	Medium	Low
Eastern Europe	Low	High	Low	Low	Low
North America	Medium	Medium	Low	High	Low
South Asia	Low	Medium	Low	Low	Medium
South-East Asia	Low	Medium	Low	Low	High

For example, in western Europe, for the average person the share of social income accounted for by the money wage was about average for the world, whereas the share coming from state benefits was high by world standards and the share coming in the form of informal transfers from the ordinary community was low. In eastern Europe, the money wage was a relatively small part of total social income, while enterprise benefits comprised a very high share. In south-east and east Asia, money wages were not only low in absolute terms but were a small share of social income, while community transfers comprised a very high share - in effect, wage workers were subsidised by their predominantly rural kinship communities.

Although crude, this disaggregation is useful analytically. The pattern almost certainly helps to explain the stagnation in state socialism. Lenin's long-term intention

---

[3] A source of income not highlighted in this decomposition is income from the sale of goods and services. These are included in W, and effectively in the flexible part of W.

was to see the withering away of the wage. But the money wage withered away to such an extent that it could not have any incentive to labour. The global incidence of social income also helps to explain the changing international distribution of production and employment. Thus, the very low money wages in east Asian economies (the NICs) facilitated industrial accumulation when those countries shifted to export-led industrialisation, because wage workers were heavily subsidised by family and community transfers.

Of course, within any country the average distribution of social income components masks considerable "class-based" and occupational differences. And both with respect to those and the international patterns, one may hypothesise with reasonable confidence that they have been changing quite dramatically, and are likely to change further in the near future. We will consider this shortly.

3. The Era of Market Regulation

In the 1970s, while state socialism was easing into stagnation that eventually brought it to collapse, the institutional arrangements of welfare state capitalism began to unravel. The model was eroded by several factors, which included:

– the inflationary pressures and the oil crises,
– the changing international division of labour (which undermined the presumption of 'competitive' trade taking place between countries with similar labour rights and costs),
– the emergence and legitimation of rational expectations theory and supply – side economics that undermined the Keynesian consensus among economic policymakers,
– the rise of libertarianism (which helped to undermine the values of social solidarity that underpinned the redistributive welfare state),
– the slowdown in economic growth that disrupted the distributional *quid pro quo,*
– the large rise in unemployment in many parts of the world,
– a widely perceived "fiscal crisis" of the state, and
– a new technological revolution, which ushered in something akin to a new ("fifth") Kondratief upswing, which disrupted the stability of production and the norms of full-time stable employment.

It is for other papers in this volume to dwell on the factors that contributed to what has since been loosely connected to the nebulous term "globalisation". For our purposes we may merely note the most relevant characteristics of what we might call the era of market regulation, which began in the mid-1970s and looks increasingly unlikely to last beyond the turn of the century, precisely because the economy has been dis-embedded from society, and because the resultant insecurities and inequalities are creating unsustainable pressures.

The emergence of supply-side economics in the 1970s and 1980s — which has underpinned IMF, World Bank and OECD programmes, and shaped the "structural adjustment" and "shock therapy" approaches — reversed the Keynesian targeting of policy instruments. Whereas under Keynesianism, governments used macro-economic policy to produce so-called full employment (male), now macro-economic policy is expected to focus on the control of inflation and monetary movements, primarily by cutting public spending. Whereas under Keynesianism, micro-economic policy was to limit inflationary pressures, now it is expected to encourage employment, through removing institutional, behavioural and regulatory "rigidities". Whatever politicians say, governments have surrendered the pursuit of full employment through economic policy. This is epitomised by the chosen independence of central banks, and delegation of authority over monetary policy to non-elected bodies. The currently orthodox economic policy places responsibility for unemployment on the behaviour of workers and firms and on "regulations". Meanwhile, governments have been trying to cut "budgetary deficits" and public spending.[4] The public sector has ceased to be "employer of last resort", and been regarded as "crowding out" private investment, employment and growth. Attempts to cut public spending include measures to make social protection more selective, conditional and privatised.

Technological changes, and the spread of informatics, have facilitated globalisation and the growth of more flexible labour processes. As far as the latter is concerned, the major point is that they have allowed many more managerial options in choice of techniques, work organisation and location of production. There has been a global growth in labour market flexibility – organisational, external (numerical), functional (internal), wage system and labour force flexibility.[5]

There has been a re-orientation of labour regulations. There is no such thing as a deregulated labour market. However, whereas in the era of statutory regulation, labour regulations were predominantly protective of workers, pro-collective and socially redistributive, in the current era the orthodox view is that regulations are justifiable if and only if they promote economic growth, following the Chicago school of law and economics. In general, there has been a strong tendency to use regulations to increase the role of "market forces", which is why it is apt to call this the "era of market regulation". The shift has been characterised by increasing emphasis placed on fiscal regulations and pro-individualistic statutory regulations, with a strong campaign against protective regulations, which have been depicted as labour market "rigidities" and the source of non-wage labour costs undermining national competitiveness. In the process, one of the great ironies of the 1990s is that the very securities that previously had been regarded as the desirable objectives of socio-economic (development) policy were regarded as undesirable obstacles to be overcome.

In the 1990s, no longer was there competition to sell welfare state capitalism and state socialism in developing countries. Both went into retreat. In their place, there was the almost hegemonic imposition of the ubiquitous "Washington consensus". This offered a model consisting of eleven main elements, with more being added as its

---

[4] As we emphasised with respect to South Africa, often this is justified, particularly in developing countries, as increasing the country's "credibility" (sic) in international capital markets. Portfolio managers use such simple indicators as "percent budget deficit" and "government share of GDP" in allocating their very substantial portfolios. Standing, G, Sender, J. and Weeks, J.(1996): Restructuring the Labour Market: The South African Challenge. ILO, Geneva.

[5] These are defined and examined in chapter 4 of the book on which part of this paper is based. Standing, G. (forthcomimng): Global Labour Flexibility: Seeking Distributive Justice.

'success' spread. Briefly, they were trade liberalisation, financial liberalisation, privatisation, "deregulation", foreign capital liberalisation (elimination of barriers to FDI), secure property rights, unified and competitive exchange rates, diminished public spending (fiscal discipline), public expenditure switching (to health, schooling and infrastructure), tax reform (broadening the tax base, cutting marginal tax rates, less progressive tax), and a "social safety net" (selective state transfers for the needy).[6] A twelfth element, which has been stridently expressed in various World Bank and IMF (and OECD) reports, is labour market flexibility, by which is meant decentralised labour relations coupled with modest or no protective or pro-collective labour regulations.

When the former Soviet bloc countries became "countries in transition" and part of a broader group of "emerging markets", they were subject to the same set of prescriptions, albeit repackaged and with additional elements under the title of "shock therapy". We need not go into the debates on "big bang" versus "gradualism", and "sequencing". However, the social and economic costs of the attempted transformations of these countries have been enormous. Although there has been some economic recovery in central Europe in the late 1990s, everywhere poverty, inequality and lack of entitlement to social protection have been spreading.[7]

However, as the end of the century approaches, we may be at the beginning of the end of this era, and far from the end of history. Here is some good news. The Chief Economist of the World Bank says that the Washington consensus is bunk and is wrong. There is one awkward problem. For over two decades, the World Bank has been devoting billions of dollars to efforts to induce countries all over the world to adopt the policies of that consensus. If there is a new attempt to re-arrange "the financial architecture" (the latest euphemism, referring to the international financial agencies), one may predict that the restructuring of international monetary policy will be devoted to stabilising capital markets.

Beyond that, we may merely note that, with a couple of exceptions, in most countries the package of policies that has been "globalised" (sic) has produced 'stabilisation' without stability – epitomised by the periodic crises that break out somewhere in the world, such as Mexico in 1994, east Asia in 1997, and Russia every six months. There has been "deregulation" that has involved many new regulations, and there have been 'safety nets' without safety, as millions more people are pushed into poverty and as inequalities have grown. No wonder Stiglitz and others are worried.

4. Fragmentation: The Social Income under Strain

The era of market regulation has ushered in a period of intense insecurity, and yet the statistical information with which most economists and commentators monitor

---

[6] Note that while property rights have been stressed, there have been no equivalent worker rights. Incidentally, in regional economic agreements, such as MERCOSUR, there has been a guaranteed right to free capital mobility, but no such right for workers.
[7] For this writer's perspective on these trends, see Standing, G. (1998):The Folly of Social Safety Nets: Why a Basic Income is Needed in Eastern Europe. Social Research, Vol.64, No.4, Winter, pp.1339-79.

economic and social change has failed to capture it. This applies to developing countries, 'transition' countries and industrialised countries. In effect, globalisation is involving "labour re-commodification". This reflects the reduction in forms of non-wage income for workers, represented by the erosion of forms of labour-related security, and the reduced prospect of receiving such components of social income for those on the edge of labour markets.

Suppose, to give an illustrative example, a man was receiving $100 as a wage, and had a long-term secure employment contract, guaranteed healthcare, subsidised canteen food and membership of a group pension scheme. The total value might actually be $200. How do we measure the value to the worker of the employment guarantee? One imagines many people would say that they would be prepared to sacrifice 10% of their income to retain such a guarantee. If an employer takes it away and gives the worker a 10% pay rise, our statistics would show wages rising by 10%, which of course is misleading because all that has happened is that the structure of social income has changed. Although we do not have good data to demonstrate this, one can be reasonably sure that in the era of market regulation and globalisation something like this has been happening all over the world – except that for many there has been no compensation for loss of security or diminished hope that they could obtain it.

Labour market insecurity has grown almost globally, with much higher levels of unemployment, slower rates of employment growth and higher levels of 'labour slack'[8]. Employment insecurity is high and rising, with growing proportions of those in the labour force having insecure employment statuses and with many more workers being without employment protection. Work insecurity has become greater, due to more people being in work statuses without coverage by protective institutions and regulations. Job insecurity has worsened, with many more workers having to switch jobs and learn new tricks of working. Skill reproduction insecurity is considerable, in part because skills become obsolescent more quickly and because few workers are receiving career skills. Income insecurity is greater for those in employment, due to flexible wages and so on, and for those outside employment, due to explicit and implicit disentitlement to benefits. Representation insecurity has been growing due to de-unionisation, erosion of effective 'tripartite' institutions and the changing character of collective bargaining.

In short, we are in one of those eras of widespread insecurity. In particular, it is worth highlighting the growth of income insecurity, and the associated changes in social income and the extent of socio-economic fragmentation. Before doing so, recall two aspects of the set of policies prescribed and implemented under the aegis of the Washington consensus — the social safety net and decentralised labour relations.

The changes in the character of social protection taking place are complex, but for our purposes the principal changes underpinning the euphemism of social safety nets are increased selectivity of state transfers, multi-tierism in modes of provision of social protection, and partial privatisation of social policy. 'Targeting' on the needy has meant a global drift away from universal benefits, more means-testing, greater

---

[8] In most types of economy, the unemployment rate has become a less reliable proxy indicator of total labour underutilisation.

conditionality in determining entitlement to state benefits, and lower "generosity" in the level of benefits provided. There has been a trend away from social insurance, both in terms of reforms of actual schemes and in terms of proportions of workers in statuses that gives them entitlement to them. Multi-tierism is spreading fast – such as a low level of state provision, a mandatory insurance-based second tier, an employment-based negotiated third tier and a private individual savings-based top tier. This sort of model has been most advanced in the sphere of pensions, but is spreading to other spheres, such as health services and schooling. Multi-tierism is linked to the partial privatisation of social protection, resulting in a cut in state coverage and in greater differentiation in access. A powerful lobby exists to extend privatisation as far as possible, and major multinational corporations are involved in this process.

For our purposes, these three trends in the character of social protection are accentuating the fragmentation of societies, since they offer very different opportunities for access to elements of social income other than wages. We will return to this shortly.

The other structural change contributing to the same set of developments is the decentralisation of labour relations, or to the trend to employment and wage 'bargains' made at the individual or small-unit level. Globalisation, with the shift in power and influence from the representatives of labour to capital, and with more labour flexibility, has contributed to this trend, and it is a global phenomenon. From the days of comprehensive 'incomes policy' in the 1960s and 1970s, the vision of national-level tripartite bargaining has faded, only kept going in a few places such as the Netherlands, where the rationale has been concession bargaining by the unions.

Sectoral bargaining has also gone into long-term decline, in part because of the ability of corporations to switch production more easily and to indulge in whipsaw bargaining. It is also declining because workers' allegiances to sectors is diminishing (and the location of firms in specific sectors has also become more flexible). On the workers' side, this lack of sectoral identity partly reflects the decline in job security and employment security, as well as the plunging decline in representation security associated with de-unionisation. Occupational bargaining has long been divisive, since Taylorism early in the century largely destroyed the base of craft unionism, while bodies to protect 'professionals' have been mechanisms for guarding the incomes and privileges of the privileged. We find that the growing sphere of bargaining is at the levels of enterprise and firm, and increasingly at the level of the individual worker and employer. The consequence of this process is that company unions and the like have been boosted, and have been the instrument for intensifying fragmentation in labour markets. The weaker elements are less likely to be protected by collective voice.

So, under the impact of economic liberalisation and "globalisation", the structure of social income has been changing. Overall, one could hypothesise that the median changes taking place in the various regions are as in Table 2, where a plus sign implies a rise in the relative contribution to total individual income, a minus sign implies the opposite. Where both a plus and a minus sign are given, one surmises that part of the growth of income differentiation is due to a shift in one direction for some groups and in the opposite direction for others. What the table suggests is that in most parts of the world there has been a shift to money wages and a shrinkage in the average share provided by state benefits and services. Perhaps most significantly – and this is an educated guesstimate rather than a statement that one can make based on substantial statistical information – there is increasing reliance on private provision (personal investment and saving) and community support (voluntary provision), or increased need for those sources to fill voids opened up by the diminishing public provision.

Table 2: Trends in components of social income since 1970s , by region.

	W	EB	SB	PB	CB
Africa	-/+	-/+	-	0	0
Western Europe	+/-	+/-	-	+	+
Eastern Europe	+	-	+/-	+	+
North America	+/-	+/-	-	+	+
South Asia	0	?	-	+ ?	0
South-East Asia	+	+	0	+	-

However, the level of disaggregation of Table 2 is not as revealing as when we consider what has been happening to the sub-components of the five components and what has been happening to distinctive socio-economic groups. Before considering this, we need to have an image of the labour fragmentation that has been taking place internationally. An essential feature of the fragmentation is that growing numbers of people are detaching themselves or being detached from mainstream national regulatory and protective systems. It is presented in descending order based on social income.

At the zenith of the globalising economy is an *élite*, consisting of a tiny minority of absurdly rich and high-earning people, whose impact is out of all proportion of their number. Some have long since reached the stage of seeing their incomes rising almost exponentially. They are global citizens. Expanding the stratum down to multi-millionaires, the relevant points are that they are detached from national regulatory and social security systems financially, neither needing nor contributing to them, psychologically, not feeling committed to their maintenance or improvement, and politically. The *élite* has very strong income security, and whatever they need of other forms of security. Their biggest danger is hubris, and being caught in criminality.

Next down is the stratum that one may call *proficians*. These are the new craftsmen of the global flexible economy. As the name implies, they are a mix of professional and technician, mostly working as consultants or in short-term employment contracts. They tend to operate in a climate of insecurity, but are well compensated for this. Perhaps their most crucial form of insecurity is work insecurity, epitomised by the frenzied pace of their erratic work schedules. They are often able to evade or avoid taxation, and are at least partially detached from state-based social protection systems.

The third stratum is what one may call the *salariat*. This consists of salaried employees, including those working in civil services, large corporations, para-statials and other bureaucracies. They have a high degree of labour security, but probably suffer from some job and skill reproduction insecurity because they may be moved around and/or gain promotion in their enterprises by leaving their technical skills behind them. Because of their reasonably high incomes and the tendency to identify with managements, employers and elements of the *élite* and profician strata, members of the salariat typically feel detached from the state social protection system, seeing their future and current income security in terms mainly of private insurance benefits and earnings from judicious investments.

The fourth stratum consists of *core workers*. These are the bulwark of what those of us with long memories used to call the working class. The welfare states were created to serve the needs of core workers, those in full-time, regular, typically unionised jobs, usually with manual skills. During the era of statutory regulation, it was implicitly presumed that these workers represented the norm and that a majority of workers in all countries would eventually belong to this stratum. The larger the proportion of people belonging to it, the more people in a position to support and benefit from the mainstream, social-insurance based social protection system and the mainstream regulatory system.

The trouble is that whereas the legitimacy of a redistributive welfare depended on core workers, they never actually comprised a majority of the economically active population in most countries and since the 1970s have been shrinking. This is not just a reflection of "de-industrialisation" in industrialised countries, and the associated dispersion of manufacturing wage labour around the world as the international division of labour evolved. It is also because of various forms of labour market flexibility. Core workers traditionally benefited from most forms of labour security, but with the growth of wage system flexibility a growing proportion of their income has come in insecure form. They have also suffered from increasing job insecurity and employment insecurity, while their unions have been weakened almost everywhere. Above all, with core workers dwindling in numbers and not expected to grow proportionately, their agenda has lacked legitimacy.

The fifth stratum in the fragmented structure consists of *flexiworkers*. These comprise a disparate group of people in non-regular work statuses, including casual workers, outworkers, sub-contracted and contractor labour, agency workers and domestic workers. Their common characteristic is labour insecurity in almost all respects. In the era of statutory regulation and welfare state capitalism it was presumed that these "informal" forms of employment would decline as economies developed. In recent years, they have appeared to be the future. Among the associated trends, a growing proportion of labour forces have lacked entitlement to mainstream statutory protection and have been disentitled to social transfers.

The sixth stratum has consisted of the *unemployed*. The number in this status has risen extraordinarily in the era of market regulation. They suffer from increased labour market insecurity, given the higher levels of unemployment, and they suffer from greater income insecurity than used to be the case, because the level of benefits has been cut, the duration of entitlement has been shortened, and the conditions for entitlement have been tightened.

The seventh, and bottom, stratum is what might be called the *detached*. This is a rapidly growing minority of the population in many countries, cut off from mainstream state benefits, lingering in chronic poverty, anomic and threatening to those above them in the income spectrum simply because others fear falling into their ranks. In recent years, politicians have been inclined to treat the victims of economic liberalisation as in need of "re-integration". They linger in the streets, in bus and train stations and in city parks. They make those above them in the social feel uncomfortable or smug, depending on where they fit. The detached represent fear. And it is fear that induces concessions - the ultimate tool of inequality.

If one divides societies (and the international economy) into these seven fragments, one sees that the top three strata are increasingly detached from state-based social protection, while the bottom three strata are increasingly detached by virtue of explicit and implicit disentitlement to its benefits and services. The analytical device also helps us to picture the growing inequality of social income and deterioration of economic security.

Table 3 is a stylised interpretation of what anecdotal evidence and reports suggest are the sources of income received by the separate strata, or the sources on which the group relies for survival. The asterisks indicate what are the main sources of income for the higher-income strata. The table's final row indicates what seems to have been the global trend for the source of income specified by the column. Thus, the base wage has tended to decline as a source of social income, the flexible part of the wage has been rising, income from private savings and investment has been rising sharply, and so on. The +/- sign means that the source has been rising for higher-income groups, falling for others.

Table 4 complements Table 3, in that it indicates how the seven strata experience various forms of security. Thus, for example, proficians have high levels of income security and skill reproduction security, being in control of their own activities, but no employment or job security. The core workers have some employment security (although diminishing), relatively high work security and reasonable entitlement to enterprise and other benefits.

One may quibble with the stylisations of Tables 3 and 4. However, they suggest a way of interpreting what is happening to income and to income security. The growing socio-economic fragmentation has produced a situation in which those in — or identifying with — the top three strata have felt increasingly detached from the mainstream state social protection system. They are thus less inclined to defend its principles of social solidarity, while the bottom three strata have felt deprived, detached by disentitlement to the benefits long offered to core workers, to whose ranks they had aspired. To them, there is no solidarity on offer, and for them, to talk about social solidarity would sound like a sick joke. The pervasive detachment and lack of social solidarity have contributed to the incipient loss of legitimation of the welfare state.

Table 3: Sources of social income, by socio-economic status.

Sources Stratum	W$_b$	W$_f$	FT	LT	NWB	IB	C	Is	D	PB/K
Élite										***
Proficians		*				+	+			*
Salariat	*	+			*	*	+	+		+
Core	+	+			+	+	+	+		
Flexiworkers		+	+	+			+	(+)		
Unemployed			+	+			+	(+)	+	
Detached				+			+		+	
Global Trend	-	+		+	+/-	+/-	-	-	+	*

Table 4: Sources of Social Income, by Socio-Economic Status.

Security Stratum	Labour market	Employ-ment	Job	Work	Skill Reprod.	Income	Benefits	Represen-tation
Élite	+	+	+	+	+	+	+	0
Proficians	(+)	-	-	-	+	+	0	-
Salariat	+	+	(+)	+	(+)	+	+	0
Core	0	(+)	0	+	0	0	+	+
Flexiworkers	-	-	-	-	-	-	-	-
Unemployed	-	-	-	-	-	-	-	-
Detached	-	-	-	-	-	-	-	-

Several trends associated with globalisation have accentuated the growing inequalities associated with social fragmentation. Multinational and potentially multinational corporations have been able to use whipsaw bargaining to induce concessions on the part of workers (i.e., if they will not make concessions, the firm will relocate). And capital has been able to persuade governments to offer huge subsidies, on the pretext of attracting foreign direct investment, or retaining such investment, or creating jobs.[9] Huge actual and implicit subsidies to rich companies (and individuals) are justified as market friendly, whereas subsidies to workers and ordinary consumers are condemned as market distortions.

---

[9] Why do so few commentators see the irony of this? There was a wonderful sequence of adverts on British TV in 1997 showing employers as heroes, with lots of them waving flags and claiming that they were making a commitment to hire workers. This was orchestrated by a New Labour Government. This is how the left has ended the century that had begun with calls for freedom from labour.

5. Towards an Era of Human Security and Distributive Justice?

The world is faced by a short period in which two "new" models of development are and will be in competition. On the right, we have the libertarians – or what are increasingly looking like the neo-liberal rump – whose vision is still fairly clear, and whose influence on macro-economic and micro-economic decision making is still pervasive. They want an economy and a society that are highly individualistic, with more constraints placed on collective bodies, with privatisation of social policy to follow the privatisation of economic activity. They offer liberty without security.

Recognising that something has to be done about the poor and the "losers" in the market economy, they offer a minimalist (residual) "social safety net" for "the deserving poor", which the state should provide through targeted, means-tested social assistance, coupled with fiscal and moral incentives to charitable disbursements from the wealthy. For the "undeserving poor", they offer the carrot and stick of "workfare", and other conditional, low-level state transfers. For the "transgressing poor", they offer a stern State prepared to uphold the law in keeping public order.

On the left (if that is the right word), the rump of the old 'labourist' and social democrats are coalescing under a delightfully appropriate euphemism – "Third Wayism". It seems to offer constrained labour market security with constrained liberty. It is unfair to caricature it, but it seems to lead to a more social, or moral ("responsible"), variant of libertarianism. It accepts and welcomes globalisation, in that it believes in economic liberalisation, favours low taxation on capital and on higher income groups, accepts the 'need' for subsidies for capital, believes in some statutory protective regulation to strengthen the rights of labour, and believes that inequality can be redressed by raising employment and by increasing the "employability" of everybody.

It too seems to divide the poor into the deserving-undeserving-transgressing categories. It advocates "welfare-to-work" schemes to integrate the victims of economic dynamism and labour market flexibility, tends to support wage and employment subsidies. It supports tax credits, such as the EITC. And it also supports "welfare pluralism", in which social protection and social services are converted into "multi-tierism". Ultimately, "Third Wayism" is suffused with the 'new paternalism' that guided US welfare reform in the mid-1990s, or the desire to have the state intervene to reduce "dependency" in deciding what is proper behaviour and what is improper.

In the light of these conflicting yet overlapping models, and in the context of globalisation and more open economies, we should reconsider what human security should entail in a Good Society of the 21st century? Of the seven forms of labour security, with more open economies and flexible labour markets (like them or not), labour market security is unlikely to return. In any case, one can argue that that particular form of security and employment security should be regarded as primarily instrumental needs. Work, job and skill reproduction security are derived needs. The really crucial forms are income security and representation security. Without effective voice, those on the margins of society, the detached and those vulnerable to impoverishing detachment, will be unable to overcome their marginalisation, and will be ignored in the increasingly supra-national policymaking. Social dumping will become pervasive. Without basic income security, freedom to make choices and develop skills and a niche in society will be impossible.

The challenge before us is to find new ways of giving voice to all interest groups and to find new ways of giving all such groups that minimal income security. The good news here is that there is growing intellectual and political unease at the morality, legitimacy and sustainability of the disembedded winner-takes-all economy. We need to spread the good news more.

11. Globalization and Social Policy Instruments in Europe

Paolo Onofri

For L60
F36

Globalization is far from being a new phenomenon. It has occurred in different forms from time to time. Referring to its alleged historical novelty is usually intended to reduce its shroud of mystery and the anxiety that the abuse of this term causes in the public opinion.

Often, in the past, when the wind of globalization started blowing, it brought with it innovations in the material civilization, which changed the daily lives of the peoples. Such innovations often triggered changes in the leadership of both world trade and standards of living. These moments were frequently the expression of a sudden jump in the progress of scientific knowledge and its technical applications.

A fear of an important change in the leadership of the advancement of the standards of living is at the basis of the insecurity we unconsciously feel when we think about the term globalization.

We, Europeans, may wonder whether the possibility for Europe, in the future, to take the lead in matching solidarity and efficiency is merely wishful thinking or a realistic expectation.

The following pages will develop the concept of globalization as a way to identify the growing openness of economies; on the face of it, this may resemble the concept of competitiveness of an economic system as a whole, but in reality the focus will be on productive capacity and its growth as well as on the possibility that social cohesion and welfare goals might interfere with the growth of the overall productive capacity. The first two European countries to try to keep this interference in check are mature and highly internationalized economies: the United Kingdom and the Netherlands.

The next step will be to inquire whether the Economic and Monetary Union will have to deal with the problem of a more sustained development for its productive capacity by following the above examples. The attempted response starts from the assumption that the EMU has two inescapable integration alternatives: an external one, owing to the ageing of its population, which requires a financial and real diversification of capital investments to prevent the possible decrease of their returns; an internal one, to achieve a single economic system in the future which might yield substantial productivity gains.

These calls for further international integration are, on the one hand, prompted by a social welfare goal and on the other raise problems of social cohesion at the European level. It is to these issues that the main considerations of this paper will be devoted.

1. Competitiveness and Productivity

The message of leadership change in the progress of material standards of living implied in the term globalization is conveyed indirectly through the more neutral expression of ability of an entire economic system to compete.

Paul Krugman, however, has long been battling against the abuse of the concept of competitiveness of a nation[1], holding that ultimately the competitiveness of a country is nothing but a "poetic license" to refer to its ability of being productive. In fact, the welfare of a country derives from the productivity level of the resources employed more than from the international competitiveness of its goods as such. In other words, Krugman emphasizes the role of comparative advantage over absolute advantage. The amount of foreign trade and its structure are not tied only to the relative international price of goods but also to the differences among the relative domestic prices of the different goods. This means that there can be a significant foreign trade both for countries with a low productivity and low salaries as well as for those with a high productivity and high salaries. Since, in general, an increase in foreign trade is associated with a positive effect on the welfare of a country, in both cases there may be a reason for being open to foreign trade.

Such a conceptual focus, closely related to the pure theory of international trade, is undoubtedly easier for an American economist, who has lived the experience of a country relatively closed to international trade that has been, and perhaps continues to be, a technology leader in different manufacturing sectors and that has benefited up to now from her seigniorage on the international reserve currency.

2. The Foreign Constraint and the Social Market Economy

The difference between competitiveness and ability of being productive may be less clear-cut for a European economist. The experience of the European countries has been such that often their internal development had to stop before the limit set by their ability to export, forcing them to endure substantial reallocations of the international purchasing power in order to revive their growth possibilities, with all the implications arising therefrom in terms of redistribution national income between labor and capital and between present and future generations.[2]

There is no need to spend many words to remember that for almost all European countries the improvement in the standards of living, the socialization of the risks of individuals in their working lives (namely, the welfare state) and the development of national identity represented a process that straddled the last two centuries and gained a strong momentum after WWII. This translated into the goals of full employment and the development of social-solidarity institutes. The expression welfare state then has taken on two different meanings: the protection of workers in the labor-salary exchange in the market and their protection against the risk of income loss,

[1] Krugman, P. (1996): Pop Internationalism. Mit Press, Cambridge.
[2] To this end, it is sufficient to recall the so-called dollar shortage in the aftermath of WWII, the ensuing Marshall Plan, the devaluation of the French Franc in the second half of the 1950s and 1960s, which occurred almost simultaneously with that of the Sterling Pound. This is just to point out those events that took place within the Bretton Woods fixed exchange rate system, without going back to the 1920s and 1930s.

sickness and poverty in old age. These protections were extended by a certain number of countries to their citizens as such. This was reinforced by the historical and political evolution over the past fifty years, which put the European countries before the need to find a social balance between labor and capital, giving rise to a social market economy that might represent the good face of capitalism that could be set against communism.

Mature economies more open to international trade (such as the United Kingdom and the Netherlands) were the first to encounter some constraints on full employment due to their balance of payments already from the fifties (throughout the fifties and sixties both had trade deficits as well as current-account deficits). Full employment, equilibrium in the balance of payments, financial[3] and currency stability started to appear in alternative to the general development of social welfare systems. This even though the growth rate of the population and the economy in general, due both to the reconstruction and to the effort to catch up with the standards of living in the US, did not fully reveal it.

In some cases the typical social and political reaction to these incompatibilities was the tradeoff between the enlargement of social citizenship rights and a centralized income policy which would make it possible to manage salary growth in keeping with the external constraint. In neo-corporatist terms, the tradeoff between salary moderation and the expansion of social welfare (both in terms of number of benefits and number of eligible recipients) validates the more general political role of trade unions.

The centralized governance of the labor market, although through the specificity of the trade unions of each country, expanded the concept of welfare state beyond the collective coverage against individual risks, strengthening the aspects of worker protection in labor relations. Labor market regulations and the enlargement of social-citizenship rights are the basic instruments of social cohesion; by reducing the likelihood of workers losing their jobs, the different forms of worker protection on the labor market make it possible to minimize the burden of the increased coverage of individual risks by making it bearable for public finances. For their part, income policies tend to replace international currency pegs, which tend to disappear, and enhance the role of trade unions in macroeconomic policy.

The oil shocks in the 70s laid bare these uncertain balances: aspirations to a higher standard of living started appearing inconsistent with the aggregate supply growth and these difficulties came to the fore in the precariousness of the external equilibrium; in the case of the two countries we are going to consider (United Kingdom and the Netherlands), thanks to the revenues generated by their national energy sources, they were characterized by a productivity development relatively lower in the sectors of international tradeables. The weight of the welfare state, in a broad sense, was beginning to be perceived as an alternative to the increase of productive capacity, thus to the overcoming of the foreign constraint. It was not only a matter of the amount of social spending, but emphasis was placed on its possible disincentive effects on the formation of the aggregate supply.

It cannot be denied that it was one country in particular, whose nature as an

---

[3] The United Kingdom, for instance, came out of WWII with a public debt equal to 175% of GDP and without the help of an inflationary burst that would reduce its weight in real terms.

open economy had stood out in Europe for decades, to be the first to suffer from a disease that originated specifically from the regulation of the labor market and on the way social spending took place: English disease. A disease revealed by the performance of the balance of payments and by the incompatibility between the growth rate of the standard of living, a desideratum of the population, and the expansion rate of the export capacity; a disease that, in the area of tradeables, was strengthened paradoxically by the discovery of the oil fields in the second half of the 70s.

The emergence of a foreign constraint as the expression of the inconsistency between aspirations and productive capacity did not in itself contradict the fact that foreign trade as such represented an opportunity to increase the population's welfare.

It is worthwhile then to look more closely at the English experience, even though very briefly, comparing it with the Dutch one, the Netherlands being the other European country with a highly open economy which also enjoyed the benefit of renewed sources of energy and suffered from a similar disease: the Dutch disease. These cases are typical of the conflicts that can be determined by the presence of inconsistencies between domestic aspirations and patterns of the productive capacity.[4]

3. The English Case

Great Britain and the Netherlands have been dealing with the internal consequences of the problem of the relationships between the socio-economic organization of a country and its productive capacity (i.e. the internal consequences of globalization) by attempting to reduce the regulation of the labor market and by setting off incentive mechanism to increase supply while preserving social-citizenship rights.

During the 1980s, in Great Britain, action on the labor market was much more vigorous than it was on the general social security system. The objective on the labor market was to have it reflect a condition of low productivity on the salary structure in different sectors, including the service one, and to foster heavy reorganizations in the manufacturing sector, supported also by low corporate income taxes and by the high inflow of foreign direct investments from abroad. Union busting and the resulting salary flexibility, capable of mirroring the demand and supply of labor, were the main intermediate results; they in turn, and after some time, made it possible for the unemployment rate to fall below that of the main countries of Continental Europe during the recovery phases of the economy. That is what happened during the economic expansion at the end of the 1980s as well as in the 1994-1997 period. The greater reduction in the 1994-97 period was due to a decrease in women's unemployment rate, which seems to be structural as well as cyclical.

As to the welfare state proper, there is evidence that the action of conservative governments during the 1979-1997 period did not change the share of social

---

[4] There is a rich literature on the experience of these two countries. Here I will recall only the two most recent analyses: Rhodes, M. (1998): Restructuring the British Welfare State: Domestic Constraints and Global Imperatives. Mimeo. European University Institute. November, Florence, Van der Veen, R. and Trommel, W. (1998): The Dutch Miracle: Managed Liberalization of the Dutch Welfare State 1985-1997. Mimeo. IPPR, October, London.

expenditure as a percentage of the GDP. On the other hand, the argument may be turned on its head and it might be said that their action held expenditure in check even though population ageing called for an increase. The modification in income support occurred through the change of some concession rules, which increased the number of those excluded, leaving basically unaltered the extent of risk coverage for middle-income groups. These latter, in fact, given the deregulation of the labour market compared with the past, have to cope with an increasing income uncertainty and job insecurity, and social cohesion could not be maintained without keeping the already existing functions of social expenditure.[5]

Other basic aspect of the welfare state reform in the United States were the growing role of the private sector in the provision of welfare benefits, a greater efficiency in the management of public healthcare and social services no longer tied to developments in technical progress but constant in terms of purchasing power.[6]

4. The Dutch Case

In the Netherlands social spending reforms pursued the goal to increase the incentives to take any kind of work and the disincentives to stay indefinitely on the welfare rolls. This reform process did not reduce significantly the level of benefits, which is definitely higher than the English one, but adopted more stringent eligibility rules and shifted part of the risk coverage, which is still mandatory, to the private insurance market. This did not reduce the cost of labor contributions *per se*. In fact, also in the cases in which benefits shrank, bargaining reinstated the benefits lost by shifting the cost on companies, which had commentators state that the Netherlands went from a centralized system of social expenditure (neo-corporatist) to a system with more elements of welfare by corporations of the American and Japanese type[7].

The most significant result obtained from the privatization of part of the risks and from the creation of a quasi-market for insurance was a lower misuse of social spending and a rise in the supply of labor. This result was attained also thanks to the acceptance by trade unions of the development of part-time work, involving at present approximately one-sixth or one-seventh of total jobs, and encouraging the participation of women in the labor market, which was very low until the mid-80s.

The degree of concentration of the interventions on the labor market was, however, lower in the Netherlands than it was in the United Kingdom and, particularly,

---

[5]Cf. Hills, J. (1998): Thatcherism, New Labour and the Welfare State. Center for Analysis of Social Exclusion, Paper n.13, August. London School of Economics, for a documentation of how social spending in the United Kingdom has remained unaltered, undergoing an internal reallocation in favour of healthcare and social security to the detriment of housing; of how the presence of the private sector has increased, though in a somewhat limited manner, both in supplying social services and in financing them; of how the role of means-testing has grown in the provision of benefits and, finally, how all this, in combination with labour market deregulation, has increased disparities in the distribution of income.

[6] Cf. M. Rhodes (1998).

[7] For a far-reaching analysis of the Dutch case, see Visser, J. and Hemerijck, A. (1998): Il miracolo olandese. Edizioni Lavoro.

it was managed with the unions' consent. In fact, the differential characteristics between the two social and political systems remain.

On the one hand, the British have kept a system of relatively lower benefits, managed mainly by the public sector, with the total disintegration of the system of political concert with the trade unions. Overall, in terms of balance of payments, the most significant results of lower unemployment translated into more significant results for the balance of current accounts than for the trade balance.

On the other hand, the Dutch focused on the preservation of the level and obligation of the benefits, justifying their defense with the contribution to efficiency that their private provision and the reduction of opportunistic behaviors would provide.

In the United Kingdom the level of social solidarity declined to focus mostly on the marginal segments of the population[8]; in the Netherlands it became more category-and company-based. In both cases, one might say with a slogan that globalization has shifted the attention more on markets than on social solidarity, but it is fair to ask whether the reduction of opportunistic behaviors is an actual injury to social solidarity.

Anyway, it is out of the question that in more recent years both countries have experienced a faster growth than the other countries of Continental Europe. It is widely known that after ten years from the initial measures this has led both countries to have an unemployment rate much lower than that in the other European countries.

5. A Lesson for the Other European Countries?

Two economies highly open to foreign trade, in a mature development phase by now, blessed with a shock that increased their rent in terms of non-reproducible energy resources; two economies whose productivity and capital accumulation in the 1970s grew at a slower pace than those of the other European countries countered these trends by overhauling their labor market regulations and welfare states. Are the main European countries headed in the same direction in the near future?

EMU countries have long been experiencing improved terms of trade, which can protect them from any deficit in their balance of payments. Taken as a whole, the EMU has a current account surplus and is not more open to foreign trade than the USA or Japan; a faster expansion would not run into a foreign constraint immediately. Also taken separately, for instance, the three main countries of the EMU show a significant current account surplus.

Despite this, there is a widespread worry for the future; there is a fear that the current trade and account surpluses with the rest of the world and the improved terms of trade that support them are hiding a potential worldwide redistribution of the ability to produce tradeables.

Are we faced with a European disease? If there is a difficulty to grow as fast as in the past, this, for the time being, does not depend on the action of the foreign constraint considered as a whole. If it is somewhat present, the foreign constraint might take the shape of some limits placed on the expansion of a number manufacturing sectors.

---

[8] For instance, single parents and potential recipients of "social" housing.

During the last thirty years the positive contribution to the trade balance of the EU countries by products that account for an increasing share of world trade has been progressively shrinking until it came to naught (e.g., the electronic industry); the contribution given to the overall trade balance by products that account for a stable share of world trade (e.g., cars and chemicals) is largely positive and stable while the negative contribution of declining products in world trade (e.g. foodstuff and textile) is decreasing.

Thus, though not compulsory on the whole, the foreign constraint might exercise its influence by prompting the reallocation of productive activities in order to sustain growth rates more in line with peoples' aspirations. To free such reallocation energies it might be necessary to review the organization of socio-economic relationships much in the way the United Kingdom and the Netherlands did.

These energies may find their way only through a national or a European channel, depending on how the integration of the EMU countries evolves.

6. Integration within the EMU

It is not at all clear what road the individual European countries will follow to govern their integration process. So far, the single European economies have been developing by becoming progressively alike and by increasing their inter-company trade. The convergence of development paths did not bring to the fore any significant specialization phenomena; actually it caused inter-company trade, as a percentage of trade among EMU countries plus the United Kingdom, to decrease by ten points, from 47 percent in the early 80s to approximately 38 percent in 1996. "Variety is the spice of life" seems to have been the motto that guided integration among the European countries. Ability to choose from differentiated products to meet the same need. In reality, the actual inter-company trade conducted under the variety principle was stable, slightly below 20 percent of the total trade among the EMU countries. What developed in a substantial manner was the type of inter-company trade that benefited from qualitative differences among products; this differentiation in turn indicates differences in terms of technology and labour quality. A sort of specialization within the qualitative array of products that satisfy the same needs.[9]

Will monetary union enhance integration through the development of inter-company trade, be it spurred by variety or by qualitative differentiation, increasingly reducing the likelihood of asymmetric shocks hitting European countries, or will greater specialization pressures emerge, which will determine the major restructuring of productive sectors and the social unrest that always result from these changes?

As far as variety and preference distribution along the range of different qualities are concerned, there seems to be no reason for consumer tastes to change; which shifts the focus of the question on the evolution of the long-term integration will evolve on the supply side of the market and how consumer preferences will affect might affect the structure of the markets.

In the presence of the development of trade relations, some believe that the

---

[9] Cf. Rapport du CEPII (1998): Compétitivité des nations. Economica, Paris.

nature of the product-diversification process, which is the other side of inter-company trade, may increase the number of firms, while according to others it may lead to industry concentration.

In the first case, inter-company trade may continue to act as the medium of real integration; in the latter case, the medium might start taking on specialization features. The stability of the share of inter-company trade supported by horizontal (or variety-based) differentiation over the last few decades, compared to an increase of vertical (or quality-based) differentiation, seems to suggest that specialization might be a development mode that should not be neglected also in the case of growth of inter-company trade[10] .

But the evolution of productive technology and market structure will not be affected only by factors of a European nature; the broader international context will play a more important role.

Thus, it is highly likely that the push toward a greater productive inter-sector specialization among the different European areas will come, at some unspecified point in the future, especially from the restructuring of international markets, regardless of the specific effects of the monetary union. This might begin to show when emerging countries will have such developed industrial structures and internal markets as to start posing a major challenge for European products on the European market.

What will the political implications of an integration development along past lines, or through a greater production specialization, be?

If integration among the countries participating in the EMU takes place mainly through an increase in trade flows among participating countries more than through the integration of market structures and if, meanwhile, the external pressures of emerging countries show up in a sufficiently slow manner, this should constitute the long-term confirmation of the current European structure and of the current monetary union. This could be defined as the minimalist monetary-union hypothesis: one monetary policy but autonomous budget policies within the limits of the stability and growth pact. The different European Councils will continue to undertake commitments for the creation of more job opportunities and more uniform welfare policies, but they will hardly be binding. Each country will feel obliged to support its competitiveness to protect, through fiscal incentives and lower social costs, the existing national-market structures, in a systemic competition supported by microeconomic policies consistent with antitrust regulations.

If the further concentration of inter-company trade, as differentiated by quality, and if the external pressures exercised by emerging countries were to appear rather fast, along with the impulses toward a greater specialization of the different areas originated from within Europe, the restructuring of production might be more intense, and sector reorganization on a continental scale more widespread. The relocation of activities will become more important than the nationality of capital, to which Europeans seem to be still so strongly attached. Social unrest resulting from the more profound restructuring of production sectors and the greater probability of asymmetric

---

[10] For an in-depth analysis of these issues, see Rondi, L. and. Sembenelli, A. (1998): Integrazione economica e aggiustamento strutturale nelle industrie e nelle imprese europee. L'Industria, n.4.

shocks might lead toward a road that today's Euro-skeptics consider self-destructive for the European Union.

Self-destruction, however, is anything but a necessary implication. It will be a difficult transition; a tension due to the union's qualitative growth. If progress of the economic and monetary union is sufficiently advanced all this might constitute a hard-to-resist encouragement to take bolder steps toward a greater political integration first and toward a single nation later. The first medium of all this would be an increasingly important supranational budget policy designed to redistribute the costs of the production reallocation on a European scale. The objective of this reallocation would be to build a truly new continental economy and not simply to fit increasingly together economies with their own specific features.

The odds economists assign to the monetary union in the long-term is strongly related to the length of time involved in the evolution of the international markets' structure and to the chance that will be given to the countries of the monetary union to place firmer roots in the bigger domestic market (captive market).

The alternative indicated, so conflicting on the logical plane, will be much more vague in reality; it will be hard to perceive on a daily basis which of the two roads is being traveled on. For instance, the same concept of inter-company trade is not so clear-cut. Its existence may end up depending on the degree of sectorial disaggregation considered. Besides, how can actual specialization be separated from the accurate segmentation of final markets? The reorganization of sectors without barriers related to a local system efficiency or to local regulations will take place on a continental scale. It will be more difficult in this case to talk about specialization or inter-company trade among nations. Where such barriers continue to operate, competition will still be systemic and the terms specialization or inter-company trade will still make sense. Establishing firmer roots in a continental market will then take place through a mix of alliances and competition where enterprises and nations will act simultaneously and it will not be always possible to interpret it in terms of general principles.

The regional repercussions of such changes will complicate these developments. The integration of the economies might increase the regional disparities within the single countries[11] and raise the level of the resources to be devoted to the regions placed at a disadvantage by this process.

7. Integration within the EMU: Competition and Harmonization

It would be rather *naïve* to think that the EMU governments will be faced with a distinct choice between specialization and non-specialization. There will be swarms of little choices to lead us in one direction rather than another.

The current contrast between the harmonization of the fiscal and contribution systems and social spending standards on one side and the competitive challenge on the other may constitute the foundation to make one of the alternatives indicated more

---

[11] Cf Giannetti, M. (1998): The Effects of Integration on Regional Disparities: Convergence, Divergence or Both? Temi di Ricerca, n. 11, Ente per gli studi monetari, bancari e finanziari, Luigi Einaudi.

feasible than another.

As was noted before, currently the EMU does not have a foreign trade constraint that limits its growth. It has a problem in mobilizing its production potential, to be stimulated on the aggregate demand side, and, a more complex task, to be made more flexible in its ability to meet demand both in terms of both quality and composition. In other words, along with the pursuit of expansionary macroeconomic policies, one may wonder if the shared need to make the overall system more productive can be filled by having each country set its own objective, on the assumption that the if each country does its best to achieve it, the result for the entire area will also be the best.

In principle, the answer to this question depends on the degree of interference among the different countries' objectives. From the standpoint of the aggregate-demand stimulus there is no difficulty in acknowledging that isolated actions may create some difficulties for the single country, thereby letting other countries reap the rewards of its action. On the supply side, each country has enough room to erode specific existing inefficiencies. Over time, the problem might become that of the limits placed on the productivity level of the European sectors by production "duplications", by the necessary mobility of workers within the EMU and probably by the need of a lower wage uniformity among productive sectors.[12]

Given the need to govern steps that the single economies might and will have to take autonomously along the competition road, an objective to be adopted with a measure of foresight might be the search for a set of minimum common standards in the area of social benefits; this in order not to waste the opportunity to implement eventually common social policies, if the restructuring of the productive sectors begins exercising its effects.

There is no doubt that the road to common standards is very complex as the starting points are highly differentiated. It is common knowledge of how this is so for the social-spending share of the GDP. Also the revenue structure shows significant differences in its composition, as indicated in Table 1 below.

---

[12] As already mentioned in this paper, the development of intra-European trade has been focusing mostly on manufactured products aimed at satisfying the same demand; even though the increase in the trade of services, integration within and without Europe might have slowed the shift of Europe toward a service economy, holding back also their sectorial specialization. In other words, it might be said that the relatively low production concentration within the European manufacturing sector might involve "duplications" that result in a higher share of manufactured goods of the total output of tradable goods and services; presumably, this translates into a lower productivity level, but in a faster growth, for the manufacturing sector so that, overall, the average productivity of the European economic system has increased more than European real salaries. In the USA, for instance, the productive concentration in the manufacturing sector generated a higher productivity level, a composition of the economy's total output where the share of services (typically little tradable) is more significant and, finally a slower productivity growth of the entire economy, more capable of supporting an increase in employment levels. For more on this, see Cellini, R. and Onofri, P. (1998): La dinamica delle quote distributive negli Stati Uniti e in Europa: una nota. Moneta e Credito, December.

Table 1: Tax-revenue structure (1998 data, estimates; percentage of GDP).

	Direct taxation	Indirect taxation	Social contributions
France	10.0	15 .4	21.7
Germany	9.8	12.8	19.8
Italy	14.5	15.4	13.4
United Kingdom	14.1	16.4	6.5

This composition reflects in highly differentiated levels and structures of the tax and contribution wedge between net salaries and the cost of labour, as can be seen from Table 2. On the whole, the size of the wedge does not differ much among the different countries of Continental Europe, while it is much smaller in the United Kingdom. In France the financing of social expenditures is higher than in the other two continental countries and it is withheld directly from salaries, which makes it possible to limit taxes on other types of income. In Germany and in Italy this financing is more evenly distributed between taxes and contributions. The overall amount of the social contribution rate in the United Kingdom does not exceed one-third that of the other countries but the average gross salary in manufacturing exceeds the German one by 17% and the Italian one by 60%. Considering that the British GDP *per capita* is not greater than that of the other countries, it seems definitely unlikely that the productivity level of the manufacturing sector, even if computed on a purchasing-power-parity basis, is higher than that of the other countries considered. From this it can be inferred that in the United Kingdom individual responsibility in risk coverage is predominant over state paternalism.

One may wonder whether there are some differential effects in case these costs arise from contracts or from legislation. It could be argued that, in the first place, in case of costs arising from contracts they are the result of arm's length transactions whereby salary payments take place in many ways (mainly in the form of money but also in the form of insurance benefits or compulsory saving) and that, in the second place, by so doing, the cost for the enterprise matches more fully the benefit for the worker and is perceived more immediately. Furthermore, the higher disposable income available to workers may affect differently the propensity to consume.

Table 2: Tax and contribution wedge in the manufacturing sector (indices, rates and average annual values for 1998).

		France	Germany	Italy[a]	U.K.
Salary after taxes and contributions (single)	Index	71.8	58.4	75.2	75.32
Absolute value	*Euro*	*15716*	*15180*	*14288*	*23000*
Salary after taxes and contributions (dependent spouse and two children)	Index	79.0	70.1	82.9	75.32[b]
Absolute value	*Euro*	*17376*	*18230*	*15751*	*23000*
Salary after taxes and contributions (dependent spouse and two children) including family allowance	Index	85.9	80.0	90.5	81.31
Absolute value	*Euro*	*18891*	*20800*	*17201*	*248000*
Gross salary	Index	100	100	100	100
Absolute value	*Euro*	*22000*	*26000*	*19000*	*30500*
Compulsory or contractual saving: retirement and precautionary	rate	23.9	27	40.3	
(present and deferred compensation):	*Euro*	*27258*	*33020*	*26657*	
Social security system		16.5	20.3	32.7	
Company contributions to pension funds		6.9	6.5		
Employees' severance fund or precautionary saving			0.2	7.6	
Contribution to debt repayment to social security		0.5[e]			
Insurance " premiums":		31.1	27.4	15.2	
Contributions to health care system		7.1[f]	13.6	4.3	
Supplementary income fund			1.7		
Occupational injuries		23	1.5	3.7	
Unemployment		8.1	6.5	5.0	
Workers' disability		13.6	4.1[c]	2.2[c]	
Solidarity contributions		11.1		3.1	
Paid maternity leave		5.4		3.1	
Other benefits (housing, transportation, training)		5.7			
Total contributions		66.1	54.4	58.6	18.03
Paid by worker		21.0	21[g]	9.2	8.35
Paid by company		45.1[d]	33.4	49.4	9.67
Cost of labor	*Euro*	*31922*	*34684*	*28386*	*33476*
Tax and contribution wedge: Cost-of-labor-to-net salary ratio		2.02	2.28	1.99	1.46

[a] for companies with more than fifty employees.

[b] this figure does not include the tax credit households can obtain to cover 70 percent of the expenses incurred for children's health care up to a maximum of 12000 euros per annum.

[c] in the case of Germany this includes costs provided for by contract paid by the company for workers to continue receiving compensation in the event of sickness.; in the case of Italy, the mandatory rate indicated refers to blue-collar workers while for clerks disability insurance is paid entirely by the company.

[d] in case of workers with an income equal 1.2 times the SMIC the rate declines to 27.02; 1.1 times the SMIC the rate is 34.18; 1.2 times the SMIC the rate is 40.16; for compensation equal or greater than 1.3 times the SMIC the rates in the table apply.

[e] non-deductible from the worker's taxable income.

[f] 2.4 points are non tax-deductible.

[g] 27% of the social contributions paid by the workers for retirement purposes are non tax-deductible; in turn, 27% of pension payments received are tax-exempt.

Sources: compiled by Paolo Bosi and Paolo Onofri on data from Inps, French Ministry of Finance, German Ministry of Labour.

Also in the case of benefits provided by public institutions and financed by mandatory contributions, explaining the size of the contribution and the corresponding benefits in an adequately transparent manner would shed light on the utility that the worker associates with such benefits, thereby reducing the perceived size of the contribution wedge[13].

Concerning this, a specific feature of our country is the lower relative cost for workers than for enterprises; but if, in reality, there is an accurate perception of the value of the benefits corresponding to the contribution, this difference may lose its importance, as would also part of the differences in the compensation level of workers from different countries; these differences, in fact, could reflect also the different distribution between workers and enterprises and the different level of the contribution costs.

To this end, the transparent organization of contributions for the benefits they finance can not only help to define a salary that does not just have a monetary component, but also encourage the materialization of insurance markets or quasi-markets for the coverage of the risks workers are subject to in their activity. An attempt was made in Table 2 to present data in a way that would prompt such a recognition. First, the contributions to the social security system and to the different types of supplementary retirement income (compulsory retirement saving), or compulsory saving of a precautionary nature, were considered, in addition to the different benefits whose contributions might be in the shape of insurance "premiums": healthcare, supplementary income (where applicable), injury, unemployment.

Other contributions are based on the solidarity among workers, with reference to allowances for dependents (France and Italy), to training, transportation, housing etc. These are more tax deductions than actual contributions for the benefits that workers receive. They are not present in Germany as they are financed out of the general tax revenue.[14]

Although it would be difficult to apply, an elementary harmonization criterion would be to agree to finance with contributions withheld from salaries only the benefits related to occupational hazards. This might strengthen the insurance principle and

---

[13] A special instrument to achieve this transparency might be the restatement of workers' payroll stubs in a way that reflects the amount paid by the employer and the employee to the funds that provide the different benefits. In the Italian case, according to this writer, these should include only a few institutes such as the Employees' Retirement Fund, the Social Safety-Net Fund (not currently existing, but whose establishment is recommended), the Income Guarantee Fund in case of Sickness and the Fund for Payments to the Worker's Family, until it is charged on the general tax revenues. Moreover, in case of tax deductibility, this would show the worker the contribution made by the state to these Funds on the worker's or the enterprise's behalf in order to keep benefits unaltered. This need is less felt in the United Kingdom where the low contribution for the different benefits, including state pensions, is included under the only item, National Insurance Contributions (NICs).

[14] For accuracy's sake it would be appropriate to underline also the net salary in the case of workers with dependents, taking into account not only the tax deductions but also the family allowances.

would implicitly determine an indifference whether the benefit, which is mandatory anyway, is provided by the public or the private sector. Pursuing this principle should not necessarily imply the privatization of the provision of these benefits; it would require, instead, the repeal of the legislation that protects them thus making their provision contestable by the private sector.

Once more consistent insurance principles have been introduced (although still based on an allocation concept) a second principle to adopt could be their indexation to prices and not to real salaries. Thus, they would remain constant in real terms but would not partake in the fruits of technical progress. The adjustments of the real levels might result from periodic discretionary reviews, but not automatic. The discretionary indexation of benefits to future prosperity is a degree of freedom that might be appropriate to leave to future generations, given the burden they are being saddled with.[15]

If the tendency of the labor markets to become increasingly local in nature continues, the adoption of these general insurance principles to cover occupational hazards would require the EMU countries to adopt a uniform scheme to provide quasi-markets large enough to allow risk to be diversified. Also the development of welfare policies is becoming more local than national in nature; in this case, contrary to the previous one, the provision of benefits might be regulated at the local level to promote the relative standards of living in a context very close to the recipients of such entitlements.

8. The EMU's External Integration: Markets for Goods and Savings

So far we have considered the possible roads to integration within the monetary union and the consequences in terms of social expenditure. We will consider now how the very difficulties arising from some aspects of social security prompt the EMU to develop real and financial integration with the rest of the world. The EMU project was completed in an external context that had undergone many changes: when the Treaty of Rome was signed, the European economy was a developing one and world trade was limited by tariff barriers of approximately 14%.

Today Europe is a mature economy, with long-term growth rates that soon will reflect the population decrease and its relative ageing. Moreover, in 2002, when the individual national currencies finally disappear from the European citizens' wallets, external tariff barriers will be about 3%. Within the EMU countries, this is regarded as one of the main sources of macroeconomic uncertainty, although at the same time there is the perception that this progressive integration is inevitable in order to cope with the problems of population ageing.

The European economies are faced with the problem of population ageing, which is symbolically represented by the baby-boomer generations that will reach

---

[15] In making the quasi-markets for social benefits contestable, it should not be forgotten that these benefits in some cases cover macroeconomic risks that can only be diversified over time and among other idiosyncratic risks that might be more so, especially in view of a European dimension of these markets or quasi-markets.

retirement in the next decade. In the long run, these economies will experience a drastic reduction of the overall population, which will reflect on GDP growth.

Whatever the social and economic organization, the consumption of the elderly who do not work is subtracted from the current production of those who work and who relinquish it for some reason. They relinquish it as a result of a moral commitment, for instance, toward the extended family; or as a result of a generational compact whose provisions are implemented through the law (allocation system); or, they relinquish it because the elderly participate in the distribution of the profits generated by the productive activity (capitalization system).

The problem an economic system has to deal with as a result of the ageing of the population is then that of the reduction of the ratio of the average pension to the average output of the active population through both lower pension promises and a higher productivity of the production factors.

The effect of the different actions already taken on the parameters of the allocation systems of the European countries is the reduction of the average expected pension; instead, other actions such as the opening to the private sector for the provision of capitalization-based retirement products aim to increase current saving.

Starting from M. Feldstein in the mid-70s, the assumption is that a greater individual responsibility in defining one's own retirement expectations, through capitalization-based private pension funds, has a positive effect on the saving rate of the economic system. The greater saving rate will translate into a higher capital and thus into a higher labor productivity. The current generation will be compensated for the loss of welfare when it retires and the economic system will be able to pay on average a higher pension than might have done with a lower saving rate.

For this to happen, it is necessary for capital accumulation not to take place in decreasing returns. The discussions still open on endogenous growth do not make it possible to state with certainty that, in the long run, the greater saving accumulation does not occur in decreasing returns. To this end, one might wonder whether in some European countries the saving rate is not already sufficiently high as to risk a dynamic inefficiency condition in the event of a further increase.

The way out of savings' decreasing returns for European countries is to invest in low-capital countries, where returns might be higher. The existence of countries with different capital endowments and at different development stages enables, in other words, generations currently active in the European countries to mortgage part of the product that the future generations of emerging countries will produce.

Given the uncertainty of the distribution between labor and capital in the next decades, European workers have begun diversifying the risk related to the distribution share with which the redistribution of consumption will take place in the next decades. The growing integration of the international capital markets and investments in the emerging countries are the channels to achieve such diversification. This in turn requires also international agreements on the regulation of capital flow toward less developed economies to avoid an excessive interference on them and, at the same time, to reduce the risk for European investors.

9. Globalization and Social Cohesion: Epilogue

Briefly, European countries are looking on the one hand for low-cost workers so as to be able to afford current consumption through the development of trade (imports), but feel threatened by this, and on the other they are searching for younger future generations with which to share consumption in the next few decades through international capital markets.

Both these situations increase the risk associated with European citizens' income. In the first case, the uncertainty affects salaries; in the second, capital returns. Given the experience of the past few decades, middle-aged middle-income Europeans are not used to a high endogenous microeconomic uncertainty. Both the constant pressure of the standard of living and the enlargement of general welfare systems have been working so far to counteract the causes and the effects of microeconomic uncertainty.

In order to reconcile growth and social cohesion, the European socio-political systems should limit the distorted effects of social protection measures and, at the same time, they should be ready to apply them on a larger scale because the individual likelihood to use them might increase. In other words the type of compensation welfare that European countries have strongly developed has actually been used so far only by marginal groups of the population, while the majority availed itself of a job security, and the protection related to it, the like of which will hardly be seen again. Social protection systems will have to make provisions to cover risks the European population is not used to dealing with, especially in view of its relative ageing which, in addition, makes it increasingly risk-avert.

In planning these institutions there will be two limits. In their operations they have to mobilize resources for the social coverage of individual risks in keeping with inter-temporal budget constraints (i.e. limit the commitments made on behalf of future generations), but they have also to be sure that the withdrawal and disbursement systems are not a disincentive to accept the challenges posed by the markets and that are at the very foundation of the risks to which the population is exposed.

The traditional channels to build consensus in European societies through the representation of categories and interests have been shaken by these trends. At times, their survival seems incompatible with the decision-making fragmentation that markets seem to impose and with the assumption of the investment risk that the diversification of the risk involving future pensions seems to require. This shows an inconsistency between the new consensus mechanisms and unions which suggests that things are going to be rather difficult for the latter. Presently, continental Europe cannot dispense with such consensus channels and is choosing a more complex alternative; that of having the unions and other representative groups internalize the new objectives, by offering them the possibility to govern the transformation process and the opportunity to define another area of common rights which might constitute a new vehicle for a European identity.

It is an ambitious objective which seems to assume again the form of a political tradeoff, this time at the continental level, between a little more deregulation of the labor market and the defense of some institutes of the general welfare systems. In any case, this requires that the entire social protection system be rid of abuses and privileges, to save effective solidarity components. Middle-income groups will have to cope with additional burdens or accept lower supports to their current income in the presence of a coverage of the risks arising from a greater uncertainty in their careers.

Their temptation to take matters in their own hands is very strong; shifting the coverage of such risks (including going through a hard life in retirement) from the sphere of political decisions back to that of individual decisions (market) in fact gives the impression of being able to incur lower costs and obtain better results. Europe's non-social right is riding this temptation of the middle classes because it feels that this is the proper way to mitigate the different intra- and inter-generational conflicts, the solutions of which require a parliamentary vote, through a slow rise of the prices that will have to be paid and/or a slow decrease of the benefits "purchased". Thus, setting those prices (corresponding to the determination of contributions and benefits) would be removed from the political arena and brought into real and financial markets, only to go back in case of changes that generate social unrest.

Thus, within the new social market economy, new instruments of the general welfare gain acceptance if the benefits they provide are produced efficiently, if the costs related to them are distributed fairly and if the different legislation levels which regulate them do not neglect exceedingly the subsidiarity principle.

Efficiency may require a more active role of the private sector in the production of benefits. A fair distribution of the costs may entail the extension of the information citizens have to provide on their financial conditions to activate an adequate means-test and, apparently, a greater encroachment by public powers.

The political difficulties to act along these lines will vary among the different European countries, depending on the different entitlement levels that each established in the past for its middle class. In this sense, Italian middle-income groups received in the past some entitlements that were beyond the European norm: low taxation, generous pension promises, regardless of the contributions made, low health care contribution (4-5% compared to 13.6% in Germany) no means-tests (compared to strict and accurate requirements in the United Kingdom, Germany etc.), higher returns on government securities, long the main investment vehicle for medium-to-high income groups, than in other European countries, in real terms as well.

In conclusion, the socio-political difficulties indicated are those that Europe will face in seeking to raise its productive capacity. This increase is dictated by the need to deal in a less confrontational way with the ageing of its population on a social plane. Such increase requires that European productions be repositioned and product markets be restructured. The competition among the nation-economies of the EMU will have a reduced function in this long-run process and will involve, at the beginning, mainly the spur to erode those areas of differential inefficiency that exist among the countries; the harmonization of the tax, contribution and benefit systems is a process that can only take place in the long run, though it will have to begin promptly, starting from a set of common policies that make the markets for benefits contestable to end up with a larger supranational budget that might redistribute the socio-political burden of the necessary production reallocations.

Acknowledgements

I would like to thank Paolo Bosi for allowing me to utilize parts of a common paper on the structure of the tax and contribution wedge, and Lucia Lambertini for some discussions on the theoretical roots of market differentiation. Neither is responsible for the use of the material presented or for the ideas expressed herein.

12. Globalization and Social Equity

Ferruccio Marzano

When dealing with problems of "Globalization and social equity", first let us make reference to the case of Europe. In terms of goals of economic policy, we can identify five (or six) objectives in comparison with at least five (or six) instruments of intervention. As for objectives, we usually have: the full utilization of labour; the real growth of the economy; monetary (and exchange rate) stability; the respect of balance in foreign payments; the fulfillment of social security (or social protection). As for instruments, we may have: fiscal policy; monetary (and exchange rate) policy; incomes policy; productivity policy (or the supply-side policies); the regulation of the labour market; measures of protection in the field of the so-called "rights of social citizenship" (which has given shape to the *Welfare State* or social security system).

In particular – whatever has been in the past the capacity of the European economies to "realize" the attainment of one or more of their policy goals by the maneuvering of one or more of the instruments – in our days we find that we need to "manage" a situation influenced by the following novelties of the global type: 1) the oil shocks; 2) the fiscal crisis of the State; 3) the technological revolution; 4) the ageing of the population; 5) the macroeconomic re-equilibrium bringing about high unemployment and recessive tendencies in many countries; 6) the "disaffection" towards the public sector that usually provides welfare-type services by means of a bureaucratically elephantine structure.

Hence, in Europe, we find ourselves in the presence of the crisis of the preceding socio-economic model; and this takes place in a context in which, at the productive level, the tendency towards the "international division of labour" becomes increasingly more pronounced, dictated by the changing specialization of production and by increasing international exchanges of the intra-industrial type. However, the resulting incentive for a profound restructuring of the productive sector – owing to "pressures" from the technological revolution – has not produced a positive trend in employment nor conditions in which (as it is said) "social cohesion" is guaranteed.

At this point, one could go on[1] to only evaluate the proposal for the European economies of the harmonization at the Union level of fiscal policy and of social protection policy versus the simpler coordination between such policies that are then carried out, so to say, at the national level.

It seems to me, however, that there are four, not two, hypotheses to consider. In fact, the harmonization versus decentralization (with possible coordination) hypothesis can concern "the re-dimensioning" or "the reform of the rules" as far as the action of the Welfare State is concerned; but, moreover, the hypotheses of harmonization versus decentralization can also refer to "the liberalization" or "the restructuring and reformulation of the rules" as to the so-called flexibility of the labour market[2]. Therefore, at one extreme we find the re-dimensioning of the Welfare State

---

[1] This is what P. Onofri does in his paper in this volume.

[2] On this see, among others, Bean, C. et al. (1995) and (1998).

together with the liberalization of the labour market, at another extreme the reform of the Welfare State together with the reformulation of the rules in the labour market, and so on as for the possible intermediary cases.

It thus seems to me that any proposal concerning the "future" of the Welfare State in Europe should be elaborated, discussed, and brought forward not in an isolated manner, but contextually with proposals relative to the functioning of the labour market, and vice versa.

As for the implications of the current technological revolution (electronics and telematics) for the employment situation in Europe[3], I maintain that – more than a three-sector model of the type "primary sector-manufacturing sector (of tradable goods)-tertiary sector (of untradable goods)" – it would be more convincing to have a model of the type "primary/manufacturing sector-sector of traditional services-sector of advanced and personalized services". In fact, if we are interested in the relationships of complementarity or of substitutability between job stability and the degree of "completeness" of social protection, it seems to me that the problem should be looked at not so much in terms of relations between the private sector (which produces tradable goods and services) and the public sector (which produces untradable goods and services), but instead at a different type of relationship. It seems to me that – whereas both the private sector and the manufacturing one are notoriously and strongly "hit" by the current technological transformations – the tertiary sector also needs to be "disaggregated" between that area that, by producing "traditional" services, is equally "shocked" by the transformations and those sectors which, by producing personalized and advanced services, are not.

In my opinion, in the first of these two productive areas there is no "protection" of jobs that will be effective, while social security continues to make complete sense; in the second area, certain rules of "protection" in the labour market continue to make sense while the social security makes less sense in comparison with the first area. Actually, in the second case we are not really concerned with "social protection" to be understood in the sense of the Welfare State, but as "social cohesion" connected to the diffusion of the so-called Welfare community[4].

It is here that a role for the so-called third sector will establish itself, in particular as to the development of that archipelago of non profit activities capable of providing personalized services. In such activities consistent new job opportunities can be realized, as well as a new way and type of social security will be based on principles of relationships, of reciprocity, and of solidarity, instead of being provided by the public sector .

Generally speaking, though, in consideration of the strong current push for the globalization of production (as well as that of markets, about which particular reference must be made to the increasingly dominant international financial markets), any hypotheses or solutions to be followed for the policy of social protection, together with those to be followed for the "functioning" of the labour market, in the European economies, must take into account the huge problems of the functioning of the labour market and of the protection of social security needs in the developing countries too.

---

[3] More generally on this, see OCDE (1998).

[4] On this, see Centro per lo studio della dottrina sociale della Chiesa (1997) and Lorenzetti, L. (ed.) (1998); more generally, see Marzano, F. (1998).

Such problems, in addition to the goal of economic development, are becoming urgent in the so-called "emerging" countries and above all in the vast world of the less developed ones.

In my way of thinking, that which we should be primarily concerned with is certainly not the so-called problem of the avoidance of social dumping, but the much more "pregnant" problem of anyhow providing at least a minimum protection in the field of labour conditions and of social security and the defense of human rights that, contextually with the measures for economic development, cannot help but see the international community committed in cooperating in the effort. Moreover, instead of reasoning in terms of problems of the protection of labour and social security in Europe in the context of economic globalization, I think we have to reason in terms of economic and social coordination, or better of cooperation, that sees the "rich" countries of the North of the world taking responsibility for a large range of problems of the "poor" countries of its South. Therefore, more than thinking in terms of the globalization of production, there is need to think in terms of "globalization of labour conditions and social protection" (or "globalization of solidarity", as Pope John Paul II has recently stated[5]). Furthermore, this is recommendable not only for ethical motives, but also for economic reasons, since we must realize that measures for nutritional assistance, health, and education of vast populations of the earth can be looked at as a real contribution to economic development. Any such initiatives are to be seen as productive activities in the countries of the "third world" and, thus, they will make a contribution to the economic growth of the entire international community.

Actually, the industrial development of "poor" countries is always to be taken as an uttermost aim in the present conditions of the world economy. However, what is required for the purpose is the genuine creation of net additional industrial capacity, factories, and firms, since so many different countries are in need of an intensive and stable process of modern economic growth. On the contrary, one cannot understand and accept a sort of "war between poor people" which would come up as a consequence of a dis-placement of plants and factories from one place to another, thus creating unemployment and distress in some places whereas new, but likely temporary, employment and industrialization are brought about in other places[6].

This is particularly objectionable when such displacements take place from one to another underdeveloped or developing country – as it has recently been the case with an American medium-sized firm in the field of the production of tennis shoes which is reported to have moved its factories from North America to Indonesia first and then from Indonesia to Vietnam in the time span of few months, just because of small differences in the wage costs per worker per day. But displacements of existing plants and factories from one area to another are also globally inefficient, if one looks at global efficiency ´– as it should be done – from a social viewpoint, in those cases in which the transfer takes place from previously industrialized to industrializing countries. Then, what really is needed in the "Northern" world, vis-à-vis the "Southern" world's needs, is an overall change in the patterns of consumption and in the international specialization of production, so that certain sectors and the respective employment be localized in the "advanced" countries and certain other sectors and the

---

[5] See Giovanni Paolo II (1994) and (1998).

[6] More generally on this, see Dunning, J.H. (1993) and Wood, A. (1994).

relative jobs be created in the "backward" countries.

Furthermore, it is strongly needed that substantial and stable flows of medium-term and long-term capital be directed from the same "rich" countries to the "poor" ones, in order that the latter countries scarce resources be supplemented with the inflows of resources taken from the surpluses of the former countries. This could be realized just because such surpluses are actually available in rich countries, but the proper "conditions" should obtain.

Hence, globalization of production is to be looked at unfavourably, in particular (so to say) from an ethically motivated point of view, if it means – as it is usually the case – that firms are intended to be fully "autonomous" in the choices and decisions to move their productive capacity from one place to another at any rate and time. In fact, the negative effects on the wealth and welfare of different people seem to abundantly overcome the positive effects which would accrue to firms as higher private short-run profits. This is so if there are no constraints or guarantees as to any "integration" of firms's decisions within an overall, long-run, coordinated action which – on the contrary – should be realistically undertaken, in support of the urgent development needs of so many "poor" countries in the world, without, though, any unrealistic "burdens" on the general living conditions in "rich" countries.

As for the globalization of finance[7], again it is to be looked at unfavourably as it is usually intended to be the process of massive and absolutely free movements of capital funds (which can even take the form of a certain movement of funds in one direction and an instantaneous subsequent movement back in the opposite direction) from one economy to another one, and more specifically from one to another financial or stock market of the world, having the following main features.

First and generally speaking, those are not meant to be medium-term or long-term capital movements, and so they do not concern the transfer of real resources, available in the surplus countries, to be utilized for growth purposes by the deficit countries, and in particular for growth purposes by the developing countries who specifically need such additional resources for stable periods of time. On the contrary, it is a question of the international movements of short-term capital, often of very short-run funds, actually of the movements of the so called "hot money", which are linked to the progressive "finanziarization" of the world economy and for which the monetarist and neoliberalist doctrines claim the absolute and complete freedom of action to be "exercized" at any rate and time.

Secondly and particularly, it must be underlined that the international "hot money" movements refer to speculative operations on foreign financial assets which, nowadays, more and more consist of the so called derivative assets or derivatives and, even, of derivatives from derivatives or the so called "synthetic assets". Now, it is known that, in general, financial assets may well "live their own life", in so far as their prices, values and returns may display a proper behaviour, quite independently from that of the "underlying" real investments. It goes without saying, then, that financial assets such as derivative and synthetic assets are to be taken as very far "removed" from any real phenomenon, and hence that real phenomena are far removed from such financial assets, in spite of the really fanciful contrary tenets subscribed by monetarist and neoliberalist theories according to which financial markets behaviour and trends

---

[7] On this, see inter alia Obstfeld, M. (1998).

always are "governed" by the well-known fundamentals, that is real phenomena, of an economy.

How much such a situation, which had been prevailing in the international financial markets for some years, rightly had to be seen as an increasing source of volatility and instability of such markets – as well as of sudden, enormous, concentrated, enrichments for some wealthy speculators, but also of "equivalent" impoverishments for others – has been understood and affirmed by some of us, mainly brought up in the Keynesian "tradition", for a long time. This opinion has now received a strong "support" from the recent and heavy "turbolences" in those markets, in particular in the case of the so called "emergent" capital markets of several industrializing countries in the Far East, Latin America, and Eastern Europe, in the last couple of years.

On the other hand, most economists and "observers", and not only those "entrenched" on monetarist and neoliberalist positions but even several "liberal-minded" colleagues, did not subscribe such critical opinions which – allow me to repeat the point – were maintained by the few of us who have never "defaulted" from a realist and open approach to economics and economic problems. Anyhow, the "contrary", monetarist and neoliberalist, opinion was based on two sets of arguments, neither of which, though, I am convinced I can show to be "well-grounded".

First, there was the "general" argument that freedom of markets is always to be an overall aim in itself. In particular, that would have to be the case as to international movements for all kinds of capital funds, since also the very short-run financial capital movements and even the "hot money" ones would provide alternative "uses of funds", in and out of different (domestic and foreign) assets, such as to be able to "furnish" the right signals with respect to the behaviour of the fundamentals or the "underlying" real variables of any economy. Secondly, the monetarist and neoliberalist very favourable positions to absolute freedom for all kinds of international capital movements, even for the extreme speculative ones, were motivated on the basis of the fact that it is true that – as I mentioned above – the sudden and substantial gains which may be realized in the financial markets do tend to be concentrated in the hands of few and rich agents, mainly speculators who act on behalf of different groups of "institutional investors" belonging to rich countries. But – the argument goes – such enrichments for some agents in some instances would then be (more or less) compensated by "corresponding" impoverishments for roughly the same agents at some other times; and so, any "speculative" movements of international financial capital will have performed their "function" at roughly no net cost for the general "people of investors" or for the economy concerned.

However, in my opinion, both lines of arguments can and must be "reasonably" and "easily" rebutted in the following ways.

As to the first argument, it is the case that – as several great "anti-monetarist" economists, like (to mention only the greatest ones) Wicksell, Schumpeter, Kalecki, and Keynes, specifically argued, contrary to the monetarists's tenets according to which money and credit are only to be seen as a "veil", even if (I may add) they may well be like a very "thick veil" so that some agents can make high gains from their management – financial flows are meant to play two specific and essential roles. These are the role of "transmitting" real resources (of which finance gives the "nominal" value) from surplus sectors that do not "use" them to deficit sectors that are in their "need", particularly for investment reasons, and at times also the role of "anticipating" the formation of real resources through the process of creation of financial funds which are needed by entrepreneurs for investment and production purposes "in advance" and which will be "counterbalanced" by the later formation of real saving with the agents who have taken advantage of the investment and production processes previously financed.

But these two processes have nothing to do with the continuous, instantaneous, speculative "in-takes" and "out-takes" of financial funds which are only looking for short-run gains and profits, are purely concerned with the "nominal" value of assets, and hence are specifically interested in "chasing" such assets that, the farther their values are "removed" from the behaviour of the "underlying" real magnitudes, the higher the levels of gains that they may provide will be. This is because, with such assets, the interplaying of speculative forecasts and forces will be stronger, hence the behaviour of asset prices will be more and more "autonomous", both in the favourable and the unfavourable cases, and the same will be true of the behaviour of capital gains. Really, one cannot understand how it is that – starting from such premises – monetarists and neoliberalists still maintain that, in any financial market, the predominant forces are represented, after all, by the fundamentals of the real economy, that is by the behaviour of production, real saving and real investment.

As to the second argument, it is true that professional speculators make gains and losses which, by and large, do compensate themselves over time. But surely this is not the case as far as "small" savers and investors are concerned who are usually induced to "gamble" on the stock and financial markets by the ascending and descending waves in assets prices (which, instead, are mainly "led" by professional speculators) without having the expertise to play their "autonomous" games, thus always buying assets in the case of positive waves and selling assets in the case of negative waves. It follows that they are "compelled" to enter the markets in the first situation and again "forced" to leave the markets in the second one, thus usually incurring heavy losses in conditions of "turbolences" and "crises" on the markets which are unlikely to be compensated by their "normal" earnings in conditions of tranquillity.

Such two points become particularly relevant ones in the case of developing countries, both owing to the more volatile and less efficient "working" of their financial markets and, mainly, because of the fact that their greater "need" of funds does bring them to offer "direct" assets – that is to say those assets which are "representative" of real investments and which constitute the "underlying" basis for the calculation of derivatives – with higher returns. These, however, may not, or at any rate not always, be regularly paid owing to the less stable and profitable process of capital accumulation and thus to the more risky behaviour of profits. The recent heavy financial crises in such different, but all "emerging", economies such as the Far East "tigers", Russia, or Brazil – as already hinted at above – give the points I have intended to argue a "sad" support.

In conclusion, globalization of finance does not at all seem to be able to "pass the test" of a comprehensive argument which attempts to be both careful in analysing finance's trends and consequences on the economic front as well as watchful in ascertaining its implications for the welfare of the different "actors" in the scene.

Actually, in this case perhaps more than in other instances, my conclusion cannot but be that its negative aspects and effects come to exceed by far the positive ones[8]. This is particularly so if we pursue the further crucial consideration that, since globalization of finance "demands" absolute and full freedom of action for any kind of international capital movements in any country and we know that shortsightedness and egoism of all sorts bring people to concentrate their choices on activities which "promise" to bring about immediate and substantial gains, it will be a specifically dangerous form of globalization for the less developed economies of the world as it is at the present. In this respect, full account is to be taken not only of the previous arguments I have tried to make, but also of the fact (already underlined above) that, in the "working" of continuously widening and deepening financial markets all over the world, a really "excessive" amount of real resources come to be assigned to the sheer "functioning" of the international capital movements of any kind, so that the amount left for the process of real accumulation and development will certainly be reduced.

References

Bean, C. et al. (1995): Unemployment: Choices for Europe, 5th Monitoring European Integration Report. CEPR, London.

Bean, C. et al. (1998): Social Europe: One for All? 8th Monitoring European Integration Report. CEPR, London.

Centro per lo Studio della Dottrina Sociale della Chiesa (1997): Scienze sociali e Dottrina sociale della Chiesa. Supplemento al Quaderno no. 4, Università Cattolica del Sacro Cuore, Milano.

Dunning, J.H. (1993): Multilateral Enterprise and the Global Economy. Addison Wesley, Reading Mass.

Giovanni Paolo II (1994): Tertio Millennio Adveniente. Libreria Editrice Vaticana, Rome.

Giovanni Paolo II (1998): Messaggio per la Celebrazione della Giornata Mondiale della Pace. Libreria Editrice Vaticana, Roma.

Lorenzetti, L. (ed.) (1998): Forum: Welfare State. Verso una Welfare Society. Rivista di Teologia Morale, XXX/117.

Marzano, F. (1998): Economia ed Etica: Due mondi a confronto. Saggi di Economia ed Etica dei Sistemi Sociali. Ed. A.V.E. Roma.

Obstfeld, M. (1998): The Global Capital Network: Benefactor or Menace? Journal of Economic Perspectives, XII/4.

OCDE (1998): Les technologies du XXIe siècle. Paris.

Wood, A. (1994): North-South Trade, Employment and Inequalities. Clarendon Press, Oxford.

World Bank (1999): World Development Report, Washington D.C.

---

[8] More generally on this, see World Bank (1999).

13. Multinational Corporations and Global and International Models of Pension Provision: Evidence from Ireland

Gerard Hughes

F 23

J 32

1. Introduction

In the debate about globalisation there are optimistic and pessimistic views about its effects on employment and conditions of work. Optimists believe foreign direct investment brings with it many employment opportunities and higher wages. Pessimists argue that it increases downward pressures on wages, conditions of employment, and social protection. Evidence on the effects of globalisation on wages, employment conditions, and social protection is limited (see Betcherman 1996). This may be because most of the countries in the Triad of North America, the European Economic Area, and Japan, which account for the bulk of foreign direct investment, do not distinguish in their statistics between domestic and foreign companies. Hirst and Thompson (1996a and 1996b) cite research by Lipsey, Blomstrom and Ramstetter (1995) which shows that the share of production by multinational corporations outside their home countries amounted to only 7 per cent of world output in 1990 and UNCTAD research which shows that the Triad accounted for 75 per cent of the stock of foreign direct investment and 60 per cent of the flow at the beginning of the 1990s.

Ireland has pursued a policy of attracting foreign direct investment for a period of almost 40 years and the activities of foreign firms now account for a significant proportion of its national output and employment. Consequently, there is statistical information available for Ireland which sheds light on the effects of multinational corporations on employment and conditions of work. In addition to presenting this evidence, we will use the results of a national survey of occupational pension schemes for employees of foreign and Irish companies to investigate whether foreign firms behave like transnational or multinational corporations in their relationship with their employees in the host country. The relevance of occupational pension schemes to the globalisation debate is that they are provided on a voluntary basis either at the instigation of the employer or through collective agreements with trade unions.

Foreign direct investment has been a feature of industrial policy in Ireland since the 1930s when protectionist measures were adopted to encourage industrialisation through import substitution. In order to protect access to the Irish market U.K. companies undertook direct investment in Ireland through partnership

---

* I am using Hirst and Thompson's (1996) distinction between transnational corporations operating in a globalised economy and multinational companies operating in an international economy.

arrangements with Irish companies. The failure of protection to develop an efficient industrial base led to the adoption of free trade policies and the removal of restrictions on foreign ownership in the 1950s. Some of the U.K. companies which invested in Ireland during the protectionist era continued to operate plants in Ireland to take advantage of the new policy of providing investment grants and a zero corporate tax rate on profits from manufacured exports. Since the late 1960s a considerable amount of foreign investment in Ireland has been in technologically advanced products for export in such sectors as electronics, office machinery, pharmaceuticals, and medical instuments and equipment. The gradual opening of the Irish economy to foreign trade since 1960 is clearly shown in Figure 1. From 1960 to 1973 national output exported increased from around 22 to 24 per cent. Since 1973 the percentage exported has doubled to its present level of 48 per cent.

Since Ireland joined the European Community in 1973 it has increased its attractiveness for foreign companies by providing access to the European market. The importance of this can be seen from the export statistics in Table 1. In 1974 firms of non-EC origin located in Ireland accounted for 58 per cent of the exports of grant-aided foreign owned manufacturing firms. By 1989 non-EC firms accounted for 82 per cent of such exports. The destinations of exports have also changed greatly (see Figure 2). In 1974 grant-aided foreign firms sent 40 per cent of their exports to the UK and 23 per cent to other EC countries. By 1989 the positions had reversed with 23 per cent of exports of grant-aided foreign firms going to the UK and 39 per cent to other EC countries.

Table 1: Manufacturing exports from Ireland of non-EC firms, 1974 and 1989.

Year	Exports of grant-aided non-EC firms/Exports of grant-aided foreign manufacturing firms	Exports of grant-aided foreign manufacturing firms to EC excluding UK	Exports of grant-aided foreign manufacturing firms to UK foreign firms.
1974	57.6	23.1	38.9
1989	82.1	49.3	22.9

Sources: O'Malley (1998).
Note: The figures for 1989 refer to all foreign firms.

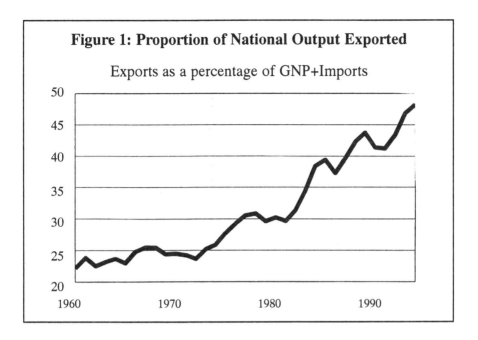

The impact of foreign direct investment on the Irish economy has been very favourable in terms of employment. Table 2 shows the growth in employment in Irish-owned and foreign-owned firms in manufacturing since 1980. Total manufacturing employment fell by nearly 17 per cent between 1980 and 1988. The bulk of this decrease was due to a fall of almost a quarter in employment in Irish-owned firms. Employment in foreign-owned firms fell by only 7 per cent during this period. Since 1988 there has been a strong recovery in manufacturing employment as the number at work has increased by almost 18 per cent. Both Irish-owned and foreign-owned firms have contributed to this growth with employment in Irish-owned firms rising by nearly 9 per cent and employment in foreign-owned firms increasing by 30 per cent. The growth in manufacturing employment in Ireland in Irish-owned and foreign-owned firms since 1988 has been remarkable by international standards, as O'Malley (1998) points out.

Table 2: Permanent full-time manufacturing employment, 1980-97

Year	Irish-owned	Foreign-owned	Total
1980	143,300	88,400	231,700
1988	110,918	82,381	193,299
1997	120,700	107,173	227,873

Sources: O'Malley (1998)

The annual average percentage change in manufacturing employment in Ireland during the period 1988-96 was 1.5 per cent. In Japan there was no growth in manufacturing employment during this period and the United States, Australia, the United Kingdom, the 15 countries of the European Union and Canada all suffered job losses in manufacturing ranging from 0.6 to 2 per cent per annum.

The strong increase in manufacturing employment in Ireland was accompanied by a gradual increase in output per person employed relative to the European average since Ireland joined the European Union in 1973 (see Figure 3). However, there was little improvement in living standards per head of population because of high dependency ratios up to 1990. Since then falling dependency ratios and strong output growth has increased Ireland's GNP per head of population from 62 per cent of the European average to 90 per cent, thus almost closing the gap between Ireland and other EU countries. The strong increase in living standards in the 1990s has been accompanied by a significant decrease in unemployment. In the period 1985-90 the average unemployment rate was 16 per cent. It fell to 12.3 per cent in the period 1995-97 (see Bradley, 1998).

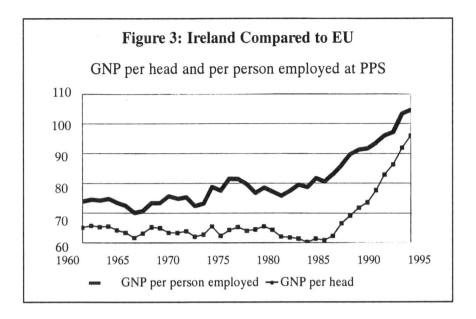

Figure 3: Ireland Compared to EU

GNP per head and per person employed at PPS

Legend: GNP per person employed — GNP per head

Foreign firms have made a significant contribution to this improvement in living standards as their skill levels are higher than in domestic firms. Measuring skill level by the proportion of staff working in technical and administrative jobs shows that 19 per cent of those employed in foreign dominated sectors in manufacturing work in such jobs compared with 14 per cent for all manufacturing sectors. One consequence of the higher skill level in foreign firms is that "the average wage in foreign industry (£16,000 in 1993) is approximately 25% higher than in indigenous industry", as Barry and Bradley (1997, p. 1802) point out.

2. Global and International Models of Pension Provision

Occupational pension schemes have existed in Ireland in the public sector since the foundation of the State in 1921. Their growth in the private sector of the economy dates from the 1960s when employment in industry began to increase and employment in agriculture continued to decrease (see Hughes, 1994). McCarthy, O'Brien and Dowd (1975) point out that: "Because most [wage] rounds in the sixties took the form of flat rate cash increases the wage structure was steadily compressed during that period." This probably created an environment in which trade unions could bargain with employers over the introduction of occupational pension schemes. What made this an attractive option for trade unions was that they could maintain solidarity on the pay front while negotiating an increase in the total compensation package by deferring the non-pay part until it could be realised in the form of pension benefits during retirement. For employers such schemes were attractive because they provided a means by which they could reduce the turnover of skilled employees and terminate their employment at a specified age without difficulty when their productivity declined. The schemes which emerged from the bargaining process were funded and they provided pension benefits for employees which were a defined percentage of pre-retirement pay. The government promoted the development of occupational pension schemes by giving generous tax reliefs on pension contributions and on the investment income of pension funds.

Irish firms which provide occupational pension schemes use them to ensure that their skilled employees will spend most of their working life with them. Consequently it makes sense for them to offer a defined benefit scheme which will give pension benefits equal to a specified percentage of pre-retirement earnings. Most defined benefit schemes will provide an income during retirement equal to two-thirds of pre-retirement earnings if the employee works for 40 years with the same firm. Foreign firms may have a looser attachment to the Irish economy than domestic firms so they do not necessarily expect that their skilled employees will spend most of their working life with them. The kind of occupational pension scheme which they are likely to provide for their employees may depend on whether they regard themselves as transnational or multinational corporations. Hirst and Thompson (1996, pp. 8-9) compare the kinds of behaviour which may be expected by companies which regard themselves as operating in a globalised economy or an international economy. In an international economy the main actors are national economies. Multinational companies "retain a clear national home base; they are subject to the national regulation of the mother country, and by and large they are effectively policed by that country". In such an economy multinational companies are likely to adapt their labour relations to the model which prevails in the host country or the mother country and to set up defined benefit occupational pension schemes. Since transnational corporations can shift their business relatively easily from one country to another they ought to have a strong preference for defined contribution schemes. Defined contribution schemes are designed to cater for a workforce which does not have long-term ties with the employer. They offer mobile companies a means of providing pensions at low cost and of transferring many of the risks associated with occupational pension provision to employees. Transnational companies which see themselves as operating in a globalised economy have a strong preference for corporate control. Hence, they may be expected to resist the imposition of controls by national governments or trade unions, as Hirst and Thompson (1996) point out. Consequently, they could be expected to have a policy of not recognising the right of trade unions to bargain for the work force.

3. Evidence from the National Survey of Occupational Pensions in Ireland

The idealised global and international economy models developed by Hirst and Thompson enable us to derive hypotheses about the kind of occupational pension schemes likely to be provided by transnational and multinational corporations which can be tested using Irish data. The evidence which is available which is relevant to these hypotheses relates to differences which should exist between foreign and Irish firms in the provision of pension schemes, in the type of employment they offer, in pension coverage rates, in relationships with trade unions, in the categories of workers covered by pension schemes, and in the type of occupational pension plan provided.

A national survey of occupational pension schemes was carried out in Ireland in 1995 by the Economic and Social Research Institute for the Department of Social Welfare and the Pensions Board (see Hughes and Whelan 1996). Evidence from this survey will be used to test the applicability to pension provision of the global and international economy models. The survey was intended to establish how many employers provide an occupational pension scheme for their employees and the nature, scope and extent of pension coverage. All employing organisations in the private and public sectors of the economy were included in the survey. For private and commercial public sector firms the sample was drawn from the Dun and Bradstreet list of 18,000 firms. These firms come from all sectors of the economy and they employ about three quarters (730,000) of all employees in the non-agricultural labour force. The sample for the non-commercial sector was drawn from the ESRI's list of all public sector organisations which employed the remaining quarter of non-agricultural employees (276,000). The list of employers was classified by firm size and industry and a stratified random sample was drawn. The stratification gave the larger firms a higher probability of being selected than the smaller firms. This ensured that valid conclusions could be drawn about the population of firms and the pension schemes they operated. Questionnaires were sent by post to 1,176 firms. Allowing for firms which had gone out of business or which turned out to be subsidiaries of other firms in the sample the valid sample was 1,064 firms and the response rate from these was 61 per cent. This response rate is somewhat above that normally achieved for a postal survey and it allows statistically valid inferences to be made about the population from which the sample is drawn.

Table 3 shows how many Irish and multinational firms provide occupational pension schemes for their employees and how many do not. Of the 145 multinational firms in our sample 121, or 83 per cent, have a pension scheme. The corresponding figure for Irish firms is 50 per cent. On the face of it multinational firms appear more likely to provide a pension scheme than domestic firms. However, this is mainly due to the fact that multinational firms are larger, on average, than Irish firms. Comparing pension provision in large multinational and Irish firms shows that 93 per cent of multinational firms employing 100 or more workers have a pension scheme while the corresponding figure for Irish firms is 90 per cent. Hence, there is little difference in pension provision between Irish and multinational firms in the same size category.

Table 3: Number and percentage of multinational and Irish firms having or not having an occupational pension scheme by firm size.

Type of company	<100	>100	Total
Pension scheme			
MNC	36	85	121
	29.8%	70.2%	100.0%
Irish	112	110	222
	50.5%	49.5%	100.0%
No pension scheme			
MNC	18	6	24
	75.0%	25.0%	100.0%
Irish	208	12	220
	94.5%	5.5%	100.0%
Total			
MNC	54	91	145
	37.2%	62.8%	100.0%
Irish	320	122	442
	72.4%	27.6%	100.0%
Grand total	374	213	587
	63.7%	36.3%	100.0%

As there is little difference between large multinational and Irish firms in the provision of pension schemes for their employees it will help to simplify the presentation of results if we confine our analysis to firms with 100 or more employees. Geographical analysis of large firms in our sample which provide pension schemes for their employees shows that over 80 per cent of them are subsidiaries of firms in the U.S. the U.K., France, Germany or Japan. Hirst and Thompson (1996, p. 80) point out that these countries were the five most important investors abroad in 1993. Since there are few Japanese firms in our sample the geographical areas we will use in our analysis are the U.S., the U.K., Ireland, and the Rest of the World. The Rest of the World category is dominated by firms from Germany and France but it also includes a small number of Japanese firms and firms from other EU countries in mainland Europe.

A common perception of multinational companies is that they are less likely to offer permanent employment than domestic firms because they are more footloose. It is also expected that they will hire proportionately more part-time and temporary employees than domestic firms to meet their need for a flexible labour force which can be expanded or contracted as fluctuations in demand require. Table 4 shows the breakdown of employment by country and employment status. Surprisingly, the table shows that Irish firms are more likely than multinational firms to have a smaller percentage of their labour force employed on a full-time permanent basis. The split between full-time permanent and other forms of employment is approximately 85/15 for multinationals whereas it is about 70/30 for Irish firms. The breakdown of employment by sex is about two-thirds male to one-third female for firms from the U.K., the Rest of the World, and Ireland and about 50/50 for U.S. firms.

Table 4: Number employed in large firms which have a pension scheme by country oforigin and employment status.

Country of origin and employment status	Number employed			Per cent of total employment		
	Males	Females	Total	Males	Females	Total
U.S.						
Full-time permanent	5.692	4.752	10.444	47.1	39.3	86.4
Part-time permanent	2	50	52	0.0	0.4	0.4
Full-time temporary	702	881	1.583	5.8	7.3	13.1
Part-time temporary	3	1	4	0.0	0.0	0.0
Total	6.399	5.684	12.083	53.0	47.0	100.0
U.K.						
Full-time permanent	7.373	3.557	10.930	59.2	28.6	87.8
Part-time permanent	64	668	732	0.5	5.4	5.9
Full-time temporary	432	274	706	3.5	2.2	5.7
Part-time temporary	12	~72	84	0.1	0.6	0.7
Total	7.881	4.571	12.452	63.3	36.7	100.0
Rest of the World						
Full-time permanent	5.818	2.784	8.602	58.0	27.8	85.8
Part-time permanent	50	596	646	0.5	5.9	6.4
Full-time temporary	329	381	710	3.3	3.8	7.1
Part-time temporary	21	52	73	0.2	0.5	0.7
Total	6.218	3.813	10.031	62.0	38.0	100.0
Ireland						
Full-time permanent	157.219	81.244	238.463	48.0	24.8	72.7
Part-time permanent	12.874	25.402	38.276	3.9	7.7	11.7
Full-time temporary	41.467	3.713	45.180	12.6	1.1	13.8
Part-time temporary	3.065	2.823	5.888	0.9	0.9	1.8
Total	214.625	113.182	327.807	65.5	34.5	100.0
Grand total						
Full-time permanent	178.048	93.258	271.306	48.7	25.5	74.2
Part-time permanent	13.017	26.796	39.813	3.6	7.3	10.9
Full-time temporary	43.034	5.338	48.372	11.8	1.5	13.2
Part-time temporary	3.140	3.016	6.156	0.9	0.8	1.7
Total	237.239	128.408	365.647	64.9	35.1	100.0

The pension coverage rate in large firms which provide occupational pension schemes is 68 per cent for U.S. firms, 87 per cent for U.K. firms, 75 per cent for firms from the Rest of the World, and 74 per cent for Irish firms. While the coverage rate for firms from the United States is somewhat lower than for other foreign firms the coverage rate for all foreign firms is actually a little higher than for Irish firms. In terms of pension coverage, therefore, large Irish and multinational firms do not differ in their willingness to include a high percentage of their employees in their pension schemes.

In Table 5 we examine whether there are any significant differences between large multinational and Irish firms in their willingness to deal with trade unions. Contrary to a widespread perception Table 5 shows that large multinational companies are as likely to negotiate with trade unions as are large Irish firms. Thus, almost 80 per cent of multinational companies have negotiating agreements with trade unions compared with 82 per cent of Irish firms. However, U.S. multinationals are somewhat less likely than multinationals from the U.K. and the Rest of the World to have a negotiating agreement with a trade union. Since the percentage of the work force which belongs to trade unions in the U.S. is much lower than in the E.U. these differences in recognition of trade unions reflect different attitudes to the organisation of work in the countries of origin.

Table 5: Number and percentage of large multinational and Irish companies having a pension scheme which have a negotiating agreement with a trade union.

Country of origin	Does company have a negotiating agreement with a trade union?		Total
	Yes	No	
U.S.	25	10	35
	71.4%	28.6%	100.0%
U.K.	26	4	30
	86.7%	13.3%	100.0%
Rest of World	22	5	27
	81.5%	18.5%	100.0%
Ireland	128	28	156
	82.1%	17.9%	100%
Total	201	47	248
	81.0%	19.0%	100.0%

While there is little difference in the propensity of large Irish and multinational companies to provide pension schemes for their employees companies may have different schemes for different categories of employees. Occupational pension schemes in Ireland were originally provided for white collar staff in the public service, the railways, banks, and insurance companies and some of the larger manufacturing firms in brewing and distilling. These schemes are generally described as "staff" schemes. Subsequently, separate schemes were introduced for blue collar workers in manufacturing and services. These schemes are generally described as "works" schemes. In cases where both white and blue collar workers belong to the same scheme they are described as "combined" schemes. In recent years some companies have introduced a new type of scheme for their senior managers. These schemes are referred to as "executive" schemes.

Broadly speaking, schemes provided by Irish companies for different groups of employees can be ranked in term of the generosity of the pension benefits they provide. The most generous benefits are provided by executive schemes. Staff schemes come next in this ranking and they are followed by combined schemes. Works schemes provide the least generous pension benefits. Table 6 shows that, on balance, large multinational companies are more likely than similar Irish companies to have the same type of scheme for all employees. Just over 55 per cent of multinational companies have combined works and staff schemes compared with 35 per cent of large Irish companies. Multinational companies, therefore, do not simply reproduce the pension arrangements they find in the host country. They provide about the same proportion of executive schemes as Irish companies but differentiate much less than Irish companies between schemes for white collar and blue collar workers.

Table 6: Category of worker covered by pension scheme provided by large multi-national and Irish companies.

Country of origin	Works	Staff	Combined	Executive	Total
U.S.	4	6	20	5	35
	11.4%	17.1%	57.1%	14.3%	100.0%
U.K.	4	12	12	2	30
	13.3%	40.0%	40.0%	6.7%	100.0%
Rest of World	1	4	19	3	27
	3.7%	14.8%	70.4%	11.1%	100.0%
Ireland	23	60	55	20	158
	14.6%	38.0%	34.8%	12.7%	100.0%
Total	32	82	106	30	250
	12.8%	32.8%	42.4%	12.0%	100.0%

Note: Totals differ from those in previous tables because some companies have multiple schemes.

Differences in the period during which the schemes were set up may be partly responsible for companies from the U.S. and the Rest of the World providing a larger proportion of combined schemes than Irish or U.K. companies. Table 7 shows that over half of the schemes provided by large Irish and U.K. companies were established before 1975 whereas 78 per cent of the schemes provided by U.S. companies and 54 per cent of schemes provided by companies from the Rest of the World were set up after 1975.

Table 7: Period in which multinational and Irish occupational pension schemes were established.

Country of origin	Up to 1960	1961-75	1976-85	1986-95	Total
U.S.	0	7	14	12	3
	0.0	21.2	42.4	36.4	100.0
U.K.	3	13	5	5	26
	11.5	50.0	19.2	19.2	100.0
Rest of World	4	7	7	6	24
	16.7	29.2	29.2	25.0	100.0
Ireland	21	55	39	3	151
	13.9	36.4	25.8	23.8	100.0
Total	28	82	65	5	234
	12.0	35.0	27.8	25.2	100.0

Developments in the organisation of work in the last two decades and changes in the skills of the labour force have lessened job demarcations between blue and white collar workers. This has made it possible for companies opening plants in Ireland to ignore job demarcations which influenced the types of scheme which Irish and British companies provided in an earlier period.

In a globalised economy in which trans-national corporations are potentially able to relocate anywhere to obtain the highest rates of return defined contribution schemes would be preferred to defined benefit schemes. Defined contribution schemes enable employers to shift the risk of a fall in pension benefits to the employees. Once the employment relationship between the employer and employee is ended by the company moving abroad, the employer has no long-term commitments to honour a pension promise as is the case under a defined benefit scheme. If the globalised model accounts better for contemporary economic developments than the international model one would expect to find a much higher proportion of foreign firms operating defined contribution plans than the proportion of Irish companies operating such plans. Table 8 presents information on the type of scheme provided by large foreign and Irish companies. It shows that on average about 14 per cent of schemes are defined contribution schemes. In Irish-owned firms almost 12 per cent of the schemes are of the defined contribution type while in foreign firms the figure is 18 per cent. There is some variation around the average for foreign firms, with almost 30 per cent of the schemes provided by U.S. companiesbeing defined contribution and only 7 per cent of the schemes provided by U.K. companies being of this type. The greater preference of U.S. companies than of other foreign companies for defined contribution plans reflects national differences in the provision of pension plans. Dailey and Turner (1992, p. 16) show in their analysis of the type of plan provided in different countries that "the United States and Australia are the only countries that have a sizable percentage of participants in defined contribution plans" and that in "Canada and the United Kingdom, by far the larger number of participants are in defined benefit plans". They also note that many employers in the U.S. use defined contribution plans as a supplement to a defined benefit plan. When allowance is made for preferences in the country of origin what emerges from the analysis of the type of scheme is that the majority of large Irish and foreign companies provide defined benefit schemes for their employees.

Table 8: Type of scheme provided by large multinational and Irish companies.

Country of origin	Defined Benefit Scheme	Defined Contribution Scheme	Total
U.S.	25	10	35
	71.4%	28.6%	100.0%
U.K	28	2	30
	93.3%	6.7%	100.0%
Rest of World	22	5	27
	81.5%	18.5%	100.0%
Ireland	139	18	157
	88.5%	11.5%	100.0%
Total	214	35	249
	85.9%	14.1%	100.0%

4. Proposals for Development of the National Pension System

The evidence from Irish national statistical sources and the survey of occupational pension schemes by the ESRI suggests that the behaviour of foreign firms in Ireland in relation to their employees is closer to Hirst and Thompson's international economy model than to their global economy model. It may be argued that this evidence tells us only about the past and that current and future behaviour is likely to be very different as the globalisation model becomes more dominant. If foreign firms are more likely to behave in the future as transnational than multinational corporations in the provision of retirement income for their employees one would expect to see some sign of this in their input into proposals which were made in May 1998 by the Pensions Board (1998) for the future development of the national pension system.

The Pensions Board proposed that the retirement needs of low paid employees should be looked after by the State while the needs of better paid employees should be catered for by employers or private pension providers. It recommends that the State should be responsible for replacing half of the gross pre-retirement earnings of the lowest paid 30 per cent of employees in the private sector. This should be done by increasing the basic flat-rate Social Welfare pension from its June 1998 level of 28.5 per cent of average industrial earnings (£83 per week) to a target level of 34 per cent over a five to ten year period. The Board also recommends that the real value of Social Welfare pensions should be preserved by indexing them in line with prices or with earnings if circumstances permit.

The Board argues that the major vehicle catering for the retirement income needs of middle and higher income groups should be a new Personal Retirement Savings Account (PRSA). It believes that private pension providers would introduce such savings accounts if they received more favourable tax treatment than existing occupational pension schemes. Personal Retirement Savings Accounts would be similar to 401(k) plans in the United States. They would be available to everyone regardless of employment status, so an employee who quits work or becomes self-employed could continue to make contributions to his or her retirement savings account. The Board proposes it should be mandatory for employers to provide facilities for their employees to contribute to PRSAs through payroll deductions if the employees wish it. However, the employer will not be obliged to contribute to these accounts. It is intended that PRSAs will be marketed by a wide range of providers including banks, insurance companies, credit unions, and the Post Office.

The philosophy behind the proposal to introduce a Personal Retirement Saving Account is similar to that underlying proposals by the World Bank (1994) for privatisation of social security. However, strengthening the social insurance component of the social protection system is not in keeping with the Bank's recommendations. The proposed increases in the basic state pension combined with ageing of the population will increase expenditure on the state pension scheme from 4.8 per cent of GNP in 1996 to 8.6 per cent in 2056, according to Hughes and Nolan's (1998) estimates. If the Pensions Board's proposals are adopted they will result in significant increases in social charges on employers. These are the only direct tax changes which are likely to lead to a significant increase in taxation on multinational corporations in Ireland because the Government has already given commitments to maintain corporation tax at a low level, 12 per cent, in the future.

Since multinational corporations are well represented in the representative body for the pensions industry (see Table 9) they could have used their influence to get the IAPF to oppose proposals which are likely to result in significant increases in social charges. However, no public statement has been issued indicating that multinational corporations are opposed to such increases and when the Pensions Board's proposals were published in May 1998 in a report entitled "Securing Retirement Income" they were welcomed by the Irish Association of Pension Funds. The Chairman of the IAPF said that: "Securing Retirement Income is probably the most significant document which has ever been published on pensions in Ireland and will set the agenda for the development of our pensions system for [the] next 20 to 25 years at least. The main ...conclusions and recommendations are broadly in line with IAPF's own thinking accordingly we are pleased to give it our support" (IAPF News Release, 7 May 1998).

Table 9: Number and percentage of large multinational and Irish companies having a pension scheme which are members of the Irish Association of Pension Funds.

Country of origin	Member of the Irish Association of Pension Funds		Total
	Yes	No	
U.S.	18	16	34
	52.9%	47.1%	100.0%
U.K.	18	10	28
	64.3%	35.7%	100.0%
Rest of World	15	11	26
	57.7%	42.3%	100.0%
Ireland	99	53	152
	62.5%	37.5%	100%
Total	150	90	240
	62.5%	37.5%	100.0%

5. Conclusions

The evidence summarised in this paper relating to the impact of foreign direct investment on employment and conditions of work in Ireland supports Hirst and Thompson's (1996, p. 198) argument that "most MNCs adapt passively to governmental policy rather than continually trying to undermine it." A significant loss of national control has, however, occurred in connection with the investment of pension funds following the internationalisation of financial markets since the 1970s.

Exchange controls were removed in Ireland in 1988. Subsequently there was a gradual shift of pension fund investment towards overseas markets. This trend will continue as Irish interest rates fall to the continental European level with the introduction of the Euro from 1 January 1999. Pension funds now operate in a global financial market in which a handful of U.S., U.K., and Swiss banks control pension assets "larger than the individual GDP of every country in the world with the exception of two – the United States and Japan – as Minns (1996, p. 74) points out. The volume of pension assets will continue to grow in the future, particularly if the European Federation of Investment Funds and Companies succeeds in getting national governments in the EU to introduce individual retirement accounts similar to those already proposed in Ireland and the U.K. (see Lessing (1997). Globalisation theorists argue that national governments have lost the power to regulate international financial flows because of the global integration of money markets. While this is so it does not mean that international financial flows are beyond control by supra-national organisations. Economic and Monetary Union provides an opportunity for the EU to promote, with the other members of the Triad, international economic governance of the World financial system which was not available in the past to individual member states.

References

Barry, F., Bradley, J. (1997): FDI and Trade: The Irish Host-country Experience., Economic Journal, Vol. 107 No. 445.

Betcherman, G. (1996): Globalization, Labour Markets and Public Policy. In: Boyer, R. Drache, D. (ed.): States Against Markets: The Limits of Globalization. Routledge, London.

Bradley, J. (1998): Interpreting the Recent Irish Growth Experience. Dublin: Economic and Social Research Institute Report Prepared for the OECD.

Dailey, L., Turner, J. (1992): U.S. Private Pensions in World Perspective: 1970-89. In: Turner, J., Beller, D. (eds): Trends in Pensions 1992. U. S. Department of Labor Pension and Welfare Benefits Administration, Washington.

Hirst, P., Thompson, G. (1996a): Globalization in Question: The International Economy and the Possibilities of Governance. Polity Press, Cambridge.

Hirst P., Thompson, G. (1996b): Globalisation: Ten Frequently Asked Questions and Some Surprising Answers. Soundings, Issue 4 Autumn 1996.

Hughes, G. (1994): Private Pensions in OECD Countries. Ireland. Paris, Organisation for Economic Co-operation and Development, Social Policy Studies No. 13

Hughes, G., Nolan, B. (1998): "Competitive and Segmented Labour Markets and Exclusion from Retirement Income. Economic and Social Research Institute, Dublin, (mimeo).

Hughes, G., Whelan, B. (1996): Occupational and Personal Pension Coverage 1995. Economic and Social Research Institute, Dublin.

Lessing, A. (ed.) (1997): Mutual Funds in European Old-Age Provision. European Federation of Investment Funds and Companies Pensions and Investment Funds Committee (mimeo).

Lipsey, R. E., Blomstrom, M., Ramstetter, E. (1995): Internationalised Production in World Output. NBER Working Paper 5385.

McCarthy, W., O'Brien, J., Dowd, V. (1975): Wage Inflation and Wage Leadership. Economic and Social Research Institute, Dublin, General Research Series Paper No. 79.

Minns, R. (1996): The Control and Investment of Pension Funds. In: Pensions in the European Union: Adapting to Economic and Social Changes. Report of a conference organised by Gesellschaft fur Versicherungswissenschaft und –gestaltung e.V. and the European Network for Research on Supplementary Pensions in Munster, Germany 13-16 June (mimeo).

O'Malley, E. (1994): The Impact of Transnational Corporations in the Republic of Ireland. In: Dicken, P., Quévit, M. (eds): Transnational Corporations and European Regional Restructuring. The Royal Dutch Geographical Society/Faculty of Geographical Sciences Utrecht University, Utrecht.

O'Malley, E. (1998): The Revival of Irish Indigenous Industry 1987-1997. Quarterly Economic Commentary. Economic and Social Research Institute, Dublin.

Pensions Board (1998): Securing Retirement Income: National Pensions Policy Initiative Report of The Pensions Board. The Pensions Board, Dublin.

World Bank (1994): Averting the Old Age Crisis: Policies to Protect the Old and Promote Growth. Oxford University Press, Oxford.

Acknowledgements

I am grateful to my ESRI colleagues John Bradley, Ide Kearney, and Eoin O'Malley for providing information on exports, imports, and relative living standards and to Frank O'Connor for comments on an earlier draft.

PART IV.

The Neo-Globalization, the Institutions and the Experience of European Integration

14. Globalization and the Reform of the International Monetary System

Carlo Azeglio Ciampi

G15 G21 F32
F34 O16 G28

1. The Causes of the Asian Crisis and the New Challenges that they Pose for the International Financial System

The starting point for my observations, other than the analytical contributions presented and discussed at the conference, stems from the experience of the last eighteen months, that is, from the beginning of the Asian crisis. Since July 1997, with the devaluation of Baht, there began a phase of financial instability that has spread to other countries in Southeast Asia; and that then widened even further, combining with other factors, to include such distant areas as Russia and Brazil.

This crisis has aspects that makes it different from similar past events. The macroeconomic policy, contrary to the past, has not been the only or even the principal cause of the crisis. The general opinion is that the detonating factors have been the "gaps" in the mechanisms of the market; these "gaps" became apparent in various forms.

In the first place, the behavior of private investors was anomalous and apparently irrational. An enormous inflow of capital towards rapidly developing countries was then followed by an unexpected and equal outflow of capital at the first sign of instability. This behavior reflects a widespread fashion of investors, specifically institutional investors, to pursue a strategy based on the repetition of benchmarks and on the imitation of successful investors in the fear that inferior performance could reduce their market share. This behavior was not stopped by the availability of clear and accurate information, by the presence of a high level of vigilance, or by clear legislation on corporate rights and bankruptcy laws.

In the second place, the price adjustment mechanisms did not operate in an appropriate manner, especially those mechanisms that should have been activated following the devaluation. The financial and macroeconomic policies were not as effective as previously thought, because they were weaker than the transmission mechanisms of the financial market. For example, in the case of Asia the devaluation of the currency, which should have stimulated the economy by means of exportation as well as allowing for an adjustment of the external imbalances, worsened the crisis. This happened because the banks, contradicting sound operating principles, assumed large overdrafts in currency without the control of the proper authorities in the accumulating of these overdrafts. The devaluation, therefore, contributed to a collapse of the banking system and to a worsening of the recession.

Other factors competed to hinder the adjustment: the dramatic slowing of the export market in these countries; the very structure of production of the local industry, strongly dependent on the importation of input and semi-manufactured goods, which were less expensive before the devaluation; and the weakening of commercial credit for local companies.

The crisis revealed that many countries developed rapidly, even at very high rates, without having an adequate market structure.

The quick liberalization of the movement of capital was not accompanied by an adequate market discipline. Capital had abundantly flowed in, without limits, in the emerging countries, attracted by momentarily favorable conditions, and it rapidly flowed out at the first sign of instability. A more gradual liberalization, in line with the development of the internal financial market, could have avoided this instability.

The recent crisis has definitely shaken the belief that the financial markets, left to the spontaneous forces in which they operate, are capable by themselves of achieving stability or of allocating resources efficiently. The crisis reminds us of a reality often obscured by an unquestioning faith in the redeeming capacity of the market; the market requires a solid foundation in the form of rules, institutions, codes of conduct of the operators, widely shared standards, and consolidated procedures.

The institutions that have presided over the international financial system now find themselves facing a partially new challenge; new because the international financial institutions, created after the Second World War, have had as a principal objective questions related primarily to macroeconomic adjustments.

The recent crises reveal that macroeconomic adjustments are necessary in the case of imbalances, but the success of these adjustments presupposes the existence of an efficient financial market.

2. The Strengthening of the International Financial System: the Nature of the Interventions and the Reform of the Institutions

The reform of the international financial system poses two problems: the type of interventions to undertake, especially in emerging countries, but also in more developed countries; and the procedures and the institutions that must promote these changes.

The nature of the interventions must correspond to the cause of the crisis. In terms of the theoretical profile, the type of analysis that puts imperfect information at the center of the failures of the market is particularly useful. Problems of adverse selection, moral hazard, free riding and herd behavior have evidently emerged during the crisis, annulling in some countries the gains in efficiency that the internationalization of finance should have produced. I will not linger on the analysis of these phenomena, on which there is a great deal of academic study. Instead it is useful to try to identify the concrete actions of public policy to adopt in order to reconcile the efficiency of allocations and the stability of the international monetary system. This is an operation that must be carried out pragmatically, without taking antithetical positions between the failures of the state and the failures of the market.

There are four areas in which to proceed on the international level:
1. the improving of universally accepted standards of transparency, of auditing and of

bank supervision;

2. the readying of safety nets, the combination of institutions, of procedures and of institutional mechanisms aimed at regulating the regimes of insolvency of financial intermediaries, and that in reality offer a public guarantee, implicit or explicit, in favor of a certain category of savers;

3. the construction of national capital markets with solid foundations;

4. the adoption of sustainable regimes of exchange.

1. As far as the first point is concerned, the international community has long agreed on the importance of transparency and its contribution to risk identification and investment selection. The Financial Ministries and the governors of the central banks of the G7 countries in the declaration of last October stressed the importance of these issues by reminding governments, the private sector and international financial institutions to strengthen the standards of transparency.

The Asian crisis has confirmed the predominant role played by the external debt of the private sector and in particular by its exposure to foreign exchange risk. This underscores the urgency of a more accurate collection and diffusion of information about the situation of the banking and corporate sector and on its sensitivity to exchange rate oscillation. Among the more important initiatives in this field are those undertaken by the International Monetary Fund: the creation of a Special Data Dissemination Standard, that will in all probability be strengthened and extended to include data on the financial sector's balance of payments exposure, as well as the development of a code of best practices on the subject of fiscal transparency.

Other initiatives that are currently underway at different international forums is the search to improve the standards of banking supervision, of corporate governance, of auditing, of payment systems and bankruptcy norms. Here I will mention only the Basle Committee on Banking Supervision, which is committed to the monitoring of the application of core principles that the Basle Committee has developed in the area of banking supervision; and the activity of the International Accounting Standards Committee, which is currently working on the identification of a set of internationally acceptable accounting standards on offerings and on cross-border listings.

2. As far as the second point is concerned, the public safety net has traditionally had two distinct objectives: to protect the small depositors; to preserve the integrity of the financial system and of payments. These objectives must be clearly balanced by the need to avoid the protection of single banks, as well as their management or shareholders, from the consequences of their actions; they must not be immune to potential failure.

The Asian crisis has provided an important example of the serious weaknesses in the public safety net. The crisis has underlined the necessity of having secure *ex ante* measures for the protection of depositors, as well as efficient and transparent institutions for the resolution of banking crises. In the absence of such measures and of transparent procedures, the Asian authorities found themselves facing the delicate question of whether or not, and to what degree, should they have offered financial support to banks and to other intermediaries hit by the crisis. The lack of well-conceived and transparent safety net planning has favored the indiscriminate extension of public guarantees, thus accentuating the risk of moral hazard. The authorities have accepted the survival of technically insolvent intermediaries, with the result of increasing both financial loss and the overall expense of public intervention.

More generally, in the recognition of the advantages in the promulgation of international standards in this area, there is still a lack of agreement on which institutions should provide the safety net. There exists, therefore, a wide variety in the extent of insured coverage by the governments of different countries.

3. As for the third point, an opening up to foreign financial flows is not, however, a substitute for the effort needed to develop internal financial markets. The existence of deep markets allows governments and the private sector to collect financing in local currency, lessening therefore the vulnerability to external shocks and risks of financial crisis. Markets that lack liquidity, on the contrary, increase the difficulty of debt management, of the activation of a monetary policy, and of the sterilization of the monetary effects of devaluation. Moreover, they demonstrate an excessive variability in prices, and are no longer faithful indicators of the scarcity of resources; they also tend, in special conditions of liquidity tension, to rapidly transmit shocks.

Although the depth and size of the markets depend to a large extent on the behavior of the operators inside these markets, it is also true that this behavior is influenced by the institutional infrastructure on which the market is based. A general agreement exists that monetary authorities and central banks have a fundamental role in the following areas: guaranteeing an ample participation, strengthening the supervision of banks, encouraging the growth of primary dealers, promulgating transparent standards, accounting principles and norms that assure the integrity of the system of payments, and maintaining a fiscal standard and macroeconomic situation that encourages saving,

Although the fundamental role of the financial sector in the development process has long been universally recognized, the actions of international financial institutions in this area have not always been incisive. Recent experience has taught that difficult reforms can be undertaken immediately after a crisis, when the resistance of the forces opposed to change is weakened by the obvious cost of inaction. Not to exploit the headway of the moment in order to get reform processes underway would be tantamount to intentionally ignoring the lessons of history and thereby missing a unique opportunity.

4. As for the fourth and last point – the subject of exchange rate regimes – the emphasis on transparency, even if justified, runs the risk of moving the exchange question into the background. Without entering into the debate about the superiority of fixed or flexible exchange rates, it is important to note that the two financial crises took place in countries that have very rigid exchange policies.

The events in Asia have confirmed, as if it were still necessary, how a fixed rate regime requires both an extremely flexible fiscal and income policy, since it is on this policy that the entire burden of adjusting to external shocks falls, as well as strong supervision in controlling the levels of foreign debt in the banking and corporate systems, which are critical elements in developing countries; an added reason for stressing the opportunity of assuring a timely alignment of exchange rates in respect to the economic fundamentals of the economy, if we want to avoid future threats to the stability of the international monetary system.

Finally, a review, however briefly, of the public actions to undertake in order to improve the management of globalization can not proceed without an analysis of the organizations institutionally in charge of crisis prevention and management. Today, the international financial institutions are criticized for not knowing how to efficiently diagnosis the size of the crisis or how to forestall it; this criticism is often ungenerous, and, in any case, should include other economic operators as well. In the case of Thailand, for example, the Monetary Fund had in fact foreseen the danger and had advised the national authorities. It is true that the architecture of Bretton Woods, devised over a half century ago on the foundations of fixed exchange rates and scarce mobility of capital, contains many aspects that require revision.

Two questions with respect to the establishment of Bretton Woods must be separated: one is legitimacy, or if you like political legitimization, and the other is competence.

As for the first, the World Bank, the Monetary Fund and the World Trade Organization are among the only international financial groups that can boast of a truly worldwide presence. For this reason they certainly seem to have legitimacy in facing problems of worldwide dimensions.

As for the second, the Monetary Fund was created to face problems in the reform of the international monetary system that are somewhat different from those that we face today. Reflection and work in the field of supervision, of accounting standards, of corporate governance and bankruptcy law are carried on by other international groups, for example the International Organization of Securities Commission, the OECD and the Basle Committee on Banking Supervision.

It is necessary to bring these efforts under a common umbrella in order to assure coordination, to impede duplication, to avoid leaving important areas uncovered, and to give voice to different events and experiences and not only to those of the industrialized countries.

The ample representation of the Interim Committee qualifies it as the body institutionally appropriate to perform the role of linkage and direction. It is necessary, moreover, to give importance to the role of the Committee, currently the principal organ of orientation for the Fund's decisions on subjects connected to the objectives of institutions, if it is to become the governmental embryo required by the global economy.

The Interim Committee should in the future be ready to discuss proposals and suggestions that come from the major international forums; to react as a sounding board for the work and study conducted in other international quarters in order to favor the diffusion and the acceptance of their recommendations; to become the principal channel of communication between the international financial community and national policy makers, as well as to strengthen the moral suasion on governments and on the private sector.

Recent experience reinforces our conviction that in a globalized economy in which there is a high risk that financial crisis will spread, it is necessary to strengthen the instruments of intervention of international financial institutions – both on the level of finance and on the level of crisis prevention and management. In terms of the former, we should greet with favor the fact that NAB has recently come into effect, since it gives the Fund the financial capacity to intervene effectively. And in terms of the latter, it is worth mentioning that thinking has already begun in a variety of official quarters (G7, G22, IMF, BIS, OSCE) on the new architecture of the international monetary system.

As already mentioned, we are proceeding along different fronts. Specifically, study continues on the possibility of introducing uniform criteria and codes of best practices in order to increase the effectiveness of the regulation and the supervision of the financial system and to harmonize national norms. In the same perspective, there is the tendency to encourage an improvement in how countries present themselves to the judgment of the market; for example, by providing complete and up-to-date information on important monetary and financial data, and by conforming to the transparency codes that the IMF has developed in the budget policy area and that have been extended to other economic policy areas.

To make these standards effective, they must be adopted worldwide; to that end, it is essential that they are defined with the full collaboration of industrialized countries and of emerging economies: their later application will be that much easier.

Strengthening the intervention capacity of international organizations does not mean to obscure the growing risk that the availability of financial help could create distortions in the behavior of investors, tempting them to pay less attention to the country's credit worthiness. In order to reduce this risk, the role of the International Monetary Fund should be evaluated in terms of crisis management and be given the capacity and the tools to involve the private sector in debt restructuring. Significant progress in this sense came about during the recent crisis in Brazil, when the pressure exerted by the direction of the Fund and by the national authorities on their own banks succeeded in bringing about an elevated rollover of short-term private loans.

An increased transparency within international financial institutions would increase the negotiating power of the Monetary Fund in its dialectic with national authorities, in the same way that an improvement in the quality and the availability of statistical information would strengthen the effectiveness and the timeliness of its recommendations. What needs to be done is to reinforce, on one hand, the capacity of moral suasion of the Fund; and, on the other, to mutually define the incentives that can promote actions that are timely, corrective, and appropriate on the part of the member countries at risk. In this area, much remains to be done.

Finally, study is underway on the possibility of increasing the array of financial instruments offered by the international financial institutions to include risk-sharing products. I refer to the eventuality that development banks will grant loans in local currency or loans that are indexed to the price of the exportable raw materials on which the country's economy chiefly depends; another possibility is to work with bank syndicates in order to create a credit line plan that can be used in situations of financial stress.

Globalization has brought to all of us not only a growth in the liberty of choice, but also new duties and tasks that would be irresponsible to neglect or to face individually. It is not possible to have a social order based on the exclusive consideration of individual preference, and it is not possible to build a global society without a culture of reciprocity, or a sustainable economy without a *polis*.

15. Globalization, Regionalism and the Nation State: Top down and Bottom up

Pier Carlo Padoan

For
HI
D71

1. Introduction

The international system is much more complex today with respect to twenty five years ago when the regime which had been set up at the end of the second world war -the Bretton Woods system- collapsed. Understanding this complexity is one the major challenges of international relations scholars and any attempt carries a high risk of adding confusion rather than clarity.

Let me first state, therefore, what this paper does not intend to do. It does not try to provide a "grand theory" of the international system today. It does not even pretend to offer indications towards such a direction. More simply it starts by noting that the evolution of the international system stems from the interaction of three levels of behavior: the systemic level, the national level, and the new intermediate level, the regional one. The distinction, and often the contrast, between the first two levels of analysis has long been one of the dividing lines among international relation scholars and only recently we are witnessing to a resurgence of the debate basically pointing at the opportunity of considering both systemic and nation state levels of analysis[1]. The discussion on regionalism has, on the other hand, followed largely a path of his own[2] with few attempts to link it to the other two levels of analysis.

Starting from this point the paper seeks to offer suggestion on how to link the three levels of analysis. This will be done largely by drawing on the existing literature and it will follow a two way approach. The "top down" approach considers the influence which the higher level influences the lower one, how the globalization[3] of the international system affects the evolution of regional agreements and how the latter influences the domestic policies of nation states. The "bottom up" approach looks at the opposite causality: how the changes at the national level influence the dimension and characteristics of regional agreements, and the development of regional agreements and their interaction shapes the characteristics of the new international system.

---

[1] See e.g. Mansfield and Milner (1997).
[2] On regionalism see, among others, DeMelo and Panagarya (1993).
[3] In this paper we define globalization as the increasing elimination of barriers that separate local and national markets of factors and products one from the other accompanied by an increasing mobility of capital.

2. The Global System in Institutional Disequilibrium

The global system is now in what has been called a post-hegemonic world (Gilpin 1987), i.e. a situation in which no single country can provide unilaterally the public goods required for the operation of the system itself. This can be restated by saying that the international system is in "institutional disequilibrium" in the sense that there is an excess demand of international public goods which, in turn, is the result of a decrease in supply because of the redistribution of power away from an hegemonic structure[4] and of an increase in demand because of increased globalization.

The current configuration of the global system, however, is also often described as "regionalism", which should be understood not so much as the result of concentration of trade and investment activities around major integrated regions (Europe, North America, Asia) but rather as a policy option pursued as a response to the failure of the post hegemonic world in providing international public goods. Regionalism may be "conflict oriented" or "cooperative". In the first case regional agreements provide collective goods for countries included in each region and exclude non members from their consumption (e.g. a discriminatory trade agreement). Cooperative regionalism, on the contrary, could be understood as the formation of regional agreements as a precondition for cooperation at a global level, i.e. towards multilateralism. To proceed on from this point one needs to consider the following aspects: a) the conditions for cooperation without hegemony, i.e. within a multipolar world, b) the interaction between domestic, regional, and international policy.

The theory of international cooperation without hegemony[5] offers a list of conditions to be met if agreements to supply international public goods have to be reached: 1) the number of actors involved must be small; 2) the time horizon of actors must be long; 3) actors must be prepared to change their policy preferences. 4) International institutions must be available. Condition 1) allows for the possibility of dealing with free riding. Condition 2) allows for repeated interaction among players, which is both necessary and unavoidable in a growingly interdependent world. Condition 3) requires the possibility that nation states adjust to the international environment to reach agreements. Finally condition 4) relates to the fact that institutions support cooperation as they facilitate exchange and information among different actors.

Conditions 1)-4) imply, among other things, that cooperation is achieved if nation states adjust both their economic and their political equilibria. This leads us to the interaction between international and domestic politics. Robert Putnam (1988) has suggested that international regime formation requires that an agreement be reached at both level I politics, i.e between national governments, and level II politics, i.e. between each national government, the legislator, and domestic

---

[4]On hegemonic stability theory the standard reference is Kehoane (1984).
[5]See the articles in Oye (1985), in particular the paper by Axelrod and Kehoane, and Guerrieri and Padoan (1989).

interest groups so while level II politics must be consistent with the agreement struck at level I politics, the opposite relation must hold as well. Level I agreements must be designed so as to be consistent with the specific level II agreements in each of the participating countries. The interaction between level I and level II politics in determining the success of international cooperation is a complex one and its implications are still being developed in the literature[6].

Regionalism adds a third level of politics, regional politics, to be understood as the definition of a common regional policy, which operates between domestic and international politics. The answer to the question whether regionalism will assume benign or malign characteristics then, requires looking at the role regional (level III) politics can play as a bridge between level I and level II politics. This, in turn, requires to look more closely at the conditions that must be met in order for regional agreements to consolidate, i.e. the conditions at which level II politics can be "melted" into level III (regional) politics. Once this is accomplished international (level I) politics interacts with regional (level III) rather than with domestic (level II) politics. De Melo, Pangaraya and Rodrik (1993) develop this point analytically. Their framework considers regional integration as both an economic and a political process which is the outcome of a relationship between national governments and domestic pressure groups (level II politics in Putnam's terminology). They show that the formation of supranational institutions -regional agreements- has a positive effect on the economic efficiency of national economies when these integrate because of the lower impact of domestic pressure groups on the policy stance of the supranational institution with respect to the impact on national governments. Without integration national governments would provide excessive intervention -with respect to the economically optimal- because of the strong influence of domestic pressure groups (the so called "preference dilution effect"). However, if there are large differences among national preferences on the degree of government's intervention, the incentive to integrate may be insufficient (the "preference asymmetry effect"). Supranational institutions (the "institutional design effect") to operate efficiently, must be designed so as to minimize the weight of countries whose domestic pressure groups demand a high amount of government intervention. The first effect relates to the increased role of national systems when international regimes are weak. The second effect relates to the role of differences in national systems in favoring or hindering international regime formation. The third effect underlines the point that regional politics requires the formation of some supranational institution, to avoid the risk of being captured by special interest action. In terms of the "level approach" the first effect indicates a predominace of level I over level II, the second effect indicates a predominance II over the remaining two, while the third effect suggest how level III could dominate level II.

The " two level" approach is a first useful step in trying to establish relations between national systemic and regional mechanisms of cooperation. The next step requires looking more closely at level III. More specifically the following

---

[6]See e.g.Guerrieri and Padoan (1992) , Mayer (1992) Mansfield and Milner (1997).

questions arise: a) why are regional agreements formed and why do they expand (or contract); b) how do countries respond to the formation of regional agreements.

3. Economic Aspects of Regional Agreements

The establishment of a regional agreement requires the selection of who joins and also of who is excluded; a number, therefore, must be determined; regionalism is much a question of cooperation as it is of exclusion. When is the "optimal number of members" reached? Why does it change over time?

Standard trade theory gives a precise answer to the question of number: the optimal size of a trade agreement is the world. Short of full liberalization, however, partial elimination of barriers following integration will improve the allocation of resources and welfare. Although the welfare gain might be partially curtailed by trade diversion, which could offset gains from trade creation, reallocation of resources generated by the integration process allows the exploitation of national comparative advantages. Differences in national resource endowments will lead to a deepening of specialization patterns which will benefit all countries involved in the integration process. Factors of production will be allocated in sectors where the country enjoys a comparative advantage while production in other sectors will stop or will be reduced. The process will, of course, involve adjustment costs and temporary unemployment, the severity and duration of which could be alleviated through appropriate financial support. Once reallocation is completed, inter-industry trade, i.e. trade of goods belonging to different sectors (like e.g. textiles and food products) within the region will increase. Note that the benefits of integration, in such a framework, could be equally obtained by the reallocation of factors among countries, i.e. by migration and/or capital movements.

Within traditional trade[7] theory the reason why the organization of international trade falls short of global liberalization, and, therefore, the reason why regional rather than global integration develops, is usually found in the presence of special interests that, given imperfect political markets, have the resources and the ability to obtain protection from national or regional governments.

"New trade theory" has pointed at another possible source of gains from integration, deriving from the exploitation of (static and dynamic) gains from trade. The larger market generated by integration allows (oligopolistic) firms to exploit increasing returns. This leads to further specialization within the same sectors as competition would rest on both lower costs deriving from expanded production and from product (quality) differentiation. Intra-industry trade, i.e. trade of similar goods between countries, will be generated. Welfare gains from integration will ensue from lower costs and broader quality range as well as the exploitation of dynamic returns to scale generated by the learning process following the introduction of new technologies.

In this case too costs from integration could emerge, however they would

---

[7]For a survey see Baldwin and Venables (1994).

be permanent, rather than temporary. In addition to the standard adjustment costs, economies of scale could generate agglomeration effects as factors, both capital and labor, would concentrate in specific areas, leading to permanent core-periphery effects within the region. Employment opportunities would concentrate in some areas exacerbating the asymmetrical distribution of net benefits.

The now again popular "gravity model" of trade flows suggests that countries are more likely to trade with each other the closer are their per capita and absolute income levels. This intuition can be given theoretical foundations according to the "new trade theory" which stresses economies of scale and diversity as a source of (intra industry) trade. The gravity model also assigns an important role to distance, predicting that geographical proximity will enhance the probability of trade between countries, ceteris paribus. While the economic justification of this element is related to transport costs it can also be suggested, (Alesina, Perotti, Spolaore 1995) that geographically close countries also share similar preferences about the provision of common policies, thus increasing the incentives to integrate. Their analysis also points to a more general topic which is increasingly being addressed in the literature: i.e. the role of social standards, in particular labor and environment standard, in setting the " comparative advantages" of countries and regions and the consequent trade offs that emerge from the pressures of globalization.[8]

In general, trade integration would increase both inter and intra industry trade and, in both cases, increased competition would activate pressures to resist adjustment and/or demand for compensatory measures on the part of countries and regions most severely hit by the asymmetric distribution of net benefits.

The emergence of inequalities generated by the process of integration brings forward the notion of "cohesion" which may be defined as "(a principle that) implies...a relatively equal social and territorial distribution of employment opportunities, of wealth and of income, and of improvements in the quality of life that correspond to increasing expectations" (Smith and Tsoukalis, 1996, p.1). An important implication is that, without cohesion, political support to a regional agreement is likely to fail.

Consensus to the regional agreement, and ultimately its size, will then depend on the cohesion among its members. Cohesion problems will be larger the larger the asymmetric distribution effects, and therefore the larger the impact of scale effects generated by integration. These effects, in turn, will be larger the larger the diversity among members of the integrating region. Once the costs for cohesion management (i.e. the costs that must be borne to offset the asymmetry effects) exceed the benefits from integration the widening process will come to an end. A number will be determined.

Monetary integration too, both when it implies fixing exchange rates and when it takes the form of full monetary union, can produce an asymmetric distribution of net benefits. (Economic) benefits from monetary integration stem

---

[8]For a recent assessment of the debate see Rodrik (1997).

from three sources[9]: the elimination of transaction costs, the elimination of currency risk, the acquisition of policy credibility for inflation prone countries. The first two benefits can be fully obtained only with monetary union. The third benefit has to be weighted against the costs of real appreciation which hits high inflation countries once they credibly enter an exchange rate agreement. If the latter are also the peripheral countries from a trade point of view, adverse effects of real and monetary integration will cumulate, leading to further demand for compensation. Low inflation countries, on the other hand, would be adversely affected by entering a monetary agreement with excessively expansionary partners, ultimately refusing permission to join to the latter (Alesina and Grilli 1993). In both cases the extension of the monetary agreement will stop short of global integration. Again a number must be determined.

To conclude, economics can provide several elements to the understanding of the number problem, however a satisfactory theory of regional integration should explain the "optimal number" of members through the interaction of economic, institutional and political variables. One way of approaching the issue is to consider regional agreements as clubs.

4. Regional Agreements as Clubs

The economic analysis of club formation started to develop in the 1960s with the contribution of James Buchanan (1965) and Mancur Olson (1965) and has been applied, since then, to several economic and political issues such as community size, production of local public goods, two-part tariffs, congestion problems, political coalitions, and more recently to international organizations (Casella and Feinstein 1990). The literature has been surveyed by Sandler and Tschirhart (1980), Frey (1984) and Cornes and Sandler (1985).

Club theory deals with problems related with the establishment of voluntary associations for the production of excludable public goods. Optimal membership is determined by marginality conditions, when the spread between an individual member's cost and benefit is maximized. Marginal costs and benefits are functions of the size of the club[10].

Costs are related to management and decision making activities, hence management costs should not be confused with congestion costs arising e.g. from cumulative effects such as those discussed in section 3 and which will be considered as factors affecting the level of net benefits from club provision.

Marginal costs are increasing with the extension of club membership because management problems rise with an the number of members. As Fratianni and Pattison (1982) stress, decision theory suggests that the addition of new members will raise the costs of finding agreements in a more than proportional manner. Costs will also rise more than proportionally for organizational reasons and because, for political balance, each new member will have to be given equal

---

[9] See De Grauwe (1992).
[10] A more extended is presented in Padoan (1997).

opportunity, irrespective of its economic size, to express its viewpoint. Institutional arrangements alter the behavior of costs. For example a shift from a unanimity rule to a majority rule in decision making within the club lowers marginal costs. On the other hand, individual members' marginal benefits are decreasing, assuming that the equal sized share of total benefits from integration increases at a decreasing rate with respect to the number of members because congestion deteriorates the quality of the club good.

Optimal club membership is obtained when marginal benefits (B) equal marginal costs (C). We can consider the following simple rule. The incentive for a change in the extension of a regional agreement emerges whenever there is a discrepancy between marginal benefits and marginal costs of the club. Note that this allows to consider possible (and not at all unrealistic) contractions in the size of the club (here determined by the number of members Q).

A trade agreement responds to some of the crucial requisites for the definition of a club: it produces freer trade, virtually a public good, and it guarantees partial exclusion of non members from free trade benefits and, in the case of a custom union, it guarantees the benefits of a common external trade policy . To the extent that standards contribute to the determination of comparative advantage groups of countries sharing common standards are forms of trade clubs.

Marginal benefits of a trade club may be thought of depending on both exogenous and endogenous components i.e. on the size of the club itself . The first include the "security" effect of trade agreements. This implies that membership in a trade club is more valuable in presence of a possible outside threat. This may be a genuine military threat as Gowa and Mansfield (1993) have argued. The present global environment, however, may present other forms of threat such as those deriving from the formation of regional and aggressive trade blocs. In such a case the incentive for joining a trade club does not only lie in the trade creation and/or scale effects benefits but, also, in the "insurance" that club membership provides against the harm that a trade bloc war could produce to small, isolated countries (Perroni and Whalley 1994, Baldwin 1993). A larger club membership will benefit existing members as well as new entrants. If the size of the alliance increases it reinforces resistance to the outside threat. This implies that the value of club arises with the degree of conflict in the global system.

Exogenous factors include purely political benefits from trade agreements. i.e. the fact that members will be admitted to the club insofar as they share the same political beliefs of the incumbents, like the full acceptance of democratic rules. This element has played a crucial role in the enlargement of the European Community to the southern countries, Greece Portugal and Spain (Winters 1993) and will play a similar role in the future enlargement of the EU.

A monetary agreement, both in the form of a currency union and of an exchange rate agreement, also responds to the requisites of a public good. The public good nature of a single currency is well established in the literature. In the case of an exchange rate agreement such as the European Monetary System -or rather its Exchange Rate Mechanism (ERM)- the public good involved is monetary stability extended to the participants of the ERM. Common intervention rules extended to members -not to unilateral peggers- allow for, at least partial, excludability of the good.

Globalization and outside threats increase the benefits of a monetary club as capital mobility and deeper financial integration increase the desirability of monetary unions as a protection against destabilizing capital movements (Eichengreen 1994).

Outside threats may come from an " aggressive" behavior (or perceived as such) of foreign monetary policies. For instance Henning (1996) argues that one of the driving forces behind European monetary integration over the last decades has been an aggressive macroeconomic policy attitude followed by the US. Finally one should include the "non economic" benefits of monetary membership which play a relevant role in the success, or failure, of monetary agreements (Cohen 1993).

Marginal benefits increase, *ceteris paribus*, with the level of economic activity. The pressure of rising inequality due to integration will be lower the more sustained is the level of economic activity as more sustained growth will benefit all club members. Another way of looking at this component is to recall that protectionist pressures increase with depressions[11]. It is widely recognized that the pressure to enlarge the EU eastward has been slowed down by the recession that has hit Europe during the first part of the decade. Finally more favorable macroeconomic conditions make it easier to implement policies that are necessary to be part of a monetary club (e.g. higher growth makes fiscal adjustment less costly).

Let us now consider the endogenous determinants of club size, i.e. the number of club members. Marginal benefits are related to club membership and decrease with club size because of rising congestion problems in club formation, as discussed in section 3. Marginal benefits, other things equal, decrease with the diversity of countries wishing to participate into the club as increasing diversity implies larger congestion costs in the case of a trade club or increasing divergencies in the preference for a stable macroeconomic policy in the case of a monetary club[12]. This explains why members of a monetary club must fulfill appropriate requirements (e.g. in terms of financial stability, witness the "Maastricht conditions") and that new members may deteriorate the quality of the public good if their monetary and fiscal policies follow non converging courses[13].

Marginal costs too include exogenous component and endogenous component (depending on club size). Marginal costs are determined by management problems. In the case of the EU, as Baldwin (1994) describes -see also

---

[11]It can be argued that the operation of an international trade regime is influenced by the operation of an international macroeconomic regime. See Guerrieri and Padoan (1988).

[12]Collignon (1997) shows that the benefits of a currency union, a clear example of a monetary club, decrease with the increasing divergence in preferences among the union members for active stabilization policies.

[13]This is also consistent with the view (Bayoumi 1994) that the incentives for non members to join a monetary union are larger than the incentives for union members to accept new countries.

Widgren (1994) - voting rules are complicated by the increase in the number of members, and hence by the increasing diversity of preferences, as each member country will use her voting power to increase the welfare of her citizens. Thus, for example, it is unlikely that the EU can successfully enlarge without a change in the voting procedure. As Fratianni (1995) stresses, the entrance of the Central and Eastern European Countries in the Union will make the formation of a blocking minority much easier, give the current voting system.

Exogenous components can be thought of being associated with the amount and quality of international cooperation already existing among club members in other areas, i.e. if institutions linking countries involved in bargaining the agreements already exist this will facilitate the formation and management of the new institutions. While several reasons can be advanced to support such a claim, a well established fact in international relations theory is that institutions provide information about other actors' behavior thus facilitating communication and information exchanges. In the case of monetary unions the exogenous component may be thought of representing the costs associated with the loss of monetary sovereignty as perceived by club members.

A simple representation of club equilibrium is offered in fig. 1. The equilibrium club size is Q^* where the marginal cost and benefits curves intersect.

Figure 1: Club equilibrium.

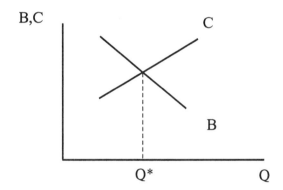

Starting from Q^* optimal club membership will vary according to a number of factors. There will be an enlargement process if: macroeconomic conditions improve; the degree of outside conflicts increases thus raising the insurance value of membership; the strength and efficiency of institutional arrangements among members other than trade relations increases; if diversity among countries -both members and candidates- decreases; the voting system becomes more flexible. The first three factors can be represented by a shift to the right of the B curve, the fourth factor may be represented by a shift of the C curve to the right[14].

---

[14] A more extended analysis is presented in Padoan (1997).

Finally, as suggested by Mansfield and Bronson (1994) the presence of a leader (or k-group in Schelling's terminology) may increase the degree of cohesion of a regional agreement. This could also be represented by a shift of both curves to the right as a regional leader would increase the vale of the club good[15] and lower management costs.

In conclusion equilibrium club size will vary because exogenous conditions change and /or endogenous conditions change. This last point, needs to be further clarified. Changing endogenous conditions here means that, given the international environment, countries outside the agreement are willing to undertake the changes in their domestic political economy so as to be " admitted to the club", i.e. to become " more similar" to the current club members thus decreasing the degree of diversity . This is the basic insight in Baldwin's (1993) " domino theory of regionalism" where the demand for integration increases in countries previously not interested in joining a regional agreement. However, the final regional equilibrium will depend on both demand and supply of membership. Linking the regional to the national level implies looking at this point.

5. Narrowing Diversity. The Demand for Integration

As just mentioned we may think of an integration "equilibrium" as the outcome of the interaction between "demand for integration", i.e. the decision of individual countries to apply for membership in integration agreements and to undergo the necessary adjustments for that request to be fulfilled, and the "supply of integration", i.e. the willingness of regional agreements to accept new members. Let us take a closer look at the determination of the demand for integration.

Economic integration delivers benefits and costs, both economic and political, to the integrating countries. In section 3 we have briefly reviewed costs and benefits as discussed in the economic literature, here we consider them from the point of view of individual countries. In other words we consider costs and benefits as country specific, i.e. as they reflect the economic and political structure of each country. If we consider this aspect we see that a given level of integration, exogenously determined[16] will deliver different costs and benefits according to the initial level of market liberalization. From integration theory we know that costs of integration -Ic- are decreasing, and benefits of integration -Ib- are increasing with the degree of integration, i.e. with the degree of liberalization of the economy -see fig.2. Costs derive from the adjustment an economy has to undergo in the reallocation process that integration requires. They are initially high as one can assume that the production structure of a closed or isolated economy is quite distant from the one that is optimal in an integration equilibrium. Hence resource allocation may be quite distant and distorted from an allocation consistent with trade liberalization. Costs can be measured both in terms of sectors that must be closed down and in terms of the political resistance to change i.e. the Ic curve

---

[15]For instance by providing monetary discipline or unilateral access to domestic markets.

[16]For instance membership in a trade agreement implies that all member countries adopt the same level of tariff.

reflects both economic and political costs. Similarly integration costs will be larger the higher is the degree of protection and the larger is the share of the economy that is not exposed to international competition, i.e. the non tradable sector. Benefits are increasing with the degree of integration as beneficial effects of international competition spread over a larger part of the economy through a better resource allocation. As for costs the Ib curve reflects political benefits in terms of the support of the interest groups that are likely to be favored by liberalization[17]. We can also consider the non economic aspects of integration, as benefits will be larger if members of the integrating region are also part of an alliance which may not necessarily be only a military one (Gowa and Mansfield 1993).

Figure 2: Costs and benefits of integration.

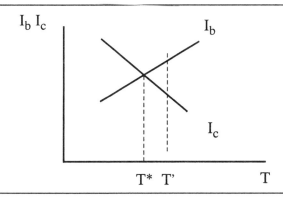

Figure 2 describes these elements. The position of the I_c and of the I_b curves, respectively, depend on the share of the non tradable sectors (a larger non tradable sector shifts the I_c curve upwards), and on the presence of an alliance, an outside threat, elements that would shift I_b upwards. The I_b curve would also shift upwards if a larger number of sectors of the economy would benefit from increased liberalization. As it is shown, there is a critical level of integration -T*- beyond which benefits are larger than costs, hence it is convenient to pursue the integration option. The level of liberalization is exogenously determined by the characteristics of the agreement (e.g. the level of the tariff for a trade club or the degree of financial liberalization for a monetary club) say at level T'. Joining the agreement implies accepting this level of liberalization. At T' net integration benefits (I_b - I_c) may be positive or negative. In the first case it would obviously be beneficial for the country to join the agreement (or to ask for membership). In the second case positive net benefits would materialize only following a shift in the position of the two curves (the I_b to the right and/or the I_c to the left) which could be seen as the consequence of a shift in domestic preferences with respect to the

---

[17]The role of interest groups in determining international agreements is analyzed in Grossman and Helpman (1996), Milner (1997).

integration option. The role of globalization is relevant in this process to the extent that increased market globalization shifts the preferences towards more open economies and away from sheltered sectors.

6. Interaction Between Supply and Demand of Integration

Net integration benefits for the single country are only a necessary condition for membership. Entering a club requires the payment of an admission fee. The justification for a club admission fee is obvious. New club members must guarantee that they will behave according to club rules and will not deteriorate the quality of the club good. Hence the admission fee requires a policy change in the country wishing to join the agreement. We may think of two simple examples for as policy change as admission fee. In the case of a monetary club the admission fee may be explicit (as in the case of the fulfillment of the Maastricht conditions for joining the European single currency). In the case of a trade club a policy change is needed to rule out that support to the domestic industry through instruments such as subsidies transfers etc. We may also think of " implicit fees". For instance we may consider the case that the adjustment entailed in the process of integration implies a macroeconomic dimension. This aspect is enhanced by globalization. Globalization is beneficial if, among other things it enhances the possibility of attracting foreign capital. This requires a " sound macroeconomic environment" . Macroeconomic stabilization must be implemented to obtain the dual objective of making the potential benefits of integration effective and of obtaining the international credibility that is necessary to attract funds from abroad, both from official institutions and from private investors. In short, the admission fee must be paid, to obtain the creditworthiness necessary to gain access to international capital markets and/or to be accepted in a club. We can assume that the cost of reputation (R) is increasing with the degree of liberalization (integration) as deeper integration requires deeper transformation in policy and/or a larger amount of funds from abroad is needed the larger the dimension of the adjustment process. In short membership in a club implies an exogenous degree of liberalization T' and a corresponding amount of reputation R* that must be obtained (the club admission fee). These two elements determine the conditions of the supply of membership.

Matching up the two elements, the level of liberalization and the reputation limit produces a new threshold in the choice process, illustrated in figure 3. The value of T' determines a critical value -R*- of reputation which must be reached in order to gain access to international finance and/or to be admitted to a club. Creditworthiness can be obtained by implementing an adjustment program, which in our framework, can be, very simply, represented by an inverse relationship between R and X, the policy variable controlled by the government. This implies that a minimum level of R requires a maximum level of X. The picture must be completed to take into account the consequences of the admission fee on domestic political equilibrium.

Figure 3: Integration and reputation.

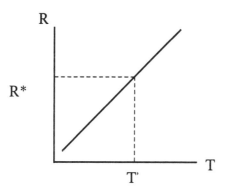

A government faces a domestic problem, which may be represented by assuming that the policy maker maximizes the probability of staying in power. In order to obtain this goal the government will use X to maximize P, the government's popularity, to which the probability of staying in power is positively related. We can assume that there is a minimum level of popularity P* which is required to stay in power for a given institutional and political setting. The way in which X influences (directly) P reflects the social and institutional characteristics of the country. The amount of X necessary to obtain a given amount of P will increase with the degree of social sclerosis in Olson's (1965) sense, (which is larger the larger is the number and strength of interest groups, and the degree of fragmentation of the society), and the size and power of the state bureaucracy, the degree of divided government (Milner 1997). A minimum level of popularity implies a minimum level of X, -X*-. The position of the P curve is influenced by the nature of the state. A strong state, where the degree of social sclerosis is low, will obtain a higher amount of P out of a given amount of X than a weak state where the degree of social sclerosis is high.

The framework is now set for its purpose, i.e. to answer the question: under which circumstances will a country find it desirable to ask for membership in an integration agreement? A positive answer requires that a positive net benefit from integration is obtained. This is larger the more market oriented is the economy, the stronger is the integration process in place (a higher value o T'), the stronger is the outside threat (e.g. regional blocs worldwide), the stronger are the non economic ties with the integration partners. As the net integration benefits must be confronted with the amount of the admission fee the pattern described boils down to one choice. The government may set the amount of X, her policy variable, at a value that is consistent with the integration option.

We may now recapitulate the steps in the domestic policy process. The intersection between benefits and costs from integration determines a minimum level of integration -T*-. This leads, to a minimum level of reputation R* to be obtained (the admission fee). Figure 4 brings together the reputation function and the popularity function, both determined, although in an opposite relationship, by the level of the domestic policy variable X. To use Putnam's (1988) terminology (see also Guerrieri and Padoan 1989) the upper and lower bounds to X, established respectively by the reputation -X(R*)- and the popularity -X(P*) - constraints, determine a "win set", i.e. a set of feasible policies that are consistent with both domestic and international policy goals.

Figure 4: Domestic equilibrium.

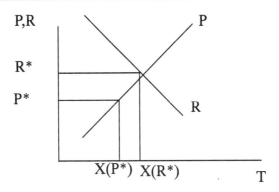

If the reputation constraint is more binding that the popularity constraint: X(R*)<X(P*) a win set does not exist. The emergence of an integration option, however, may be exploited by the government to force an adjustment on the domestic economy by lowering the popularity constraint below the reputation constraint. This is the familiar case where international politics is used as a leverage to impose change in the domestic political and economic arena. This option will be more attractive the larger are the benefits promised by integration. This option will also be more easily pursued the more powerful are the domestic interest groups that will benefit from integration (whose relative position and size determines the relative position of the I_b and I_c schedules). As the country adjusts towards the liberalization level T' and the reputation level R* requested by club membership the diversity between existing and candidate members decreases and this allows for an expansion of club size (the endogenous component of club size determination increases).

7. From Top down to Bottom up

In the sections above we have followed a "top down" approach, suggesting some linkages between the collapse of the post war international (hegemonic) system-which has produced a state of institutional disequilibrium-towards the emergence of regionalism, which can be thought of as partial response to the excess demand of international public goods. We have then suggested that the formation of regional clubs, has increased both the supply of and the demand for integration. The latter is signaled by the willingness of an increasing number of countries to adjust their domestic political economy in order to pay the entry fee to regional clubs (the " domino effect").

It is now appropriate to follow a " bottom up" approach to look at what is the initial point raised in section 2: is the spreading of regionalism leading to a more cooperative global system - i.e. to the formation of a " global multilateral regime" - ?

This issue can be addressed by reconsidering the conditions for cooperation without hegemony. Discussion in section 2 suggests that the willingness to adjust, hence the willingness to change national preferences (condition 2) is fulfilled to the extent that the supply of integration generates positive net benefits from integration to the domestic economy and that the club admission fee is not inconsistent with domestic political equilibrium. The same discussion suggests that (condition 3) - a long time horizon- is also fulfilled, by definition, to the extent that club membership is seen as a long time commitment. This is the case for participation to trade agreements and monetary unions[18] as they both imply large sunk costs to be paid in order to make the national economies consistent with club requirements. Condition 4) - the role of institutions- is fulfilled if we consider that regional agreements are usually based on strong issue-linkages, e.g. between economy and security, between monetary and trade relations etc. Issue linkages may be explicit as in the case when members of an economic agreement (like the EU) are also part of a security agreement (like NATO) or may be implicit when e.g. security goals are pursued through economic integration. In general, issue linkages provide information about partner's behavior in an area that is different from the one in which the agreement is being sought thus fulfilling the role of institutions in international cooperation.

Condition 1) -a small number of actors- is also, by definition, fulfilled by the spreading of regionalism. What is less clear is whether such a condition does indeed lead to deeper global integration. For example Krugman (1993) has argued that the formation of regional blocs will lead to conflict rather than cooperation and he has also shown that, under specific conditions, the number of regional actors less conducive to cooperation is three. Condition 1) then becomes the crucial one. To see whether a small number of actors leads to more or less global cooperation one must introduce hypothesis about the behavior of regional clubs facing each other in the international system.

One approach has been suggested by Oye (1992). He posits that, in a post-hegemonic, multipolar, regional (and national) actors tend to pursue " unrestricted", i.e. selective, bargaining *vis-à-vis* each other in order to obtain selective market

---

[18]The same is not true for currency arrangements such as pegged exchange rates which, on the contrary, tend to be increasingly short lived in a world of deep financial integration. See Eichengreen (1994).

access and, to this purpose are ready to reciprocate with their partners to obtain liberalization of their domestic market. He also notes that a strong incentive to pursue unrestricted (selective) bargaining comes from globalization as selective market access is a form of competition in global markets (which are not uniform markets). In addition, selective market access reinforces the incentives of third parties to barter over market access as the formation of preferential agreements increases the costs of exclusion. This line of argument (which is very similar to the " domino approach" to regionalism) may be reinforced by the issues explored in the recent literature on the political economy of protection and liberalization. Grossman and Helpman (1996) suggest that domestic lobbying for domestic liberalization will come from pro free trade groups that see domestic opening as a condition to obtain market access abroad as the result of reciprocal bargaining. They also suggest that the predominance of protectionist interest groups comes from the fact that industries seeking protection are usually declining industries where the prospective market size is simply not enough to compensate for entry costs, hence the potential for free riding is much lower and the possibility of organizing collective action larger. On the contrary, industries that benefit from liberalization usually face expanding markets where free riding firms would be able to enter without contributing to the lobbying effort. However, if sunrise markets expand fast enough the incentive to pursue reciprocal domestic liberalization may overcome the free riding costs. In addition the value of sunk costs investment in lobbying for protection declines over time in sunset industries. This point can be extended to bargaining between regional agreements by noting that, if reciprocal liberalization is carried out on a regional basis it will benefit firms belonging to the regional agreement which, in principle have already paid an admission fee[19].Therefore participation to a regional agreement that engages in selective bargaining partially offsets the free riding problem. In other words, reciprocal bargaining between regions may be more efficient than reciprocal bargaining between countries. On the other hand regionalism may make the multilateral system more fragile because, among other things, countries joining a regional agreement are doing so because they want more and not less protection, hence they would oppose regional policies leading to a more open and multilateral system.

Globalization can speed up the process towards a more open direction. The most powerful forces of global integration are represented by the activities of multinational firms (MNE). One relevant aspect is that these activities not only increase the degree of economic interdependence, but may also lead to convergence in governments' polices (through reciprocity).

The relevance for economic convergence derives from the fact that MNE are powerful vehicles of innovation diffusion. In a world in which technological progress is the key determinant of growth and competitiveness the degree of diffusion of knowledge is the crucial factor for the dissemination of the benefits of growth[20].

---

[19] The admission fee is "paid" by governments but this obviously reverberates on the country's firms.

[20] A formal assessment is provided by Grossman and Helpman (1991).

MNE, however, may also become a powerful factor in "political" convergence. As Froot and Yoffie (1991) have shown, MNE activities decrease the incentives national governments face in supplying protection to their economies. In a world of highly mobile capital, MNE activities are one typical response to protectionistic barriers -be they erected to protect nations or regions. As the amount of foreign investment in protected areas increases, the rents from protection increasingly accrue to foreigners, i.e. to the owners of foreign capital in the region rather than to domestic residents. Hence protectionist governments receive a decreasing share of political support in exchange for their intervention and their benefit from this form of political exchange decreases. On the other hand the benefits from both reciprocal market access and international diffusion of knowledge increase. In short, in a world of countries or regions, each pursuing a policy of protection, international mobility of capital tends to weaken the strength of protectionistic policies and, indirectly, to decrease the differences in national or regional political economies.

However this is true as long as this process is symmetrical, i.e. if capital mobility is a two way activity. If capital flows only in one direction the government of a region or country where foreign capital does not penetrate will be able to preserve the political benefits of protection. Only as long as investment flows in both direction global market forces represent a powerful vehicle of economic integration. Further, if capital integration is not symmetrical, the region where foreign investment does not penetrate will also loose part of the (potential) benefits of innovation diffusion and of growth associated to it. It follows that in a world of high mobility of capital new incentives emerge to attract foreign MNE activities. This reinforces the incentives of industrial sectors to obtain liberal policies on a reciprocal basis.

Support may come not only from business groups. Lobbying activity by trade unions interested in creating new employment opportunities, not necessarily generates a request for more protection. Rather unions would be interested in policies that attract capital. The opposite may be true as the request to the governments will be for more rather than less openness. This is one of the consequences of the fact that globalization has produced a new form of competition - competition for location sites - which requires (and is also dependent on) regulation. In the first place, because location advantages may be created by investment of regional development funds the overall amount of which may be excessive ex-post. Secondly because this will take the form of "competition among rules", i.e. regulations affecting locational incentives such as environmental and labor market regulations. The attempt to attract foreign investment might create the incentives towards a "deterioration" of rules, or of rule enforcement, so as to decrease the private costs of investment at the detriment of social costs, a problem facing both NAFTA and Europe. To summarize, increasing capital mobility may indeed represent a powerful element of convergence to the extent that it creates incentives in domestic politics to pursue more open and less protection oriented (more "market" oriented) policies, which tend to favor more cooperative international policies. This last and crucial point stems from the fact that, by definition, MNE operations are global and MNE themselves, to a increasingly lesser degree, can be considered as tied to a specific country or region. This reinforces the need, however, to establish regimes that will facilitate the operation of market forces at a global level; i.e. globalization increases the demand for international public goods.

8. Summary and Conclusion

The points developed in this paper may be summarized in the following steps.

step1: The international system is in a state of " institutional disequilibrium" in the sense that there is an excess demand of international public goods. This is the result of a decrease in supply because of the redistribution of power away from an hegemonic structure and of an increase in demand because of increased globalization

step 2: The excess demand of international public goods spurs the formation of regional agreements Regional agreements are a source of supply of (partially excludable) international public goods (club goods). At the same time globalization provides incentives to the formation of regional agreements based on norms and standards that contribute to the build-up of regional comparative advantage. To the extent that globalization brings forward market instability it is itself a source of spreading regionalism.

step 3: Regionalism and globalization increase the demand for integration and support structural adjustment at country level. The demand of integration increases because access to the global market (globalization) requires new standards for the domestic economy and regional standards are a source of comparative advantage but also because clubs offer protection against global instability. Domestic adjustment and demand for integration will respond positively to the supply of integration (as provided by existing regional agreements) to the extent that they are not inconsistent with domestic political equilibrium.

step 4: As a growing number of countries joins regional agreements regionalism provides a new equilibrium in the production of international public goods. It also leads towards the fulfillment of conditions of cooperation under anarchy since: a) the time horizon increases as regional agreements are by definition long term commitments, b) the propensity to adjust increases, c) issue linkages increase the exchange of information.

step 5: The fulfillment of the fourth condition - a small number of actors- does not necessarily imply that regionalism leads to the construction of a new global system (to be understood as a global equilibrium between the supply and demand of international public goods). However this might be obtained under unrestricted bargaining (Oye). The incentive to pursue unrestricted (selective) bargaining comes (also) from globalization as selective market access is a form of competition in global markets.

As presented the sequence above can easily deliver the impression that almost inevitably a new global order will emerge from the collapse of the old one. We should be careful to accept this view. What has been suggested in the paper is only one possible reading of the existing literature in the attempt to establish linkages between the different levels of analysis. Several other approaches, and sequences, are possible leading to different conclusions about the evolution of the international system.

References

Alesina, A., Grilli, V. (1993): On the Feasibility of a One-Speed or Multi-Speed European Monetary Union. Economics and Politics, 5.

Baldwin, R. (1993): A Domino Theory of Regionalism. CEPR Discussion Paper n 732.

Baldwin, R., Venables, A. (1994): Regional Economic Integration. In: Grossman, G., Rogoff, K. (eds): Handbook of International Economics. Vol. 3, North Holland, Amsterdam.

Bayoumi, T. (1994): A Formal Model of Optimum Currency Areas. CEPR Discussion Paper n 968.

Buchanan, J. (1965): The Economic Theory of Clubs. Economica 37: 1-14.

Casella, A., Feinstein, J. (1990): Public Goods in Trade: on the Formation of Markets and Political Jurisdictions. NBER Working Paper n.3554, December.

Cohen, B. (1993): Beyond EMU: The Problem of Sustainability. Economics and Politics, vol 5.

Collignon, S. (1997): European Monetary Union, Convergence and Sustainability. The Sustainability Report, AUME, Paris.

Cornes, J., Sandler, T. (1985): The Theory of Externalities, Public Goods and Club Goods. Cambridge University Press, Cambridge.

De Grauwe, P. (1992): European Monetary Integration. Oxford University Press, Oxford.

De Melo, J, Panagariya, A. (eds) (1993): New Dimensions in Regional Integration. Cambridge University Press, Cambridge.

De Melo, J., Panagariya, A., Rodrik, D. (1993): The New Regionalism, a Country Perspective. In: De Melo, J. Panagarya, A. (1993).

Eichengreen, B. (1994): International Monetary Arrangements for the 21st Century. Brookings. Washington.

Fratianni, M. (1995): Variable Integration in the European Union. Mimeo. Indiana University.

Fratianni, M., Pattison, J. (1982): The Economics of International Organisations. Kyklos, Vol.32.

Frey, B. (1984): International Political Economics. Basil Blackwell, New York.

Froot, K., Yoffie, D. (1991): Strategic Policies in a Tripolar World. The International Spectator n.3.

Gilpin, R. (1987): The Political Economy of International Relations. Princeton University Press, Princeton.

Gowa, J., Mansfield, E. (1993): Power Politics and International Trade. American Political Science Review, vol 87.

Grossman, G., Helpman, E. (1991): Innovation and Growth in the World Economy. MIT Press, Cambridge.

Grossman, G. , Helpman, E. (1994): Protection for Sale. American Economic Review, vol 84.

Grossman, G., Helpman, E. (1996): Sunk Costs and Liberalization Policies. European Economic Review, May.

Guerrieri, P., Padoan, P.C. (eds) (1988): The Political Economy of International Cooperation, Croom Helm, London, Sidney.

Guerrieri, P., Padoan,P.C. (eds) (1989): The Political Economy of European Integration: Markets, States and Institutions. Wheatsheaf, Brighton.

Henning, R. (1996): Europe's Monetary Union and the United States. Foreign Policy, Spring.

Keohane, R. (1984): After Hegemon. Princeton University Press, Princeton .

Krugman, P. (1993): Regionalism. Some Analytical Notes. In: De Melo, J, Panagaraya, A.(1993).

Mansfield, E., Branson, R. (1994): Alliances, Preferential Trading Arrangements and International Trade. Paper presented at the annual meeting of the American Political Science Association, September 1-4, New York.

Mansfield, E., Milner, H. (eds) (1997): The Political Economy of Regionalism. Introduction Columbia University, New York.

Mayer, F. (1992): Managing Domestic Differences in International Negotiations: the Strategic Use of Internal Side-payments. International Organization, 46 Autumn.

Milner, H. (1997): Interests, Institutions, and Information. Princeton University Press, Princeton.

Olson, M. (1965): The Logic of Collective Action. Yale University Press, New Haven.

Oye, K. (ed.) (1985): Cooperation under Anarchy. Princeton University Press, Princeton.

Oye, K. (1992): Economic Discrimination and Political Exchange. Princeton University Press, Princeton.

Padoan, P.C. (1997): Regional Agreements as Clubs. The European Case. In : Mansfield, E. and Milner, H. (1997).

Putnam, R. (1988): Diplomacy and Domestic Politics: the Logic of Two-Level Games. International Organization, 42, Summer.

Perroni , C., Whalley, J. (1994): The New Regionalism: Trade Liberalization or Insurance? NBER Working Paper n. 4626.

Rodrik, D. (1997): Has Globalization Gone too Far? Institute for International Economics, Washington D.C.

Sandler, T., Tschirhart, J. (1980): The Economic Theory of Clubs: an Evaluative Survey. Journal of Economic Literature, XVIII.

Santos, P. (1993): The Spatial Implications of Economic and Monetary Union. European Economy n.54.

Smith, A., Tsoukalis, L. (1996): Report on Economic and Social Cohesion. Mimeo, College of Europe, Bruges.

Snidal, D. (1991): Relative Gains and the Pattern of International Cooperation. American Political Science Review, September.

Widgren, M. (1994): The Relation between Voting Power and Policy Impact in the European Union. CEPR Discussion Paper n 1033.

Winters, A. (1993): Expanding EC Membership and Association Accords: Recent Experience and Future Prospects. In: Anderson, K., Blackhurst , R.(eds): Regional Integration and the Global Trading System. Harvester Wheatsheaf.

Acknowledgements

I would like to thank Gerard Roland for a number of stimulating comments. The usual disclaimer applies.

16. Financial Liberalization, the European Single Currency and the Problem of Unemployment

E 42

F33 F36

F41

F43

Annamaria Simonazzi and Fernando Vianello

1. Financial Liberalization: Origins and Consequences

The idea that the era of the self-regulating market had come to an end once and for all with the Great Transformation of the 1930s, and that a return to the past, as attempted in the 1920s, could no longer be contemplated found its most consummate expression in Karl Polanyi's great book, published during World War II (Polanyi, 1944). But the idea in itself (by no means the only important thing in the book) was, in reality, widespread and indeed dominant in both Europe and the United States. Thus, even though reconstruction of the international economic order was placed under the aegis of free trade, it was certainly not inspired by that "market fundamentalism" whose destructiveness is condemned today in terms worthy of Polanyi by his fellow countryman George Soros (cf. Soros, 1998). Three aspects, in particular, are worth mentioning:

(a) an attempt was indeed made to reunite the world market in the form of a return to multilateralism and the dismantling of administrative controls on foreign trade (as well as on domestic prices), but with a gradual, step by step approach; nor was there any question of doing away with customs duties in the individual countries, and certainly not along the boundaries of the two great regional economic areas the formation of which was being actively promoted, namely the Western European and Japanese areas;

(b) the United States alleviated the financial difficulties of the rest of the world through massive loans and aid, the role of which as a source of international liquidity was later taken over by the chronic deficit of the US balance of payments;

(c) the total freedom of action enjoyed by international finance until World War I, and then again for a short period of time before the great crisis, was not restored, the reason for this being not only to protect the economies from the disruptive consequences of the movements of hot money, still burning in the memory, but also – as we shall see more clearly later – to make exchange rate management compatible with the autonomy of national monetary policies.

European and Japanese protectionism (in the face of the openness of the American market), powerful injections of international liquidity and restrictions on capital movements represented, as it were, the external defences of the post-war social pact, which took on very different forms from one country to another, but was in all cases based on low interest rates, labour market regulation and high levels of employment and social protection. In the particular case of capital controls, it is worth emphasising the role they played not only in the peripheral countries, but also in the central one. Under the umbrella of capital controls, both the American government and the Federal Reserve (despite their notorious differences) followed a policy of low interest rates, aiming both at immediate redistribution and at securing affordable financing for the public debt, thus widening the scope for the expansion of social expenditure.

Behind these choices, one factor that seems to emerge fairly forcefully (along with the influence of wartime interventionism and solidarism, and the memory of the disasters *laissez faire* had exposed both the individual economies and the international economic order in the period between the two wars) is the calling into question of the capitalist mode of production prompted by the Soviet revolution and the attraction the Soviet model exerted on the working classes all over the world. A sense of the precariousness of the existing social order and the challenge represented by the Soviet Union and its economic successes – in contrast with economic crisis in the West – dominated debate in the 1930s and played a major role in determining both the success of the theoretical position of Keynes (who was himself convinced that capitalism could not survive mass unemployment) and, closely bound up with it, the rise of the welfare state. Suffice it to recall the title of the Beveridge Report, *Full Employment in a Free Society*, amounting to the assertion that a non free society, namely Communism, was not the only alternative available to mass unemployment, and the warning, serving as an epigraph, that "Misery generates hate".

In this respect, the "neoclassical synthesis", following upon the straight Kenynesianism of the immediate post-war period, offered a compromise between various needs. On the one hand, unlike the "Keynesians of the first generation"[1], the authors subscribing to the new orthodoxy embraced the canonical view of the market as capable of securing allocative efficiency, which was precluded to a planned economy (and which, some argued, the latter might seek to achieve by simulating market behaviour). This provided the United States with a banner under which to muster forces against the renewed challenge of the Soviet economy – which was growing at a steady pace and, according to Khruschev's ambitions, would be catching up with the American economy and even outreaching it in a decade or two – and to react to lost ground in the technological field, which the spectacular Sputnik launch seemed to reveal. On the other hand, they recognised the incapacity of the market to secure full employment and a fair distribution of income, thus furnishing a functional theoretical framework for the post-war social pact.

The theoretical fragility of the compromise was clear from the outset to anyone who really wanted to see it, but the crunch came only much later, thus reinforcing the conviction that the reasons for its staying power lay elsewhere. "As Darwin's theory states", it has been said of the evolution of literary forms, "the context does not generate new forms, but only selects them. The dominant forms (or ideas) are not, therefore, the forms or ideas of the dominant class, but more simply the forms the dominant class has selected" (Moretti, 1988, p. 221).

The context was, however, to change rapidly as a result of the progressive erosion of the United States economic supremacy over Europe and Japan. The continued American balance of payments deficit eventually shook confidence in the

---

[1] The expression is by S. Steve. Cf. Steve (1977), p.98.

dollar, plunging the international monetary system into crisis in the early 1970s and opening the way to the audacious devaluation strategy of the Nixon administration. With transition to flexible exchange rates one significant justification for capital controls no longer applied. In fact, in the complex architecture of the Bretton Woods system capital controls played a role complementary to that of adjustable exchange rates. While the possibility to adjust the exchange rates side-stepped the social costs of deflation together with the threat to freedom of trade represented by competitive devaluations, capital controls freed the interest rate from the task of defending the existing parity (until modification was deemed necessary), thus safeguarding the autonomy of monetary policy – and, to some extent, fiscal policy, given the constraint imposed on the latter by the level of interest rates. It is true that in a flexible exchange rate system autonomy of monetary policy is fully guaranteed only on condition that no limits are set to the size of exchange rate variation one is prepared to accept, but this limitation gives capital controls nothing like the importance it has in a fixed exchange rate system.

As for the destabilising effects of hot money in flexible exchange rate systems, a quarter of a century of adjustable exchange rates had dimmed the memory (while the memory of the obstinate resistance of governments to apparently inevitable devaluation remained vivid). At the same time, acceptance grew of Milton Friedman's argument that the fact that speculators make profits suffices to prove that speculation is a stabilising factor (cf. Friedman, 1953, pp. 174-6). Two observations can be made here. The first is that the above argument neglects the fact that speculators can indeed make profits by forcing a country to rapid acceptance of a currency depreciation which it could in no case avoid, but they can also make profits by imposing a perfectly avoidable depreciation, which would be offset by an increase in prices in the future. The second observation is that the argument in question does not take account of the investors' expectations of some sort of bailing out should things take a negative turn. Such expectations normally prove well-founded, given the need facing the monetary authorities (in the country whose currency is the object of speculative activity or in the country the speculation originates from) to ward off a financial crisis of vast proportions. To the two manners of making profits mentioned above we must thus add another, which does not consist in forcing a country to accept depreciation of its currency, justified or not, but in bringing in vast amounts of capital, thus offering the exchange rate undue support, and paving the way for future catastrophes (indeed, measures to limit the entry of capital are increasingly being proposed – and sometimes successfully adopted, as in the case of Chile).

With the rise in the price of oil in late 1973 began the golden age of the great American (and British) banks, which found a fruitful field of action in the recycling of petrodollars. When their international orientation appeared incompatible with a persistently weak dollar, they were able to settle the conflict with the Carter administration to their own advantage and impose a sharp restrictive turn in monetary policy. At the same time the banks became ever more intolerant of constraints imposed upon their freedom of action by their own and other countries. Consensus on financial liberalisation was rapidly obtained thanks to a series of domestic and international circumstances. On the domestic level, as we shall soon be seeing, the foundations of the post-war social pact were by now somewhat worn down. At the international level, financial supremacy was (along with military supremacy) becoming the tool to which American hegemony, shaken on the industrial ground, would entrust its own self-perpetuation (cf. de Cecco, 1987, pp. 8-9) – and financial supremacy both demanded financial liberalisation and made it possible to impose it on the rest of the world. Of the Bretton Woods system the International Monetary Fund was practically the only element to remain viable, although no longer, at least principally, in the role of supplier of international finance to countries facing balance of payments problems. This role was increasingly being taken over by the private banks, while the IMF became more a guarantor, on behalf of the banks, of the reliability of the countries on which they had lavished loans, often urging them to borrow beyond their real needs, and which now found themselves stifled by rising interest rates. IMF conditionality represented an important vehicle for the spread of domestic deregulation as well as capital liberalisation.

The rise in interest rates and the recession following on the second oil shock reversed the upward trend in the price of raw materials that had marked the 1970s. This had devastating effects on producer countries[2], particularly those deeper in debt, which saw the burden of the service of the debt grow as the means to tackle it dwindled. But it also brought the benefit of a sharp and lasting improvement in terms of trade for the industrialised countries. The fall in prices of raw materials was the hidden protagonist (the attention of the economists being mainly turned elsewhere) of the great disinflation of the 1980s (cf. Ginzburg and Simonazzi, 1998), which for the United States was also helped by considerable appreciation of the dollar up to the mid-eighties.

While improving the terms of trade, the appreciation of the dollar tightened the constraint of foreign competition. Thus the drive to increase profit margins prompted by the rise in interest rates had to be partly re-routed in the direction of reduction of costs[3]. Here the drive came up against the old institutions of the labour market, and swept them away or, where it could not, bypassed them by moving production to other parts of the country, thus bringing to completion the process of dislocation in industrial relations that had set in during the previous decade.

On top of the increasing flexibility of labour and inequality in income distribution came drastic rescaling of the welfare state and the progressive system of taxation. What this actually suggests is that the dominant classes suddenly felt that the old set of policies aimed at organising consensus no longer served much purpose. Not only did it stand in the way of that freedom of action in the productive

---

[2] Regarding oil in particular, in the United States the interests of the domestic producers – penalised by the high cost of extraction – were sacrificed to cheap importation policy (when the price of oil fell, too): a distinctly "Ricardian" choice which, like the British abandonment of corn protectionism in the nineteenth century, calls for control over supply sources and sea routes (a circumstance that did not fail to condition American foreign and military policy in the following years; cf. Ginzburg, 1991a and 1991b).

[3] On the reduction of costs as a way of reacting to an increase in interest rates, especially when the alternative way of price increase is precluded, cf. Bonifati (1991) and Bonifati and Vianello (1998).

field that the high cost of money and mounting competition seemed to be making more necessary than ever; not only was it found an excessive burden on tax-payers and firms but, above all, the truly new and exciting sensation was that it could be dispensed with: control over the use of the labour force could be imposed instead of negotiated and the governance of social tensions exercised more through repression (for which it is always easy to find funds) and less through consensus.

If we go back to the origins of the post-war social pact, it does not seem inappropriate, or merely dictated by a love of symmetry, to observe that by the time the pact entered into crisis the need to respond to the challenge of the Soviet Union had long since waned away. Indeed, the Soviet Union was now a giant with feet of clay, a great military power resting on a paralysed economy and rotting state structure, and the idea hatched to drag it into a new arms race that would finally exhaust all its resources (while for the United States it represented an extremely useful means to boost demand and a rich source of technological innovation, thus offering textbook illustration of the different functioning of a market economy and a planned economy; cf. Pivetti, 1989, pp. 63-6).

In a way, it was a return of American capitalism to its origins (if this is not taken too literally), free from the conditioning of history. "America, you are more fortunate/ than our continent, the ancient one:/ you have no castles in ruins", as Goethe sang. To a country made by people who have cut all possible umbilical cords and whose only common trait is their equality, and fungibility, as Marx would say, as suppliers of "labour in general", creator of abstract wealth: " this abstraction of labour in general is not only the mental result of a concrete totality of labours. Indifference towards specific labour corresponds to a form of society in which individuals easily move from one type of labour to another, and in which the particular type of labour they actually perform is for them a matter of chance, and thus indifferent. Labour here has become a means of creating wealth in general, not only in the category, but also in reality.... This state of affairs finds its greatest development in the most modern form of existence of bourgeois society, the United States. Here, therefore, the abstraction of the category 'labour', 'labour in general', labour *sans phrase* becomes for the first time practical truth" (Marx, 1859, p. 635). And so the United States once again became the "promised land" of capitalism, as Sombart (1906) called it: a disjointed society, where the principle of *cash-payment for the sole nexus* (cf. Carlyle, 1976, p. 32) has more literal significance than elsewhere (which by no means contradicts its breaking-down into community and ethnic groups, just as the present resurgent nationalism is to some extent the other side of globalisation), and which places no obstacles to the free play of the destructive forces (creative or otherwise) of competition.

It is this return to the origins that finds its theoretical counterpart in the switch to monetarism and neoliberism. The latent conflict between neoclassical microeconomics and Keynesian common sense – the latter incapable of realising its potential as alternative theory – was abruptly settled in favour of the former: but why precisely then? As always, the problem is not the ways in which the new theoretical positions mature, but how they become established, thus leading to the development of a new orthodoxy. And, as always, the answer is to be sought in how they suit the environment in which they seek acceptance. Keynes referred to this principle to account for the success of 'Ricardian' theory (in reality the economic orthodoxy of his times). "The completeness of the Ricardian victory is something of a curiosity and a mystery. It must have been due to a complex of suitabilities of the doctrine to the environment into which it was projected. That it reached conclusions quite different from what the ordinary uninstructed person would expect, added, I suppose, to its intellectual prestige. That its teaching, translated into practice, was austere and often unpalatable, lent it virtue. That it was adapted to carry a vast and consistent logical superstructure, gave it beauty. That it could explain much social injustice and apparent cruelty as an inevitable incident in the scheme of progress, and the attempt to change such things as likely, on the whole, to do more harm than good, commended it to authority. That it afforded a measure of justification to the free activities of the individual capitalist, attracted to it the support of the dominant social force behind authority" (Keynes, 1936, pp. 32-3). Without changing a single word, these are considerations that seem equally applicable to the economic theory in vogue today.

Keynes seems to be forgetting the selection of economic theories on the basis of suitability to the characteristics of the environment when, in an oft-quoted passage, he describes the ideas of economists and political philosophers as more important than vested interests (cf. Keynes, 1936, pp. 383-84) and "practical men" as "usually the slaves of some defunct economist" (Keynes, 1936, p. 383). This brilliant, but superficial remark overlooks the essential point of the problem: *which* economists are practical men unknowingly slaves to? And it also disregards the possibility those in power knowingly choose under which theoretical banner to march, rapidly embracing the ideas of living economists, and making very free – not to say, frankly expedient – use of them. Thus, the vaunted monetarism of the Bundesbank or Volcker's Federal Reserve did not prevent the former from keeping an eye on the mood of the German trade unions at least as much as on variations in the money supply, nor the latter from adapting its policy to circumstances pragmatically, just as commitment to "supply-side economics" did not prevent the Reagan administration from vigorously boosting demand with a boldly expansive fiscal policy ("military Keynesianism"), unperturbed by the increased burden high interest rates meant for the government budget.

Here we must point out that in the US expansionary policies were, paradoxically, facilitated, and at the same time made more necessary, by the crisis of the post-war social pact. Let us take these two aspects one by one. The transformations undergone by the system of industrial relations were aptly summed up in such formulae as "intimidated labour force" (Krugman) or "cowed labour market" (Samuelson)[4] while, in statements reported by the press, A. Greenspan, present chairman of the Federal Reserve, indicated in the fear of losing the job (perhaps to find another, but losing out in income and social prestige) the factor that could account for the capacity of the American economy to conciliate high levels of employment with the absence of any inflationary drive, thus allowing for the

---

[4] Cf. for both expressions Samuelson (1977), p. 11.

perpetuation of an expansionary monetary stance. At the same time, it is the insufficiency of the social safety net which makes high unemployment both socially and politically intolerable. It has been observed that "American society does not tolerate unemployment" (Fitoussi, 1998, p. 58)[5] – and the mix of fiscal, monetary and exchange rate policies adopted has constantly taken this into account. Similarly, we might say that in Europe the existence of a vast, highly organised social safety net has not caused a high level of unemployment, as has all too often been stated, but has made it tolerable, thus proving functional to a highly restrictive mix of policies. It is this mix of policies, and the reasons behind it, that we shall now address.

2. The Macroeconomics of the European Union

The collapse of the Bretton Woods system caught the European countries in a phase when the idea of closer economic co-operation was very much on the upswing. In 1968 duties and quantitative restrictions on intra-community trade had been abolished. True, non-tariff barriers and capital controls still remained. But at the Hague summit (December 1969) the heads of state had approved the Werner Report calling for the institution of a monetary union by 1980. Well aware of the essential role of capital controls, the Report prescribed elimination only at the end of the process, when exchange rates would become fixed.

If the monetary turbulence of the early 1970s soon made the project utopian, it did however reinforce the conviction that it was necessary to construct an area of stable exchange rates and forge ahead on the road to integration. The decision taken in the spring of 1972 to institute the "monetary snake", or in other words to contain the fluctuations of the European currencies within a narrower band than that contemplated by the December 1971 Smithsonian Agreements, and the decision of the Council of Europe (Bremen, 1978) to substitute the above mechanism – which had long since entered into crisis – with a more ambitious exchange rate agreement (the EMS) are manifestations of this conviction.

The EMS owes its origins to the converging interests of various countries, reflecting both economic and political considerations[6]. As far as Germany is concerned, the attempt to make (real) exchange rates stable in a geographical area accounting for 50% of its foreign trade (if we include Austria and Switzerland, following a unilateral policy of pegging their currency to the D-mark), rising to 60% with the joining of Great Britain and Spain, constituted a response to the continual decline of the dollar and the American government's refusal to take action against it ("benign neglect"). As for the other countries, the reason why they accepted to give up autonomy

---

[5] This statement should be taken gingerly for various reasons, among which it is worth mentioning the fact that the percentage of unemployed is significantly altered by the great number of people swallowed up by the prison system. Between the mid-1970s and the mid-1990s the male prison population nearly tripled. In 1993 the number stood at 1,350,000, or little less than 2 per cent of the male labour force. Cf. Heise (1997), p. 50. Cf. also Freeman (1995) and (1996).

[6] See Simonazzi and Vianello (1994), pp.47-51 for detailed analysis of the positions of the various countries and the events that led to the EMS.

in exchange rate policy is probably to be found in their worry that a high degree of exchange rate instability would block the process of creating a single European market (as we have seen, the Bretton Woods system, too, was meant to protect freedom of trade from the risks associated with competitive devaluations) and jeopardise the survival of the Common Agricultural Policy.

Once the worries of the Bundesbank about the obligation to intervene in defence of the parities were assuaged, the creation of an area of exchange rate stability could answer to its needs, too, by spreading capital inflows over all the European currencies, thus easing the task of avoiding excessive appreciation of the D-mark over the dollar. During the 1970s, not even the Bundesbank had, in fact, been able to totally disregard the effects of exchange rate appreciation on the competitiveness of German industry; indeed, it was forced to intervene heavily in support of the dollar – first in 1971-73 and then again as from late 1977, faced with further decline in the American currency – getting itself into a position where it had to reabsorb the liquidity thus created.

Various factors helped in the cohesion of the EMS. To begin with, the first period of operation coincided with a phase of dollar appreciation. Moreover, the system was initially managed in a flexible manner: up to 1987 there were no fewer than 11 realignments, with an overall appreciation of 38% of the D-mark over the other currencies (and 45% over the French franc), while the pressure on exchange rates was limited by placing severe restrictions on the mobility of capital. Last but not least, the monetary policy of a growing number of countries took pegging to the D-mark as a major criterion until – with the "new EMS" phase beginning in 1987 –the principle extended to the entire area, whose monetary policy came thus to be determined by German monetary policy.

Along with the exchange rate policy, the latter constituted an integral part of the "neo-mercantilist" model adopted by Germany, which may be outlined as follows. The major force behind Germany's growth was its exports (with the exception of a few periods like the late 1970s, when Germany accepted to play, as they put it then, the "locomotive", and the unification phase). The country's trade surplus strengthened the D-mark and encouraged capital inflows serving to finance a large flow of trade credits, direct investment and aid in support of Germany's export of investment goods. Moreover, appreciation in the exchange rate allowed for reductions in the prices of imported raw materials, consumer goods and intermediate goods, thus helping curb the increase in domestic prices and safeguard the social pact upon which the system of industrial relations rested. If, however, this pact was called into question with wage demands seen as excessive, the Bundesbank intervened, threatening to raise interest rates and thus signalling its unwillingness to accommodate price increases[7]. This threat worked as a deterrent to trade unions and employers associations alike: in fact, higher interest rates would mean appreciation of the D-

---

[7] Commenting on the 1973-74 monetary squeeze, Giersch et al. (1992. p. 187) note that "the Council of Economic Experts endorsed the monetary policy as an unpleasant but necessary step towards breaking inflation and towards demonstrating to the public that excessive wage increases would not be given the monetary leeway to be shifted on to prices".

mark with a consequent loss of competitiveness for German products and falling profits, investment and employment.

The success of this model rested on the specific characteristics of the German productive structure and industrial relations system. The highly centralised nature of industrial relations made it possible for the Bundesbank to influence wage policy much more directly than could, for example, the Federal Reserve (cf. Carlin and Soskice, 1996), while industrial sectors whose capacity to penetrate the world market was not simply a matter of price competitiveness had considerable weight in the German productive structure. It was above all the interests of the other sectors, more exposed to foreign competition, that were now taken care of by promoting the creation of an area of exchange rate stability within Europe. However, the overall design rested on a delicate balance between potentially conflicting objectives: on the one hand, a strong currency, necessary to curb import prices and finance investment good exports and, on the other hand, stable exchange rates within the European trade area. Excessive appreciation of the D-mark over the other European currencies would, in fact, undermine the competitiveness of the German industry in the European Market, as actually happened in the latter half of the 1970s, and again in the years immediately following on the EMS crisis of 1992[8]. The need to defend the sectors exposed to foreign competition led the German government to foster institution of the EMS in the first case, and accept − albeit reluctantly − more flexible interpretation of the criteria for admission to the monetary union in the second. At the same time, exceedingly restrictive economic policies on the part of the other European countries would have reduced the growth capacity of their economies, and thus of the export markets for German industry. It was for this reason that the German government insisted on a system of *adjustable* exchange rates.

As we have already pointed out, in the latter half of the 1980s all the countries subscribing to the EMS adjusted their macroeconomic policies to the German model, as from 1987 foregoing further realignments. The adoption of orthodox policies, not supported by the system of industrial relations and the type of products and markets on which German supremacy rested, inevitably had results that were very different than those hoped for. Thus, even though the convergence of French macroeconomic policy towards the German one − the "competitive disinflation model" − succeeded in curbing inflation, it not only failed to secure the return of full employment through enhanced competitiveness, but led to a dramatic increase in unemployment. The high interest rates and the restrictive budget policies needed to achieve exchange rate stability in the "new EMS" period entailed such high costs for certain countries that the market could no longer regard them as sustainable in the medium term. Italy and Great Britain were forced to abandon the EMS, and France itself was only able to remain with a greatly widened band of fluctuation. Nor did the small and open economies of northern Europe, closely integrated with the German area as they were, escape the costs of a policy of exchange rate stability and financial orthodoxy, which could be truly heavy as the case of Belgium demonstrated.

---

[8] Between September 1992 and March 1995 the lira was devalued by 50% against the D-mark, fuelling demands for protectionist measures in the rest of Europe.

The restrictive stance of the European countries' macroeconomic policies and, in fact, the adoption of an export-led growth model by such a vast economic area transformed the low growth rate of the 1980s into generalised deflation which eventually drew even Germany along with it. That this was by no means an inevitable course of events is demonstrated by the whole story of the EMS in the preceding period, when the member countries seemed well aware of, and worried over, the consequences that too rigid a discipline – with persistent and sizeable divergences in the "fundamentals" – could have on growth and employment, and ultimately on the very sustainability of the exchange rate agreements. Thus, thanks to the far-sightedness of Paolo Baffi, on joining Italy negotiated and obtained a wider band of fluctuation. Shortly after, France ventured on an experiment in reflation; Germany accepted (when it did not urge) changes in the parities aimed at offsetting differences in inflation; capital controls were maintained and when necessary stiffened. What brought about the change? Various social and industrial policy designs (use of the exchange rate as an instrument for discipline and stimulus for restructuring) and others more frankly political (as, in the case of France, binding Germany ever more closely to Europe or, in the case of the Bank of Italy and its allies, cutting off funding of the party-led grabs system then in power, accelerating its undoing[9]) wove together, as also with the evolution of economic theory, where support and justification were sought.

The advent of monetarism brought an end to justifications for capital controls, even within a system of pegged exchange rates like the EMS. Since the only consequence of a restrictive monetary policy, it was now being argued, would be a lowering of the inflation rate, without any lasting loss of employment, free capital movements would represent a healthy factor of monetary discipline, without any substantial contraindications.

Immediately after the crisis of the international monetary system, the ideas dominant at the time had been distilled into the brilliant formula stating that fixed exchange rates, freedom of capital movement and autonomous national monetary policy formed an "irreconcilable triad" (Wallich, 1973, p. 297). Now the formula was being repeated with a few variations (Padoa-Schioppa, 1982, pp. 38-9), but its meaning had undergone a radical change. In the new theoretical framework foregoing the autonomy of monetary policy in favour of freedom for capital movements no longer meant sacrificing employment and the formation of new productive capacity, but only foregoing the freedom to create inflation. Aligning inflation rates at the lowest level, namely that of Germany – it was later to be added – would render useless the parity changes so frequently resorted to in the early phase of the EMS, and favour transition to a system of irrevocably fixed exchange rates. Moreover, as long as inflation rates differed, commitment to keeping the exchange rate with the D-mark fixed (a commitment that could be broken only at very high political costs) would lend credibility to intentions to reduce inflation (bringing it to a level low enough to trigger such a depreciation in the real exchange rate as to offset the previous loss of

---

[9] See Simonazzi and Vianello (1998) for a more complete treatment of the reasons behind transition to the "new EMS" and monetary union.

competitiveness). This credibility would in turn reduce expectations of devaluation, making it less costly to finance balance of payments deficits.

While the economic journals filled with such arguments, the difficulty of securing exchange rate stability in the absence of capital controls seems to have remained ever present to those responsible for economic policy and among EEC experts. In a report prepared for the EEC Commission in 1986-87 (i.e. just before the advent of the "new EMS") the question was raised as to whether financial liberalisation would not entail the need to adopt flexible exchange rates within the Community, too (Padoa-Schioppa, 1987, p. 87), although the conclusion reached with some heart-searching was that it would not. Not wishing to take this path, fraught as it was with dangers for the very survival of the Common Market (on its way to becoming the Single Market), another, more courageous path lay open: monetary unification. As a result of the huge social costs borne by France in keeping the exchange rate with the D-mark stable – and the fact that speculation nevertheless gave no respite to the French franc, counting on the unsustainability of these costs in the long run – the French government became the main champion of this solution. And this was the solution that Germany, anxious to win over French assent to the country's reunification and extension of the European Union to include the former communist countries of central Europe, finally agreed to.

3. Industrial Restructuring and Unemployment

Given the macroeconomic polices adopted, it is hardly surprising that the history of the European Union, from approval of the exchange rate agreements to the launch of the single currency, is one of slow growth and increasing unemployment, with the exception of the latter part of the 1980s – a result that appears all the more disappointing when compared with the considerable growth in income and employment shown by the United States. However, the explanation given for the low growth rate – an explanation long dominant in Europe – put it down to the rigidity of the labour market and the generosity of the welfare system.

In time, and with change in the economic situation, the concept of "flexibility" held relevant saw progressive modification (cf. Simonazzi and Villa, 1999). In the 1970s, it was the rigidity of real wages that was held to set a limit to the rate of growth of income compatible with the inflation target. When, as from the mid-1980s, the share of wages in income began to shrink, other causes were sought to account for the persistence of unemployment in Europe: on the one hand, excessive regulation of the labour market, protecting those in employment (insiders) and reducing their mobility, and on the other hand a far too generous welfare system which reduced both incentives for job-searching and the competitive pressure exerted by the unemployed (outsiders). Rising long-term unemployment and the concentration of unemployment among unskilled workers were for their part accounted for with the rigidity of the wage structure. Technological progress and competition from developing countries, it was argued, shifted labour demand towards skilled labour, creating a mismatch between demand and supply. This could only be remedied by reducing the cost of unskilled labour, which could, in turn, be obtained either with wage cuts, as in the United States, or with subsidies or tax relief – as was suggested for Europe in an attempt to escape from what appeared as a trade-off between employment and equality. Attention subsequently turned to another aspect of European unemployment, namely its uneven geographical distribution and the widening gap between areas experiencing sustained growth and areas marked by backwardness or de-industrialisation. Again, the differences were accounted for with the lack of labour flexibility. And so yet another concept of flexibility was invoked, namely geographical flexibility, in terms of both wage differentials and labour mobility.

Thus the labour market was called upon to take care not only of the macroeconomic problems concerning the level and distribution of income, but also of the structural problems facing the industrialised nations. Intensified competition from developing countries – particularly keen in the heavy industry and in labour intensive sectors or processes, and fed in no small measure by the delocalisation of production (one of the forms taken on by competition between firms in the industrialised countries) – gave rise to a process of rationalisation and reorganisation of production, elimination of obsolete or excess capacity, further delocalisation and intensification of competition. The capacity to meet this challenge required a high level of flexibility in the productive structure: promptness in introducing product and process innovation and ability to adjust rapidly to changes in demand, exiting from mature sectors to enter new ones. This type of flexibility has often been identified with flexibility in the use of the labour force, so that the greater dynamism of the American economy, its capacity to develop new sectors and success in combining structural change with growth in employment were ascribed to differences in labour market institutions. Now, it is indeed true that a rapidly changing social-economic context (seeing changes not only in the characteristics of labour demand, but also of labour supply, particularly in the form of a higher female participation rate and the attendant new demands regarding the organisation of time) requires a certain degree of flexibility in labour market institutions, but to ascribe the flexibility of the productive structure and its capacity for upgrading mainly, if not solely, to the flexibility of the labour market means, on the one hand, attributing the latter with a task it is not able to perform while, on the other hand, diverting attention from the complexity of factors influencing the capacity of response of a productive structure. And yet flexibility seems to be the only policy prescribed, even when the problem is to promote real convergence between the various areas in the countries participating in the European Monetary Union. We shall now focus on this aspect, leaving examination of the problems posed by the differences in the economic and social conditions among the member states for the next section.

In the first place, there are situations of unemployment deriving from the rescaling of mature sectors that no amount of labour flexibility can take care of. Analysis of the restructuring process in two areas marked by industrial decline (Wood, 1997) reveals that workers in these areas have shown considerable capacity to adapt to new forms of labour organisation and new productive processes. When, however, the structural modifications are such as to lead to plants being closed down and whole sectors being rescaled or relocated, the industry-specific skills of laid off workers prove useless. In the areas most heavily affected by restructuring (like the Rhur and the eastern Länder in Germany, the north-east of England, the northern part of France, Belgium and certain areas of north-west Italy) the professional skills of the population, once the region's major asset, becomes a serious obstacle to conversion towards new sectors. Moreover, the loss of employment extends from the firms in crisis to the whole network of their suppliers. It has been estimated that the loss of one job in the Ruhr iron and steel industry leads to the loss of 2.7 jobs in related industries (Wood, 1997, p. 196). At the same time, growth in employment is concentrated in the services, and accounted for largely by female, often part-time, employment substituting full-time, predominantly male employment in manufacturing [10].

Secondly, the capacity for restructuring depends on factors such as cost and market structures, relations between banks and firms, and government policies, which have little to do with the flexibility of the labour market. For example, exit from a sector entails the loss of material and immaterial assets (equipment and machinery, sales networks, knowledge of the market and the technology). Such "sunk" costs can make firms more determined to remain in the market, resorting to measures of rationalisation, decentralisation of stages of production and other forms of cost reduction[11]. Close relations between bank and industry, as in Germany and Japan, facilitating access to the resources necessary to finance the restructuring process and/or helping firms through possibly long periods of low profits, may have the effect of delaying closures. The abandonment of declining sectors is, moreover, facilitated by the existence of expanding ones, but where this does not obtain the lack of alternatives will mean greater demand for protection, coming both from workers and firms. The birth and growth of new sectors also presuppose the existence of a social context of knowledge, competence and experience, necessary to feed the continuous exchange of information sustaining and stimulating the innovation process (cf. Bonifati, 1999). And, of course, they presuppose the existence of demand, which in some cases can only be secured by creating a protected internal market.

That the institutional context plays a primary role in determining the comparative advantage of a country in new sectors has been widely recognised at least since Veblen's (1915) classic study on the rise of German industrial power. Attention to this aspect has vigorously revived in the light of the extraordinary dynamism marking highly innovative sectors such as telecommunications, electronics and biotechnology in the United States. This dynamism (following on a phase of considerable pessimism on the dynamic capacities of American industry) was made

---

[10] Striking evidence of the new social situation developing in areas of industrial decline, where the men have lost their jobs in industry and remain unemployed while the women find jobs in the services, is offered by a whole series of British and French films. According to the flexibility thesis, it was excessive regulation of the labour market (in the form of minimum wages, unemployment benefits, but also high taxation on labour) that allowed workers to decline job opportunities offered at the lower wages justified by the loss of human capital.

[11] The American iron industry's technological lag *vis-à-vis* the Japanese and European industries, which had been largely reconstructed in the post-war period, might, for example, explain the decision to close down old plants and substitute them with smaller ones (*"mini-mills"*) located in regions other than the older industrialised regions (cf. Bradbury, 1987).

possible, it is worth stressing, by factors like the close relations between industry and the university, the development of technical disciplines, the availability of venture capital and, last but not least, the support given to the American industrial system by heavy military spending, both through procurements and with R&D funding[12]. Military spending in the United States did, indeed, represent an effective form of industrial policy: "*laissez faire* was planned" as A. Amsden ironically reminds us[13].

The flexibility of the labour market therefore represents far too easy a shortcut to account for the happy combination of conditions favouring American industrial dynamism. The irrelevance of rigidity factors as obstacles to change is, moreover, demonstrated by what has happened in the areas of growth within the European countries. A system of guarantees and social protection in many cases superior to the national average does not seem to have posed any real obstacle to the continued renewal of the productive structure, the development of new products and new sectors and the spread of innovations in those areas where favourable social and economic conditions exist (the district areas in Italy, the southern part of Germany and England, the more dynamic areas of Ireland).

Contrary to what happened in the United States, in Europe both the Community and the individual governments intervened above all in the mature sectors, applying a vast range of instruments, from financial aid for firms to measures designed to limit competition (such as quotas and crisis cartels) (Nevens and Vickers, 1992). Such interventions did not prevent decline in areas highly specialised in mature industries but, at least in part, saved the crisis-stricken communities from the dramatic consequences marking the American (and, to some extent, British) restructuring process. The Japanese government also took active steps to intervene in the restructuring of industries in crisis. Unlike European industrial policy, however, Japanese industrial policy was not confined to these industries, but also boosted the development of new sectors, favouring the dissemination of (American) know-how and promoting the creation of a basic nucleus around which the comparative advantages of the national high-tech industries could be developed.

In Europe the conflict of interests pitting the various national productive systems one against another and the consequent lack of an autonomous decision-making centre may have stood in the way of a coherent industrial policy[14], but the philosophy behind the industrial policy that ultimately prevailed seems to have been just as important. Indeed, growing scepticism about the possibility of combining

---

[12] Harrison (1994, ch. 5) indicates the Defence Department and Stanford University as the two institutions behind the success of Silicon Valley. The role played by military spending in the creation and defence of American hegemony in the electronics field, which boosted American companies to proceed along the learning curve at a faster pace than their rivals, is stressed, among others, by Gordon and Krieger (1990), while Florida and Kenney (1990) put the stress on the role of venture capital in financing the explosion of new high-tech companies in the early 1980s.

[13] The phrase in Amsden (1993) is cited in Harrison (1994), p. 117.

[14] According to Neven and Vickers (1992) the defence of national interests seriously hampered the process of reorganisation in the mature sectors – but also, it should be added, the development of a strong European industry in the new sectors.

sectoral policies with efficiency (a scepticism partly justified by the results of industrial policies in the 1970s and 1980s), caused reliance to be increasingly placed on the operation of the market. In some European countries demand restraint was resorted to as an anti-inflationary policy and a means to discipline the labour market (as in the case of French competitive disinflation); others (like Italy in the late 1980s) used a strong exchange rate policy as a surrogate for industrial policy. In general, faith was placed in the drive to efficiency that the tougher competition resulting from the creation of the single market would mean for European firms. That the contemporaneous reduction of the possibility to intervene in support of national industries – coming on top of the growing competition of countries with low labour costs brought about by the investment policy of the European companies themselves – would inevitably add to the pressure on the more exposed sectors was judged a price to be paid for progress along the road to efficiency.

Thus, added to macroeconomic policies penalising growth was the lack of an adequate industrial policy. It is therefore hardly surprising that the measures introduced in all the European countries in the 1980s and 1990s to increase flexibility in the labour market – and which significantly reduced the obstacles placed in the way of the free functioning of that market by the guarantees and social protection provided by the welfare state – did not produce the desired results in terms of employment.

In the United States action taken against the labour market institutions (well documented in Harrison and Bluestone, 1988, for example) and the reduction of welfare benefits were accompanied not only, as we have just argued, by efficient, systematic support for industrial restructuring but also, as we saw in the first section of this paper, by a mix of fiscal, monetary and exchange rate policies designed to safeguard growth. It is precisely this complementarity of policies that appears to be missing in Europe, where flexibility is in fact the field that has seen the greatest efforts to approach the American model, while no such efforts have been made on the other two fronts, i.e. industrial and macroeconomic policy[15]. Of industrial policy enough has been said. On the subject of macroeconomic policy a few considerations remain to be added.

---

[15] The authors of *An Economists' Manifesto on Unemployment in the European Union* (Modigliani, et al., 1998), although not holding it "possible or advisable to push reforms [of job security legislation] as far as the American system, where job security provisions are largely absent", and acknowledging Europe's progress towards greater flexibility (from this point of view "the situation has generally improved"), advocate "a marked liberalisation of the ability of firms to eliminate surplus labour and some with respect to dismissal of individual workers for cause". This being the authors' conviction, all the more reflection is merited by their recommendation that "these reforms be postponed to a more suitable time" since "to carry them out now, when the demand is greatly depressed and there is plenty of unemployment, probably a good deal of redundant labour in many firms and few vacancies would have simply the effect of condemning many workers to join the rank of the unemployed, initially reducing instead of increasing employment" (p. 354).

The "prudent" fiscal policy of the 1980s (especially in Germany[16] and later also in France) became decidedly restrictive by the 1990s, in a context marked by high real interest rates and weak economic growth. Unlike the approach adopted in the United States, reduction first of inflation and then of the public debt were the priority objectives to which the defence of employment was sacrificed. Recovery in the latter part of the 1980s was rapidly thwarted by the tightening of German monetary policy, designed to prevent the effects it was feared the unification boom and growing wage claims would have on inflation[17]. Commitment to defending the exchange rate forced the other EMS countries, too, to raise interest rates and thus nip economic recovery in the bud, before they could benefit from German expansion. Things went even worse in the 1990s, when the slow-down in economic growth in Europe was aggravated by the deficit reduction measures imposed by the Maastricht treaty and implemented in the blindest of manners, with no consideration for the changed macroeconomic situation or the disastrous cumulative effects such policies must surely produce when simultaneously adopted by a whole set of countries bound together by intense trade relations. (To this must be added – for Germany and those countries, like France, whose currency remained pegged to the D-mark even after 1992 – the negative consequences of the strengthening of the D-mark relative to the dollar, which could have been avoided with a different monetary policy in Germany, and those, felt particularly in France, of the depreciation of the lira.)

The uncertainty of the European macroeconomic picture characterising the last decades has been responsible for the sharp drop in investment as a share of potential income – a point that F. Modigliani [18] has called attention to on various

---

[16] In the autumn of 1982 a centre-right coalition led by Chancellor Kohl took over from Helmut Schmidt's centre-left government. In the following spring the new coalition based the election campaign on a programme of fiscal austerity, which was immediately implemented. "All in all", we read in Geirsch et al.(1992), "demand management virtually disappeared from the policy agenda in the West Germany of the 1980s" and despite international protest over the growing German balance of payments surplus, "both the West German government and the Bundesbank by and large stuck to their course"(pp. 194-5).

[17] After the long period of wage moderation in the 1980s, which led to a reduction in labour cost per unit of output (cf. Giersch et al., 1992, pp. 132 and 211), in the early 1990s wages began to rise sharply. It should however be noted that the Bundesbank had already reverted to a policy of higher interest rates as from the mid-1988 (i.e. with the first signs of a slow down in the fall of inflation).

[18] In the previously cited "*Manifesto*" (Modigliani et al., 1998) we read, for example: "We believe that one reason for the drastic European decline in the demand for labour relative to its available supply – and the resulting rise in unemployment – has been a decline in investment relative to full-capacity output" (p. 335). Reference here to the share of investment in full-capacity output is worth emphasising. Actual production does in fact, *ceteris paribus,* vary in the same direction as investment, which makes the investment to actual output ratio a poor indicator of the intensity of accumulation. It must, however, be added that, when prolonged, stagnation in investment slows down not only the rate of growth of actual output, but also that of potential, or full-capacity, output, so that even the indicator adopted by the authors of the '*Manifesto*' leaves part of the problem in the shade.

occasions. It should be noted that slow growth jeopardises future growth capacity, both discouraging investment and making the social cost of productive restructuring less bearable. As far as the first point is concerned in particular, it is worth noting that a capacity constraint such as to preclude the possibility of any considerable and immediate increase in industrial employment in Europe has been signalled by various authors, who associate the insufficient formation of productive capacity with the profit squeeze of the 1970s (cf. for example Rowthorn, 1995) or the high real interest rates of the 1980s (cf. Fitoussi, 1995). The weakness of these explanations appears evident, however, when we consider that the same causes did not produce the same effects in the United States, where macroeconomic policy was able to keep the prospects for growth in demand encouragingly open. But we must also note that the insufficient formation of productive capacity – and the ensuing transformation of "Keynesian" into "structural" unemployment (cf. Garegnani, 1979, p. 79) – is perhaps less important (in that sustained and lasting expansion of demand is in general enough to provide a remedy) than the investment opportunities lost and the delays thus accumulated.

In the 1990s intensified competition in a context of stagnant demand and scant technological dynamism led to an intensive process of rationalisation, decentralisation of production and shedding of labour, which meant a dramatic drop in manufacturing employment in all the European countries. Even the German model of internationalisation, hitherto based on the export of domestically produced goods, underwent transformation, approaching the Japanese model of the 1980s based on decentralisation of production. There was, however, an important difference. While Japanese decentralisation, carried out in a context of economic growth and supported by shrewd industrial policy, led growth throughout the region (thanks to the continued upgrading of the Japanese productive system and the room thus made for the industries of the late-comer countries), the shift of industries and stages of production from Germany to the vast low labour cost area opening up with the fall of the communist regimes occurs in a context of stagnation and difficulty in entering the more technologically advanced sectors. While direct investment abroad soars, domestic investment stagnates. Delocalisation of production and restructuring thus lead to decline in industrial employment hitting laggard regions harder, and meeting with considerable resistance.

These processes have already gone ahead to such an extent as to threaten Germany's tried and tested system of industrial relations. Paradoxically, this is happening at the very moment when the glaring failure of flexibility policies – along with the contradictory results of empirical studies on the actual degree of rigidity in the European labour market and the relevance of the individual rigidity factors to employment[19] – are beginning to prompt an alternative view, ascribing the major reasons for Europe's high unemployment rates to the macroeconomic policies followed by the European countries and the low growth rates they produced, together with the lack of an adequate industrial policy.

---

[19]Nickell (1977, p. 73) notes that "many labour market institutions that conventionally come under the heading of rigidities have no observable impact on unemployment".

4. The Economic Prospects for Europe

With the creation of the EMU the national currencies of the member countries cease to exist, and with them the need to defend the exchange rates and the constraint on each country's monetary policy this need imposes in the absence of capital controls. The national central banks no longer need to keep reserves (or to borrow) in order to finance the deficits with the other countries of the Union, and the external constraint of each country no longer manifests itself in the need to curb loss in reserves.

An excess of payments by residents in Italy to residents in Germany, for example, leads as before to a fall in the deposits of Italian residents with the Italian commercial banks and an increase in the deposits of German residents with the German commercial banks (here, and below, a few obvious simplifications are made). And, as before, the deposits of Italian commercial banks with the Bank of Italy diminish, while the deposits of the German commercial banks with the Bundesbank increase. However, unbalances between the Bank of Italy and the Bundesbank are no longer regulated through transfer of international reserves – with doubts possibly arising over the solvency of the debtor central bank – but through the transfer of euro-denominated assets.

If it is always the same countries that run deficits, their central banks' debt will increase. Would indefinite prosecution of the process be tolerated by surplus countries? We shall suppose that it would, given that no limit is officially set (although there does seem to be some justification for the doubts expressed by Kenen, 1998, p. 8)[20]. Let us now go on to suppose that liquidity is redistributed spontaneously within the European banking system or, alternatively, that the creation of liquidity in surplus countries and its destruction in deficit countries are completely sterilised by the national central banks. In this case the financing of a deficit of one EMU country with another does not pose greater problems than are posed within one and the same country by financing the deficit of one region with another.

The old financial constraint no longer applying, the fact remains – of course – that deficits do have to be financed. Let us imagine there were no other regions in Italy apart from Calabria and Veneto, and that the Italian economy had no foreign trade. If the Calabrian families and firms buy from the firms in Veneto more than the families and firms in Veneto buy from the Calabrian firms, the difference will result in an equal increase in the net debt of the Calabrian families and firms taken as a whole. And if their capacity (and will) to borrow is limited, as indeed it cannot but be, their capacity to import from Veneto will also prove limited. We shall call this the external constraint of Calabria.

If we now suppose that Italy trades with another country, Germany, importing more than it exports, and that the two countries have the same currency, the story

---

[20] Cf. also Kenen (1995), p. 53 and in particular note 7 (cited in his more recent work) where the author reports the doubts of a central bank executive. At the time, however, he held that the system adopted would, like the American system, be based on the transfer of public debt securities, which in the case of Europe could only be those of the various national governments.

can be re-told in exactly the same terms putting Italy in the place of Calabria and Germany in the place of Veneto. Between the external constraint of Calabria (represented now by its capacity to import from Veneto and Germany) and that of Italy (represented by its capacity to import from Germany) there exists, however, an important difference. To make it clear, let us suppose that the Region of Calabria, as an administrative body, enjoys no fiscal autonomy. What we have called the external constraint of Calabria is, then, no more than the result of an exercise in aggregation. Indeed, we might equally well speak of the external constraint of the families in a block of flats. In the case of Italy, the situation is quite different. In fact, if the operation of the Italian fiscal system results in a transfer from Veneto to Calabria, this will increase the import capacity of Calabria (from Veneto and Germany) and reduce the import capacity of Veneto (from Calabria and Germany). The external constraint of Italy is not, therefore, the result of a pure operation of aggregation. The import capacity available for redistribution among Italian families and firms can be referred to as the import capacity of Italy in a different, more meaningful sense than had reference to the import capacity of Calabria [21].

The national fiscal system does not, however, confine its operations to transferring purchasing power from one region (or area, however defined) to another. An expansive fiscal policy increases (and a restrictive fiscal policy reduces) the import capacity of each region from the others, and of all of them from abroad. The constraint the central government encounters in implementing such a policy is represented by its borrowing capacity on the financial market[22] (or from the Central Bank: but this possibility is ruled out for the governments of the EMU countries).

Now, a government's borrowing capacity and the costs involved depend, in general, on the size of its existing debt and on the market assessment of its capacity to increase tax revenues and/or cut spending in the future. As for tax revenues, if there can be no counting on some expansion in demand (such as so effectively helped the American government on the way to balancing its budget), increasing revenues will remain a matter of increasing tax rates. However, capital mobility severely limits the possibility of increasing tax rates on capital incomes. And if, as happens, certain countries reduce such rates in order to attract foreign investment, it will be difficult

---

[21] To make the point clear, let us take the example of a family. Like any other body, a family can purchase from outside (import) more than it succeeds in selling outside (exporting), provided it borrows, and can continue to do so until its borrowing capacity runs out. But what is it that makes us refer the constraint to the family rather than to its individual members? Evidently we assume that among the family members there exists a basic principle of solidarity on the basis of which the family redistributes within itself the import capacity of its members. If, whenever the imports of a member of the family exceed his or her individual import capacity, the others make over to him or her part of their own, then the family will have a single external constraint, represented by the import capacity of all of its members taken together. It should be noted that what determines the oneness of the constraint is not the fact that relations with the outside are referred to a unique subject, which may or may not be the case (the purchases may be made, and debts taken on, by the individual members), but lies solely in the redistribution of import capacity.

[22] For the sake of simplicity the expansionary effects of a simultaneous increase in government spending and taxes are disregarded here.

for the others even just to hold them steady, let alone raise them. Since, at least in Europe, labour mobility is incomparably lower, it might seem possible to tax labour more heavily. However, the tax burden on earned incomes has reached a limit hard to exceed without proving socially intolerable, on the one hand, and increasing labour costs on the other, thus jeopardising competitiveness and eventually becoming yet another disincentive to invest in the country (as indeed is, more directly, the high level of social security contributions, now seeing competitive reduction). As far as government spending is concerned, it seems fairly clear that unemployment-related expenditure will long resist squeezing. It is therefore on health care and pensions that demands for reduction come particularly thick and fast, although generally with the aim of making room for other expenses and, above all, for cuts in taxes and social security contributions.

On the basis of these considerations we would argue that there are scant chances for a heavily indebted government to finance an expansionary fiscal policy at acceptable costs, even regardless of the restrictions imposed by the Stability Pact. It is a point to bear in mind in particular should such restrictions – the absurdity of which is ever more widely recognised[23] – eventually be relaxed in one or another of the ways proposed (referring the limit to the structural deficit, exempting capital expenditure, etc.). Incidentally, we may also note that the single currency eliminates one of the two causes of interest differentials, namely the exchange rate risk, but not the other, which is associated with the creditworthiness of the debtor. If at times the market seems to forget this, it is on account of the confidence that "fluid" investors place (rightly, more often than not) in their ability to quit the market in good time (cf. Simonazzi e Vianello, 1994 and 1997). A heavily indebted country that wishes to avoid orthodox fiscal policies can therefore – for a certain period – enjoy some apparent credibility which allows it to borrow cheaply, but there can be no escaping the day of reckoning, which must loom up sooner or later. And the later it comes, the more gruelling it will be. No longer able to play on exchange rates, speculation will force down security prices, thus making debt service unsustainable and exposing the country to the risk of insolvency. The opinion then beginning to circulate in the markets that it is better for the country to abandon the monetary union and seek escape from its woes in inflation will aggravate the crisis further, and aggravated crisis will reinforce the opinion.

The external constraint which, as we have seen, continues to apply to the individual countries can be alleviated by a supranational redistributive system analogous to that operating in each country through the national fiscal system. But fiscal redistribution is not – or is only marginally – among the tasks that the EU sees as its own (and yet Germany claims that it does all too much of it, calling for a fairer balance between what one country gives and what it receives).

---

[23] How is a rule to be judged if not absurd when it requires restrictive adjustment of fiscal policy in times of recession (when the budget deficit rises with falling tax revenues) and allows a more expansionary policy in times of recovery (when the deficit falls) – and ignores the repercussions of the fiscal policy of one country on the level of demand, and thus on tax revenues, of the others?

The theory of optimum currency areas has clarified how the existence of a centralised fiscal system, both through automatic and discretionary intervention, alleviates the negative consequences of foregoing exchange rate adjustments – and how the lack of one stands as the great disadvantage of a monetary union as compared with a federal state (cf. Mundell 1961; for an application to the European case see the MacDougall Report of 1977, which envisages dire consequences such as to jeopardise the process of integration itself, for a monetary union that does not contemplate measures of compensatory financing; cf. Commission of the European Communities, 1977, p. 60.)[24]

The theory of optimum currency areas focuses on the case of asymmetric shocks, like the two associated with the rise in oil prices (but also the shock caused by its subsequent reduction) and like the shock that will come with the extension of the European Union to the former communist countries of central and eastern Europe. Reference to asymmetrical shocks is, however, a reductive way of posing the problem since it suggests that at the root of the difficulty there is necessarily a specific, clearly identifiable event, and not a steady flow of events and a process of cumulative causation. The various countries are not only subject to asymmetric shocks. They are, first of all, different from one another, with different histories and susceptible of different future developments. The implications of this are beginning to be recognised with reference to the financial system and the possibility of de-synchronisation of cyclical phases: owing to differences in the ways of raising finance, an increase in short term interest rates can be particularly burdensome for Italian firms, while having little significance for German firms; an increase in interest rates could hurt countries burdened with a sizeable public or private debt[25], but not the others; finding themselves in different phases of the cycle, some countries could benefit, and others suffer, from a certain trend in monetary policy. However, there are many other important differences. For reasons connected with its colonial history, France has adopted a more generous immigration policy than Germany, and cannot send back its workers of Algerian origin as if they were Turkish *Gastarbeiter*[26]. Italy has an exorbitant number of self-employed workers and small businesses that evade taxes to varying degrees, and might not be able to survive if they did not, which makes it all the harder (on those who cannot escape paying taxes or are affected by cuts in welfare spending) to exercise financial austerity – and attract capital by cutting taxes and social security contributions. Moreover, in certain countries or areas where the family (in some cases the extended family) maintains its traditional functions, a reduced or at any rate inadequate social welfare system proves more tolerable. Neither should we forget the differences in industrial relations in the various countries, in their political culture and the differing degrees and ways in which they look to social conflict as a source of active democracy. Nor have we considered the backward areas – differing in size and features in the various countries – and requiring different forms

---

[24] Attention is called to the report in Pivetti (1998), pp. 12-3.
[25] The hardship caused to British families by the high interest rates needed to defend the exchange rate proved a significant obstacle to the pound's remaining in the EMS in 1992.
[26] At the time this text is being revised for publication impassioned debate is growing in Germany on broadening criteria for granting citizenship.

of government support.

The list could go on, but we shall stop here to point out quite simply that the impossibility of exchange rate variation, a common monetary policy and the lack of compensatory finance combine to create a sort of straightjacket, which the various economies must strive to fit. The choice made can be summed up as a decision to ignore diversity, imposing a constraint and waiting for the heterogeneous economic and social structures to reorganise around it, no matter what the cost.

Let us now briefly consider the two re-balancing tools which should be taking the place of exchange rate variation: labour mobility and wage flexibility. An interesting book by a European on the city of Chicago (d'Eramo, 1995) dedicates one of the first chapters to describing, amazement touched with amusement, the constant whirl of Americans moving from county to county and state to state, and to illustrating one of the means – indeed, the very symbol – of this perpetual wandering: a prefabricated wooden house travelling the interstate highways on an immense trailer truck. For Europeans it is different: they do not speak the same language, do not share the same customs, do not feel at home beyond their national borders, nor do they find neighbours just like the ones they left thousands of kilometres behind[27]. We must also recognise the fact that unemployment is a Europe-wide problem (a case not considered in the theory of the optimum currency areas), and that the chances of finding a job are no higher in Germany than in Italy.

It is true that devaluation is an imperfect tool for fighting unemployment when the latter is concentrated exclusively in certain areas of the country, particularly if these areas are not the ones which would benefit from an increase in foreign demand. This does not mean, however, that a population shift is any more effective. On the one hand, to bring about a significant reduction in the unemployment of the depressed areas, the shift would have to be on a scale far exceeding the absorption capability of the region showing economic growth while, on the other hand, the experience of domestic migration itself (which, at any rate, could never return to the high levels of the past) has taught us that, besides creating congestion in the areas of destination, migrants deprive their own regions of their best energies, thus jeopardising their growth potential.

The point, then, is to take production where labour is available rather than the other way round. And it is precisely this objective that is being pursued with wage cuts. However, the question to ask is just *how much* wages must fall to attract production activities to an area they have no reason to go to spontaneously (or have good reasons not to go to). If, moreover, the increase in competitiveness thus obtained does lead to some increase in employment, it will be in the low value-added sectors. The competitiveness of the area will come to depend increasingly on low wages, in a vicious circle steadily widening the gap between the various regions.

Nor must it be forgotten that what increases the competitiveness of the products of one country or area is reduction in wages *relative to those paid in other countries or areas*. But any attempt to influence the relative levels by altering the

---

[27] A. Portelli (1991, p. 175) aptly points out that in America everything is organised in such a way as to make newcomers feel at home everywhere.

absolute levels can only be successful, according to a now classic objection, if the other players in the game do not behave in the same way. If they did, a devastating downward race would ensue (the same applies to tax cuts aimed at attracting foreign investment). We may well understand, therefore, why former German Finance Minister Lafontaine proposed a European income policy, no longer to restrain wage increases, but rather to prevent competitive reductions.

A more articulated proposal has been put forward by Modigliani (1996): to plan wage changes differentiated among the various countries, so as to modify their degree of competitiveness and redirect demand towards those with greater unemployment problems (in the countries losing in competitiveness demand would be sustained, according to the author, by the increase in the real income of the countries gaining in competitiveness, as also by the improved terms of trade and an appropriate European monetary policy). However, cutting money wages is, as Fitoussi (1998, p. 60) points out, by its very nature a non co-operative strategy, and it may not be very realistic to expect to make it co-operative, and to turn it into a refined tool for economic policy.

The conclusions we come to are not very encouraging. It is to be hoped that favourable conditions be created for those who wish to move from one country to another or from one area of a country to another, but it is ludicrous to think that the unemployment problem can be solved in this way. Competitive wage cuts are a danger to be avoided, not a strategy to follow. A European fiscal policy geared to redistribution appears politically unfeasible. To find some more promising prospect we must look to the capacity the EU has to sustain demand for all the member countries, just as a national government can do for all the regions of one country. Indeed, the EU enjoys a distinct advantage over its member countries in that the degree of openness of its economy to imports from the rest of the world is much lower than that of the economies of the individual countries (many of whose imports come from other countries in the Union). What this amounts to – especially if combined with a policy of "benign neglect" towards the euro-dollar exchange rate – is a relaxation of the external constraint, which leaves ample scope for expansionary fiscal policy.

This could take the form of an investment programme financed with the issue of EU securities (as suggested by Delors). Moreover, interdependence between the various countries might at last be recognised, leading to a policy of co-ordinated reflation. In both cases the rise in aggregate demand would result directly or indirectly in a rise in the imports of each of the EU countries from the others, while the increase in tax revenues (much greater, in proportion to expenditure, than if the latter were increased in only one country) would mitigate the impact of the expansionary measures on the budget. Co-ordinated reflation would, however, have the advantage of allowing for differences in the level of employment to be taken into account in deciding how much each country should reflate.

Once this therapy began to pay off, triggering sustained and lasting recovery, budget deficits would spontaneously tend to diminish and any structural intervention, regarding taxation or government expenditure, could be addressed in due time and only if deemed desirable in itself, free from the perverse logic of budget cuts that has led to so many of the present disasters. Unless, of course, the design is to remain in a state of emergency until – in the name of the emergency itself – such sacrifices have been imposed as would be hard to justify under normal conditions.

References

Amsden, A. H. (1993): Beyond Shock Therapy: Why Eastern Europe's Recovery Starts in Washington. American Prospect. Spring.
Beveridge, W. H. (1944): Full Employment in a Free Society. Report by William H. Beveridge. George Allen and Unwin, London.
Blotevogel, H.H., Fielding, A.J. (eds) (1997): People, Jobs and Mobility in the New Europe. John Wiley and Sons, Chichester.
Bonifati, G. (1991): Saggio dell'interesse e distribuzione del reddito. Rosenberg & Sellier, Torino.
Bonifati, G. (1999): The Capacity to Generate Investment. An Analysis of the Long-term Determinants of Investment. In: Materiali di discussione. Department of Political Economy, University of Modena, n. 266.
Bonifati, G., Vianello, F. (1998): Il saggio dell'interesse come fenomeno monetario e il saggio di rendimento del capitale impiegato nella produzione. In: De Vecchi, N., Marcuzzo, M. C. (1998).
Bradbury, F. H. (1987): Technical Change and the Restructuring of the North American Steel Industry. In: Chapman, K., Humphrys, G. (1987), pp. 157-172.
Carlin, W., Soskice, D. (1996): Shocks to the System: the German Political Economy under Stress. National Institute Economic Review, n. 159, February.
Carlyle, T. (1976): Past and Present. Dent, London.
Chapman, K., Humphrys, G. (eds) (1987): Technical Change and Industrial Policy. Blackwell, Oxford.
Commission of European Communities (1977): Report of the Study Group on the Role of Public Finance in European Integration. Bulletin of the European Communities, April.
Cool, K., Neven, D. J., Walter, I. (eds) (1992): European Industrial Restructuring in the 1990s. Macmillan, London.
de Cecco, M. (1987): La liberalizzazione valutaria: riflessioni di un economista. La Comunità Internazionale, n. 4.
d'Eramo, M. (1995): Il maiale e il grattacielo. Chicago: una storia del nostro futuro. Feltrinelli, Milano.
De Vecchi, N., Marcuzzo, M. C. (eds) (1998): A cinquant'anni da Keynes. Teorie dell'occupazione, interesse e crescita. Edizioni Unicopli, Pavia.
Eichengreen, B. (1993): European Monetary Unification. Journal of Economic Literature, 31, September.
Fitoussi, J. P. (1995): Le débat interdit. Monnaie, Europe, pauvreté. Editions Arléa, Paris 1995.
Fitoussi, J. P. (1998): Il dopo Euro: quali "modelli" di economia politica per i paesi europei nello spazio della moneta unica. Info-Quaderni, IV, n. 21.
Florida, R., Kenney, M. (1990): The Breakthrough Illusion. Basic Books, New York.

Freeman, R. (1995): The Limits of Wage Flexibility to Curing Unemployment. Oxford Review of Economic Policy, 11, n. 1.

Freeman, R. (1996): Why so Many Young American Men Commit Crime and What We Might Do about It? Journal of Economic Perspectives, 10, n. 1.

Friedman, M. (1953): The Case for Flexible Exchange Rates. In: Friedman, M.: Essays in Positive Economics. The University of Chicago Press, Chicago.

Garegnani, P. (1979): Notes on Consumption, Investment and Effective Demand. Part II. Cambridge Journal of Economics, 3, September.

Giersch, H., Paqué, K. H., Schmieding, H. (1992): The Fading Miracle. Four Decades of Market Economy in Gemany. Cambridge University Press, Cambridge.

Ginzburg, A. (1991a): Le cause economiche della guerra. Politica ed economia, n. 4.

Ginzburg, A. (1991b): Approvvigionamenti sicuri: una risposta – a volte – militare. Politica ed economia, n.12.

Ginzburg, A., Simonazzi, A. (1997): Saggio di interesse e livello dei prezzi: i paradossi della disinflazione. Rivista Italiana degli Economisti, 2, n. 1.

Gordon, R., Krieger J. (1990): Anthropocentric Production Systems and US Manufacturing Models in the Machine Tool, Semiconductor and Automobile Industries. Vol. 18, FOP 262, Research Paper Series, Commission of the European Communities, Brussels.

Harrison, B. (1994): Lean and Mean. Basic Books, New York.

Harrison, B., Bluestone, B. (1988): The Great U-Turn: Corporate Restructuring and the Polarizing of America. Basic Books, New York.

Heise, A. (1997): A Different Transatlantic View. The American Job Machine. Challenge, 40, n. 3.

Kenen, P. B. (1995): Economic and Monetary Union in Europe: Moving Beyond Maastricht. Cambridge University Press, Cambridge.

Kenen, P. B. (1996): Sorting Out Some EMU Issues. Jean Monnet Chair Paper N. 38. Princeton Reprints in International Finance, n. 29.

Keynes, J. M. (1936): The General Theory of Employment, Interest and Money. In: The Collected Writings of John Maynard Keynes, vol. 7. Macmillan, 1973, London.

Marx, K. (1859): Einleitung zur Kritik der Politischenökonomie. In: Marx, K., Engels, F., Werke, Band 13, Dietz Verlag, Berlin, 1964.

Modigliani F. (1996): The Shameful Rate of Unemployment in the EMS: Causes and Cures. De Economist, 144.

Modigliani, F., Fitoussi, J.P., Moro, B., Snower, D., Solow, R., Steinher, A., Sylos Labini, P (1998): An Economists' *Manifesto* on Unemployment in the European Union. Banca Nazionale del Lavoro Quarterly Review, n. 206.

Moretti, F. (1988): L'evoluzione letteraria. Nuova Corrente, 35.

Moss, B.H., Michie, J., (eds) (1998): The Single European Currency in National Perspective. A Community in Crisis? Macmillan, London.

Mundell, A. R. (1961): A Theory of Optimum Currency Areas. American Economic Review, 51.

Neven, D.J., Vickers, J. (1992): Public Policy Towards Industrial Restructuring: Some Issues Raised by the Internal Market Programme. In: Cool, K., Neven, D. J., Walter, I. (1992).

Nickell, S. (1997): Unemployment and Labour Market Rigidities: Europe versus North America. Journal of Economic Perspectives, Summer, 11.

Padoa-Schioppa, T. (1982): Mobilità dei capitali: perché la Comunità è inadempiente? In: Padoa-Schioppa, T. (1992).

Padoa-Schioppa, T. (1987): Dopo l'Atto Unico: efficienza, stabilità ed equità. In: Padoa-Schioppa, T. (1992).

Padoa-Schioppa, T. (1992): L'Europa verso l'unione monetaria. Einaudi, Torino.

Pivetti, M. (1989): Military Expenditure and Economic Analysis. Contributions to Political Economy, 8.

Pizzuti, F.R. (ed.) (1994): L'economia italiana dagli anni Settanta agli anni Novanta. Pragmatismo, disciplina, saggezza convenzionale. McGraw-Hill Libri Italia,Milano.

Polanyi, K. (1944): The Great Transformation. Holt, Rinehart & Winston Inc., New York.

Portelli, A. (1991): Taccuini americani. Manifestolibri, Rome.

Rowthorn, R. (1995): Capital Formation and Unemployment. Oxford Review of Economic Policy, vol. 11, no. 1.

Samuelson, P. A. (1997): Wherein Do the European and American Models Differ? Temi di discussione del Servizio Studi, Banca d'Italia, n. 320, November.

Simonazzi, A., Vianello, F. (1994): Modificabilità dei tassi di cambio e restrizioni alla libertà di movimento dei capitali. In: Pizzuti, F. R. (1994).

Simonazzi, A., Vianello, F. (1996): Credibility or "Exit Speed"? Reflection Prompted by the 1992 EMS Crisis. Rivista Italiana degli Economisti, n. 1.

Simonazzi, A., Vianello, F. (1998): Italy towards European Monetary Union (and Domestic Socio-economic Disunion). In: Moss, B.H., Michie, J. (1998).

Simonazzi, A., Villa, P. (1999): Flexibility and Growth. International Review of Applied Economics, no. 3.

Sombart, W. (1906): Warum gibt es in den Vereiningten Staaten keinen Sozialismus. Tübingen.

Soros, G. (1998): The Crisis of Global Capitalism (Open Society Endengered). Bbs Public Affairs, New York.

Steve, S. (1977): Politica fiscale keynesiana e inflazione. Rivista internazionale di scienze economiche e commerciali, February.

Veblen, T. (1915): Imperial Germany and the Industrial Revolution. Macmillan, London.

Wallich, H.C. (1973): La crisi monetaria del 1971 e gli insegnamenti da trarne. Bancaria, n. 3.

Wood, G. (1997): Social and Economic Restructuring in Old Industrial Areas: a Comparison of North-East England and the Rhur District in Germany. In: Blotevogel, H.H., Fielding, A.J. (1997).

Acknowledgements

We thank Paola Masi for her patient discussion of the fourth section. The research on which this paper is based was made possible by a grant from the Italian Ministry for University (MURST).

17. Monetary Policy and Competitiveness in the Euro Area

Francesco Farina

(Ɛ_ropul

1. Introduction

F33 F36

F31

The European Monetary System (EMS) was a fixed exchange rate agreement designed to remove the main obstacle to the creation of that public good which is monetary stability, the high inflation of the countries of Peripheral Europe. Section 3 of this paper analyzes the interest-rate parity condition for a country representative of Peripheral Europe[1], showing that the inflation differentials with Germany lay at the foundation of the low degree of credibility attributed to the fixed exchange rates by the market, and pointing to Peripheral Europe's "currency risk" as the reason why its interest rate differentials with Germany are higher than the depreciation against the DM. In order to reduce the instability that the currencies of Peripheral Europe transmitted to the exchange-rate mechanism (ERM) it was necessary for the monetary authorities of these countries to enjoy the same anti-inflationary reputation as the Bundesbank, thus lending credibility to their disinflation policies. This was the rationale that led the DM to take on the role of nominal anchor of the system. This pivotal role, however, did not imply as its necessary corollary the "asymmetric" working that characterized the European exchange rate mechanism, namely the "hegemonic" solution, instead of the cooperative one, that was given, within the EMS, to the so-called $(n - 1)$ problem, (the autonomy enjoyed by the nth country to join an exchange rate agreement in setting the money supply[2]). In the 1980s, this German "hegemony" within the EMS caused the burden of the adjustment necessary to keep exchange rates stable to fall on the countries of Peripheral Europe, whatever the "divergent" currency in the fixed exchange rate mechanism[3].

F32

---

[1] At least from its establishment up to the 1992 crisis, the EMS has been usually divided into Core Europe – made up of Germany, the countries of the DM area (Benelux and Denmark, whose financial markets have integrated fast with Germany's and in whose foreign trade Germany plays a dominant role) and France (after a few years with a high inflation, this country has progressively achieved a monetary and financial stability equal to Germany's) – and Peripheral Europe, which includes Italy, Spain, United Kingdom and the least-developed countries (Ireland, Portugal and Greece).

[2] A country can exploit the degree of freedom existing in a fixed exchange rate system [the fact that only (n-1) monetary policies are constrained to maintaining the fixed parities] by determining the money supply in full autonomy. The literature on the EMS is almost unanimous in arguing that the Central Bank of the EMS's "leading" country has enjoyed such autonomy. See, for instance Giovannini and Giavazzi (1989). However, Fratianni and von Hagen (1990) disagree with the thesis whereby Germany's monetary policy is "dominant" within the EMS.

[3] Support interventions in favor of the currencies under speculative attacks have always been asymmetrical. In the 1980s, in the face of devaluation expectations due to their inflation differentials with Germany, the countries of Peripheral Europe supported their currencies by selling the DM obtained through the VSTF (very short term facility). The Bundesbank never intervened to defend weak currencies and normally isolated the impact of the flows of DM into Germany resulting from the support interventions carried out by the monetary authorities of the currencies under attack for fear of the inflationary pressures generated by a higher money supply.

As interpreted by the "new classical macroeconomics", discussed in section 4, the low degree of credibility of the EMS exchange rates, indicated by the interest-rate parity condition, is related to the idea that the threat to the stability of the exchange rates derived essentially from the fact that Peripheral Europe was less "inflation-avert" than Core Europe, owing to the incentive in those countries to make "unannounced" increases in the money supply. The expectations of a divergent behavior by the Central Banks of Peripheral Europe would then have dictated that the nominal anchor role played by the DM in the EMS be accompanied by the "asymmetry" which allowed the Bundesbank to exert control over the money supply of the entire area.

This vision of the EMS is set against the argument that while the monetary authorities of Peripheral Europe pegged their currencies to the DM – in order to achieve a faster disinflation and at a lower cost in terms of output and employment – it did not follow that they were devolving monetary sovereignty to the Bundesbank. Thus, in section 5 the argument is set forth whereby Peripheral Europe's "currency risk" might have been originated not by the lower "inflation aversion" disposition of the monetary authorities of these countries, but by the progressive loss of competitiveness determined by their inflation differentials with Germany, which resulted in current account deficits that raised devaluation expectations due to the inability to sustain a fixed exchange rate with the DM.

Section 6 illustrates how within the Euro area there might appear again the causation relationship between a diverging economic cycle in Germany and deflationary trends in Peripheral Europe that was at the root of the 1992-93 EMS crises. This time the conflict of interest between the two areas would involve the Euro/dollar exchange rate. Germany's interest in preventing inflationary tensions from spreading internally and in maintaining the competitiveness of its exports might lead the European Central Bank (ECB) to adopt a conservative approach to monetary policy – through a nominal appreciation of the Euro *vis-à-vis* the dollar – with the risk of widening the real divergence of Peripheral Europe.

2. The EMS: Some "Stylized Facts"

Figures 1, 2 and 3 depict some "stylized fact" that marked the working of the EMS[4]. Figures 1 and 2 divide member countries as follows: Core Europe (see footnote 1); the group of the larger and more advanced economies in Peripheral Europe (Periphery A: Italy, Spain and United Kingdom); and the group of the least-developed and smaller economies in Peripheral Europe (Periphery B: Ireland, Portugal and Greece); Fig. 2 introduces the distinction among the first phase of the EMS (1979-86), characterized by frequent realignments and controls on capital flows, the second phase of stable exchange rates (1987-92) and the third phase (1993-97) of parities held formally fixed (with the shift, following the 1992-93 crises, from the "narrow" fluctuation band to the "enlarged" 15% band), which ended with the definition of the countries participating in the monetary union and in the launch of the Euro.

---

[4] The figures were prepared based on statistical data by Eurostat and the OECD.

Fig. 1. Inflation rates and unemployment rates.

Fig. 2. Inflation rates, growth rates real GDP, short term real interest rates.

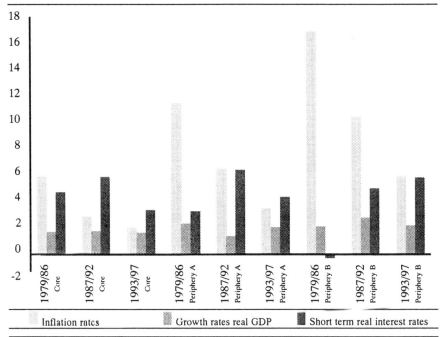

Fig. 3. Current accounts (as a percentage of GDP).

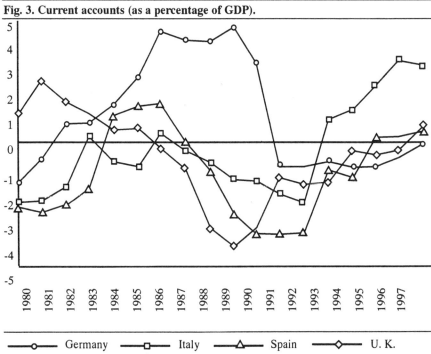

The following are the most important pieces of empirical evidence: 1) the slow inflation reduction in the countries of Peripheral Europe. Following the initial decline between 1982 and 1986 (which was due also to the effect of the oil counter-shock), the inflation rate rose in the late 80s and neared or reached the low German inflation rate only after the 1992-93 EMS crises; 2) the unemployment increase. Following the decline of the years 1987-89, unemployment stabilized at a high rate, particularly in Periphery A where income growth rates showed a steep decrease while short-term interest rates became increasingly higher. These data lead to believe that the devolution to Germany of the power to set the money supply entailed a monetary contraction greater than was warranted to reduce inflation, namely a "deflation bias" for Peripheral Europe; 3) the mirror pattern that characterizes the Current accounts/GDP ratios in the leading country on the one hand and in Periphery A on the other. From the creation of the EMS up to the asymmetric shock caused by the unification, Germany's surplus grew constantly; this was matched by a slowdown and strong deficits in the three economies of Periphery A, especially in the 1987-1992 phase of stable exchange rates.

In the years that followed the 1992-93 crises, instead, the negative values of the Germany ratio, due to the reunification process, were matched by a remarkable recovery in Periphery A, with a shift to substantial surpluses in the case of Italy. It can be assumed that this strong correlation existing between the trade flows of the Core and Peripheral Europe was the outcome of the trend whereby the DM experienced a real depreciation and the currencies of Peripheral Europe a real appreciation as a result of the inflation differentials with Germany in the presence of fixed exchange rates. This correlation also shows that the countries that started the monetary union are a relatively "closed" area. Since trade within the EMS was a crucial factor in determining the activity level, competitiveness undoubtedly represented a very important indicator when financial markets evaluate the credibility of fixed exchange rate systems.

3. Peripheral Europe and the "Interest Rate Parity" Condition

To understand how inflation, unemployment, growth rates and interest rates (as implied by "stylized facts" 1) and 2)) are connected as a result of the fixed exchange rate it is appropriate to dwell on the degree of credibility of the EMS as an engine of convergence toward a low inflation.

Figures 4, 5 and 6 show the differentials of the short - and long - term interest rates and of the inflation rates of Italy, Spain and UK *vis-à-vis* Germany[5].

The trends indicate a progressive reduction of the interest-rate and inflation- rate differentials with Germany. In the second phase of stable exchange rates of the EMS (1987-92) there was also a greater correlation, especially for Italy and Spain (the United Kingdom joined the fixed exchange rate mechanism only in 1990). The reduction of the two differentials, however, was rather slow and, most of all, there were still wide differentials of Peripheral Europe *vis-à-vis* Germany as for interest (short and long term) rates and inflation rates. These divergences widened for short-term interest rates in the period of stable exchange rates (which indicates a tighter monetary policy) and for long-term interest rates in the third phase (attesting to inflationary expectations following the shift to the wider fluctuation band). We now proceed with an in-depth analysis of the "interest rate parity" pattern for the countries of Peripheral Europe.

---

[5] The charts were prepared based on statistical data by European Economy, European Commission.

Fig. 4. Italy.

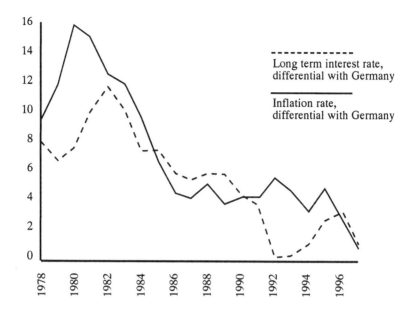

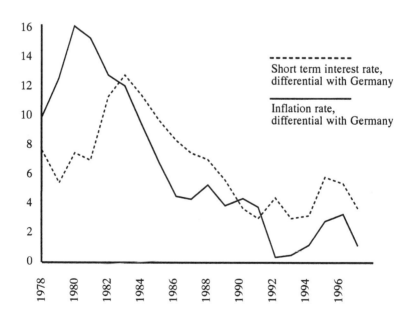

Fig. 5. Spain.

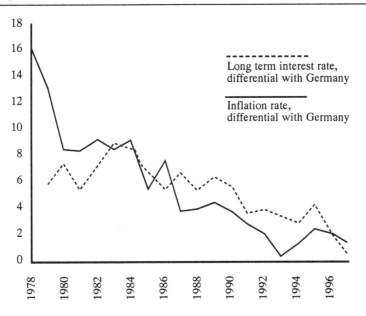

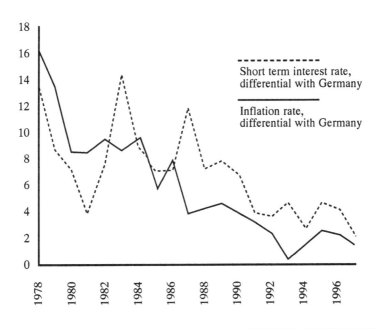

Fig.6. United Kingdom.

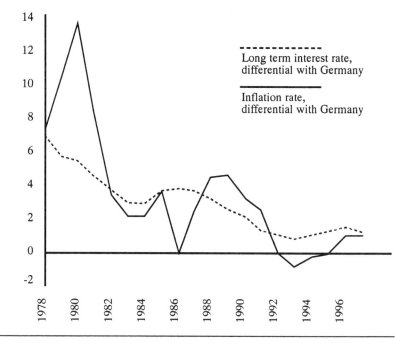

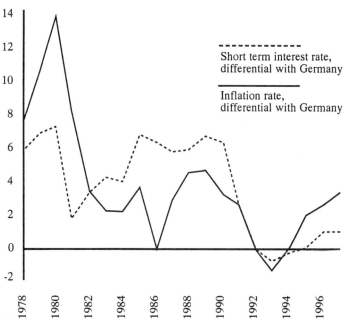

In measuring the credibility of the exchange rate within the EMS through interest rate differentials, no account will be taken of that part of the exchange rate expectations of Peripheral Europe's currencies *vis-à-vis* the DM which concerns the depreciation within the fluctuation band[6]. This makes it possible to consider such interest rate differentials a reliable indicator of the expected change in the exchange rate. In Equation 1, assuming that the first term on the left side indicates the difference between the interest rate (i) of the country representative of Peripheral Europe – e.g. Italy – and that (i*) of the EMS's leading country – Germany – and the second term on the right side represents the expected depreciation of the currency against the DM ($_ts_t+1$ - s_t) / st, where st is the prevailing exchange rate. Empirical evidence shows that the values of the first term have been systematically exceeding those in the second term[7].

$$(1) \quad (i - i^*) - (_ts_t+1 - s_t) / s_t = [(i - i^*) - (f_t - s_t) / s_t] + (f_t - _ts_t+1) / s_t$$

A possible divergence between interest-rate differential with Germany and depreciation against the DM depends on the value other than zero of one or both the terms that appear on the right side of the equation: the first term is the so-called "covered" interest differential (where f is the forward exchange rate), which can assume a negative value whenever there is a country risk (the risk incurred by an investor in case controls on capital flows are put in place). This is what happened at the start of the first phase of the EMS (1979-87). The degree of freedom enjoyed by monetary policy from administrative controls in some countries of Peripheral Europe led to the opening of a wedge between onshore and offshore interest differentials with Germany. In fact, the restrictions on capital outflows did allow interest rates in the internal market (onshore) to stay constant instead of rising after the wider interest rate differentials with Germany – approximated by the percentage changes of the "forward premium" on the currency *vis-à-vis* the DM (f_t - s_t) / st the market expectation of the future spot rate – that materialized on international markets (offshore).[8] After having reached even high values at the eve of the realignments prompted by the speculative attacks on weak currencies, this wedge began declining as a result of the removal of the controls on capital flows, until it disappeared in the second half of the 1980s.

Before examining the second term on the right side, which indicates the "currency risk" (the premium required by an investor to hold assets denominated in a

---

[6] The expected change in the exchange rate (s) may be divided into the sum of two components: the expected depreciation of a currency within the fluctuation band (D) and the expected realignment rate of the central parity (C). ($_ts_t+1$ - s_t)/ s_t = ($_tD_t+1$ - D_t)/ D_t + ($_tC_t+1$ - C_t)/ C_t. In assessing the credibility of the exchange rate, consideration should be given, in addition to the expected realignment, to the expected change within the fluctuation band. Since the "full credibility" assumption of Krugman's "Target Model" does not apply to the EMS, the ratio between exchange rate and interest rate differential is a positive one. When the exchange rate reaches the upper limit of the band, speculators do not think that authorities will intervene and accelerate the realignment by selling the currency. This seems to explain why, in measuring the expected realignment, subtracting the estimated expected change in the exchange rate within the band from the interest rate differential yields results approximately equal to the simple measurement of the exchange rate credibility through interest rate differentials. [Rose and Svensson (1993)].

[7] Farina (1990), pp. 371-81 and Frankel, Phillips and Chinn (1993), pp.273-279. Based on the rational expectations hypothesis, the expected depreciation is measured by approximating the expected change in the exchange rate $_ts_t+1$ to the *ex-post* exchange rate st_t+1.

[8] Farina (1993), pp. 449-454.

given currency), let us look at equation 2: it expresses a possible error in forecasting the exchange rate (difference between the forward exchange rate f and the future exchange rate s_t+1) as the sum of the deviation of the forward exchange rate from the expected exchange rate (the first term) and a forecasting error due to the absence of rational expectations in financial markets (the second term):

$$(2) \quad (f_t - s_t+1)/s_t = (f_t - {}_ts_t+1)/s_t + ({}_ts_t+1 - s_t+1)/s_t$$

Thus, adopting the rational expectations hypothesis, the second expression on the right side ($_ts_t+1 - s_t+1$) / st) is equal to zero. Since now both expected and actual exchange rates are equal, the first term on the right side represents the deviation of the forward exchange rate f_t from the *ex-post* exchange rate s_t+1 and corresponds to the second term on the right side of equation 1: $(f_t - s_t)/s_t - ({}_ts_t+1 - s_t)/s_t$. Now, this difference can be written in terms of observable magnitudes: $(f_t - s_t+1)/$ st. A positive value on the left side of equation 1: $(i - i^*) - (s_t+1 - f_t)/s_t > 0$, due to a possible excess of the interest rate differential over the depreciation may be explained in the excess of the forward exchange rate over the *ex post* exchange rate: $(f_t - s_t+1)/s_t > 0$.

In fact, empirical evidence suggests that in the years included between the end of the decade and 1992, the difference on the left side of equation 1 for countries of Periphery A deviated from zero again, showing now positive values because of the second term of the right side of equation 1[9]. The positive difference between forward rate and spot rate with the DM suggests the presence of a "currency risk" which determines a positive difference, on the left side of equation 1, between the interest rate differential with Germany and the *ex post* depreciation of the currency against the DM.

The possible explanations for a persistence of the excess of the interest rate differential over changes in the exchange rate are basically two: either a change over time in the credibility of the exchange rate or a "risk premium"[10], namely a compensation for the risk of domestic financial assets (determined for instance by expectations about the sustainability of public debt and thus by a forecast of its future monetization). As the empirical evidence shows that "risk premiums" are negligible[11], Peripheral Europe's excess interest rate differential *vis-à-vis* Germany should be attributable to a variable though persistently low credibility, which determines interest rate differentials with Germany that do not reflect in the subsequent depreciation of the exchange rate of weaker currencies against the DM. Sections 4 and 5 will cover two different interpretations of the low credibility that – in light of the empirical evidence mentioned – characterized the EMS's fixed exchange rate system.

4. The "Classical" Interpretation of the EMS

The interpretation under the "new classical macroeconomics" sees the EMS as a purely cooperative game between the two distinct groups of countries of Core Europe and Peripheral Europe, designed to achieve the public good of monetary stability. The choice of the European countries in favor of a complete liberalization of capital flows

---

[9] Frankel, Phillips and Chinn (1993), pp. 273-79.

[10] The equation for the uncovered parity of interest rates may include a premium for the "currency risk": $i = i^* + ({}_ts_t+1 - s_t)/s_t - \gamma$, where γ represents the premium for the "currency risk". The expected exchange rate then will tend to exceed the forward exchange rate for an amount up to the product between the current exchange rate and the absolute value of the "risk premium": $_ts_t+1 = f_t + s_t \gamma$.

[11] Frankel, Phillips and Chinn (1993), p. 281.

reflected the "perfect markets" theoretical conception adopted by the "new classical macroeconomics". As they have a better knowledge of the "fundamentals", financial markets are in a position to evaluate the degree of credibility of monetary authorities by monitoring the consistency of these countries' macroeconomic policies with their maintenance of fixed exchange rates. The "forward premium" over the DM, expressed by the interest rate differentials with Germany, became in its own right the signal of the financial markets' opinion on anti-inflationary policies, and a "discipline effect" on the convergence process of Peripheral Europe toward the country with the lowest inflation rate was attached to it.

As can be seen shortly, the peculiarity of the classical approach to the EMS – termed the "monetary discipline approach" – lies in the idea that at the origin of Peripheral Europe's devaluation expectations there was always the expectation of "divergent" behaviors by their monetary authorities and not also the macroeconomic instability resulting from the high interest rates linked to the "asymmetric" working of the EMS.

The analytical scheme of "monetary discipline" may be built as follows. In equation 3, the "natural" unemployment rate is determined through the traditional Phillips curve augmented with expectations, where p is the inflation rate , p^e the expected inflation rate, U the unemployment rate, U_n the "natural" unemployment rate while the parameter α represents the slope of the curve that indicates how unemployment reacts to "unexpected" inflation.

$$(3) \qquad U = U_n - \alpha \, (\, p - p^e \,)$$

The equation indicates that the higher α, the flatter the Phillips curve. As this implies that a higher inflation results in a substantial employment increase, a high value of this parameter signals the presence of an opportunity for a "surprise" inflation. The common assumption is that in the interaction between Central Bank and private sector agents monetary authorities set the monetary base after wage contracts have been signed. Hence the well-know "time-inconsistency" problem: the time sequence of the events creates for the Central Bank the incentive to implement an "unannounced" expansion of the monetary base in order to achieve temporary production and employment increases. Every "unexpected" increment of the money supply is met with an upward adjustment of the inflation rate on the long-term Phillips curve, in correspondence of an upper short-term curve. Thus, the main condition to lower the inflation rate on the long-term Phillips curve is the credibility of an anti-inflationary monetary policy announcement by the monetary authorities, namely a high value of the parameter that expresses "inflation aversion" in the social loss function.

$$(4) \qquad L = [\, \beta \, (\, p - p^*)^2 + (U - U^*)^2]$$

In the quadratic function of social loss represented by equation 4, U^* is the target of the unemployment rate, π^* is the target inflation rate and the value of parameter β indicates the importance monetary authorities attribute to the inflation target, namely that "inflation aversion" which the credibility of monetary authorities should depend on. This parameter determines the slope of the curve: the steeper the indifference curve – as happens with curves (I) and (I') in Figure 1 – the lower the loss attributed to a higher inflation rate and the lower the incentive to create inflation in order to reduce unemployment.

A higher money growth rate in order to generate a "surprise" inflation is usually related to low "independence" of Central Banks from Government pressures for a looser monetary policy. The time succession between union bargaining and decision to create money undermines the credibility of every announcement of a "zero rate of inflation". In Figure 1, every "surprise" monetary expansion is followed by: the movement starting from A along the short-term Phillips curve up to point of tangency B with indifference curve (I) which depicts the trade-off between inflation and unemployment; the upward adjustment of inflation expectations through an upward shift of the curve and the resulting reinstatement of the "natural" unemployment level at point C; further increase in the money growth rate with successive equilibrium points (for instance, point of tangency D on the new short-term Phillips curve and indifference curve (I'), up to point E on the long-term Phillips curve.

The "credibility" theory aims to increase the degree of confidence in a low but positive average inflation rate, resulting from a trade-off between credibility – the condition whereby inflationary expectations are revised downward – and flexibility – the discretionality in setting the parameters that makes it possible to stabilize income in case of a negative shock. A change toward a strictly anti-inflationary monetary policy should be signaled by the appointment of "conservative" monetary authorities who in turn determine a shift in the trade-off between inflation and unemployment[12]. The application to the EMS of the "credibility" theory saw the convergence toward the low German inflation as a goal that was not logically inconsistent as it referred to inflation rates higher than zero. In the case of Peripheral Europe's monetary authorities, a high threshold for "inflation aversion" may be associated to the end of the realignments and to the so-called "change of regime" toward stable parities which took place in the EMS starting in 1997.

The greater "inflation aversion" is expressed by the increase of parameter β in the social loss function of equation 4 and in figure 1 by the flatter slope that marks indifference curve (I") compared to (I) and (I'). The anti-inflationary monetary strategies adopted by conservative authorities in Peripheral Europe, however, was not followed by a rapid disinflation, due to the stickiness of inflationary expectations which prevented the short-term Phillips curve from shifting downward. This can be seen in Fig. 7: since tight money cannot reduce inflationary expectations, the only effect of an anti-inflationary monetary strategy, given the flatness of the curve, is to increase the unemployment rate (from E to E') along the same curve (with a negligible decline of the inflation rate).

However, the "classical" interpretation underscores how the greater credibility obtained by the central banker, once a high value for β has been established, is not sufficient to solve the "time inconsistency" problem. The possibility, in the name of flexibility, that both an inflation and an employment target have been set causes inflation rates greater than zero, such as those announced by the monetary authorities of Peripheral Europe, to have a "credibility" problem even though they are not subject to "time inconsistency". Although the countries of Peripheral Europe appointed conservative Government aimed at achieving the public good of monetary stability, the

---

[12] According to this well-known theory a country may improve its social welfare – a reduction of inflationary expectations, thus of the inflation rate – by appointing a "conservative" Governor, who in other words places a higher priority on inflation stabilization than on income and employment stabilization. The main works on the "credibility" of monetary authorities include Rogoff (1985), Flood and Isard (1989) and Lohmann (1992).

Fig. 7. Monetary policy credibility and disinflation.

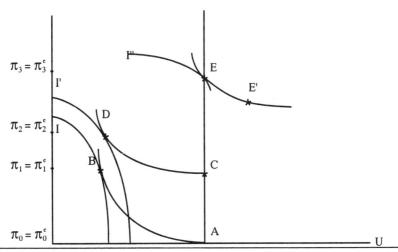

prerogative of monetary authorities to determine a "surprise" inflation remained untouched, and with it the possibility for each member country to renege on the agreement and revert to the "competitive devaluations" strategy. Consequently, according to the "classical" approach, for a strategy of convergence toward the low German inflation to be successful in reducing inflationary expectations was that financial markets be placed in the position to express a vote of confidence on the commitment of the Central Banks of Peripheral Europe to give up flexibility altogether, in accordance with the "classical" proposition whereby every deviation from "zero" inflation represents a social loss (a permanent increase of the rate of inflation could not be matched by any permanent benefit in terms of output and employment levels)[13].

The financial markets could not give such vote of confidence. There was in fact the incentive to make "unannounced" increases of the money supply which would exploit the determination of nominal wages before deciding on money creation: the rise of the unemployment rate which took place during the phase of stable exchange rates in 1987-92[14]. The assumption is that the current distortions in the labor market, starting from the rigidity of nominal wages, prevent the operation of the classical adjustment mechanism after a negative shock (such as for instance a wage increase greater than productivity growth). This market "imperfection" was possibly

---

[13] This theoretical position gave rise to the argument in favor of a rapid transition to the single European currency, partially accepted in the Maastricht Treaty. The "new classical macroeconomics" maintained that the time inconsistency problem, the obstacle that stood in the way of Peripheral Europe's pursuit of "zero inflation", could be solved through an "institutional" innovation whereby the creation of money should not diverge from that of the Bundesbank: the shock therapy consisting in a transition to the Central European Bank and to the single currency without waiting for the full convergence of all the member countries. The underlying rationale was that the ECB should "inherit" the reputation of the Bundesbank so that it might achieve in Europe the "zero inflation" objective without running into the "time inconsistency" problem.
[14] Among the different contributions to the "new classical macroeconomics" strand, see for all Alesina and Grilli (1992) and (1993).

responsible for raising the "natural" rate to abnormal levels in Peripheral Europe. The credibility of the EMS might then have been impaired due to the fact that the Central Banks of Peripheral Europe could at any time ignore the "ineffectiveness of the monetary policy" proposition and plan the reduction of the unemployment rate below the "natural" level[15]. The persistence of an excess interest rate differential with Germany compared to *ex post* depreciation was then univocally attributed to the expectation of a devaluation of the currencies against the DM, variable in magnitude but always pessimistic.

This "classical" interpretation of the reasons for the low credibility of the monetary authorities of Peripheral Europe should be explored. In fact, it is grounded on the rather strong assumption of the existence, for the monetary authorities of Peripheral Europe, of a clear incentive to "surprise" inflation: the possibility to raise employment through price increases aimed at lowering the real wage.

This thesis can be expresses by supposing that the "peripheral" country sets an unemployment target related to "natural" unemployment by coefficient $(1 - \delta)$, where $0 < \delta < 1$:

$$(5) \qquad\qquad U^* = (1 - \delta)\, U_n$$

A value close to 1 of parameter δ reflects the monetary authorities' expectation that "active" policies are capable of bringing the "natural" unemployment rate back to the preceding lower level.

By substituting equations 3 and 5 in equation 4 the following social loss function is derived:

$$(6) \qquad\qquad L = \{\beta\,(p - p\,^*)^2 + [\,\delta\, U_n - \alpha\,(p - p^e)^2]\,\}$$

where the target inflation rate p^* is equal to zero.

The monetary authorities' minimization of the social loss function (equation 6), under the constraint that agents have a perfect forecast of the inflation rate $(p = p^e)$[16], yields the following rational expectation solution:

$$(7) \qquad\qquad p = \alpha\,(\delta\, U_n)/\beta$$

Thus, the equilibrium inflation rate has a positive relationship with parameter α (the higher α the less steep the short-term Phillips curve and the greater the incentive for a "surprise" inflation) and with parameter δ (the higher the divergence of the unemployment target from its "natural" level, the higher the equilibrium inflation) and a negative relationship with the degree of "inflation aversion" (β), the parameter to which the function to foster the reduction of the inflation rate is attributed.

True, the policy of pegging the DM allowed the anti-inflationary commitment of the Central Banks of Peripheral Europe – which can be summarized in the high value

---

[15] "This wedge between the market generated, "natural" level of output (...) and the target level (...) can be justified by the existence of various distortions in the labor market, such as income taxation or labor unions. These distortions keep employment and output below the levels that would be achieved in an undistorted economy. Thus, the policymakers have an incentive to circumvent these distortions by generating "unexpected" inflation which increase the level of economic activity" (Cf. Alesina and Grilli (1993), p.147).

[16] In formal terms $p^e = E\,(p/\lambda-1) = p + \varphi\ E(\varphi) = 0$, where the inflation rate is based on information λ-1 available in the preceding period and φ is a white noise.

of parameter β at the denominator, producing a reduction of the inflation rate – to benefit from the Bundesbank's reputation. But, according to this view, the "monetary discipline" strategy was weakened by the labor market distortions. The "stylized facts" that characterized the EMS functioning might then be explained through a sequence of causation relations whose first mover is the rigidity of the labor market, which hobbles the adjustment mechanism of the classical model through the reduction of wages and prices and causes the persistence of an "inflation bias". The more the adjustment takes place with unemployment increases along a short-term downward rigid Phillips curve rather than through price and wage reductions, the more the "natural" unemployment rate tends to increase. This real factor might have reduced the independence of monetary authorities from Government pressures for an "unannounced" monetary expansion. The logical chain then is as follows: the greater the distortion of the labor market, and then the higher the "natural" unemployment rate, the greater the deviation from the existing "natural" rate of the set unemployment target.

The monetary authorities of a country of Peripheral Europe will then be led to attribute a higher value to δ . If the agents anticipate the higher value for δ, namely the establishment of an unemployment target too low, they will also expect the monetary authorities to be tempted to produce a "surprise" inflation, so that inflationary expectations will remain sticky. Thus, the higher the "currency risk" of the high-unemployment countries the higher will have to be the rise of interest rates in these countries, so as to determine an excess of the differential with Germany compared to the *ex post* changes of the exchange rates against the DM[17]. According to the "classical" interpretation, the reason for the permanence of Peripheral Europe's inflation rates at a higher level than Germany's was the static nature that a value of δ closer to one than to zero produced in inflationary expectations.

5. Real Appreciation and Deflation Bias in Peripheral Europe

Thus, the "new classical macroeconomics" denies the existence of a connection between the first two "stylized facts" – the slow pace of disinflation and the unemployment increase – and German "hegemony" in the EMS. Instead, there might have been a fundamental independence between the countries of Core Europe and those of Peripheral Europe with respect to the benefits received and the costs incurred. In other words, there was no causation relationship between the benefits obtained by the former – such as the real depreciation of the DM – and the costs borne by the latter – such as the strong decline of the growth rate and the loss of competitiveness that characterized the second phase of the EMS (1987-92), especially in Periphery A (see Figures 2 and 3).

The "classical" interpretation, however, is not satisfactory, as the different assumptions adopted do not seem to be consistent with one another. The argument whereby the "credibility" of monetary policy is low due to the existence of an incentive to make "unannounced" increases in the money supply derives from the assumption of a downward real wage flexibility. Nominal wage rigidity, that is the lack of reaction to price increases in the short term, would allow output and employment levels to temporarily increase. Instead, the assumption of a too high "natural"

---

[17] The existence of a causation relationship whereby increases of the unemployment rate led to wider interest rate differentials with Germany, was put forth by Drazen and Masson (1994) on the basis of tests that would rule out the possibility that these variables are now endogenously determined.

unemployment rate due to distortions in the labor market implies the existence of downward-rigid real wage: non-economic constraints which distort the working of the labor market would make it impossible to bring wage growth back in line with productivity growth. The assumption that the real wage level in Europe is downward flexible has been disproved by empirical evidence. In fact, the results of a series of studies show that the necessary condition of nominal wages being sufficiently sticky as not to react promptly to every price increase did not occur[18].

Thus, consistently with the empirical evidence and contrary to the classical vision depicted in Figure 7, the Phillips curve in Figure 8 is very steep. Even adopting in equation 7 the classical "assumption" of a high value of δ caused by the rigidities existing in the labor market, the value of α is low. This value indicates that any temporary increases in output and employment that can be achieved with a "surprise" inflation would be totally negligible: the low value of α, in fact, is capable of

---

Fig. 8. Monetary policy credibility and disinflation with nominal wage rigidity.

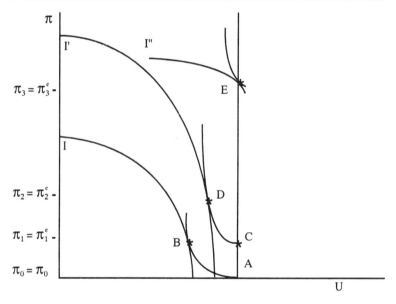

---

completely offsetting the effect of a rise in the inflation rate due to a high value of δ.

The downward rigidity of the real wage raises strong doubts about the "classical" theory whereby at the origin of the low EMS credibility (as shown by the excess of its interest rate differential with Germany compared to the depreciation against the DM in Peripheral Europe) there may have been an incentive to make "unannounced" increases in the money supply. As a result, the causation relationship which, according to the "classical" interpretation, was deemed to exist – during the stable exchange rate

---

[18] "Nominal wage rigidity is a good deal lower in the EU than in the US: estimates of the parameter β in the EU are only about 1/8 of the US value (…)" (Loockwood, Miller and Zhang (1996), p.253-5). Also Grubb, Jackman and Laylard (1983) and Obstfeld and Peri (1998) reached the same conclusions.

phase in the EMS – between the rise in the unemployment rate and the wider interest rate differential with Germany is not proven[19]. The only thing which survives of this interpretation is the tenet – compatible with the downward rigidity of real wage – that the labor market's distortions caused a structural increase of the "natural" unemployment rate compared to the rate prevailing in macroeconomic equilibrium with perfectly working markets.

Let us review then a different interpretation of the low EMS credibility: the loss of competitiveness of Peripheral Europe's countries as a reason for expecting a devaluation against the DM. Figure 9 depicts in a stylized manner the macroeconomic equilibrium achieved in Peripheral Europe once the EMS – in the phase of stable exchange rates in 1987-1992 – definitely became a fixed exchange rate system, thereby rejecting both realignments and capital flow controls. Figure 9b shows the deviation of the macroeconomic equilibrium of a country representative of Peripheral Europe (Italy) from that of a country representative of Core Europe (Germany). The macroeconomic equilibrium of Peripheral Europe is represented by A', at the intersection between aggregate supply that has shifted upward from AS to AS' [the price divergence with the German level (p*), created by the negative shock of the increase of labor cost per unit of output at the end of the 1970s, was eventually fed continuously by the inflation differential with Germany] and aggregate demand that has shifted downward as a result of a tight monetary policy.

In Figure 9a. in correspondence of point A', there is the IS-LM equilibrium point A, which results from a backward shift of IS to IS' (corresponding to the shift from AD to AD') and from a backward shift of LM to LM". This latter shift – greater that the one that would result simply as a consequence of a conservative monetary policy (from LM to LM') – indicates the reduction of liquidity in Peripheral Europe caused by a price level higher than in Germany and shows the presence of an interest rate differential between Italy (i) and Germany (i*).

The equilibrium between current accounts (CA)[20], which makes it possible to usher the third "stylized fact", completes the description. Due to deflationary monetary and fiscal policies, Peripheral Europe witnesses a progressive fall in absorption, which is represented by the backward shift to CA'. Section 2 showed the disequilibria of the balances of trade between Germany on the one hand and Italy, Spain and United Kingdom on the other (see Figure 3).

The origin may be due to the stickiness of disinflation. The slow reduction of inflation differentials with Germany of Periphery A's countries - by determining a wider price level differential with Germany in the presence of stable exchange rates in the second EMS phase (1987-1992) – caused the continuous appreciation of those currencies and an increasingly unsustainable current account deficit. The opposing patterns of the Current Account/GDP ratios witness the continuous loss of competitiveness by Peripheral Europe in favor of Core Europe. In Figure 9a, a decrease of the aggregate demand (from AD to AD') greater than that of the current account equilibrium line (point A lies on the left of CA') represents a loss of output (and of employment) greater than the absorption reduction. Thus, Figure 9 describes

---

[19] De la Croix and Lubrano (1996) showed that in most European countries real interest rates and unemployment rates are co-integrated variables, with the first causing the second.

[20] The equilibrium between current accounts is defined as: $p_D Y = p_A A$ (where p_D is the level of domestic prices; Y domestic output, p_A the average price level of domestic goods, A the absorption). The negative slope of CA depends on the fact that for every increase of p_D, p_A increases less-than-proportionally, which makes it necessary for domestic output Y to decline (De Grauwe (1997), pp.30-1).

Fig. 9. Macroeconomic equilibrium in the Peripheral Europe.

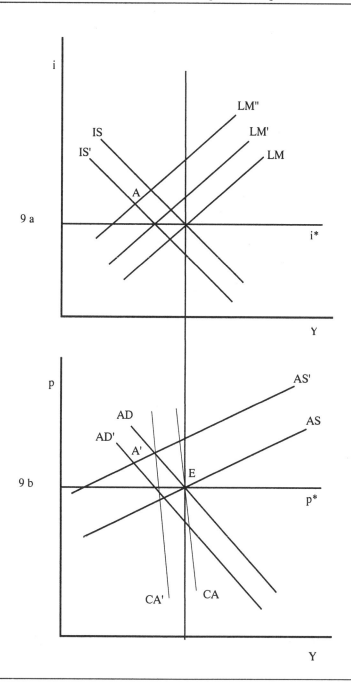

the EMS's "deflation bias", determined by the high interest rates level (as shown in Figure 2) and the deterioration of price competitiveness (as indicated by the trend of the Current account/GDP ratio in Figure 3).

In the light of this interpretation, the low credibility of the monetary policy of Peripheral Europe's countries – instead of "surprise" monetary expansions for which, as was seen, the incentive of a downward flexibility of real wage was lacking – could be attributed to a lack of confidence by the markets in these countries' ability to balance their current accounts without resorting to a devaluation against the DM. On the other hand, the "asymmetric" working of the EMS, and the upward pressures on real interest rates put by Germany's "hegemony" in determining the monetary policy of the fixed exchange rate area, produced a remarkable macroeconomic instability in Peripheral Europe. The destabilizing effects of such "asymmetry" became incompatible with the stability of the EMS's exchange rates when – as a result of the asymmetric demand shock originating from the unification process – Germany's economic cycle reversed its trend in the face of the deflationary pattern prevailing in Europe.

Had the EMS been a symmetrical system, both the leading country and the peripheral countries should have tackled – through interventions to sustain their currencies – the trend of weak currencies to move toward the upper limit of the fluctuation band against the DM. Instead, the countries of Peripheral Europe had to raise interest rates to the extent required not only by the goal of internal disinflation but also by the strong monetary restriction that a higher inflation had made inevitable in Germany[21]. When the financial markets assigned a higher "currency risk" to the countries of Periphery A, the interest rate increases that would have been necessary to widen the differentials with Germany to defend their currencies became unsustainable for their domestic macroeconomic equilibrium.

The "classical" argument of a lower "inflation aversion" in Peripheral Europe as the main factor of a crisis within the EMS is contradicted by the fact that, at least in Periphery A, the monetary authorities were following "correct" monetary and fiscal policies firmly devoted to achieve disinflation. Thus, it can be stated that the speculative attacks in the summer of 1992, which led Italian lira and the pound to abandon the EMS, arose from the markets' belief that Peripheral Europe as a whole could not live with the asymmetric shock of the German unification without resorting to exchange rate realignments to adjust their Current Account balance. The fact that the "asymmetric" working of the EMS made it impossible to determine interest rates independently of the Bundesbank's monetary policy – namely to avoid further unnecessary increases to defend the currencies – caused speculative attacks to be self-fulfilling[22].

After the relevant widening between real interest rates and growth rates that characterized the stable exchange rates phase in 1987-1992 (see Figure 2), the third phase of the EMS (1993-97) provides an indirect indication of the "deflation bias" in Periphery A during the preceding phase. The histograms of figure 8 show that in the third phase the growth rate experienced a remarkable increase while real interest rates fell considerably. The exit from the fixed exchange rate mechanism (as far as Italy and the United Kingdom are concerned) and the end of the "narrow band" EMS (as far as

---

[21] De Grauwe (1996), pp. 10-7.
[22] On the self-fulfilling nature of currency speculation in a fixed exchange rate regime see Obstfeld (1986). The devaluations of the Italian lira and the pound in September 1992 seem to confirm Obstfeld's model.

Spain is concerned) made it possible to achieve a non-inflationary demand recovery. This process may be described in Figure 9 as a return of both AS and AD to the initial position, thanks to a lower rigidity of real wage[23].

Figure 3 highlights how the countries of Periphery A improved their Current Account/GDP ratios (mirroring the deterioration of such ratio in Germany), which confirms that the recovery did not go hand in hand with such a rise in prices and wages as to jeopardize the competitiveness of Periphery A's countries. It can then be surmised that the strong deflation which had taken place in Periphery A in 1987-1992 determined a situation of path dependency: as shown in Figure 9b, in absence of a boost to aggregate demand, the adjustment mechanism providing for a reduction in prices and salaries would not have been able to restore the previous macroeconomic equilibrium. As a matter of fact, due to the marked shift backward of the AD line, an adjustment consisting merely in the reversal of AD toward the starting position would have entailed a limited income increase, with a fall of Peripheral Europe's price level below Germany's (p*).

6. Competitiveness and Euro/Dollar Exchange Rate

With the introduction of the Euro, the surpluses and deficits of the balances of payments among the Euro-11 turned into surpluses and deficits related to domestic trade and the problem of the loss of competitiveness against Germany caused by pegging Peripheral Europe's currencies to the DM disappeared. On the other hand, the possibility that non-synchronized growth paths might cause again macroeconomic instability continues to exist. In fact, it is possible that the European Monetary Union might make it increasingly likely that different growth-rate and/or production specialization trends create a conflict of interest on the setting of a common monetary policy by the ECB. This section will analyze one of the possible reasons for divergence among the productive systems of Core Europe and Peripheral Europe that might arise in the short-to-medium term.

In line with monopolistic competition prevailing in European production, the economic integration process that has been taking place hand in hand with monetary integration is grounded mainly on product differentiation and on the growth of intra-industry trade. There is a wide consensus that the change that will be spurred by the single currency – such as mergers and the further expansion of intra-European trade – will lead monopolistic competitive firms to a more rapid exploitation of increasing returns to scale. The fiercer competition and the increase of the average size of firms should hasten concentration and the production specialization of the different areas[24].

It may be assumed that these changes in the productive structures related to the EMU will foster the development of an endogenous growth mechanism especially in the Germany-influenced economic area, paving the way for a productivity, thus an inflation, differential between Core Europe and Peripheral Europe. Germany's concern with a deterioration of the tradeoff between inflation and unemployment should not then be ascribed entirely to the presence in the ECB Board of the less "inflation avert" monetary authorities of Peripheral Europe[25] but also to possible internal inflationary

---

[23] The export-led recovery that took place in Italy between 1992 and 1995 would indicate that, if a recession is due to a lack of effective demand, a nominal devaluation can be successful. (Dornbusch (1996), p.32).

[24] See for instance Krugman (1993), pp. 243-255.

[25] Claassen (1996), pp.231-4.

tensions[26]. The conflict that arises on the degree of tightness of monetary policy is thus the consequence of the different monetary manouvres required by real economies which follow different growth paths despite sharing the same currency.

In a two-country model representing respectively Core Europe (Germany, indicated by the asterisk) and peripheral Europe (Italy), we express the general price indicators as the sum of the indicators of the *tradable* PT and the non tradable PN sectors:

(8) $p^* = a^*PT + (1 - a^*) PN$
(9) $p = a\,PT + (1 - a)\,PN$

where (a) and $(1 - a)$ represent the share of the tradable and non tradable sectors on the total.

The real exchange rate (e) may be written as $e = [PT / PN]^{(1-a)} / [PT / PN]^{*(1-a^*)}$.

Assuming the shares in the two countries to be equal, $a = a^*$, the rate of change of the exchange rate (ε) will be equal to the product between the share of the non tradable sector and the difference between the inflation rates (π) of the two sectors in each country:

$\varepsilon = (1 - a)\,[(\pi T - \pi N) - (\pi T^* - \pi N^*)]$

Assuming that the equilibrium prices in each sector equal the labor cost per unit of output, the inflation rate (π) is the difference between the rate of change of nominal wages (ω) – equal in both countries by assumption – and rate of change in productivity (ξ):

(10) $\pi T^* = \omega T - \xi T^*$ (12) $\pi N^* = \omega N - \xi N^*$
(11) $\pi T = \omega T - \xi T$ (13) $\pi N = \omega N - \xi N$

Assuming also that the rates of change of nominal wages in the two sectors are equal $\omega T = \omega N$ (as it is assumed for instance in the so-called Scandinavian model[27]), from equations 10 to 13 we obtain

(14) $(\pi N^* - \pi T^*) = (\xi T^* - \xi N^*)$
(15) $(\pi N - \pi T) = (\xi T - \xi N)$

Thus, in each country, there is an inverse relationship between the inflation and the productivity differentials between the two sectors.

Expressing equations 8 and 9 in terms of growth rate and substituting in them equations 10 and 12 and equations 11 and 13, we obtain:

$\pi^* = a\,(\omega - \xi T^*) + (1-a)\,(\omega - \xi N^*)$
$\pi = a\,(\omega - \xi T) + (1-a)\,(\omega - \xi N)$

Rearranging, we have:

(16) $\pi^* = a\,\pi T^* + (1-a)\,(\pi T^* - \xi T^* - \xi N^*)$
(17) $\pi = a\,\pi T + (1-a)\,(\pi T - \xi T - \xi N)$

---

[26] The strategy to admit to the initial stage of the single currency only a limited number of countries was inspired by the "classical" vision of the deadlock risk that the common monetary policy would have incurred once the ECB Board would have included also monetary authorities not "independent" from their governments (see De Grauwe (1997), pp.150-4).
[27] Lindbeck (1979).

Given that in the two countries the growth rates of productivity in the non tradable sectors are equal, $\xi N = \xi N*$, subtracting equation (16) from equation (17) yields:

(18) $\pi - \pi* = a(\pi T - \pi T*) + (1-a)(\pi T - \pi T* + \xi T - \xi T*)$

In the "purchasing power parity" equation: $\varepsilon = \pi T - \pi T*$ (where ε is the rate of change of the exchange rate between Italian lira and DM, πT Italy's inflation rate and $\pi T*$ Germany's inflation rate), the introduction of the Euro sets $\varepsilon = 0$, whence, given perfect market competition, $\pi T = \pi T*$.

Equation (18) then becomes:

(19) $\pi - \pi* = (1-a)(\xi T - \xi T*)$

Equation (19) shows how the end of the variability in the exchange rate following the transition to the Euro sets a direct causation whereby a differential of productivity growth in favor of Germany in the tradable sector determines a higher inflation rate in Germany than in Italy (for a given share of the non tradable sector).

Let us transfer the main relations on a 4-quadrant graph. In quadrant 2, the common value of the ratio of the inflation rate of the tradable sector to that of the non tradable sector (σo), together with the line representing equation $\pi To = \eta o - \pi T^U$ (where ηo is the rate of change of the Euro/dollar exchange rate, πTo is the inflation rate in the tradable sector common to the two countries and πT^U is the inflation rate in the tradable sector in the United States) and the line representing the overall inflation rate (πo), determines the equilibrium (E) existing at the time the Euro is introduced. Moreover, let us assume that, in addition to the wage level the two countries have the same growth rate in the tradable sector (ξTo).

Let us suppose now that the faster integration among the productive systems of the Euro-11 determined by the introduction of the Euro leads to a general increase of the growth rate on a *per capita* basis in the countries of the monetary union; let, however, the productivity rise in the tradable sector [starting from line (ξT)o in quadrant 3] be greater in Core Europe, as a result of the more pronounced dynamism of those countries to achieve economies of scale. Quadrant 3 then shows a gap ($\xi T* - \xi T$) in the growth rate of productivity between Germany's tradable sector ($\xi T*$) and Italy's (ξT).

As it was assumed that the wage increase extends to the non tradable sector, also without any corresponding productivity increase (the common growth rate of productivity in the non tradable sectors of the two countries is assumed to remain constant), then the inflation rate of the non tradable sector must rise. The fact that it was assumed that productivity increases in the tradable sectors are matched by wage rises in both sectors, so that wage increases in the non tradable sector reflect on prices, then lies at the foundation of the higher inflation rates in the non tradable sector, in proportion for each country to the productivity growth in the tradable sector.

Hence the gap between the inflation rates of the two sectors within each country: according to equations (14) and (15), this gap stands in an inverse relationship with the gap between the growth rates of productivity in the two sectors. Differing increases, $\xi T*$ and ξT (keeping ξN constant), in quadrant 3 are matched, through the line of quadrant 4, by differing productivity gaps ($\xi T - \xi N$) in the two countries.[28] Through the line of quadrant 1 these differentials determine the new inflation levels in the non tradable sector $\pi_N *$ and π_N (holding πT constant). In quadrant 2, the line depicting the ratio between the inflation rates in the non tradable

---

Fig. 10. Inflation differentials inside the EMU and the Euro/US Dollar exchange rate.

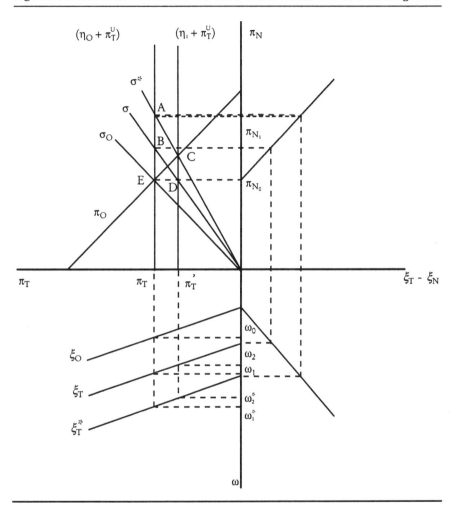

---

and tradable (σ_0) reflects the different inflation increases in the non tradable sectors of the two countries through a more marked rotation for Germany ($\sigma*$) than for Italy (σ). At the intersection between straight lines ($\sigma*$) and (σ) and the line depicting the Euro/dollar exchange rate $\pi T_0 = \eta_0 - \pi T^U$, there are new inflation rates – both

---

[28] The inflation level for the non tradable sector is obviously greater in the country "representative" of the area with the higher per capita growth rate (Core Europe) compared to the level of the country representative of the area with the lower per capita growth rate (Peripheral Europe).

higher than the initial level – in the two "representative" countries (point A for Germany, point B for Italy).

From the gap that might open, following the monetary union, between the two areas in the productivity growth of the tradable sector ($\xi T^* > \xi T$ in quadrant 3), the model described originates an inflation differential between the two countries (A> B in quadrant 2), in accordance with equation (19). Let us turn now to the possible courses of action the ECB might take in light of a positive inflation differential for Germany (and, possibly, for the Core Europe) with respect to Peripheral Europe. The prospect that an "accomodating" monetary policy by the ECB might cause an inflation differential to occur between Germany and Italy would obviously be opposed by Germany. Unchanged though the inflation rate in the tradable sector may be at level πO (as can be seen in quadrant 2), inflationary tensions might spread throughout the production system undermining the competitiveness of German exports to the rest of Europe.

The most likely scenario is that the Bundesbank is capable of exerting on the ECB's monetary policy as effective a control as that it had on the monetary stances of the EMS Central Banks. The ECB might then be led to set as its target the preservation of monetary stability in Germany by appreciating the Euro against other currencies (which for simplicity's sake we may identify with the dollar area). In this case, as we will see shortly, the effects on peripheral Europe may be as deflationary as those that the German "hegemony" produced on the creation of money in the whole EMS area.

A foreign exchange policy by the ECB intent on preserving Germany's monetary stability consists in having the Euro appreciate against the dollar so much as to prevent Germany's inflation rate to rise. This is shown in Figure 10 by the lower inflation rate of tradable sector $\pi T1$ and by the appreciation of the Euro against the dollar which would follow from a deflationary stance of the ECB: the line $\pi To = \eta_o - \pi T^U$ shifts to the right up to $\pi T1 = \eta_1 - \pi T^U$ and the rotation from σ to σ^* is such as to determine an intersection with line πTo at C (inflation held constant at the initial level)[29]. However, a monetary policy whereby the ECB pursues Germany's internal goals – exactly as happened in the EMS – places the representative country of Peripheral Europe at a loss. As a matter of fact, the appreciation provokes a deflationary process in Italy: inflation must necessarily decline as the new line ($\eta_1 - \pi U$) intersects the line σ (point D) below inflation rate πo[30].

The level at which this initial inflation rate lies is not indifferent to the possible deflationary outcomes of an Euro-appreciation strategy. In the presence of inflation rates in Core Europe and Peripheral Europe close to zero – the "classical" vision whereby social welfare is reached in correspondence of "zero inflation" – such strategy might turn deflation into a recession. As can be seen in Figure 10, in case of an Euro-appreciation strategy *vis-à vis* the dollar, the wage differential between the

---

[29] The condition for this equilibrium is that the deflation caused by the appreciation triggers a decline of inflation rate πT^* and a weaker increase of inflation rate πN^* such that inflation rate π^* in Germany is unchanged. According to Claassen [(1996), pp.231-4], instead, in case of a higher growth rate in Germany than in the other countries of the monetary union, a lower Euro/dollar exchange rate could not in any case prevent Germany from experiencing the unpleasant effect of a higher inflation.

[30] If in the ECB Board the interest of Peripheral Europe were to prevail, calling for a Euro/dollar exchange rate that would avoid deflation and leave room for an export expansion such that the growth gap with Germany stops widening, it would be necessary to maintain the exchange rate unaltered and allow inflation rates in Core Europe and Peripheral Europe to exceed level πo (points A and B, respectively). The inflation rise in non tradable sector πN would then be lower than πN^*, with constant inflation rates πT^* e πT in the tradable sector.

two countries, due to the gap between the growth rate of productivity in the tradable sector, remains unchanged. Wage rate levels, however, must adjust to the lower inflation in the tradable sector and experience a proportional reduction to lower values compared with those prevailing with the previous Euro/dollar exchange rate: $\omega_2^* < \omega_1^*$ and $\omega_2 < \omega_1$. If the ECB reputation is such that the operators' inflationary expectations do not entail an "inflation bias", so that the inflation rate in the tradable sector is $\pi T = 0$, then in Peripheral Europe prices are due to fall in absolute terms.

Despite the lower prices, however, labor unions might not accept that wage increases should be lower than productivity gains[31]. Since "zero inflation" makes the adjustment of real wages through price increases impracticable, the increase in the real wage level might stabilize, thus determining such a loss of competitiveness in Peripheral Europe's productive systems as to trigger de-industrialization phenomena.

7. Conclusions

The interpretative framework outlined in this paper differs from the "classical" interpretation in two respects: 1) the slow decline of inflation differentials with Germany in the late eighties, causing the gap between the price levels of the two areas to widen, resulted in the real appreciation of peripheral Europe's currencies. The low credibility of the EMS was thus linked to the devaluation expectations determined by the growing difficulty that Peripheral Europe's countries had in keeping a fixed exchange rate in the face of an increasing current-account deficit, as witnessed by the mirror pattern of the Current account/GDP ratios of Germany and Periphery A. The high level of interest rates in Periphery A – especially in the phase of stable exchange rates (1987-92) – should not be then related to "surprise" inflation expectations but to devaluation expectations arising from the continuous loss of competitiveness; 2) the higher unemployment rates attained in Peripheral Europe during the phase of stable exchange rates (1987-92) might be the consequence, rather than of a rise of the "natural" unemployment rate due to labor market distortions, of the "deflation bias" generated in Peripheral Europe by the worsening of the "external constraint" problem of these countries (as a consequence of the loss of competitiveness and of the wide interest rate differentials with Germany dictated by the "asymmetric" working of the EMS). The macroeconomic instability generated in Peripheral Europe by the German "hegemony" in the EMS was due mainly to the inability to cancel the interest rate differentials between Peripheral Europe and Germany, which in turn made it impossible to counter deflationary trends and then caused the system to collapse in the presence of the asymmetric shock of German unification.

Germany's strategy to tie Peripheral Europe to the conservative monetary policy of the Bundesbank through the EMS agreement then was conducive to the creation of a competitive advantage in favor of Core Europe. Given this interpretation perspective, the "asymmetric" functioning of the EMS – contrary to the role as nominal anchor of the DM, which was necessary to accelerate the disinflation process – was not "neutral" to the trade competition between Germany and Peripheral Europe. Parallel depreciation trends against the DM, the dollar and other European currencies have represented a constant problem in the aftermath of the second World War, due to

---

[31] Near-zero inflation means that real wages can only be reduced through a cut in nominal wages (not through price increases). The goal of "zero inflation" was criticized by Akerlof, Dickens e Perry (1996) as a possible cause for the revival of the long term trade-off between inflation and unemployment.

Germany's strategy to keep its inflation low by supporting demand through the foreign component of aggregate demand.

The public good of monetary stability, realized in Europe by the monetary integration process, meant for Germany the creation of a less uncertain economic environment for the development of its export. On the one hand, the common fluctuation *vis-à-vis* the dollar prevents German exports from being penalized during the dollar depreciation trends by the fall of other European currencies, with the loss of competitiveness of German goods in the US market also accompanied by lower opportunities in the European markets[32]. On the other hand, the exchange rate stability during the EMS and the single currency today, that is the condition for a common fluctuation against the dollar, allow, such a real appreciation of Peripheral Europe's currencies against the DM – given the wide inflation differentials – as to encourage the penetration of German goods in European markets. Thus, the opportunity offered by the Euro for a common fluctuation of the Euro-11 *vis-à-vis* the dollar represents the accomplishment of Germany's trade strategy.

The quicker pace that should accrue to Germany's productive system following the coming of the Euro could represent a new asymmetric shock, with a tendency to a higher productivity – and price – growth rates in Germany than in the rest of the EMU, which could give rise to a conflict between the two areas as for the monetary stance. The German opposition to a monetary policy that "accommodates" inflationary tensions and weakens the competitiveness of German products – which was ultimately responsible for the EMS collapse in 1992 – might then materialize again in the EMU. If the ECB were then urged to follow a tight monetary policy, Peripheral Europe could be exposed to deflationary pressures greater than those that were determined by the asymmetric functioning of the EMS, so as to widen the real divergence between the two areas.

References

Akerlof, G., Dickens, W., Perry, G. (1996): The Macroeconomics of Low Inflation. Brookings Papers on Economic Activity, 1.

Alesina, A., Grilli, V. (1992): The European Central Bank: Reshaping Monetary Policy in Europe. In: Canzonieri, M., Grilli, V., Masson, P. (eds): Establishing a Central Bank: Issues in Europe and Lessons from the US. Cambridge University Press, Cambridge.

Alesina, A., Grilli, V. (1993): On the Feasibility of a One-Speed or Multispeed European Monetary Union. Economics and Politics, 5: 145-165.

Cepr (1995): Europa: l'integrazione flessibile. Il Mulino, Bologna.

Claassen, E-M. (1996): Global Monetary Economics. Oxford University Press, Oxford.

---

[32] With the creation of the EMS, Germany could halve the overall loss in competitiveness against the United States and the other European countries arising after the parallel depreciation of the dollar and the European currencies. In fact, the correlation between the indicators of global "competitiveness" and of Germany's competitiveness within the ERM is both high and negative in the first two phases of the EMS (1979-1992). This result shows that, by preventing the other European currencies to follow the dollar in its revaluation against the DM, the EMS fostered the improvement of the competitiveness of German goods in Europe. The correlation became negative in the years following the 1992-93 crisis, once the exchange rate stability was abandoned along with the "narrow" fluctuation band [Cf. Cepr, (1995), pp. 169-71].

De Grauwe, P. (1996): Monetary Policies in the EMS: Lessons from the Great Recession of 1991-93. Cepr Discussion Papers Series N.1047.

De Grauwe, P. (1997): The Economics of Monetary Integration. Oxford University Press, Oxford.

Dornbusch, R. (1996): The Effectiveness of Exchange-Rate Changes. Oxford Review of Economic Policy, 12: 27-38.

Drazen, A., Masson, P.R. (1994): Credibility of Policies versus Credibility of Policymakers. Quarterly Journal of Economics, 109: 735-54.

Farina, F. (1990): I tassi di cambio SME e l'autonomia della politica monetaria. Rivista di Politica Economica, XII Suppl.

Farina, F. (1993): From the EMS to the EMU: The Role of Policy Coordination. In: Baldassarri, M., Mundell, M. (eds): Building the New Europe. Macmillan, London.

Flood and Isard (1989): Monetary Policy Strategies. IMF Staff Papers, 36, n.3.

Frankel, J.A., Phillips, S., Chinn, M. (1993): Financial and Currency Integration in the European Monetary System: the Statistical Record. In: Torres, F., Giavazzi, F. (eds): Adjustment and Growth in the European Monetary Union. Cambridge University Press, Cambridge.

Fratianni, M., von Hagen, J. (1990): German Dominance in the EMS: The Empirical Evidence. Open Economy Review, 1: 86-87.

Giavazzi, F., Giovannini, A. (1989): Limiting Exchange Rate Flexibility: The European Monetary System. MIT Press, Cambridge (Mass.).

Grubb, D., Jackman, R., Layard, R. (1983): Wage Rigidity and Unemployment in OECD Countries. European Economic Review, 21: 11-39.

Krugman, P. (1993): Lessons of Massachusetts for EMU. In: Torres, F., Giavazzi, F. (eds): Adjustment and Growth in the European Monetary Union. Cambridge University Press, Cambridge.

Lindbeck, A. (1979): Imported and Structural Inflation and Aggregate Demand: the Scandinavian Model Reconstructed. In: Lindbeck, A. (ed.): Inflation and Employment in Open Economies. North Holland, Amsterdam.

Lohmann, S. (1992): Optimal Commitment in Monetary Policy. American Economic Review, 82: 273- 286.

Loockwood, B., Miller, M., Zhang, L. (1996): Central Banks and Reputation: some Transatlantic Contrasts. In: Canzonieri et al. (eds): The New Transatlantic Economy. Cambridge University Press, Cambridge.

Obstfeld, M. (1986): Rational and Self-fulfilling Balance of Payments Crises. American Economic Review, 76: 72-81.

Obstfeld, M., Peri, G. (1998): Asymmetric Shocks. Economic Policy, 10: 207-47.

Rogoff, K. (1985): The Optimal Degree of Commitment to an Intermediate Monetary Target. Quarterly Journal of Economics, 100: 1169-90.

Rose, A., Svensson, L. (1994): European Exchange Rate Credibility before the Fall. European Economic Review, 38: 151-79.